# Introducing Autodesk® 3ds Max® 2011

# Introducing Autodesk® 3ds Max® 2011

**Autodesk®**
Official Training Guide

RANDI L. DERAKHSHANI | DARIUSH DERAKHSHANI

Wiley Publishing, Inc.

**Acquisitions Editor:** Mariann Barsolo
**Development Editor:** Lisa Bishop
**Technical Editors:** Jon McFarland ; Nick Poznick
**Production Editor:** Dassi Zeidel
**Editorial Manager:** Pete Gaughan
**Production Manager:** Tim Tate
**Vice President and Executive Group Publisher:** Richard Swadley
**Vice President and Publisher:** Neil Edde
**Book Designer:** Caryl Gorska
**Compositor:** Kate Kaminski, Happenstance Type-O-Rama
**Proofreader:** Candace English
**Indexer:** Ted Laux
**Project Coordinator, Cover:** Lynsey Stanford
**Cover Designer:** Ryan Sneed
**Cover Image:** Randi Derakhshani; Dariush Derakhshani; Federico Esparza; Nick Poznick; Ghazaleh Pourkazemi; Jesse Doyle

Library of Congress Cataloging-in-Publication Data

Derakhshani, Dariush.
  Introducing Autodesk 3ds max 2011 / Dariush Derakhshani, Randi L. Munn.—1st ed.
      p. cm.
  ISBN-13: 978-0-470-91615-5 (pbk)
  ISBN-10: 0-470-91615-X (pbk)
  ISBN: 978-0-470-94422-6 (ebk)
  ISBN: 978-0-470-94424-0 (ebk)
  ISBN: 978-0-470-94423-3 (ebk)
  1. Computer animation. 2. 3ds max (Computer file) 3. Three-dimensional display systems. I. Munn, Randi. II. Title.
  TR897.7.D463 2010
  006.6'96—dc22
                    2010031877

Dear Reader,

Thank you for choosing *Introducing Autodesk 3ds Max 2011*. This book is part of a family of premium-quality Sybex books, all of which are written by outstanding authors who combine practical experience with a gift for teaching.

Sybex was founded in 1976. More than 30 years later, we're still committed to producing consistently exceptional books. With each of our titles, we're working hard to set a new standard for the industry. From the paper we print on, to the authors we work with, our goal is to bring you the best books available.

I hope you see all that reflected in these pages. I'd be very interested to hear your comments and get your feedback on how we're doing. Feel free to let me know what you think about this or any other Sybex book by sending me an email at nedde@wiley.com. If you think you've found a technical error in this book, please visit http://sybex.custhelp.com. Customer feedback is critical to our efforts at Sybex.

Best regards,

Neil Edde
Vice President and Publisher
Sybex, an Imprint of Wiley

*To Max Henry*

# Acknowledgments

*We are thrilled* to be updating *Introducing 3ds Max* for a third edition in honor of version 2011. Education is an all-important goal in life and should always be approached with eagerness and earnestness. We would like to show appreciation to the teachers who inspired us; you can always remember the teachers who touched your life, and to them we say thanks. We would also like to thank all of our students, who taught us a lot during the course of our many combined academic years. Equally, we would like to extend many thanks to the student artists who contributed to this book; many of them are our own students from The Art Institute of California—Los Angeles. Thanks to the AI faculty for their help in gathering the inspiring work for the color insert and for their support in writing this book. ■ Having a good computer system is important with this type of work; so a special thank you goes to HP for keeping us on the cutting edge of workstation hardware. Special thanks go to Mariann Barsolo, Lisa Bishop, Dassi Zeidel, and Candace English, our editors at Wiley who have been professional, courteous, and ever patient. Our appreciation also goes to technical editors Jon McFarland and Nick Poznick, who worked hard to make sure this book is of the utmost quality, as well as contributed elements to the writing of a few chapters. We could not have done this revision without their help. ■ In addition, tremendous gratitude again goes to Jon McFarland for his fantastic contributions to the previous editions of this book, some of which have been updated over to this edition. Finally, thanks to Dariush's mother and brother for their love and support, not to mention the life-saving babysitting services.

# About the Authors

*Randi Lorene Derakhshani* is a staff instructor with The Art Institute of California—Los Angeles. She began working with computer graphics in 1992, and was hired by her instructor to work at Sony Pictures Imageworks, where she developed her skills with 3ds Max and Shake, among many other programs. A teacher since 1999, Randi enjoys sharing her wisdom with young talent and watching them develop at The Art Institute. Currently, she teaches a wide range of classes, from Autodesk 3ds Max to compositing with Apple Shake and Adobe After Effects. Juggling her teaching activities with caring for a little boy makes Randi a pretty busy lady.

*Dariush Derakhshani* is a visual effects supervisor and head of CG with Radium, a creative design and VFX boutique, and a writer and educator in Los Angeles, California, as well as Randi's husband. Dariush used Autodesk's AutoCAD software in his architectural days and migrated to using 3D programs when his firm's principal architects needed to visualize architectural designs in 3D on the computer. Dariush started using Alias PowerAnimator version 6 when he enrolled in USC Film School's Animation program, and he has been using Alias/Autodesk animation software for the past 14 years. He received an M.F.A. in Film, Video, and Computer Animation from the USC Film School in 1997. He also holds a B.A. in Architecture and Theatre from Lehigh University in Pennsylvania. He worked at a New Jersey architectural firm before moving to Los Angeles for film school. He has worked on feature films, music videos, and countless commercials as a 3D animator, as a CG/VFX supervisor, and sometimes as a compositor. Dariush also serves as an editor and is on the advisory board of *HDRI 3D*, a professional computer graphics (CG) magazine from DMG Publishing.

# About the Contributors

*Jon McFarland* is an adjunct faculty member at two colleges where he teaches AutoCAD, 3ds Max, Revit, and several other courses to students seeking degrees in Visual Communications, Interior Design, and Construction Management. He also writes and edits books on a variety of technical subjects. Jon lives in Cleveland, Ohio, with his wife and two sons.

*Nick Poznick* is a lighter at Radium in Santa Monica, California. He worked previously at Speedshape in Detroit, modeling and lighting CG environments. Nick also has an interest in dynamics and other visual effects, has created fluid pipelines, and headed up projects involving such techniques as weather effects for various clientele.

# CONTENTS AT A GLANCE

# Contents

# Introduction

*Welcome to* *Introducing 3ds Max 2011.* The world of computer generated imagery (CG) is fun and ever-changing. Whether you are new to CG in general or are a CG veteran new to 3ds Max, you'll find this book the perfect primer. It introduces you to Autodesk 3ds Max and shows how you can work with the program to create your art, whether it is animated or static in design.

This book exposes you to all facets of 3ds Max by introducing and plainly explaining its tools and functions to help you understand how the program operates—but it does not stop there. This book also explains the use of the tools and the ever-critical concepts behind the tools. You'll find hands-on examples and tutorials that give you firsthand experience with the toolsets. Working through these will develop your skills and the conceptual knowledge that will carry you to further study with confidence. These tutorials expose you to various ways to accomplish tasks with this intricate and comprehensive artistic tool.

Finally, this book explains the 3ds Max workflow. It explains how specific tasks are accomplished and why—that is, it explains how the tasks fit into the larger process of producing 3D animation. By doing that, these chapters should give you the confidence you need to venture deeper into 3ds Max's feature set, either on your own or by using any of 3ds Max's other learning tools and books as a guide.

Learning to use a powerful tool such as 3ds Max can be frustrating. You need to remember to pace yourself. The major complaints CG book readers have are that the pace is too fast and that the steps are too complicated or overwhelming. Addressing those complaints is a tough nut to crack, to be sure. No two readers are the same. However, this book offers the opportunity to run things at your own pace. The exercises and steps may seem confusing at times, but keep in mind that the more you try and the more you fail at some attempts, the more you will learn how to operate 3ds Max. Experience is king when learning the workflow necessary for *any* software program, and with experience come failure and aggravation. But try and try again. You will find that further attempts will always be easier and more fruitful.

Above all, however, this book aims to inspire you to use 3ds Max as a creative tool to achieve and explore your own artistic vision.

## What You Will Learn from This Book

You will learn how to work in CG with 3ds Max 2011, but moreover, you will learn how CG works and you will be able to apply the basic techniques and concepts to any software package to accomplish anything you need, from modeling to animation. The important thing to keep in mind is that this book is merely the beginning of your CG education. With the confidence you will gain from the exercises in this book, and the peace of mind you can have by using this book as a reference, you can go on to create your own increasingly complex CG projects.

## Who Should Read This Book

Anyone who is interested in learning 3ds Max should start with this book. No other series of books provides a better, more solid foundation than the Introducing series. *Introducing 3ds Max 2011* will give you more than just the basics of software operation; it will also explain how CG productions are accomplished.

If you are new to CG, or you are a veteran looking to pick up another program, *Introducing 3ds Max 2011* will give you the foundation you will need to progress further into Autodesk's 3ds Max software.

If you are an educator, you will find a solid foundation on which to build a new course. You can also treat the book as a source of raw materials that you can adapt to fit an existing curriculum. Written in an open-ended style, *Introducing 3ds Max 2011* contains several self-help tutorials for home study, as well as plenty of material to fit into any class.

## How to Use This Book

*Introducing 3ds Max 2011* approaches teaching CG by first giving you an informal look into the core concepts that make up this art form. The book aims to create a solid reference for you by showing you the commonly used toolsets and interfaces you will need to navigate to accomplish your goal. To reinforce the concepts, *Introducing 3ds Max 2011* gives you hands-on exercises and tutorials, letting you flex your muscles and giving you a chance to try for yourself.

The process can be a bit daunting when you begin to learn a CG program. In that light, it's best to explore the material in this book at your own pace, and allow yourself to digest not just the nuts and bolts, but also the workflow and concepts behind how *and* why 3ds Max artists work the way they do.

Once you have a firm grasp of the concepts introduced in this book, you will be ready to tackle more advanced material in the form of an intermediate class or even another book. Learning CG is a tough hurdle to get over, and you can rest easy knowing that this book is targeted to give you the tools you need to begin a longer, deeper study of the craft.

## How This Book Is Organized

Chapter 1, "Basic Concepts," begins with an introduction to the basic concepts of CG production as well as its terminology and general workflows and pipelines. This chapter gives you an overview of how CG is created and how 3ds Max relates to the overall process.

Chapter 2, "Your First 3ds Max Project," creates a simple animation to introduce you to 3ds Max's workflow and give you a sense of how things work. By animating a simple mobile, you will learn the basic concepts of creating and animating in 3ds Max.

Chapter 3, "The 3ds Max Interface," presents you with the entire 3ds Max interface and shows you how to access all the tools you will need for a CG production. Beginning with a roadmap of the 3ds Max screen, this chapter gives you a rundown of the icons and explains their uses. You can use this chapter as a reference to which you can return for UI refreshers whenever they're needed.

Chapter 4, "Modeling in 3ds Max: Part I," is an introduction to modeling concepts and workflows in general. It shows you how to model using 3ds Max tools with polygonal meshes and modifiers to create various objects, including a bedroom dresser.

Chapter 5, "Modeling in 3ds Max: Part II," takes your modeling lesson a step further by showing you how to model a complex object. You will use and add to the tools you learned in Chapter 4 to create a toy rocket model. You will learn how to loft and lathe objects, as well as how to use Booleans.

Chapter 6, "Character Poly Modeling," rounds out your modeling lessons by showing you how to create organic, low polygon count models such as a soldier character you might find in a game.

Chapter 7, "Materials and Mapping," shows you how to assign textures and materials to your models. You will learn to texture various objects, such as the toy rocket from Chapter 5, as you learn the basics of working with 3ds Max's materials and UVW mapping. New to this edition is UV and pelt mapping to texture the soldier model, an important step in production.

Chapter 8, "Introduction to Animation," covers the basics of animating a bouncing ball using keyframes, and moves on to creating a more complex animation such as a knife thrown at a target. You will also learn how to use the Track View—Curve Editor to time, edit, and finesse your animation.

Chapter 9, "Character Studio and IK Animation," expands on Chapter 8 to show you how to use Character Studio to create and edit a walk cycle using the soldier model. You will also learn how to use 3ds Max's IK system to rig a tank model's gun.

Chapter 10, "3ds Max Lighting," begins by showing you how to light a 3D scene with the three-point lighting system. It then shows you how to use the tools to create and edit 3ds Max lights for illumination, shadows, and special lighting effects. You will light the toy rocket to which you added materials in Chapter 7.

Chapter 11, "3ds Max Rendering," explains how to create image files from your 3ds Max scene and how to achieve the best look for your animation by using proper cameras and rendering settings. You'll also learn about different ways to implement ray-tracing, atmospheric effects, and motion blur when you render the toy rocket. New to this edition is the inclusion of mental ray rendering and a brief intro to HDRI lighting.

Chapter 12, "Particles and Dynamics," introduces you to 3ds Max's particle systems and space warps, as well as the reactor physics simulation system. You will animate dynamic objects colliding with one another using rigid body dynamics, and you will learn how to use soft body dynamics.

The companion web page to this book at www.sybex.com/go/intro3dsmax2011 provides all the sample images, movies, and files that you will need to work through the projects in *Introducing 3ds Max 2011*, as well as a demo version of the program.

## Hardware and Software Considerations

Hardware changes constantly, and it evolves faster than publications can keep up. Having a good solid machine is important to a production, although simple home computers will be able to run 3ds Max quite well. Any laptop (with discrete graphics) or desktop PC running Windows XP Professional, Windows Vista, or Windows 7 (32- or 64-bit) with at least 1GB of RAM and an Intel Pentium Core2 Duo/Quad or AMD Phenom or higher processor will work. Of course, having a good video card will help; you can use any hardware-accelerated OpenGL or Direct3D video card. Your computer system should have at least a 2.4GHz Core2 or i5/i7 processor with 1GB of RAM, a few GBs of hard drive space available, and an

NVIDIA GeForce FX or ATI Radeon video card. Professionals may want to opt for work-station graphics cards, such as the ATI FirePro or the NVIDIA Quadro FX series of cards. The following systems would be good ones to use:

- Intel i7, 4GB RAM, NVIDIA Quadro FX 1400, 400GB 7200 RPM hard disk
- AMD Phenom II, 4GB RAM, ATI FirePro V5700, 400GB hard disk

You can check the list of system requirements at Autodesk's website at `www.autodesk`
`.com/3dsmax`.

## The Next Step

The next step is really up to you. *Introducing 3ds Max 2011* is meant to give you a kick-start into learning CG. Your education beyond this primer can be from DVDs, classes, or more books, all bundled with a good amount of playing around and creating your own 3D pro-ductions. There is no better way to learn CG than to create something for yourself. Use these tools as a reference to help you get there.

You can contact the authors through Wiley or at `http://koosh3d.com`.

# Basic Concepts

*Any way you cut it,* everyone learns in different ways, especially when they are learning about Autodesk 3ds Max 2011 or any other computer graphics (CG) package. You should realize that the best education you'll get is through months or even years of working with the software in different capacities. Ask any successful student, and they will tell you one thing: There is no such thing as book smarts when it comes to good CG production—it all comes down to what you can achieve.

Achievement comes only from practice. You can't avoid the many pitfalls of production work without falling into and climbing out of them. Some readers may find this idea frustrating, but it is an intractable truth. The more you work with 3ds Max, the better you will become with it. And the more you struggle, fail, and recover, the more you will learn.

This chapter introduces you to basic concepts in computer graphics production. Topics in this chapter include the following:

- ■ **How to read this book**
- ■ **What is CGI?**
- ■ **Production workflow**
- ■ **CG workflow**
- ■ **CG specialties**
- ■ **Core concepts**
- ■ **Coordinate systems**
- ■ **Basic 3ds Max terms and concepts**
- ■ **Basic animation concepts**

## How to Read This Book

First and foremost, you don't need to read this book cover to cover and front to back to get the most from it. If you are the type who loves to jump right into the pool to learn to swim, then skip this chapter and jump into Chapter 2, "Your First 3ds Max Project" to start working with the interface. If you already know how to navigate 3ds Max, you can begin with any of the other chapters. You can leave this chapter for bathroom reading or for when the TV goes out.

If you like slowly dipping your toe in the water first, then by all means sit back and have a long soak in this chapter. It covers a lot of basic concepts and core topics with which you may or may not already be familiar. It will gently ease you into the powerful program that is Autodesk 3ds Max 2011, and into computer graphics in general.

No matter how you choose to read this book, it is crucial that you approach the lessons as a way to *begin* the learning process. This book aims to give you a solid foundation in many aspects of 3ds Max so that you can take this beginning and move on to more study. In keeping with that ideal, you will need to understand that you will not necessarily become proficient in any one aspect of 3ds Max *just by reading* this book. Instead, you'll gain an understanding of how it works and how you can work with the program to create animations and models.

Frequently, students are annoyed by tutorials that don't seem to lead them to perfection in the first go-around. This is the case for all tutorials, and indeed for all books that purport to teach anything. The key is to use the lessons as a guideline not just once, but repeatedly. Doing a lesson multiple times will help you understand the concepts better and give you opportunities to try out a few different methods, stray a little from the dictated steps, and try your own ideas on for size. Ideally, you will obtain a stronger education this way, but doing so will perhaps be slower and require you to be more patient. However, getting a good education always requires this sort of dedication.

## What Is CGI?

In addition to standing for computer graphics, *CG* is sometimes used as an acronym for *computer generated*. You may have heard the term *CGI* (computer-generated imagery). These terms refer to any image or images that are created with the aid of a computer. In this day and age, you'd be hard-pressed to find anyone with any computer experience who hasn't messed around with electronic images such as scanned pictures or digital photos. Learning a CG package such as 3ds Max is just an extension of the simple concept of playing around with a digital photo. The obvious difference is that 3ds Max adds the dimension of depth as well as control over time.

Computer graphics is a more common toolset in the hands of the masses than it was just a few years ago. Within the next decade or so, 3D rendering will be as ubiquitous as

"Photoshopping" a photo is today. Artists who are not in the 3D or CG industry are finding that programs such as 3ds Max are valuable tools for generating elements for their own work, digital or not. Let's take a look at the concepts behind 3D creation.

The following sections break down the fundamental concepts behind CG.

## 3D Space

*3D space*, the virtual canvas in which you create 3D objects, is a simulation of space that is divided into three axes—*X, Y,* and *Z*—representing (in loose terms) left/right, up/down, and in/out. Figure 1.1 shows 3D space in a Max viewport.

So what the heck do you with 3D space? In many ways, setting up a scene in CG is like setting up a photo shoot. With a photo shoot, you gather your subjects and pose them in your composition. You set up lights to illuminate them as dramatically or naturally as you need them to look and then take pictures with your camera, framing the composition as you like it. Next, you develop and fine-tune your photos or adjust them with tools such as Photoshop before you print them. Finally comes the happy part of showing them off and sharing your work with others.

Computer graphics production has much the same workflow, although with CG you create nearly everything from scratch in your 3D space. Instead of running out and hunting down the perfect models and all the props and settings you need for a photo, you create them. You model everything first and then apply colors and texture to the surfaces you created. Once you lay out your scene with all the settings and props you need, you set up your CG lights to illuminate the models. Lighting is perhaps the most important aspect of CG, as this stage of CG production really makes or breaks a scene.

Figure 1.1

**3D space looks good enough to eat!**

Once your lighting is ready, you *render* the scene. This is akin to developing your photos. Knowing what the end result should be will dictate how you decide to render. You can choose several settings for quality and output, for example, so you can show off your scene to your friends (although a QuickTime movie can't be hung on the fridge the way a photo can).

Of course, with CG you also have control over time, because you can animate your scene. The workflow we'll discuss in this chapter is best illustrated with a film production example. The next section will briefly describe a film production workflow and how it relates to CG production.

## Production Workflow

There are three major stages to producing films and videos: preproduction, production, and postproduction. In preproduction, the script is written, storyboards are drawn up to outline the action, costumes and sets are designed and built, the actors are cast and prepared, and a production crew is put together. During the production phase, the scenes are set up and shot according to a production schedule that lays out everything in the most efficient manner possible. Finally, in postproduction, everything else happens. The film is printed and edited, a score and soundtrack are laid, any digital effects are added, and scenes are colored to match an overall aesthetic. When all of this is finished, the film is distributed for people to see.

Although the specific tasks of CG for narrative or even game development are vastly different from those of live-action photography, understanding this framework is useful to understanding CG in general.

### Preproduction

Preproduction for a CG workflow requires that the artist or artists gather together all the reference materials, motion tests, layout drawings, model sketches, and other components to make the actual CG production as uncomplicated as they can be.

Because everything is essentially made from scratch, you have to formulate a strong plan of attack. You can't just take some actors into the park and begin shooting. With CG, you have to make it all from nothing, or at least acquire assets such as models from places such as TurboSquid.com. The time spent in preproduction planning is vital to smooth production and postproduction, and it helps the overall outcome of the project. Never underestimate how much time and planning you should put into a CG project.

You will seriously sandbag your project if you don't plan it effectively. Although you may get sick of hearing this, it will always be true.

As you do the exercises in this book, you will work with sketches and other files supplied on this book's accompanying web page, www.sybex.com/go/intro3dsmax2011. These are your preproduction assets. Additionally, you are strongly encouraged to put together as much information as you possibly can about your intended project, no matter how short it may seem.

A poorly planned production will always fall short of its potential and give you many headaches throughout your project.

### Writing a Script

Whether a CG project has a ton of dialogue or doesn't have a single spoken word, both the project and you will benefit from having at least a rudimentary script. Even abstract animations can benefit from a script that presents a highly detailed explanation of timing and colors, whether that script is typed neatly or scribbled on a cocktail napkin.

A script serves as your *intention*. Without having a clear intention of what you wish to say with your film, your production time may as well be spent lying on a lounge chair drinking iced tea; you will not get much done in either case.

### Storyboards

A storyboard is the next step in defining the action laid out in the script. It shows the timing and framing for the camera, as well as the action and dialogue (if any). To create an effective storyboard, you should dissect your script into scenes, and further dissect the scenes into shots, with each shot presenting a distinct view from the camera or a distinct cut of action. Each storyboard panel describes what is happening in that shot. The panels show you the overall action of the project in a linear, shot-by-shot fashion, and how it should come together in editing.

Even if your storyboards are simple ones composed of stick figures, they are important to preproduction.

### Concept Art

*Conceptuals* (also called *concept art*) are the design elements that are needed for a CG production. If you don't have concept art—whether it's your own drawings, or photos or images grabbed from the Internet—you are in trouble. You must have an idea of how you want your CG to look; otherwise, you are just burning calories and not saying anything.

If you have CG characters, create character sheets for each character that show them in at least three different neutral poses: from the front, from the side, and from an angle called a ¾ *view*. You can even sculpt reference characters in clay or Play-Doh if you need to have a better idea of how they should look in 3D space. In Figure 1.2, you can see a character sheet with four poses generated for a student-produced short at The Art Institute of California—Los Angeles.

Figure 1.2

**A character sheet with four poses**

Sketch or download images of the props and sets you need in your scene. You should map out the "look" for everything that you need to have in your scene. When you are working on your project, you won't be limited to the things you picked out at this stage; however, you will find that knowing how things should look will help enormously in getting you to your final product. The better your concept art and research, the smoother the production and the better your end result will be.

## Production

Production is the meat of any project. Film production begins when you start filming your project. In the case of CG, production begins when you start creating assets for your projects, such as models or textures, based on well-researched reference materials. The production phase lasts until the rendering phase, where you actualize your scene into image files.

Animation, texturing, and lighting are all performed between the modeling and rendering phases. Later in this chapter, we'll divide the CG production phase into more stages; however, most of the techniques you'll learn in this book are components of the production phase.

## Postproduction

Postproduction begins when your scene elements and animation are all set up and raring to be completed. Postproduction for a CG project is very similar to postproduction for a film. When you click the Render button, you'll end up with several image files or movie files that are then edited and put together to make your project. You add sound, correct color, combine elements, and add any finishing touches in postproduction. Here is a quick rundown of the CG postproduction pipeline.

## Rendering

All CG scenes need to be rendered to their final image or movie files. Again, this is the process by which the computer calculates how everything in the scene should look, and displays it. Rendering makes your computer work hard. It usually requires the full attention of your PC and can take a lot of time. As you'll learn throughout this book, the decisions you make, such as how much detail you give the objects you create for a scene, can make a big difference in the rest of the process and can affect the rendering speed.

You can render one scene while another scene is in production, but working on a system that is rendering is not advisable unless you're using a multiple-processor or multiple-core machine with plenty of memory. Once everything has been rendered properly, the final images will be sorted and the CG project assembly will begin. Rendering is the subject of Chapter 11, "3ds Max Rendering."

Compositing, editing, and adding sound are advanced postproduction activities, and a detailed discussion of them is beyond the scope of this book. However, a multitude of books is available for further study.

## Compositing

CG is often rendered in different layers. These segments ultimately need to be put back together. For example, in a scene where multiple characters interact, each character can be rendered separately from the others and from the setting. *Compositing* is the process of bringing together rendered elements to form the final scene, usually using compositing software such as Autodesk's Composite 2011, Adobe's After Effects, or The Foundry's Nuke.

Compositing can greatly affect the look of a CG project, and professionals consider it to be an integral part of CG creation. Compositing programs allow you to compose CG elements together, but they also give you additional control over color and timing, and a host of other additions and alterations you can make to a scene.

> A lot of students assume that they need to render a scene in a single pass and create its intended look on the first try. This is not the case. CG has an inherently modular nature. You can render items separately and composite them in the finishing stage while retaining the ability to make changes in the project without rendering everything again. Rendering a project in different layers (sometimes called passes) also gives you much greater control over the project's look.

## Editing

During editing, rendered and composited CG footage is collected and edited to fit the script and storyboards. This process is usually more straightforward for a CG film than for a live-action movie, provided that you made good storyboards during preproduction to follow when assembling the finished film.

With live-action shoots, you shoot much more footage than will ultimately end up in the film. You do this to make sure you have enough material for all your scenes and to leave extra room for creative editing. Additionally, you have to run through all the footage and choose which takes will be in the final product.

Because CG footage is generally much more time-consuming to generate than live action, scenes and shots should be tightly arranged in preproduction storyboards. The entire production can be edited beforehand in storyboards, so the scenes that are built and animated can match the story almost down to the frame. If your preproduction was done well, it can be just a matter of putting the shots together using an editing program such as Adobe's Premiere or even Apple's Final Cut Pro. (If you don't have an editing program, you can use the Video Post module in 3ds Max.) This functionality is not covered in this introductory text, however.

### Sound

Sound design can add an entirely new dimension of reality or mood to any CG. The audience needs to associate visuals with audio. Even a basic soundtrack adds a boost to a simple animation by enhancing realism, mood, narrative, and other aspects of its "feel." A good music soundtrack and well-placed sound effects can be very powerful.

Sound effects, such as footsteps, can be added to match the action in the animation; this type of sound effect is also known as *Foley sound*. Just as with any film, adding music to most animations can help with pacing as well as mood. In this case, music and live action sound design are pretty similar. Once you combine everything, you assess the sound needs.

The one glaring difference between CG and live action sound relates to dialogue. When you shoot live action, you generally capture the sound and dialogue live as you shoot. With CG, all dialogue needs to be recorded and edited at the beginning of the production phase. In other words, dialogue is a part of the CG preproduction and postproduction phases. This is because animators need to hear dialogue spoken so they can animate images to match the lips of the characters speaking (this is known as *lip-sync*). Recording the dialogue with actors also helps you animate the CG characters because you can imitate the gestures and actions of the live actors to help make your animation more real.

## Game-Development Workflow

Very simply put, game-development workflow is not very different from the workflow of a narrative film or video as outlined earlier. After the scripting, designing, and conceptualizing that any creative project undergoes, assets are created for the game following the concepts previously laid out. Assets describe the models used for props, settings, characters, and so forth, as well as textures for those models. For games, assets are created with polygon count in mind. (Low poly modeling aims to create models with fewer polygons to increase a game's efficiency and playability since the console or PC has to process less geometry to keep the game running efficiently.) Additionally, animation clips may be created through keyframe animation, motion capture, or, usually, a combination of the two.

Rendering and compositing are traditionally not part of a game's workflow (not accounting for cinematics and other such playback sequences). Instead of rendering the assets created for a scene, they are typically fed into the game engine by technical directors, software engineers, and/or programmers. A game engine renders the game as you play it, allowing for real-time feedback. How that engine accepts CG assets for the game depends on the game engine and the programming behind it.

The worlds of real-time rendering (such as for games) and traditionally produced and rendered CG are converging as time passes. But by and large, the same workflow is used when creating CG for any creative production, whether for a game or not.

## CG Workflow

CG is a collaborative effort in which all the stages of production work hand-in-hand to achieve your final images. Because of how CG comes together, following a structured production pipeline or workflow generally works best. The layout of this book and its exercises follow this overall workflow. You begin by modeling, texturing, animating, lighting, and then rendering. You can texture after you animate, if you wish; however, for most projects, the workflow described here is best. What is universally true is that you will go back and forth between these stages several times throughout the process as you assess and further define your needs. For example, you may have to change some textures once you see the lighting, or change a model according to an unexpected animation need.

### Modeling

Modeling is the topic of Chapters 4 through 6 of this book. Modeling is usually the first step in CG creation, and it can sometimes take the longest time. You probably already know that modeling and modeling tutorials are popular on the Internet, where you will also find a generous number of free and fee-based models. You might be able to find a lot of the props and characters you need for your scene there. Unless you enjoy modeling, take a look through Google (or another search engine) and see what's already available, especially at sites such as www.turbosquid.com.

When you model, of course, you'll be faced with many choices about how to proceed. Most 3ds Max modeling is done using *polygons* (geometric representations of surfaces and objects); however, the specific tools you use to create the models will depend on how you like to work. The process of modeling can be easier when you have a good idea of your whole story via a storyboard and you copiously reference the object you are modeling. If you identify your project needs as fully as you can at the outset, you'll be able to fulfill them more easily when you start modeling or gathering models.

With forethought, you will know how detailed your models need to be. In many cases, you can add sufficient detail to a model through texture. If a park bench is shown in a wide shot from far away, there is no need for abundant detail or complicated surfacing. If you create a highly detailed model for that far-away shot, you will have wasted your time and will also increase your rendering time. However, if you have to show that park bench prominently in a close-up, it will need as much detail as possible. In such cases, viewers will see more of the bench and have more of an opportunity to question it. The more you use models in scenes, the better you will be at sensing exactly how much detail to give a specific model. As you begin with CG, however, it's better to give too much attention to detail than to give too little. The detailing process will teach you a majority of what you need to learn about modeling. This, in turn, will benefit your overall speed and technique. With more experience, you will be able to discern the level of detail you really need and work more efficiently.

Here is a quick rundown of some different kinds of modeling.

### Character Modeling

Character modeling includes the modeling of any characters in your scene, from humanoids to animals to ordinary objects that are animated to life. Most characters are organic forms, such as animals, humans, aliens, and so on. However, a talking cheese sandwich is just as much a character as the person holding it. As a good character modeler, you need to keep in mind the animation needs of a character when you're modeling. It's important to know what you need from your shot way ahead of time so you can model appropriately.

Traditional characters, such as humans, need to appear seamless once they're modeled. Character animation usually requires the model to deform in some way, such as bending and warping at certain points, such as the elbows. The pieces that make up the model may tear apart if the character is not built to accommodate deformation and movement.

Like the park bench we talked about earlier, your character must be built with the level of detail required by the scene. As a matter of fact, you could wind up with multiple models for a single character that are built to account for differences in detail level. Using different versions of the same character can help keep the scene efficient and workable. A low-resolution model of a character (one that uses few polygonal faces) can easily be placed in wide shots, and a more detailed, higher-resolution model can be used in close-ups.

Game characters are not much different from characters in a typical film. However, game characters are usually created with efficiencies in mind (such as low polygon count) because they are later imported into the game engine and its real-time renderer. Some game engines require specific file outputs, but the vast majority of off-the-shelf game engines accept models from the very game-friendly 3ds Max.

## Architectural and Environmental Modeling

3ds Max is a natural tool for architectural and environmental modeling. In fact, architects and engineers use it to model and render designs for previsualizing. This type of modeling includes the generation of backgrounds for sets and environments. To do this, you model any buildings or interiors, as well as mountains and other required scenery, such as trees, roads, lampposts, and mailboxes.

Do not create overly detailed environments when they are far off in the background. The biggest common mistake new CG practitioners make is overcreating detail. Doing this adds more geometry to a scene, creates inefficiency, and can crash a scene. The more geometry that is used in a scene, the more slowly the computer will run and the more time you will need to render the scene.

> You can create a good deal of the environment using clever textures on simple geometry. Detailed maps on bare surfaces are used frequently for game environments.
>
> Because your computer stores everything in a scene as vector math, the term *geometry* refers to all the surfaces and models in a scene.

## Props Modeling

A *prop* is any object in a scene that is actively used by a character in his or her action. Props are useful to the narrative of the story. They help the characters' actions. A prop can be anything from a baseball bat that a character is swinging to a purse that a character is carrying.

Any objects not used by the characters as props are called *scenics*, as they are often used to add realism to the set by "setting the scene." Think about it. If your scene takes place in front of a desk, that desk will need scenics such as pens, notebooks, and papers to make it look more realistic. Just showing an empty desk may not be enough to make the scene believable. You usually can find the props and scenics you need on the Internet, frequently in a format for 3ds Max.

# Texturing

Once you have created a model, you'll want to finish its look. You can apply materials to its surface(s) to make it look right, whether it is supposed to look "real" or not. *Texturing* is typically applied immediately after modeling, and heavily tweaked when the scene is lighted. The process of texturing essentially applies colors and tactile feeling to models. 3ds Max automatically assigns simple colored materials to objects as you create them.

You don't need to finalize every texture at the beginning, because you'll be coming back and making adjustments all the time. Remember that the materials you create for your scene will probably look different when you light and animate everything.

You'll learn more about texturing in Chapter 7, "Materials and Mapping."

## Animation

Animation puts your scene into action and adds life to your characters. *Animation* is *change over time.* Anything in a scene that needs to change from one second to another will need to be animated to do so.

Everyone has their own reflexive sense of how things move. This knowledge is gleaned through years of perception and observation. Therefore, your audience can be more critical of a CG scene's motion than lighting, coloring, or anything else. You know when something doesn't look right. So will your audience.

Animation takes quite a lot of setup, sometimes more than just modeling. For a character, you will need to create a *rig* (a character's setup or digital armature used to drive character animation, such as a Character Studio Biped, which is featured in Chapter 9, "Character Studio and IK Animation") to attach to the model and then create controls to make animation easier to operate.

It's thrilling to see your hard work on a scene come to life with animation. On the flip side, it can be extremely aggravating to see your creation working improperly. Making mistakes is how you learn things, and your frustrations will ease over time. Your first several attempts at animating a scene will not look like Pixar films, but that should not dissuade you from working on more animations and scenes. You will get better with more practice.

Chapter 8, "Introduction to Animation," and Chapter 9 cover basic animation techniques in 3ds Max.

## Lighting

Lighting is the most important aspect of CG production, whether for narrative stories or for games. This area is where you get to see your models and textures, as well as set the mood of the project. During lighting, you set up virtual lights in 3D space that will illuminate the objects in your scene when it comes time to render to images or within a game engine. In the case of games, the game engine helps define (if not fully define) how the lighting is created, and may not be congruous with traditional lighting within 3ds Max. This book will not cover gaming render workflows but rather will cover general lighting and rendering within 3ds Max and mental ray. If your interest lies only with gaming, it's important to note that learning how to light within 3ds Max or mental ray is as important as lighting specifically for the game engine itself, as it gives you a solid understanding of how a scene should look when rendered in or out of a game engine.

Lighting can drastically change how your scene looks. Using lighting wisely is a learned skill, and it takes tons of time to master; there are no shortcuts to becoming a good lighter. Not only are you dealing with the aesthetics of getting your shot to look great, but you are also dealing with rendering issues and bottlenecks that could make rendering your shot a nightmare. These issues come up with much larger scenes than the ones you will be using in the first years of your CG education; however, it's important to start learning how to use lighting efficiently as well as aesthetically.

Lighting can make or break all your hard work. You can use lighting to affect the believability of your models and textures as well as to create the proper mood and tone.

In this stage of the pipeline, the lighting workflow begins when you are texturing your objects. You need to light your scene initially to evaluate how your textures are progressing. However, the final lighting and look really happen after everything else is done, and you are left to go back and forth with the render to check and recheck, fix and refix issues that come up in the rendered images. You may even find, for example, that a model you've built needs to be altered because a lighting scheme works for everything but that model. Therefore, a back-and-forth workflow with lighting does not apply just to texturing.

The more experience you gain with lighting, the more you will start to notice that lighting affects every stage of CG creation. Once you start mastering the subtleties of lighting, and after years of modeling, you may change how you model to accommodate how you now light. Even your animation and texturing preferences may take a backseat to how a scene needs to be lighted.

CG is fundamentally all about light. Manipulating how light is created and reflected is what you're doing with CG.

Luckily, in 3ds Max lighting is set up to mimic the behavior of real lights used in live action (at least in principle), making the lighting process easier. You will learn how to light in 3ds Max in Chapter 10, "3ds Max Lighting."

## Rendering

You've modeled it all, textured it, and lit your scene like a pro. Now you are ready to render your scene, unless you are creating assets for a game. *Rendering* is the stage where your computer makes all the computations necessary to create images from your 3D objects. Depending on how much stuff is in your scene, rendering may be superquick or painfully slow. The amount of geometry (the number of polygons) you used to model, the number and types of lights, the size of texture images, and the effects in your scene all affect render times. When time or resources are limited, you need to build your scene intelligently so that you don't spend hours rendering a single frame. The more efficient your scene is, the faster the rendering will go.

Having said that, there is really no magic formula to figure out how long is too long for a render. Some scenes require a massive amount of time to render, for whatever reason, and you are stuck with that—but most do not. In time you'll be able to ascertain for yourself how long is too long for your renders.

A good gauge for render times is to identify what computers you have to render with and how much time you have before a project has to be completed. With a little simple math, you can determine an acceptable render time for your scenes and adjust your quality and output settings, as well as your lighting setup, to fit within your constraints.

The general rule in production is this: You're always out of time. Therefore, the most efficient pipeline will be your savior, because eventually your producer or boss will tire of hearing, "But I'm still rendering...."

For now, go ahead and use as much geometry and lighting as you think is necessary. With more experience, you'll start pruning your scenes and getting more efficient renders. Right now, knowing *how* a scene is put together is more important than knowing how efficient it needs to be.

## CG Specialties

Like most professionals, CG professionals specialize in specific areas. Those areas coincide with the stages of CG production outlined earlier in this chapter.

Modelers create models for shows or projects. They need to have a keen eye for detail, as well as a sense of how objects come together. Environment modelers create settings, and character modelers specialize in creating organic surfaces for characters such as people. In all cases, professional modelers need to understand form and function and be experienced in lighting, rendering, and texturing to effectively model professionally.

Animators are artists who work directly with the animation of a project. Character animators specialize in character movement, ranging from mimicking human movement to outlandish cartoon animation. There are also animators who specialize in mechanical objects. Frequently, good animators can span the divide between character animation and other types of animation because they inherently understand motion and timing.

In some cases, great animators are also great *riggers*. Studios hire character TDs (technical directors) who specialize in rigging characters for motion. This usually includes creating skeleton structures, such as Bipeds or Bones, for the character as well as skinning the model to such a system before handing it off to the animator(s). Character TDs can also work with motion-capture systems to transfer motion to a character. They use recorded data from a live-action stage where actors are outfitted in special equipment that records their movements.

Effects TDs are specialists who typically animate special effects such as tornadoes, clouds, or explosions. These specialists generally rely on particles and dynamics, as well as textures, lights, and rendering tricks to perform their effects. This specialty requires a strong eye in all stages of CG production and a strong ability to troubleshoot and come up with solutions that are frequently not standard techniques in a program such as 3ds Max.

Lighters light and render a scene once it is completed. Lighters specialize in being able to *final* a shot; in other words, to complete a shot for final approval and output. A good lighter needs to understand how models and textures behave in a scene and sometimes must remodel or retexture an object to make it work. Good lighters also need to be good compositors, because so much of CG can be broken into elements that later need to be put back together. For example, the shadows in a scene may be rendered separately from the rest of the scene.

Compositing as a specialty requires less knowledge of CG than a CG artist has, although today's competitive compositors should know as much as they can cram in their brains about CG. Compositors not only have to assemble and *color time* (make final color decisions about) CG shots, but they also have to work with live-action footage that needs to be altered or affected. For example, a compositor will need to remove a green screen from behind an actor and "place" that actor into a virtual rendered set. With color correction and other tools at their disposal, the compositors must make sure everything looks as though it belongs in the shot. In many cases, the line between lighter and compositor is blurred, and the two specialties can become one.

Generalists are CG artists who can do everything. This is not to say they are the be-all and end-all of all things CG. Many studios and boutiques have short-term jobs that are small in scale (as compared to a production of the Pixar film *Up,* for example). When a short turnaround is required, you need artists who can take a shot from beginning to end by modeling, texturing, lighting, animating, and rendering a scene. Generalists are more likely to work on commercials, for example, than feature films.

## Fundamental Concepts

CG touches many disciplines, and you will come across many different concepts as you learn CG. You'll need to understand something about physics, computer output, film, photography, sculpting, painting, and other disciplines. This section introduces several key concepts that will make it easier for you to understand how CG is created. Again, if you've been around the block a few times, you can skip large parts of this chapter. However, you never know when you might come across a little tidbit that fills in an educational gap you never thought you had.

### Computer Graphics Basics

Here are some general terminologies and methodologies used in computer graphics. Understanding them will help you understand how 3ds Max works. First on our plate is the critical distinction between *raster* (bitmap) and *vector* graphics and how this distinction affects you as a 3ds Max user.

#### Raster Images

Raster images (also known as bitmap images or bitmaps) make up the world of computer images today. In raster images, colored pixels are arranged to display an image on a screen; these pixels come together to form the image like a tapestry. The same is true of printouts, where dots of ink serve as pixels to form the printed image. The printed dots, like each colored pixel, come together to form the overall image.

When you work in a program such as Photoshop, you are editing the pixels of an image directly by adjusting existing settings such as color, size, and position for all or part of an image. In this manner, you can bring a scanned photo or a digital picture of your house into Photoshop and paint one wall red just to see how it would look before you buy paint at the store.

Essentially, a raster or bitmap image is a mosaic of pixels, with each pixel corresponding to a mosaic tile. The *resolution*—fineness of detail—of an image is defined by the number of pixels per inch (or other unit of measure) in the horizontal and vertical directions. Because raster images are based on a fixed grid, these images do not scale larger very well. The closer you zoom into a raster image (or the larger a raster image is scaled), the larger the pixels seem, which makes the zoomed or enlarged image blocky, or *pixelated*. To use larger raster images, you need to start with a higher resolution when the image is created. The higher the resolution, the larger the file size will be. Figure 1.3 shows what happens when you blow up a raster image.

So why are raster images even used if you can't scale them up well? Most common displays and output methods, such as television or computer screens or even printers, are actually raster displays. The display devices need raster images to display the pictures properly. The term *raster* originally referred to the display area of a television or computer monitor. To form an image, the electronics in these devices "paint" it as a grid of red, green, and blue pixels on a glowing screen. Every image generated by a computer, therefore, must either begin as a raster image or be *rasterized* as part of rendering for display.

Figure 1.3

**A raster image does not scale up very well. Here is the front of a stereo receiver that has been blown up by several hundred percent. The pixels look blocky.**

## Vector Images

Why does the interface for 3ds Max look so different from a paint program such as Photoshop? Autodesk 3ds Max and other 3D programs work with vectors. Vectors are created using mathematical algorithms and geometric functions. A vector program defines its images using coordinates and geometric formulas to plot points that define *areas, volumes,* and *shapes* instead of defining the color of each and every pixel in a grid of a raster image.

Popular vector-based image applications include Adobe Illustrator and Adobe Flash, as well as practically all computer-aided design (CAD) programs, including AutoCAD and SolidWorks. These programs let you define shapes and volumes and add color and texture to them through their toolsets.

Vector files store the scene in 3D space using coordinates and equations of points in space; and the color values are assigned through materials. Therefore, when a vector image is scaled up, the image does not suffer from the same blocky limitations as a raster image would. As you can see in Figure 1.4, vectors can be scaled with no loss of quality. They will never pixelate because they always redraw at the new scale.

Figure 1.4

**A vector image of a girl at its original size (left) and blown up to a few hundred percent (right) shows no loss in quality. The curves are not stepped or pixelated.**

Motion in a raster movie, such as a QuickTime movie, is stored in a long sequence of image files that, when played back, show animation or movement. By contrast, motion in vector programs is stored in the changes in the coordinates of the geometry and in the math that defines the shapes and volumes.

When a Flash cartoon plays on a web page you are visiting, for example, the information for that cartoon is downloaded into your computer in vector form. The data contains the position, size, and shape of all the elements of the animation. The vector information is then converted into raster images (called *rasterization*) so you can view the final image or animation. Your computer *renders* this information on the fly, in real time, into a raster display that you can enjoy on your screen.

This is roughly how things are done with 3D programs such as 3ds Max. You begin your work in 3ds Max's 3D space in vectors. When you are ready to render, 3ds Max renders the scene contents into raster images or movie files that you can display. You use the tools in 3ds Max to change the geometric information, which in turn changes the scene, and then re-render to show the output. Changing a raster image, such as retouching a digital photo, alters that original image once you save your work because it directly affects the pixels of the image.

### Image Output

When you're done with all your CG, you will probably want as many people as possible to see your work. To accomplish this, you will need to import the CG images into a game engine or render the scene out to a sequence of image files or a movie file. Game engines have specific import requirements, and image and movie files can be output and saved in many different ways. The kind of file output you will use will be determined by a combination of disk space, personal preference, project needs, and output requirements.

### Color Depth

Aside from the specific needs of print work, an image file stores the color of each pixel as three values, representing red, green, and blue. Image type depends on how much storage is allotted to each pixel (the *color depth*). These are the color depths common to image files in CG production:

**Grayscale**  The image is black and white with varying degrees (typically 256) of gray in between. Grayscale images are good for rendering out black-and-white subjects because no extraneous color information is stored in the image file.

**16-Bit Color Display or High-Color 5-Bit Image File**  Each color channel (red, green, blue) gets 5 bits of space to store its value, resulting in an image that can display a maximum of 32,768 colors. Each color channel has a limited range of shades, but still gives a nice color image. You might notice the gradation in the different shades of each color, which can result in *color banding* in the image. There is little use of these limited-color images in CG work, though you will find them used in web pages to maximize efficiency.

**8-Bit Image File**  This format is referred to as 24-bit color display or True Color, especially in Microsoft Windows desktop settings. Each color channel is given 8 bits, for a range of 256 shades each in the red, green, and blue channels. A total of 16 million colors are available to use in the image. This color depth gives the best color quality for an image and is widely used in most animation applications. The human eye cannot see quite as many shades of color as there are in a True Color image. Most of your renders from 3ds Max will be 24-bit color files.

**16-Bit Image File**  Used primarily in film work using such file types as TIFF 16, this type of image file holds 16 bits of information for each color channel, resulting in an astounding number of color levels and ranges. Each file can exceed several megabytes even at low resolutions. These files are primarily used in the professional workplace and are more standard for film work because outputting CG to film can require high levels of color and brightness range in the image.

**Floating-Point/32-Bit Image File**  Thirty-two-bit floating-point images are commonly used in film production to give the utmost attention to color depth. Most computers are capable of rendering a huge range of tones and colors, and 32-bit floating-point images capture that range effectively. These files (such as EXR and HDR images) are easy to work with using such tools such as Photoshop CS5 and usually require some tweaking in compositing to output properly.

EXR (based on the OpenEXR format pioneered by Industrial Light & Magic for high-end film work) and high dynamic range (HDR) images are usually in 32-bit float format and are incredibly detailed in the range of contrast they store. Therefore, they are very helpful tools in creating lighting for scenes using renderers such as mental ray.

## Color Channels

As mentioned, each image file holds the color information in channels. All color images have a red, green, and blue (RGBA) color channel. Each channel is a measurement of the amount of red, green, or blue in areas of the image. A fourth channel, called the *alpha* channel, is used as a transparency channel. This channel, also known as the matte channel, defines which portions of the image are transparent or opaque. Not all image files have alpha channels.

Some file types, such as OpenEXR, can have multiple channels within the single-image file. For example, an OpenEXR file can contain not only the RGBA channels to define color and transparency, but also channels to describe surface normals, depth in Z space, motion blur vectors, ambient occlusion, shadows, etc. We will explore image channels in more depth in Chapter 11.

### FILE FORMATS

In addition to image types, several image file formats are available today. The most common is probably JPEG (Joint Photographic Experts Group), which is widely used on the Internet for its small size and reasonable image quality. However, JPEGs are too compressed and lossy (meaning they lose color detail when compared to the original) to be used in most CG renders.

The main difference among file formats relates to how they store images. Some formats compress the file to reduce file size; however, the greater the compression, the poorer the image's color.

The popular formats to render into from 3ds Max are Tagged Image File Format (TIFF), Targa (TGA), and OpenEXR (EXR). These file formats maintain at least a good 24-bit color depth using an 8-bit or more image file, are either uncompressed or hardly compressed (*lossless* compression), and are frequently used for broadcast or film work. These formats also have at least an alpha channel, giving you better control when you later composite images together.

To see an animation rendered in a file sequence of TIFFs, you will need to play them back using a frame player, such as 3ds Max's RAM Player, or you can compile them into a movie file, such as a QuickTime file.

Your final image output format will depend on the project's needs. If, for example, you need to composite your CG together, you will need to output in a format that can be used in your compositing or editing program. TIFF files are perhaps the best format to use as they are widely compatible, store uncompressed color, and have an alpha channel. EXR files are quickly gaining widespread popularity for their multichannel capability and high color fidelity. More and more compositing packages are supporting EXRs. EXR files (especially at a high bit depth and with multiple channels) can be quite large.

### MOVIE FILES

Animations can also be output to movie files such as AVI or QuickTime. These usually large files are self-contained and hold all the images necessary for the animation that they play back as frames. Like image files, movie files can be compressed to keep their sizes to a minimum, but they suffer from quality loss as well.

3ds Max can render directly to an AVI or QuickTime movie file. This may seem like it saves you the hassle of rendering out large sequences of image files. In reality, you shouldn't render directly to a movie file, at least for your final output. It is best to render a sequence of files, because image sequences can easily be compiled into a movie file later using a program such as Autodesk Combustion, Adobe After Effects, Premiere, or even QuickTime Pro.

Rendering to images is less risky than rendering to a movie. In addition to having a sequence you can easily manipulate, you do not have to worry about crashing and losing rendering time. If your render crashes or your machine freezes while you are rendering to a movie file, you'll need to restart rendering from the beginning, because you can't append content to a half-rendered QuickTime movie. With a file sequence render, you can simply pick up the render from the last good frame. With a sequence, you also have the option of reordering the frames or easily adjusting a few individual frames' properties, such as hue or saturation, without affecting the entire movie file.

## Color

Color is how we perceive the differences in the frequency of light. The wide range of colors that we see (the visible spectrum) can be replicated (on a screen, for example) when any of three *primary colors* of light—red, green, and blue—are mixed together. Color can be mixed in two ways: subtractive and additive. These color definitions are most often displayed in *color wheels*, which place primary colors equally spaced around a ring, and place in between the appropriate primaries the colors that result when the primaries are mixed.

Understanding how color works will help you gain more from your CG's color scheme and help you design your shots with greater flexibility and better outcomes.

### SUBTRACTIVE AND ADDITIVE COLOR

Subtractive color mixing is used when an image will be seen with an external light source. It's based on the way reflected light creates color. Light rays bounce off colored surfaces and are tinted by the different pigments on the surface. These pigments absorb and reflect only certain frequencies of the light hitting them, in essence subtracting certain colors from the light before it gets to your eyes. Pile up enough different colors of paint, and you'll get black; all the color is absorbed by the pigment and only black is reflected.

With *subtractive color* mixing for painting, the traditional color wheel's primary colors are red, blue, and yellow. These three pigments can be mixed together to form any other color pigment. This is the basis for the color wheel most people are exposed to in art education. However, in the world of print production, a CMYK (cyan, magenta, yellow, and black) color wheel is used, which places cyan, magenta, and yellow ink colors as the primary colors used to mix all the other ink colors for print work.

Projected light, however, is mixed as *additive color*. Each light's frequency adds upon another's to form color. The additive primary colors are red, green, and blue. These three colors, when mixed in certain ratios, form the entire range of color. When all are equally mixed together, they form a white light.

A computer monitor uses only additive color, mixing each color with amounts of red, green, and blue (RGB). Output for print is converted to a CMYK color model.

*Warm colors* are those in the magenta to red to yellow range, and *cool colors* are those in the green to cyan to blue range of the additive color wheel. Warm colors seem to advance from the frame, and cool colors seem to recede into the frame.

### HOW A COMPUTER DEFINES COLOR

Computers represent all information, including color, as sets of numeric values made up of binary 0s and 1s (bits). With a 24-bit RGB color depth, each pixel is represented by three 8-bit values corresponding to the red, green, and blue "channels" of the image. An 8-bit binary number can range from 0 to 255; therefore, you have 256 possible levels for each primary color. With three channels, you have $256 \times 256 \times 256$ (16.7 million) possible combinations of each primary color mixed to form the final color.

Color value need not be expressed in values for red, green, and blue. It can also be set on the hue, saturation, and value (HSV) channels of a color. Again, each channel holds a value from 0 to 255 (in an 8-bit image) that defines the final color. The hue value defines the actual tint (from red to green to violet) of the color. The saturation defines *how much* of that tint is present in the color. The higher the saturation value, the deeper the color. Finally, value defines the brightness of the color, from black to white. The higher the value, the brighter the color.

HSV and RGB give you different methods to control color, allowing you to use the method you prefer. All the colors available in 3ds Max, from textures to lights, are defined as either RGB or HSV values for the best flexibility. You can switch from HSV to RGB definition in 3ds Max at any time.

### CMYK COLOR

A CMYK color wheel is used for print work. This is referred to as the four-color process. Color inkjet printers produce color printouts by mixing the appropriate levels of these inks onto the paper.

All output from an RGB-based computer to a printer goes through a CMYK conversion as it is being printed. For professional print work, specially calibrated monitors are used to better preview the CMYK color of an RGB image before it is printed. Fortunately, only print professionals need to worry about this conversion process because most of it is handled by graphics software to a fairly accurate degree.

### VIEWING COLOR

The broadcast standard for North America is called *NTSC,* which stands for National Television Standards Committee. Industry folks sometimes refer to the acronym as Never The Same Color, calling attention to the fact that the color you see on one TV screen will inevitably look different on another TV. The same is true for computer monitors, especially flat panel displays. Unless calibrated to do so, different screens do not show the same color the same way, so what you see on one screen will display differently on another screen. If it is paramount that the color appear as you see it on a specific screen, it makes sense to finalize the work and show it on that screen. You can also download color bars from the Internet to display on monitors in an attempt to calibrate them to your eye. This is not the best way to go, but at least it will help a little without the costs and trouble of using color calibration equipment.

## Resolution, Aspect Ratio, and Frame Rate

*Resolution* expresses the size of an image by the number of horizontal and vertical pixels it contains, and usually is stated as $x \times y$; an example of this would be $640 \times 480$. By and large, the higher the original resolution of an image, the finer the image detail will be.

You will adjust your final render size to suit the medium for which you are creating the animation. Table 1.1 lists some typical video resolutions.

| STANDARD | SIZE | NOTES |
| --- | --- | --- |
| VGA (Video Graphics Array) | 640 × 480 | Formerly the standard computing resolution and still a popular television resolution for tape output. |
| NTSC D1 (National Television Standards Committee) | 720 × 486 | The standard resolution for broadcast television in the Americas and Japan. |
| NTSC DV | 720 × 480 | Close to the NTSC D1 resolution, this is the typical resolution of digital video cameras. |
| PAL (Phase Alternate Line) | 768 × 576 | The standard broadcast resolution for most European countries. |
| HDTV (High Definition TV) | 1920 × 1080 | The emerging television standard, sometimes also referred to as 1080i or 1080p. |
| 1K Academy (1K refers to 1,000 pixels across) | 1024 × 768 | Typically, the lowest allowable resolution for film production at Academy ratio. Because film is an optical format (whereas TV is a raster format), there is no real set resolution for film. Suffice it to say, the higher the better. |
| 2K Academy (2K refers to 2,000 pixels across) | 2048 × 1556 | Most studios output CG for film at this resolution, which gives the best size-to-performance ratio. |
| 4K Academy (4K refers to 4,000 pixels across) | 4094 × 3072 | A high resolution for film, used for highly detailed shots. |

Table 1.1

**Typical Video Resolutions**

Any discussion of resolution must include the matter of *aspect ratio*. Aspect ratio is the ratio of the screen's *width* to its *height*. There is a variety of standard aspect ratios (Table 1.2).

| STANDARD | SIZE | NOTES |
| --- | --- | --- |
| Academy Standard | 1.33:1 or 4:3 | The most common aspect ratio. The width of an image is 1.33 times its height. This is the NTSC television aspect ratio. |
| Widescreen TV | 1.78:1 or 16:9 | With HD and widescreen TVs gaining popularity, the 16:9 standard is commonplace now. This aspect ratio is used in HD programming and is also the aspect ratio of many widescreen computer monitors and laptops. This aspect ratio is very close to how most films are displayed (1.85:1, as seen in the next row). |
| Widescreen Film (aka, Academy Flat) | 1.85:1 | The most often used 35mm film aspect today. When it's displayed on a standard television, horizontal black bars appear above and below the picture so that the edges are not cropped off (This is called letterboxing). |
| Anamorphic Ratio | 2.35:1 | Using a special lens (called an anamorphic lens), an image originally captured on 35mm film is squeezed. When played back via a projector with an anamorphic lens, the image is projected at a width 2.35 times its height. On a standard TV, the letterboxing would be more severe to avoid cropping the sides. |

Table 1.2

**Standard Aspect Ratios**

The number of frames that are played back per second determines the *frame rate* of an animation. This is denoted as *fps*, or frames per second. The three standard frame rates for media are as follows:

- NTSC: 30fps
- PAL: 25fps
- Film: 24fps

Knowing what your final output medium is going to be before you begin your project is pretty important. It is not crucial by any means, but knowing what the screen will look like (i.e., whether it will be a small web window or a large television) will help you better compose your scenes. You can always change your frame rate and render resolution later, but it is much simpler to begin with it already worked out.

Playing back a 24fps animation at 30fps will yield a slower-moving animation and will require either repeating some frames to fill in the gaps or ending the animation early. Conversely, playing a 30fps animation at 24fps will create a faster-moving animation that will either skip some frames or end later than it should.

Games do not typically have a set playback rate for animation. When a scene is created for a game, the assets in the scene are rendered and played back on the user's computer system in real time; therefore, many factors contribute to the playback speed of scenes created for games. The game's engine and game playback hardware, such as graphics card or console type, determine the frame rate. Also, on the Internet playback speeds vary according to the content and the delivery method.

## Coordinate Systems

Coordinates are numerical representations of where an object is in 3D space. Every object in 3ds Max has a coordinate of where it exists. Without this coordinate, it would be gone—*poof*—into thin air! Max's 3D space is organized with the Cartesian coordinate system, which uses a three-pronged axis to define width, height, and depth as *X*, *Y*, and *Z*, respectively. The overall coordinate system in 3ds Max is called the *world coordinate system*. It is an absolute coordinate system that is fixed and unchangeable.

Objects in 3ds Max can have their own coordinate systems as well. When an object is created, it has its own width, height, and depth, again expressed as *X*, *Y*, and *Z*. Upon creation, the local coordinate system (belonging to the created object) and the world coordinate system are aligned. However, when the object is rotated, its local coordinate system rotates with it. Because of this, an object created in a Front viewport (for instance) will have a different Local axis than if it were created in the Top viewport.

Figure 1.5 shows a box. The *X*-, *Y*-, and *Z*-axes of the box are displayed in the center of the base of the box and align with the axes of the world coordinate system (which shows the World Space axes) displayed in the lower-left corner of the window.

When the box in the scene is rotated, 3ds Max retains them as Local space instead of substituting its own axes. The *X*-axis of the box does not change. Now the Local axis and the World Space axis are not aligned. This is a very good feature because it allows you to manipulate the box based on its original Local axes.

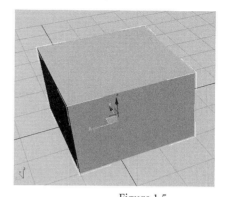

**Figure 1.5**

**The local space of the box aligns with the World Space axes.**

## Animation Fundamentals

A wealth of information regarding animation concepts and techniques is available on the Internet. Also, there are tons of books out there that teach the basics of animation. In this very brief section, you will be exposed to a few important concepts behind animation. These concepts will help you better understand what you're doing in 3ds Max.

### Frames, Keyframes, and In-Betweens

Animation is based on change over time; so you need a unit of measure for time. In animation, time is almost always expressed in *frames*. One frame is a single rendered image in an animation, or a single drawing in a traditional animation. *Frame* also refers to a single unit of time in your animation. The exact length of that time depends on the final frame rate at which the animation will be played back. For example, at film rate (24fps), a single frame will last $\frac{1}{24}$ of a second. At NTSC video rate (30fps), that same frame will last $\frac{1}{30}$ of a second. Therefore, a video based output will require more frames for the same amount of time as would a film.

*Keyframes* are points at which the animator creates a pose for a character (or whatever is being animated). A keyframe, in CG terms, is a frame in which a pose, a position, or some other parameter's value has been saved in time. Animation is when the object travels or changes between keyframes. Because the change happens between *keys*, these frames are called *in-between* frames. The computer extrapolates what needs to happen to get the object from its state in keyframe 1 to its state in keyframe 2. You will have plenty to keyframe in the coming chapters of this book.

In 3ds Max, a keyframe can be set on almost *any* parameter of an object, such as its color, position, or size. In reality, you can set several keys on any one frame in CG animation. Figure 1.6 illustrates a keyframe sequence.

Figure 1.6
In the first frame
of this sequence,
a keyframe is set
on the position,
rotation, and scale
of the cone. On
frame 30, the same
properties are again
keyframed. The
computer calculates
all the movement in
between.

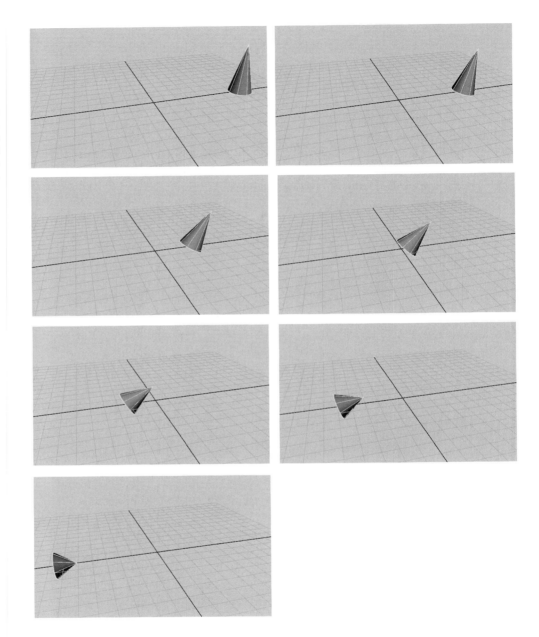

## Weight

*Weight* is an implied facet of design and animation. Weight denotes the heaviness or presence of an element in a design. The more weight an element has, the more power it has in the composition. The weight of an object in a composition is affected by its color, its contrast, its background, its position in the frame, and other variables.

The weight of an object in animation roughly follows that idea, but more pragmatically denotes the actual weight of the object as it relates to its environment. Giving an object a good weight in animation is critical to the believability of the animation. You will have a chance to animate an object and edit the animation to give it weight in Chapter 8's Bouncing Ball and Knife exercises.

*Weight in animation is a perception of mass.* An object's movement and how it reacts in motion and to other objects are critical to conveying the feeling of weight. Otherwise, the animation will look bogus or "cartoonish." Over the years, animators have created a set of techniques to give their subject weight in animation. Manipulating these concepts correctly in your work will greatly help your animations.

## Squash and Stretch

"Squash and stretch" is a cartoon concept that allows a character to physically squash down when he is landing from a jump, or stretch out thin while he is jumping up. The overall mass of an object should never really change. When you squash an object down, you should also reduce its height to make it seem as if it's squashing down. Similarly, when you stretch an object up, you should also thin it. This technique will make a character seem to respond to gravity. You will see how this applies in the Bouncing Ball exercise in Chapter 8.

## Ease-In and Ease-Out

Things in the real world don't immediately come to an abrupt stop. There is always a slowing before a stoppage, no matter how fast the stop may be. This is called *ease-out*.

Just as objects don't suddenly stop, they don't immediately start moving either. Pretty much everything needs to accelerate, no matter how fast it begins moving. This is called *ease-in*. The mechanics of *ease-in* and *ease-out* will also be illustrated in the Bouncing Ball exercise in Chapter 8.

## Follow-Through and Anticipation

Exaggerating the weight of an object in animation is sometimes necessary. Objects ending an action usually have some type of *follow-through* motion. For example, a ponytail on a girl jumping down from a chair will continue to move after she lands on the floor. There should be a slight resting follow-through to her action. For example, she may bend slightly at the waist to center herself once she lands.

You can also create a small amount of movement before your action is in full swing. Before committing to an action, a character may "wind up" to a greater or lesser extent. Doing so will create a slight *anticipation* in the movement (for example, a hammer cocking back slightly before it strikes or a cartoon superhero that bends down before he jumps up to fly away). These concepts are covered in Chapter 8.

# 3ds Max Fundamental Terms and Concepts

Any 3D program has terms and concepts you need to learn to become a good artist in that tool. Most of these concepts are fairly transferable, meaning they apply to more than one CG package, although their names may vary depending on which package you are using. Here are several terms and concepts you will encounter in the world of CG as they relate to 3ds Max. If you are not already familiar with 3ds Max's interface, running through this list before diving into the next chapter might be a good idea.

**Objects** An element in your 3ds Max scene is called an *object*. An object may be converted to a more easily Editable Mesh at any time. You will learn about this concept in Chapter 4, "Modeling in 3ds Max: Part I."

**Primitives** *Primitives* are basic 3ds Max objects such as spheres or boxes. Primitives can be shaped and altered to suit the needs of the model.

**Sub-objects** Many (though not all) objects are made up of components called *sub-objects*. You can select and manipulate sub-objects in 3ds Max to alter the look or function of an object. Types of sub-objects include vertices, faces, polygons, edges, gizmos, and centers. The types of sub-object you are able to manipulate depends on the type of object you are manipulating. See Chapter 4 for more on sub-objects.

**Normals** Each face of a polygon has a direction in which it points. A *normal* is a vector that defines which way a face is oriented.

Figure 1.7

**Spinners allow you to change the value of a parameter**

**Spinners** *Spinners* are a function of the user interface (UI) in Max. Spinners are the little arrows to the right of value readouts; they allow you to adjust the values either by clicking up or down on the arrows or by clicking and dragging the values to change. A spinner for a sphere's radius value is shown in Figure 1.7.

**Flyouts** Another UI term, a *flyout* is an icon in 3ds Max that is actually several icons in one. If you press and hold a flyout icon, the other icons "fly out" and display themselves. Scroll to the icon you need and click to activate its flyout properties. A flyout icon has a black triangle in its lower-right corner (as here: ⚓). Flyouts are further covered in Chapter 3, "The 3ds Max Interface."

**Home Grid** The *Home Grid* is a gray grid that displays the origin (0, 0, 0). It is useful for grounding yourself in the viewports, and it helps with proportion and direction as well. A Perspective viewport Home Grid is shown in Figure 1.8.

**Absolute/Relative** *Absolute* refers to an adjustment on an object that is based on a fixed reference, such as World Space. An absolute scale of 2 will scale the object to a flat unit of 2. *Relative* refers to an adjustment made to an object that takes its current state into account. Scaling with a relative value of 2 will make that object twice its current size.

Figure 1.8

**The Home Grid in the Perspective viewport**

**Track** In 3ds Max a *track* is a display of animation data for an animated object. When an object has animation on several parameters, such as Move $X$ and $Y$, as well as Scale in $X$ and $Z$, it is said to have four tracks. One track defines one animation on one parameter of that object on one axis.

**SUGGESTED READING**

The more you know about all the arts that are used in CG, the more confident you'll feel among your peers. To get started, check out the following excellent resources:

**ART AND DESIGN**

These books provide valuable insights into the mechanics and art of design. The more you understand design theory, the stronger your art will be.

Bowers, John. *Introduction to Two-Dimensional Design: Understanding Form and Function*. New York: John Wiley & Sons, 2008.

Itten, Johannes. *Design and Form*: The Basic Course at the Bauhaus and Later. New York: John Wiley & Sons, 1975.

Ocvirk, Otto G., and others. *Art Fundamentals: Theory and Practice*. New York: McGraw-Hill, 2008.

Wong, Wucius. *Principles of Form and Design*. New York: John Wiley & Sons, 1993.

*continued*

**SUGGESTED READING** *(continued)*

**CG**

CG has an interesting history and is evolving at breakneck speeds. Acquiring a solid knowledge of this history and evolution is as important as keeping up with current trends.

Kerlow, Isaac Victor. *The Art of 3-D: Computer Animation and Imaging*. New York: John Wiley & Sons, 2000.

Derakhshani, Dariush. *Introducing Maya 2011*. San Francisco: Sybex, 2010.

Kuperberg, Marcia. *Guide to Computer Animation for tv, games, multimedia and web*. Burlington, MA: Focal Press, 2002.

Masson, Terrence. *CG 101: A Computer Graphics Industry Reference*. Indianapolis: New Riders Publishing, 1999.

Birn, Jeremy. *Digital Lighting and Rendering (2nd Edition)*. Indianapolis: New Riders Publishing, 2006.

**FILM**

Block, Bruce. *The Visual Story: Seeing the Structure of Film, TV, and New Media*. Burlington, MA: Focal Press, 2001.

**PERIODICALS**

These magazines offer great topical insights into the industry, and product reviews as well as some tutorials for further study.

*Computer Graphics World* (free subscription for those who qualify): www.cgw.com

*Cinefex*: www.cinefex.com

*3D World*: www.3dworldmag.com

**WEBSITES**

You'll find a wealth of information at your fingertips at these websites.

www.autodesk.com

www.animationartist.com

www.awn.com

## Summary

In this chapter, you learned the basic concepts that drive the CG field. Starting with production workflow and moving into CG workflow, we discussed how productions are generally run. Next, you learned the different types of tasks used in CG production and the professional specialties that have arisen from them. After that, you learned about core computer concepts, color space, and output formats. Finally, you saw a preview of some of the key 3ds Max terms and concepts that are covered in depth in the following chapters.

No matter how you use this chapter—or even if you skip it entirely to get right to the action—there is a lot of background information here that can be useful in your overall knowledge of CG production. Although it takes some extra time to develop a good foundation, having one is an excellent idea because gaining true understanding of a subject is fundamental to its mastery. Having said this, take the rest of the book as it comes, enjoy the challenges of the exercises, and remember that *some* frustration with an exercise will inevitably help you learn the concepts better, so keep at it.

# CHAPTER 2

# Your First 3ds Max Project

*This chapter gets your engine revving* right away. It begins with an overview of the user interface (UI) and starts you off with an exercise that will expose you to a few 3ds Max workflows and practices. The goal of the chapter is to put some concepts from the previous chapter into production so you can get going quickly and get experience with the interface.

Topics in this chapter include the following:

- **Getting around in 3ds Max**
- **Project and file-management workflow**
- **The 3ds Max interface**
- **Jumping headlong into production**

# Getting Around in 3ds Max

At this point, it's important not to get caught up in the details of this great machine. Don't worry about the steps, buttons, menus, switches, and levers; just allow yourself to become comfortable with the tools that you use to create your artwork. Creating art is never about which button to press; it's about what to create. Always remember that, and your studies will be a great deal more successful.

Jumping straight into an exercise without knowing how to get around the interface might seem a little weird. However, you'll find everything you ever wanted to know, and then some, in Chapter 3, "The 3ds Max Interface." Learning is an experimental art, and there's no better way to learn than to start experimenting as soon as you can. The overall goal of this chapter is to expose you to the UI and show you how to get some things done in Max. Then you can proceed to the next chapter for a debriefing. (If you prefer, you can skip ahead to Chapter 3, get a tour of the UI, and then come back to this chapter for your first experience.)

# Project and File-Management Workflow

3ds Max provides several subfolders automatically grouped into projects for you. Different kinds of files are saved in categorized folders under the Project folder. For example, scene files are saved in a Scenes folder and rendered images are saved in a Render Output folder in the Project folder. The projects are set up according to what types of files you are working on, so everything is neat and organized from the get-go. 3ds Max will automatically create this folder structure for you once you create a new project, and its default settings will keep the files organized in that manner.

The conventions followed in this book and on the accompanying web page (`www.sybex.com/go/`) will follow this project-based system so that you can grow accustomed to it and make it a part of your own workflow. File organization is extremely important for professional work. If you do a lot of CG for fun or profit, it pays to be organized.

The exercises in this book are organized into specific projects, such as the one you will tackle in this chapter, *Mobile*. The Mobile project will be on your hard drive, and the folders for your scene files and rendered images will be in it. Once you copy the appropriate projects to your hard drive, you can tell 3ds Max which project to work on by choosing Application menu → Manage → Set Project Folder. This will send the current project to that project folder. For example, when you save your scene, 3ds Max will automatically take you to the Scenes folder of the current project.

Before we begin any project, we'll briefly explain the naming conventions and suggest a folder structure. Using these naming conventions and structures is a good habit to develop.

## Naming Conventions

Every studio and professional production company worth its salt has an established *naming convention* for its files and folders. This is a documented procedure that dictates how to name files and (usually) where to store them. Most organizations have different conventions, but the point is to have a convention and stick to it.

Students, in particular, tend to forgo any semblance of organization in their file-naming procedures. A common mistake is to save files to the local disk on the school computer, only to have the files erased by the support teams during the school's weekly purge. Designating a specific place on your PC or server for all your project files is important.

In addition to finding a suitable place to store your files, you need to name the files following some sort of convention. Your files will not only look neat when you're browsing, but they'll make sense months later when you try to figure out where you saved that finished scene file that you need. Typically, you should name a scene file with a project name or an abbreviation of such, then a brief description of what the file is, and a version number.

Figure 2.1

**Click Make New Folder and enter the folder name.**

For example, if you are working on a project about a castle, begin by setting a new project called *Castle*. Choose Application menu → Manage → Set Project Folder. On your hard drive, click the Make New Folder button (Figure 2.1) to create a folder named **Castle**. 3ds Max will automatically create the project and its folders.

Once you save a scene, one of your scene filenames should look like this: `Castle_GateModel_v05.max`. This tells you right away it's a scene from your Castle project, and that it is a model of the gate. The version number tells you that it's the fifth iteration of the model and possibly the most recent version. Following a naming convention will save you oodles of time and aggravation.

## Version Up!

The naming convention just mentioned used a version number appended to the end of the filename. After you've spent a significant amount of time working on your scene, or after you've made a major change or big breakthrough in your work, you will want to *version up*. This means you save your file using the same name, but you increase the version number by one to tell yourself or your colleagues that there was a big change since the last version. Version numbers are also useful for keeping track of your progress.

Version numbers can also save your hide. If you start down a path on your scene, but discover after hours of work (and saving your work as you went along, versioning up as you went) that this was in fact the wrong way to go, you can simply close the scene and open one of the previous versions that you created before you started going in the wrong direction. This happens a lot more than you might think.

Disk space is cheap and scene files, even huge ones, aren't all that big in the face of terabytes of space that you can buy for around $100. Keep a notebook and a pen next to your workstation so that you can take notes on your progress and record exactly what you did during your work sessions. Professionals do this regularly; those who don't should. They can't afford to waste time trying to figure out what file they should load to access a particular chunk of work.

## The Basic Project Structure Used in This Book

Each exercise in this book will be its own 3ds Max project. Pick a place on your hard drive and start there. Create a folder called **Max Projects** on your C: drive (you can create one anywhere you want, including your My Documents folder). Place all of your projects in this folder. This will make it easy to find your files and back them up to DVD or backup drive.

Let's create the first project we'll be working on, *Mobile*. Select Application menu → Manage → Set Project Folder, navigate to your 3ds Max Projects folder (or My Documents folder), and then click Make New Folder. Name the folder **Mobile**. 3ds Max will create the subfolders for the project once you click OK, as shown in Figure 2.2.

Figure 2.2

**Standard subfolders for the Mobile project**

That's pretty much it. Having a naming convention is easy; sticking to it is not, especially when you're first starting out. Make sure you stick to it.

## Saving Your Scenes in Max

Save your scene frequently to protect yourself from mistakes and from losing your work. Choosing Application menu → Save updates the current scene by overwriting the last save of the scene. If the scene was not previously saved, this command opens the Save File As dialog box. Using it, you can select where to save the scene and enter your scene's name. If you are working in a scene file already, I recommend using Save As so you do not accidentally overwrite your current work. You can also use an incremental save function, discussed shortly.

To version up, you can save by using Application menu → Save As and manually changing the version number appended to the end of the filename. 3ds Max also lets you do this automatically by using an increment feature in the Save As dialog box. Simply name your scene file and click the Increment button (the + icon) to the right of the filename text (Figure 2.3).

Clicking the Increment button will append the filename with 01, then 02, then 03, and so on as you keep saving your work using Save As and the Increment button. In the previous example, the scene's base filename was SceneName_v. Clicking the Increment button added the two-digit version number after the _v. Adding the _v is a personal preference, of course, but it keeps with the naming convention set up in this book. It looks nicer, and you can easily determine the version number for your file by reading the number after the _v.

Figure 2.3

**Click the Increment button to version up.**

# The 3ds Max Interface

Here is a brief rundown of what you need to know about the UI and how to navigate in 3ds Max's 3D space. We will cover the interface in more detail in the next chapter, so feel free to jump back and forth if you need to know more about the UI.

Figure 2.4 shows theUI. At the very top left of the application window is a large icon (with 3ds Max's logo) called the Application menu (aka Application button) which gives access to many file operations such as Save and Open. Running along the top also is the Quick Access toolbar, which provides access to common commands, and the InfoCenter for various Autodesk applications' support. Just below that is the menu bar, which runs across the top of the UI. The menus give you access to a ton of commands—from basic scene operations, such as Undo, to advanced tools you may need for a scene. Immediately below the menu bar is the Main toolbar. It contains several icons for functions such as the three Transform tools (Move, Rotate, and Scale). You will use some of these icons for the Mobile exercise. They are more fully explained in Chapter 3.

Quick Access toolbar · InfoCenter · Command panel
Application menu · Menu bar · Main toolbar · Modeling ribbon (Graphite Modeling tools) · ViewCubes · Viewports · Time slider · Track bar · MAXScript Mini-Listener · Prompt line · Animation keying controls · Animation playback controls · Viewport navigation controls

Figure 2.4

**The 3ds Max 2011 Interface**

Some of the most important commands in the Quick Access toolbar are the Save File and Open File commands as well as the all important Undo Scene Operation and Redo Scene Operation functions. If you do something and then wish you hadn't, click the Undo Scene Operation icon (the icon on the left in Figure 2.5) or press Ctrl+Z. To redo a command or action that you just undid, click the Redo Scene Operation button (the icon on the right in Figure 2.5) or press Ctrl+Y.

Figure 2.5

**The Undo Scene Operation and Redo Scene Operation buttons**

## The Command Panel

A tremendously important part of the 3ds Max UI is the Command panel, a vertical column or panel on the right side of the UI. It is segmented into tabs, as shown in Figure 2.6. Each tab displays the buttons and icons for a particular part of your workflow, such as creating objects, modifying objects, and animating objects. In each tab, the functions are grouped under headings that can be expanded or collapsed by clicking on the heading title. A plus sign next to the heading name, known as a rollout, means that you can expand the heading's view; a minus sign means that you can collapse the heading to save space.

If the Command panel is longer than what you can see vertically on your screen, you can mouse over a blank area of the Command panel, and the arrow pointer will change to a hand pointer, as shown in Figure 2.6, when it is not on a button or icon. While the pointer is a hand, you can click and drag to move the current panel up and down in the Command panel to see more functions in that space. You can also click on the far right side of the panel to scroll up and down if you don't want to use the hand.

The viewport controls (Figure 2.7), which contain icons for various options for the 3D world windows (called *viewports*), are in the lower-right corner of the UI. These functions allow you to navigate the windows and their 3D space. However, you may find it easier to use hot keys rather than icons to invoke most of these functions. We will cover navigating 3D space and the appropriate hot keys next.

## Viewports

You'll be doing most of your work in the viewports. These windows represent 3D space using a system based on *Cartesian coordinates.* That is a fancy way of saying "space on $X$-, $Y$-, and $Z$-axes." All CG programs, including 3ds Max, are based on this coordinate system.

You can visualize $X$ as left–right, $Y$ as up–down, and $Z$ as in–out (into and out of the screen). The coordinates are expressed as a set of three numbers such as $(0, 3, -7)$. These coordinates represent a point that is at 0 on the $X$-axis, three units up on the $Y$-axis, and seven units back on the $Z$-axis.

### Four-Viewport Layout

3ds Max's viewports are the windows into your scene (Figure 2.8). By default, there are four main views: Front, Top, Left, and Perspective. The first three—Front, Top, and Left—are called Orthographic (2D) views. They are also referred to as *modeling windows.* These windows are good for expressing exact dimensions and size relationships, so they are good tools for sizing up your scene objects and fine-tuning their layout.

The name of each viewport is listed in the viewport's upper-left corner between a plus sign and a display-mode name.

Command panel tabs

Rollout

Hand pointer

Rollout

Scroll bar

**Figure 2.6**

**The tabs in the Command panel are segmented into headings called** *rollouts* **that group similar functions and icons.**

**Figure 2.7**

**The viewport controls**

Figure 2.8

**The 3ds Max viewports**

The Perspective viewport displays objects in 3D space using perspective. Notice in Figure 2.8 how the distant cubes seem to get smaller in the Perspective viewport. In actuality, they are the same size, as you can see in the Orthographic viewports. The Perspective viewport gives you the best representation of what your output will be.

To select a viewport, click in a blank part of the viewport (not on an object). If you do have something selected, it will be deselected when you click in the blank space. You can also right-click anywhere in an inactive viewport to activate it without selecting or deselecting anything. When active, the view will have a mustard yellow highlight around it. If you right-click in an already active viewport, you will get a pop-up context menu called the *Quad menu*. You can use this shortcut menu to access some basic commands for a faster workflow. We will cover this and other shortcut menus in the next chapter.

### Display of Objects and Axes in a Viewport

Viewports can display your scene objects in a few different ways. If you click the viewport's name, you can switch that panel to any other viewport angle or point of view. If you click the viewport display mode name (shown as [Smooth + Highlights] in Figure 2.9), a menu will appear (Figure 2.9) to allow you to change the display mode. The most common view modes are Wireframe mode and Smooth + Highlights mode. Wireframe mode displays the edges of the object. It is the fastest to use because it requires less computation on your video card. The Smooth + Highlights mode is a shaded view where the objects in the scene appear solid. You will get the chance to experiment with different display modes in the upcoming Mobile exercise.

Each viewport displays a ground plane grid (as shown in the Perspective viewport), called the *Home Grid* (Figure 2.10). This is the basic 3D-space reference system. It's defined by three fixed planes on the coordinate axes (*X, Y, Z*). The center of all three axes is called the *origin*. This is where the coordinates are (0, 0, 0). The Home Grid is visible in 3ds Max's default settings when you start the software, but it can be turned off in the right-click Viewport menu. You can also toggle the grid by pressing the G key.

The Perspective viewport has a red, green, and blue axis marker in which the *X*-axis is red, the *Y*-axis is green, and the *Z*-axis is blue. 3ds Max uses this red, green, and blue color scheme to represent the *X*-, *Y*-, and *Z*-axes throughout the interface.

> Most 3D packages use red, green, and blue to represent *X*-, *Y*-, and *Z*-axes, respectively. It's not just a 3ds Max thing.

Figure 2.9
**Click to see the viewport display mode options.**

Figure 2.10
**The Home Grid in the Perspective viewport**

## Selecting Objects in a Viewport

Selecting objects in a viewport is as easy as clicking them. If the object is displayed in Wireframe mode, its wireframe will turn white while it is selected. If the object is displayed in a Shaded mode, a white bracket will appear around the object as shown in Figure 2.11.

To select multiple objects, hold down the Ctrl key as you click additional objects to add to your selection. If you Ctrl+click an active object, you will deselect it. You can clear all of your active selections by clicking anywhere an empty area of the viewport.

> The Alt key can be used to subtract objects from a selection set.

Figure 2.11
**The white frame indicates the object is selected.**

### Changing/Maximizing the Viewports

To change the view in any given viewport—for example, to go from a Perspective view to a Front view—click the current viewport's name. From the menu, select the view you want to have in this viewport, as shown in Figure 2.12.

A faster way to change viewports is by using keyboard shortcuts. To switch from one view to another, press the appropriate key on the keyboard, as shown in the following table:

| VIEWPORT | KEYBOARD SHORTCUT |
|---|---|
| Top view | T |
| Bottom view | B |
| Front view | F |
| Left view | L |
| Camera view | C |
| Orthographic | U |
| Perspective view | P |

If you want to have a larger view of the active viewport than is provided by the default four-viewport layout, press the Maximize Viewport Toggle icon ( ) in the lower-right corner of the Max window. You can also use the Alt+W keyboard shortcut to toggle between the maximized and four-viewport views.

## Viewport Navigation

To work effectively, you will need to navigate in 3D space. 3ds Max allows you to move around its viewports either by using key/mouse combinations, which are highly preferable, or by using the viewport controls found in the lower-right corner of the 3ds Max

Figure 2.12
**Click to change the view.**

UI. A full explanation of the viewport controls is in the next chapter. However, to navigate within the views, you should become familiar with the key/mouse combinations now.

Open a new, empty scene in 3ds Max. Experiment with the following controls to get a feel for moving around in 3D space. If you are new to 3D, this may seem odd at first, but it will become easier as you gain experience, and it should become second nature in no time. If you are coming to 3ds Max from another 3D package, such as Maya, you will notice several things that will take a little getting used to, but you will also notice similarities. With time and practice, you should be able to hop back and forth between packages with little confusion.

**Pan** Panning a viewport will slide the view around the screen. Using the middle mouse button (abbreviated in the remainder of this text as MM), click in the viewport and drag the mouse pointer to move the view.

**Zoom** Zooming will move your view closer to or farther away from your objects. To zoom, press Ctrl+Alt and MM+click in your viewport, and then drag the mouse up or down to zoom in or out, respectively. It is more common to use the scroll wheel to zoom, however.

> Zooming is sometimes called dollying in other packages; 3ds Max also has a dolly function, but it is active only when you are in a Camera viewport. (3ds Max differentiates between Camera viewports and Perspective viewports, unlike other packages.)

**Orbit** Orbit will rotate your view around your objects. To arc rotate, press Alt and MM+click and drag in the viewport. By default, Max will rotate (or *tumble*, as it's called in some other CG programs) about the center of the viewport to change your perspective.

> The arc rotate move is used primarily in the Perspective viewports and is not used in the Orthographic viewports. If you accidentally arc rotate in one of the orthographic views, you will be given a new orthographic view that shows your model in a 3D view that is not actually in perspective. This view will be similar to a perspective view. However, it will remain orthographic, meaning that there will be no vanishing point or perspective shift in the view; it is not a real camera view. You can reset the view back to your straight orthogonal view by right-clicking the User viewport's name and selecting your original view.

# Jumping Headlong into Production

Let's get busy and dive right into 3ds Max and create a scene that we will animate later using very simple objects so you can become familiar with the UI. You may not understand the reasons for all the things you're about to do, but you will get a quick trial by fire by getting into the program and following these steps, which will guide you through some of the basic workflows for 3ds Max.

For your first experience, we will create a simple mobile. This example will teach you the basics of object creation and manipulation and in Chapter 8, "Introduction to Animation," you will learn about hierarchies and about setting and editing keyframes to create animation.

## Plan of Attack for Making Objects

It's always a good idea to go into something with a goal in mind. Knowing, even roughly, where you are headed will make things much easier. In production work, setting down a plan and having clear goals for your animation is very important. Without a good idea of where you need to go, you'll end up floundering and losing out on the whole experience.

With that in mind, our goal in this chapter is to create a finished mobile like the ones that hang over baby cribs. You will animate the mobile in Chapter 8. Because this is ostensibly your first foray into 3ds Max, let's start with a simple object so we won't be bogged down with the specifics of creating masterful models. Instead, we'll use simple objects that are very easily created in 3ds Max.

### Hierarchies

Once we model the mobile, we'll set up the pieces for animation. We will do this by creating proper hierarchies within the scene. The concept of *hierarchy* is a common feature in almost all CG packages. The hierarchy in a CG scene deals with how objects are arranged in a scene in relation to each other. *Parents* in a hierarchy lead *children*; where a parent goes, the children follow. When you *translate* (move) or rotate or scale a parent object, its children will move, turn, or scale along with it.

However, children retain the ability to move individually under their parent's supervision. The Mobile exercise is a perfect way to demonstrate the idea of hierarchies, and we'll revisit it for that purpose in Chapter 8. Our task here is to create the scene and setup the mobile's parts.

Take a look at Figure 2.13, which displays the completed mobile. The top bar (the parent), from which the other bars hang, rotates and takes the lower bars (its children) with it. In Chapter 8, we will animate the mobile parts to rotate individually, just as a real mobile would.

The dangling shapes on the lower bars are the children of their respective bars. Those lower bars are children of the bars above them, and so on up to the top bar that controls the rotation of the entire mobile. Once you begin working on it, it will make more sense. As you can see now, hierarchy will play an important part in animation.

Don't get hung up on all the steps and what they mean. This is a quick dip in the pond to get your feet wet. In the next chapters, we will explain everything you did here.

### Making the Mobile's Bars

To begin, we'll create the simple objects that are the parts of the mobile. The mobile comprises horizontal bars, and shapes that hang from the ends of each bar. We will forgo the strings used in

Figure 2.13

**The completed mobile object**

an actual mobile and just make do with the bars and the shapes. To create the bars for the mobile, follow these steps:

1. In the Command panel, activate the Create panel (as shown in Figure 2.14) by clicking on the Create tab ( ). The Create panel is usually enabled by default. Click the Geometry button ( ) to display the Standard Primitives pull-down menu and the Object Types rollout; it is usually enabled by default. You will see a number of ways to create various objects. You will begin most, if not all, of your Max models in this panel.

2. With Standard Primitives selected in the Create panel's pull-down menu, as shown in Figure 2.14, click the Cylinder button. The Cylinder button will turn dark blue, and your cursor will turn from the default arrow to a cross.

3. Go to the Perspective viewport. On the Home Grid, click and drag the mouse in any direction to begin the radius of the cylinder. Drag the mouse until it makes a circle, as shown in Figure 2.15, and release the mouse button.

   You'll notice that as you move the mouse up or down, 3ds Max will pull the circle into a cylinder. Settle on a height for the cylinder and click to create the cylinder (Figure 2.15). Don't worry about the size of the tube; we will modify it in the following steps to turn this cylinder into the top hanging bar for the mobile. Any size cylinder is fine for right now.

4. With the cylinder still selected, go in the Perspective viewport and click the Modify tab ( ) in the Command panel to bring up all the nifty tools you can use to modify objects in 3ds Max.

   You will rename the cylinder and size it to be a bar for the mobile. At the top of the panel, you'll notice a text box with Cylinder001 and a colored square next to it, as shown in Figure 2.16. The color swatch is the object color, and it helps you organize your elements in a scene. The color is easily changed by clicking on the swatch and simply choosing another color from the window that pops up (as shown in Figure 2.17). This color is not necessarily the color your object will render in the final output of your animation (for more on rendering in 3ds Max, see Chapter 11, "3ds Max Rendering"). However, we are not too interested in the color of the bar right now, so you can leave the cylinder the way it is, or you can change it if you desire.

Figure 2.14

**The Create panel**

Figure 2.15

**Drag out a circle, then drag up a cylinder.**

Figure 2.16

**The Modify panel allows you to change the name of the selected object and its color in the scene.**

Figure 2.17

**The Object Color dialog box helps you organize the scene by letting you assign colors to your objects.**

Figure 2.18

**The parameters of a selected object (in this case the Main Parent cylinder) can be changed to suit your needs.**

5. You do need to change the name of the cylinder, however. Click in the text box and change it from Cylinder001 to Main Parent. This name signifies that the cylinder will be the top bar of the mobile, and the top parent to the rest of the objects in the scene. For more on hierarchies, see the "Hierarchies" section earlier in this chapter.

6. You need to size the cylinder (Main Parent) to make it a bar. Under the Parameters heading in the Modify panel, you'll notice a handful of parameters for Main Parent, as shown in Figure 2.18. If you don't see anything there, make sure the cylinder is selected. The Modify panel will display the parameters for the selected object only. To adjust the parameters for the bar, you can type values directly into the appropriate boxes. You can also use the up and down spinners on the right either by clicking the arrows or by clicking and dragging up or down on the arrows. Change the Radius to 1, Height to 100, and Height Segments to 1 (as shown in Figure 2.18). Your cylinder should look like a bar, as shown in Figure 2.19, though you may need to zoom out your viewport to see it all.

Every object in 3ds Max will have parameters that define it geometrically in the scene. The exact parameters that are available for editing depend on the object that is being edited. For this cylinder, for example, you've already seen what the Radius and Height parameters do. The Height Segments, Cap Segments, and Sides parameters determine how many polygons you will use to define the shape, and hence how smooth it appears. Because the bar will not bend, you do not need extra polygons along the length. Therefore, the Height Segments parameter was changed from the default of 5 to 1.

---

### NAMING OBJECTS AND KEEPING THE SCENE ORGANIZED

In 3ds Max, and in any CG package, it is incredibly important to keep things organized and as clean as possible. It's no fun to pick up a scene from a colleague and waste tons of time trying to figure out exactly what is in it. Many artists will touch the same digital files and assets during a production. This is why many professional studios have strict naming procedures and conventions to minimize the confusion their artists may have when working in a pipeline. Even if you are the only person who will ever see a scene in 3ds Max, it is still an incredibly good idea to name and organize your objects. Get into the habit of naming your objects and keeping a clean scene. You will waste a lot of time if you don't—not to mention the dirty looks you'll get from other artists handling your cluttered scenes.

Figure 2.19
**Your cylinder should be a thin bar.**

### Positioning the Bar

Now you need to position the first bar, and then create copies for the other bars of the mobile, as shown in the following steps:

1. Click the Select and Rotate icon (⟳)—we'll call it the Rotate tool from now on—in the Main toolbar just below the menu bar. (You can also use the hot key E to enable Select and Rotate.) Click on the Main Parent cylinder to select it, and enable the Rotate tool. Notice that the Rotate gizmo appears at the base of the cylinder.

2. Clicking and dragging one of the axes will rotate the cylinder on that axis. For this step, click on the *Y*-axis *rotate handle*, which is the green circle, and drag the mouse to rotate the cylinder to the right of the screen, as shown in Figure 2.20. The green *Y*-axis handle will turn yellow when you move the cursor over it. (A gizmo's active axis handle is yellow.)

Figure 2.20

**The Rotate gizmo allows you to rotate the selected object.**

Figure 2.21

**Set the rotation to exactly 90 degrees in the *Y*-axis in the Transform Type-In box.**

3. The bar needs to be rotated a perfect 90 degrees, and that is usually difficult to do by hand using the gizmo. Look at the bottom middle of the 3ds Max UI, and you will see the orientation of the bar in three text boxes called the Transform Type-In boxes. With the Rotate tool selected, you can enter a value of **90** in the *Y*-axis Transform Type-In box to set the bar to exactly 90 degrees, as shown in Figure 2.21.

### Copying the Bar

In the next set of steps, you will copy the bar to make the other bars. Because the bar is already the size and orientation we need, it'll be much faster to copy three more bars and place them. Copying objects in Max is quite easy if you follow these steps:

1. Click the Select and Move Tool icon (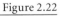)—we'll call it the Move tool from now on—and select the bar. You can also invoke the Move tool with the hot key W.

> You can also access the Move/Rotate/Scale and Select tools easily by right-clicking on the intended object to transform and picking the tool from the Quad menu that appears.

2. With the bar selected, hold down the Shift key and move the bar down in the *Z*-axis (by clicking on and dragging the *Z*-axis of the Move gizmo) by about five units, or grid squares. A second copy of the bar will form because you held down the Shift key as you moved. Move the copy down in the *Z*-axis with your cursor. As soon as you release the mouse button, the Clone Options window will ask you what kind of copy you want to make (Figure 2.22). We will cover the different types of copies and what they mean in Chapter 4, "Modeling in 3ds Max: Part I."

3. In the Clone Options window (Figure 2.22), keep the Copy button checked, enter **3** for the number of copies, and change the Name to **Parent001**. Click OK. 3ds Max will create three copies for you and position them as far down in the *Z*-axis as you moved the original clone while you had the Shift key pressed.

4. Use the Move tool to position the lower bars as shown in Figure 2.23; just don't move the bars off the *Z*-axis; instead move them only in the *X*- and *Y*-axes by clicking on just those axes on the Move gizmo. (We will keep all the bars in the *Z*-axis plane for simplicity's sake. After all, this is your first 3ds Max project; there will be plenty of time for confusion later.)

**Figure 2.22**

**The Clone Options window asks you the type and number of copies to make.**

Try to position the bars so that the second bar's center lines up with the left end of the top bar. The third bar's center should be lined up with the top bar's right end. The fourth bar can line up with the top bar. Each level of the bars should be about five units (or grid squares) down in the *Z*-axis from the last bar. Now you're ready to make the simple hanging objects.

Figure 2.23

**Position the bars for the mobile.**

## Creating the Mobile's Objects

What kind of mobile has only four sticks hanging on a string? You'll have to make some objects to hang from the ends of the bars. These objects will be simple shapes you can create with the following steps:

1. Activate the Front viewport by right-clicking inside it (by right-clicking, you will not affect any of your selections and you'll still be able to activate the viewport). Maximize that viewport with the Maximize Viewport Toggle icon ( ) in the bottom-right corner of the 3ds Max UI.

2. In the Command panel, click the Create tab and then click the Shapes button ( ) to display the creation options for various shapes. The Splines option should appear in the Category drop-down list, as shown in Figure 2.24.

3. Let's start with a circle. Click the Circle button. Your cursor will turn to a cross as it did when you created the cylinder. This time, expand the Keyboard Entry rollout. Enter a value of **20** for the Radius under the Keyboard Entry rollout in the Create panel, as you can see in Figure 2.25. Click the Create button. A circle with radius 20 should appear at the origin. This is a way to make objects with precise dimensions, as opposed to clicking and dragging as you did to create the cylinder.

4. 3ds Max has given the circle you created the name Circle001, which is fine, so there is no need to change its name. Use the Move tool to position it under the second bar, lining up its center with the left end of the second bar, as shown in Figure 2.26. Splines, including the circle you just created, are not renderable

Figure 2.24

**Creating spline-based shapes**

Figure 2.25

**Under the Keyboard Entry rollout, you can enter the exact radius to use for the circle.**

Figure 2.27

**Modifier List
pull-down menu**

Figure 2.26

**Position the circle under the second bar.**

shapes by default. This means they will not render when you output your scene unless you specify otherwise. The circle will be displayed as a wireframe, even when the viewport is in Smooth + Highlights, mode (also called Shaded mode) when objects are shown as solid in the viewport. For more on display modes in viewports, see the "Viewport Modes" sidebar.

Spline shapes, such as our lovely circle, are curves that need to be given a surface to be able to render as solid objects. To make the circle solid, you will *extrude* it by following these steps:

1. Select the Circle001 object (the circle) and click the Modify tab (  ) in the Command panel.

   Under the Circle001 name text box, click the Modifier List pull-down menu to access the many modifiers you can add to the circle (Figure 2.27). Under the Object-Space Modifiers heading, select Extrude.

2. In the box below the Modifier List pull-down menu, a new entry called *Extrude* should appear above the existing Circle entry for the selected Circle001 object. This box, called the *Modifier Stack,* is shown in Figure 2.28. The Modifier Stack displays all the modifiers that are contributing to the selected object, in this case the circle. The Circle Modifier Stack entry holds the original parameters of Circle001, while the new Extrude modifier entry holds the parameters for the extrusion you just applied to the circle. The circle now has a surface and should display as solid in the Perspective viewport (Figure 2.29).

**VIEWPORT MODES**

In Smooth + Highlights mode, you see the objects in your scene as solid objects. This is the default mode for all the 3ds Max Perspective viewports, but not for the Modeling viewports such as the Front viewport. To switch from one view mode to another, click on the display mode label in the upper-left corner of the viewport, next to the viewport's name. A menu will appear, as shown here. You can also use keyboard shortcuts to change from one viewport to the next.

From the menu, you can select the view mode for that viewport. Additional display modes are listed under Other Visual Styles on the menu.

3. In the Modifier Stack, click the Extrude entry to bring up its parameters. Play with the Amount parameter to give the circle extrusion some depth and make a cylinder.

4. Let's go off topic just for a second to cover something a bit more general about 3ds Max. Go into Wireframe view mode in your Perspective viewport by clicking the Smooth + Highlights mode name in the upper-left corner and selecting Wireframe from the menu (you may also press F3).

Now that you see the wireframe of the extruded circle, change the Segments of the Extrude modifier to see what happens. Figure 2.30 shows the extruded circle with Segments of 1 on the top, and Segments of 4 on the bottom. You'll see that now there are more geometry divisions (called *subdivisions*), which make the object smoother lengthwise. Because you don't need to bend this extruded cylinder, you do not need extra subdivisions along the length, so set the Segments back down to 1.

5. Back to the topic at hand, we need the circle to remain a flat disc, so set the Amount to 0.01 and keep the Segments at 1 as in the previous step.

6. Set the Perspective viewport back to Smooth + Highlights by clicking the Wireframe mode name, and selecting Smooth + Highlights from the menu. You may also press F3 to toggle between the two display modes. You should now see a flat solid disc, as shown in Figure 2.31.

Figure 2.28

**The Modifier Stack shows the Extrude modifier you just applied.**

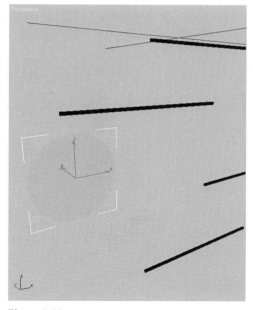

Figure 2.29

**The circle is now a flat disc.**

Figure 2.30

**The extruded cylinder with a Segments value of 1 on the top and a Segments value of 4 on the bottom**

Figure 2.31

**The flat disc in Smooth + Highlights mode**

Figure 2.32

**Setting parameters
for the hexagon**

7. Create a hexagon for the second shape. Go back to the Front viewport. In the Command panel, click the Create tab, then click the NGon button as shown in Figure 2.32. In the Parameters rollout, set the Sides to 6 for a hexagon. (An *NGon* is a polygon with *N* number of sides. In this case, *N* is 6 to make a hexagon.) In the Front viewport, click and drag to create the hexagon to a radius of about 20.

8. In the same way you created the disc using an Extrude modifier on the circle, make a hexagon into a solid shape by adding an Extrude modifier to it. Select the hexagon (named NGon001). In the Modifier tab, click the Modifier List menu and select Extrude (as was shown in Figure 2.28). The NGon001 object will now have its own Extrude modifier in the Modifier Stack.

9. Use the Move tool ( ) to place the NGon001 hexagon below and lined up with the other end of the second bar. Figure 2.33 shows the solid NGon001 surface in position.

10. Create four more shapes and place them to line up under the ends of the remaining bars, as shown in Figure 2.34. You will need to create and extrude the remaining four shapes all at about the same size (radius of 20). The following table shows you the remaining shapes, what Object Type button to use to create them, and what their names will be in the scene. To avoid any confusion when we begin to set up the hierarchies for animation, keep the naming as shown here:

| MOBILE OBJECT | CREATION TYPE | OBJECT NAME |
| --- | --- | --- |
| Square | Use the Rectangle button. | Rectangle001 |
| Star | Use the Star button. | Star001 |
| Triangle | Use the NGon button, specifying three sides, and rotate to the orientation in Figure 2.34. | NGon002 |
| Donut | Use the Donut button. | Donut001 |

You should already have created these first two shapes:

| MOBILE OBJECT | CREATION TYPE | OBJECT NAME |
| --- | --- | --- |
| Circle | Use the Circle button. | Circle001 |
| Hexagon | Use the NGon button, specifying six sides. | NGon001 |

If you click and drag to create a shape in the Perspective viewport and nothing happens, you will need to switch to one of the orthographic views. In this Mobile example, make sure to create all the shapes in the Front viewport for simplicity's sake.

There you have it—a completed mobile model ready to set up and animate in Chapter 8. This exercise should have warmed you up to the 3ds Max UI as well as gotten you more familiar with the workflow. Go put your feet up and watch something dumb on TV for a little while; you've earned a break. It's actually important to take a break at this point, and make sure what you've gone through makes some sense before moving on to Chapter 3 (about the UI) or Chapter 4 (where you start creating more complex objects). Feel free to go back and redo the exercise in part or in whole for a little more practice.

Save your progress, making sure to version up so that you don't overwrite any previous scene files you might need later. You can check your work against the `Mobile_v01.max` scene file in the Mobile\ Scenes folder on `www.sybex.com/go/intro3dsmax2011`.

Figure 2.33

**The solid hexagon is in place.**

Figure 2.34

**The shapes are now in position for the mobile.**

## Summary

In this chapter, you learned how project management and file workflow help you keep things organized. You learned how to navigate the user interface to create and manipulate objects in the viewports, and you got a little hands-on experience to get to know 3ds Max better before plunging deeper into it in the following chapters.

# CHAPTER 3

# The 3ds Max Interface

*This chapter explains* the 3ds Max interface and its most commonly used windows and panels. You already mucked about in the UI when you built your mobile in the previous chapter. This chapter will go into more depth regarding some of the tasks you performed, and it will give you an overview of where things are and what they do. Furthermore, we'll take a look at the commonly used windows and panels in 3ds Max and discuss how to operate them.

You can use this chapter as a reference as you work through the rest of this book. As you progress, you might want to check back here to review some of the information. It's important to be in front of your computer when you read this chapter, so you can try things out as we discuss them in the book.

Topics in this chapter include the following:

- **What am I looking at?**

- **Screen layout**

- **Command panels**

- **Controls at the bottom of the UI**

- **The viewports**

- **Managing scene objects**

- **Scene explorer**

- **The Quad menu and the caddy interface**

## What Am I Looking At?

When you start up 3ds Max, you will be looking at a screen full of buttons, icons, menus, tabs and panels, and an empty work area—how daunting! Although it may seem that there is no end to the switches and levers in 3ds Max, you'll be able to master the UI with just a little experience. The more you use 3ds Max to create, the more comfortable you'll become with the UI and all of its nuances. Before you know it, the UI will be a nonissue for you—just give it time and patience.

As with many other 3D applications, almost any command or tool can be accessed in a few different ways. For example, you can access some tools through icons in the Command panel by selecting them from the menu bar, by pressing a hot key, or by using context-sensitive Quad menus that appear when you right-click in the interface.

With so many different ways to perform any single function, how can you keep it all straight? Having a function or tool in several different places may seem like overload, but ultimately it gives users the most freedom to discover their preferred workflow. You may prefer to work mostly through the Command panel; others may find the menu bar easier to use. In either case, it's important to first experience the most common way to use 3ds Max and then branch out and find your own preference. In this book, we will first present the most obvious way to access a function; later we will give you alternative ways (such as hot keys) that you can use to access that feature.

Please don't obsess about all the information you're about to encounter. It's best to peruse this chapter at your own pace in front of your PC. Don't worry about memorizing all the information on every button and panel. Each of the exercises in this book contains short descriptions of the UI elements you'll use in that exercise. You can always refer back to this chapter for a more thorough explanation of a particular element. You should read through this chapter once to become familiar with where everything is and how everything works. Experience—and only experience—will show you how to make the tools work effectively; this chapter just shows you where they are.

In this chapter, you will find a fairly comprehensive explanation of 3ds Max's UI that expands on what you learned in Chapter 2, "Your First 3ds Max Project." If you skipped Chapter 2, please go back to it now and read the section called "The 3ds Max Interface" for a run-through of how to work in 3ds Max's UI. Because experience will teach you so much more than just reading a text, it's wise to give the UI a whirl. Go ahead and click on things and move around in the UI using this and the previous chapter as a guide.

## Screen Layout

Let's take a quick look at how the screen is laid out. Figure 3.1 shows the initial 3ds Max screen.

Along the top of the UI, to the left, is the Quick Access toolbar where you have access to some of the most frequently used tools, including Open File, Save File, and the Undo

Scene Operation and Redo Scene Operation buttons. Along the top of the UI, to the right, you will find the tools used to access the help files and to search for Autodesk-related content. At the top-left corner of the UI is the important Application Menu button with the 3ds Max logo on it (  ). The Application menu is the starting point for many operations in 3ds Max.

The menu bar runs from left to right near the top of the 3ds Max UI, just as with many other applications. Here you can access tons of features to help you with your scene creation and manipulation. Immediately under the menu bar is the Main toolbar, which contains the most frequently accessed tool icons. Everything from selecting objects to rendering the scene is in the Main toolbar for easy access.

Running down the right side of the 3ds Max UI is the Command panel. Object creation and manipulation tools are gathered here for your access. The Command panel, as you discovered in the previous chapter, is divided into tabs. Each tab has its own specific panel of tools, ranging from Create to Utilities.

The meat of the UI is in the viewports. These portals give you access to 3ds Max's 3D space through orthographic and perspective views. These viewports are where you'll do the bulk of your work. By using the mouse and key combinations, as you saw in the previous chapter, you can navigate through 3D space and around your scenes quite easily.

Figure 3.1

**The default
3ds Max screen**

Running across the bottom of the UI are the tools for changing time values , viewport navigation controls, and controls for animating.

Each of these UI sections is explained in more detail in the following pages, with a breakdown of the major components.

> The following conventions are used throughout this book: *Click*—click with the left mouse button; *MM click*—click with the middle mouse button; *RM click*—click with the right mouse button.

## The Application Menu

Common to many Autodesk products is the Application menu shown in Figure 3.2. From 3ds Max's Application menu, you can access many file-related tools, including opening and saving files, importing other file types into 3ds Max, or exporting 3ds Max scenes in formats suitable for other programs. The Application menu is also where you will set up your project's file structure and access information about the current scene.

When you first open the Application menu, the right pane lists the last 10 projects that were open. If you click the pin icon to the right of any file name (  ), that file's position in the list becomes fixed until you unpin it to release it and allow the filename to scroll off the list as new files are accessed. Pausing the cursor on an item in the left pane displays that menu's content in the right pane. You can use the Options button at the bottom of the Application menu to open the Preference Settings dialog box (Figure 3.3) and adjust the many file and system settings available in the program. You will use the Application menu considerably while working in 3ds Max.

Figure 3.2

**The Application menu**

Figure 3.3

**The Preference Settings dialog box**

## The Menu Bar

If you've ever played with a computer, you should be familiar with the layout of the menu bars, so let's keep this brief. Here is a rundown of what to expect in each of the menus shown in Figure 3.4. Feel free to click along with the text to see for yourself what is in each menu.

Figure 3.4

**The menu bar**

**Edit** This contains the commands for editing and selecting objects in your scene. This is one of the areas where you will find the Undo/Redo functions, as well as easy selection methods such as Select All. Under the Select By submenu heading you can select objects in the scene using a certain criteria, such as by their color or name. Tools such as Move, Rotate, and Scale (transforms) are found here as well.

**Tools** This menu is where tools to manipulate your objects, such as Mirror and Align, are located. Many of these tools and functions are found on the Main toolbar and are also found in the Command panels. You'll see how several of these tools operate in the coming chapters.

**Group** Grouping lets you combine two or more objects into a single grouped object. Groups can be open or closed, depending on how you want the user to access objects inside the group. You can also permanently break up the group by ungrouping or exploding (a command that dissolves all nested groups).

**Views** Options to set up and control viewports are located in this menu. From here, for example, you can disable the view of your gizmos (visual aids for using the transforms) in the viewports or toggle the ViewCube and SteeringWheels Viewport Navigation tools on and off.

> If many of your tools, including the Main toolbar, Command panels, and viewport controls, disappear, you're probably in Expert mode. Click Expert Mode on the Views menu to restore these tools or use the Ctrl+X shortcut key combination.

**Create** This menu gives tools for creating objects and is very extensive, with many submenus. Everything that you would ever want to create for your 3D scene is found here. Some of the objects you created in the previous chapter for your mobile can be created through this menu as well as through the Command panel's Create panel, which you used in the Mobile exercise.

The Create menu is divided into 16 submenus. The main ones we will be using in this book are Standard Primitives, Extended Primitives, Shapes, Helpers, Lights, Cameras, and Particles.

**Modifiers** A modifier is a 3ds Max feature that controls and changes the basic structure of objects. Modifiers are used for modeling, animating, and adding special effects to objects. Through the Modifiers menu you can apply modifiers to selected objects in the scene. Once applied, modifiers are edited through the Modify panel.

**Animation** This menu has features for animation, constraints, controllers, and Inverse Kinematics (IK), a feature that is used for character animation.

**Graph Editors** These are floating windows for managing a scene, hierarchy, and animation. Graph Editors give you access to scene components in graphical layout for easy use. Everything from nodes (a node represents an object in 3ds Max) to animation curves are displayed. Animation curves are representations of animation expressed in mathematical graphs. It sounds harder than it is. You'll see plenty of curves later in the book.

**Rendering** These commands are for scene rendering, setting up an environment and render effects, accessing video post for in-program compositing, and using a RAM player. The Material Editors are also accessed under this menu, as is the Material/Map Browser.

**Customize** This menu is for all things relating to user interface customization. This book will, for the most part, use the default layout for the 3ds Max UI, as that is most universal. Once you get a feeling for 3ds Max and are more comfortable with it, you'll find yourself customizing the UI to your tastes.

**MAXScript** These are commands for working with MAXScript, which is a scripting language for 3ds Max. MAXScript allows you to automate certain functions and program parts of your scene as needed. MAXScript will not be covered in this book because it is an advanced feature set.

**Help** This provides access to online references, tutorials, and online support, and it is perhaps the most important menu in the program.

## Main Toolbar

The Main toolbar puts the tools most commonly used in 3ds Max in a convenient location at the top of the interface (see Figure 3.5). This toolbar can be rearranged as a floating palette or docked on the bottom, left, or right side of the interface. To do this, place your cursor to the far-left side of the toolbar over the embossed vertical line. An icon of white boxes will appear next to your cursor. Click and drag to create a floating toolbar, or drag the toolbar to one side of the UI to dock it.

You can also right-click on the embossed vertical line for a pop-up window, giving you options for docking and floating the toolbar, as shown in Figure 3.6. All palettes and bars in the 3ds Max interface can be rearranged in this fashion.

Selection tools
Coordinate systems
Named Selection Sets editor/display
Graphite Modeling Tools
Select and Link/Unlink Selection
Snap tools
Align
Bind to Space Warp
Transform tools
Mirror
Material Editor
Manipulators
Pivot point
Manage Layers
Keyboard Shortcut Override toggle
Graph editors
Rendering

**Figure 3.5**

**The Main toolbar**

If your screen does not show all the icons on the Main toolbar shown in Figure 3.5, don't panic. Your display is probably set to a lower resolution than the width of the toolbar. In this case, you can scroll the toolbar left and right to expose the missing end of the toolbar. Place your cursor over an empty part of the toolbar (not on an icon), and it will turn into a hand icon. Click and drag to scroll the toolbar as needed.

**Figure 3.6**

**You can float toolbars easily in 3ds Max.**

The icons for the Main toolbar are as shown in the following tables. You should use them as references while you use this book; you don't need to memorize everything here. For the most part, you will learn tools and functions in 3ds Max as you come across them in your work. Trying to memorize all the icons and their functions at the outset will just drive you nutty. Grab your mouse and click along through the examples in this chapter to get a feel for the icons.

Some icons, characterized by the small triangle in the lower-right corner, have flyouts. *Flyouts* are additional options for the tool that appear as a context menu of new icons when you click and hold the icon, as shown here for the Scale tool.

## Linking and Hierarchy Icons

Linking and Hierarchy tools are used to parent objects for animation; this is covered in the Mobile exercise in Chapter 8, "Introduction to Animation." The icons are detailed here:

| ICON | NAME | FUNCTION |
|---|---|---|
| | Select and Link | Allows you to create a hierarchical link of child and parent between objects. |
| | Unlink Selection | Allows you to remove the hierarchical link of child and parent between objects. |
| | Bind to Space Warp | Allows you to bind an object to a space warp effect (like gravity, wind, or displace). |

## Selection Tool Icons

Selection tools allow you to select objects in a scene using different methods. The icons are detailed here:

| ICON | NAME | FUNCTION |
|---|---|---|
| | Selection Filter | This drop-down list allows you to screen out certain objects that can be selected. For example, if you choose Geometry from the list, you will not be able to select anything other than geometry. This is particularly helpful when you have a very crowded scene. You can also create filter combinations such as cameras and lights together. |
| | Select Object | Allows you to select any object in your 3D scene by clicking it. |
| | Select by Name | Allows you to select an object from a list within the Select from Scene dialog box, shown in Figure 3.7. The list contains objects currently in your scene and has filters for easy selection. For more on Select by Name, see the following section. |
| | Selection Region flyout | Gives you different ways to select objects by defining a region, which is done by clicking and dragging in a viewport. There are five region selection methods: Rectangular (the default), Circular, Fence, Lasso, and Paint. |
| | Window/Crossing Selection | Switches between Window and Crossing modes when you select by region. If you are in Window mode, it will select only objects that are entirely inside the window's region. The default Crossing mode allows selection of objects that are touching the edge of the region. This tool will also work when you are selecting polygons in sub-object mode. |

Flyout icons show all the icons stacked below the current tool's icon. This results in the current icon appearing twice in the flyout.

*Figure 3.7*

**The Select by Name icon opens the Select from Scene dialog box.**

### SELECT BY NAME ICON

When you click the Select by Name icon in the Main toolbar, 3ds Max will bring up the Select from Scene dialog (Figure 3.5). With the Select from Scene dialog box, you can select any object in your scene by name, which is mighty handy if you have an extensive scene or need to select objects that are difficult to select in a viewport. While the window is open, you cannot edit anything in your scene until you click the Select button in the dialog to close the window. As you can see in Figure 3.7, the Select from Scene dialog box gives you information about the objects, such as their hierarchy and scene color.

This dialog box is a trimmed down version of the more powerful Scene Explorer window, covered at the end of this chapter.

## Transformation Tools Icons

As you saw in the previous chapter, transformation tools move, rotate, and scale your objects. Their icons are detailed here:

| ICON | NAME | FUNCTION |
|---|---|---|
| | Select and Move | Selects and moves objects. For all the transform tools (Move, Rotate, and Scale), you can click and drag a region box around the object or objects to select them. You can also invoke this tool with the W hot key. |
| | Select and Rotate | Selects and rotates objects. Clicking and dragging a region box around the object or objects selects them. You can also invoke this tool with the E hot key. |
| | Select and Scale flyout | This icon leads to a flyout where you can access two other Scale tools. The default Scale tool is the Uniform Scale tool (top icon), which allows you to scale along all three axes evenly. The middle icon in the flyout is the Non-uniform Scale tool, which allows you to scale along the axis you choose. The bottom icon is the Squash tool, which is a type of scale used mainly for the "squash and stretch" style of animation found in cartoons. When you are scaling down in one axis, it scales up in the other two, and vice versa. You can also invoke this tool with the R hot key. |

## Coordinate Systems, Center Pivots, and Manipulator Icons

As you saw in the first chapter, coordinate systems define the axes that you use. The icons for this section of the Main toolbar are detailed here:

| ICON | NAME | FUNCTION |
|---|---|---|
| | Reference Coordinate System menu | Allows you to choose which coordinate system you want to use. Coordinate systems are covered in depth at the end of Chapter 1, "Basic Concepts." |
| | Use Center flyout | The tools accessed through this flyout allow you to determine the pivot point of an object for its transforms. The default setting, Use Pivot Point Center, is adequate for nearly all situations and is used throughout this book; however, this tool has a flyout that lets you relocate the center point of your transformation tools. You can use the tool if you have multiple objects selected. |
| | Select and Manipulate | Allows you to edit the parameters of certain objects, modifiers, and controllers by dragging manipulators in viewports. Manipulators are similar to the gizmos you've already used. Manipulators are not covered in this book. |
| | Keyboard Shortcut Override Toggle | Determines which set of keyboard shortcuts are currently useable; when it is disabled, only the main UI shortcuts are recognized. When it is enabled, the main UI and the functional area shortcuts are recognized. |

## Snapping Icons

Snapping functions allow accurate placement of objects in your scene. When you enable a Snap function and then move an object, for example, 3ds Max will "snap" the object to points on the Home Grid or to other geometry in the scene. Because they let you snap to specific locations during creation and transformation of objects or sub-objects, Snaps give you control when you're creating, moving, rotating, and scaling objects.

There are several different types of snaps; you can snap to a grid, pivot, or vertex among others. You can turn snaps on and off by clicking their icons in the Main toolbar or by pressing the S key while you are in the middle of a transform. We will be using snaps in the following chapters. Right-clicking on the Snaps Toggle button will open the Snaps tab of the Grid and Snap Settings dialog box shown in Figure 3.8. In it, you can select exactly how you want to snap.

| ICON | NAME | FUNCTION |
|---|---|---|
| | Snaps Toggle flyout | The 2D Snap (top) icon allows you to snap to the Home Grid or to any shapes or geometry on the grid. The 2.5D Snap (middle) icon snaps vertices or edges of an object, but actually places the cursor at the projection of that point on the grid beyond it. The 3D Snap (bottom) icon will snap to any geometry in 3D space. |
| | Angle Snap Toggle | Allows you to set the increment of rotation for rotating an object in a given axis. To set the increment you want to snap to, right-click the icon to open the Options tab of the Grid and Snap Settings dialog box, as shown in Figure 3.9. |
| | Percent Snap Toggle | Allows you to define a set scaling increment when you are scaling an object. |
| | Spinner Snap Toggle | Causes spinners to adjust in specific increments. You will run into spinners constantly in 3ds Max. Right-click the Spinner Snap Toggle to set the increment by which you want to increase or decrease a metric. |

Figure 3.8

**The Grid and Snap Settings dialog box for the Snap functions**

Figure 3.9

**Right-click the Angle Snap toggle or Percent Snap toggle to set their parameters.**

## Named Selection Sets Icons

Selection sets are a way to easily select several objects at once. To create a selection set for your workflow, choose the objects you want it to contain, and then type a name for the set in the Named Selection Sets field. That name will be added to the drop-down menu so you can select all those objects in the set by selecting the set's name. We will explore selection sets further in Chapter 5, "Modeling in 3ds Max: Part II."

**Figure 3.10**

**You can edit selection sets using this dialog box.**

| ICON | NAME | FUNCTION |
|---|---|---|
| | Edit Named Selection Sets | Launches a menu that allows you to organize your selection sets and the objects that are members of those sets. Click the plus (+) or minus (–) symbol to expand or collapse the object list for each set. The buttons along the top allow you to create or delete sets and add or remove objects. See Figure 3.10. |
| Gun Items | Named Selection Sets | To create a named selection set, choose the objects for the selection set and enter a name for that set. |

## Align and Mirror Icons

The Align and Mirror icons are next up in this Main toolbar discussion. The Mirror dialog box (Figure 3.11) allows you to mirror an object about a specific axis. In the dialog box, you can choose a mirror axis and the Offset amount—that is, how far the axis is from the pivot point. Before accessing the Mirror tool, use the Reference Coordinate System menu to select the coordinate system used to define the axis. You can either mirror the object or create a clone that is mirrored.

**Figure 3.11**

**The Mirror dialog box**

| ICON | NAME | FUNCTION |
|---|---|---|
| | Mirror | Mirrors the selected object in the chosen axis. Can also copy a mirror of the object. |
| | Align flyout | The flyout gives you access to all the Align functions discussed in the following table. This Align icon is displayed by default. |

The Align tools found in the flyout allow you to line up your object as discussed in the following table. Select the object you want to align, click the appropriate Align tool icon from the flyout, and then click the target object to which the object is to be aligned.

| ICON | NAME | FUNCTION |
|------|------|----------|
| | Align | Once you click on the target object to align to, 3ds Max will open the Align Selection dialog box shown in Figure 3.12. Here you can choose which axis to align your selected object to as a function of position, rotation, or even scale. |
| | Quick Align | Lets you instantly align the position of the current selection to that of a target object. |
| | Normal Align | Lets you align two objects based on the direction of the normal of a face or selection on each object. A normal is an imaginary line that is perpendicular to a surface. |
| | Place Highlight | Lets you align a light to another object so that its highlight can be precisely positioned. |
| | Align Camera | Lets you align a camera to a selected face normal. |
| | Align to View | Lets you align an object with the current viewport. |

## Editing and Organizational Icons

Manage Layers, Graphite Modeling Tools, Curve Editor, and Schematic View are four editing and organizational tools in 3ds Max. We will cover each of them later in this chapter. Their icons are explained in this table.

| ICON | NAME | FUNCTION |
|------|------|----------|
| | Manage Layers | Lets you manage sets of objects in layers. Very useful for large scenes and complicated setups. |
| | Graphite Modeling Tools | Displays or hides the Graphite Modeling Tools ribbon and panels shown in Figure 3.13. |
| | Curve Editor | Allows you to edit animation by manipulating mathematical curves representing the changes over time. |
| | Schematic View | A node-based display of the objects in a scene that allows you to edit parameters as well as hierarchies. |

Figure 3.13

**The Graphite Modeling tools**

## Graphite Modeling Tools

The Graphite Modeling tools is a section of the UI that provides you with a wide range of tools to make building and editing models in 3ds Max fast and easy. All the available tools are divided into tabs that are organized by function, and then further divided into panels. For example, the Graphite Modeling Tools tab contains the tools you use most often for polygon modeling and editing, organized into separate panels for easy, convenient access. In the following chapters, you will make copious use of the Graphite Modeling tools (see Figure 3.13). The panels found in the Polygon Modeling tab are:

- Polygon Modeling Panel
- Modify Selection Panel
- Edit Panel
- Geometry (All) Panel
- [Sub-object] Panel
- Loops Panel
- Additional Panels

The Material and Rendering Editors give you access to materials for shading and texturing, as well as options for rendering your scene. These functions will be covered later in this chapter, along with other commonly used dialog boxes and panels. Their icons are as follows:

| ICON | NAME | FUNCTION |
| --- | --- | --- |
| | Material Editor flyout | Accesses materials you can add to scene objects to give them their final look when rendered. The top icon opens the Material Editor and the bottom icon opens the newer Slate Material Editor. |
| | Render Setup | Opens the Render Setup dialog box, where you set the parameters for the next rendering. |
| | Rendered Frame Window | Displays or hides the Rendered Frame Window that shows the result of the last rendered frame |
| | Render flyout | Lets you render the scene using the current render settings without displaying the Render Setup dialog box. Render Production (top) uses the settings in the Render Setup dialog box. Render Iterative (middle) ignores settings that output the file and ActiveShade (bottom) keeps a constantly updated rendered window open. |

## The Quick Access Toolbar

At the top-left corner of the UI is the Quick Access toolbar. This toolbar contains some of the most often-used, file-related tools in 3ds Max.

### The File Control Icons

Rather than accessing the nested tools in the Application menu, the Quick Access toolbar contains the New Scene, Open File, and Save File tools, and, at the right end, the Project Folder tool. The icons are as follows:

| ICON | NAME | FUNCTION |
| --- | --- | --- |
| | New Scene | Starts a new 3ds Max scene. Existing objects and hierarchies can be carried over to the new scene. |
| | Open File | Opens an existing 3ds Max scene. |
| | Save File | Saves the file using the same filename. If the file has not been saved yet, the Save File As dialog box opens so that a filename and location can be entered. |
| | Project Folder | Opens the Browse for Folder dialog box, where the project folder is defined. |

### Undo/Redo Icons

The Undo Scene Operation and Redo Scene Operation buttons (we'll call the Undo and Redo from now on) are extremely useful in 3ds Max. You will find yourself painted into a corner many times—especially when you are first starting out—and Undo will let you back out of those corners. The icons are as follows:

| ICON | NAME | FUNCTION |
| --- | --- | --- |
| | Undo | Reverses the effect of the last action. Clicking the small arrow to the right shows a list of the previous actions that can be undone. |
| | Redo | Cancels the last Undo. Clicking the small arrow to the right shows a list of the previous actions that can be undone. |
| | Customize Quick Access Toolbar | At the far end of the Quick Access toolbar, this button is where you can set which tools are shown. |

## The Information Center

Autodesk provides the Information Center, at the top-right of the UI, as the source of information from Autodesk regarding your software. This is also where you can manage your software subscription, if you have one, access the 3ds Max help files, and define a list of favorite articles to access quickly.

| ICON | NAME | FUNCTION |
| --- | --- | --- |
| *Type a keyword or phrase* | Search field | Type in a word or phrase to search for. |
| | Search | Searches the several locations for the word or phrase entered in the search field. |
| | Subscription Center | Displays links used to manage the software subscription program. |
| | Communication Center | This is where you access software-specific communications from Autodesk. |
| | Favorites | Contains links to user-specified articles for quick access. |
| | Help | Click the icon to access the 3ds Max help file or the arrow to display a list of the available help files. |

## Whoa! Did You Get All That?

That was a lot to take in! Don't worry. There is absolutely no need to memorize all this material. You will see most of these tools in action in the next few chapters, and before long, using them (and recognizing their icons) will be second nature to you. This part of the book is designed as a reference guide, so bookmark these pages for easy access later.

# Command Panels

Everything you need to create, manipulate, and animate objects can be found here. As you saw in the previous chapter, the Command panel (shown in Figure 3.14) is divided into tabs according to function. This lets you access several commands and functions through the different panels that comprise a quick workflow in 3ds Max.

The function or toolset you need to access will determine which panel you need to click. The division of panel tabs is very instinctive and easy to decipher.

You can scroll up and down a panel to access tools that are not visible on the screen because the panel is too long vertically. When you encounter a panel that is longer than your screen, 3ds Max will display a thin vertical scroll bar on the right side. Your cursor will also turn into a hand that lets you click and drag the panel up and down.

You will be exposed to more panels as you progress through this book. Here is a run-down of the Command Panel functions and what they do. They are discussed in more detail in later sections of this chapter.

Figure 3.14

**The Command panel**

| ICON | NAME | FUNCTION |
|---|---|---|
| | Create panel | Lets you create objects, lights, cameras, etc. |
| | Modify panel | Lets you apply and edit modifiers to objects. |
| | Hierarchy panel | Lets you adjust the hierarchy for objects and adjust their pivot points. |
| | Motion panel | Lets you access animation tools and functions. |
| | Display panel | Lets you access display options for scene objects. |
| | Utilities panel | Lets you access several functions of 3ds Max, such as motion capture utilities and the Asset Browser. |

## Create Panel

The first panel, the Create panel, is used primarily for creating various objects for your scene. You can create seven categories of objects. The panels under the Create panel are detailed here:

| ICON | NAME | FUNCTION |
|---|---|---|
| | Geometry | Lets you create renderable objects, such as primitives or parametric objects. |
| | Shapes | Lets you create 2D lines and splines of various shapes. |
| | Lights | 3ds Max lights can simulate real-world lights to illuminate objects in the scene. |
| | Camera | Lets you create cameras to view and render your 3D scene. |
| | Helpers | Helper objects are aids to constructing a scene. |
| | Space Warp | Space Warp objects deform the appearance of other objects. |
| | Systems | Catch-all panel containing functions such as Bones and Biped Animation tools, as well as lighting systems to simulate sun and daylight. |

Figure 3.15

**The Create Geometry category for the Create panel**

Figure 3.15

**The Create Geometry category for the Create panel**

## Geometry

The Geometry category in the Create panel is responsible for renderable objects, also known as primitives or *parametric objects* (objects whose parameters may be changed at any time to adjust their original shape or appearance). The default is Standard Primitives. Click on the drop-down window to access more object types, such as Extended Primitives, Compound Objects, and Particle Systems.

When you created the mobile in the previous chapter, you made the cylinders from the Geometry panel. You can access many other objects through the Create menu as well (Figure 3.15).

Figure 3.16

**Creating shapes in the Create panel**

## Shapes

Shapes are 2D lines or splines that can be used as is. You can also use them to create 3D objects using modifiers, such as Extrude, as you saw in the Mobile exercise. You can use stock shapes, such as a circle or rectangle, or you can use the Line tool to create free-form shapes. Lines are used as components to create other objects. You can use splines to create motion paths, extrusions, lathes, lofts, and 3D objects. The drop-down menu will give you access to NURBS and Extended Splines. Figure 3.16 shows the Shapes Creation option.

Figure 3.17

**Creating lights**

## Lights

Lights in 3ds Max, just like lights in the real world, are used to illuminate objects. You can create lights that simulate indoor lights (such as incandescent or florescent lights), outdoor lights (such as the sun or street lights), or lights that don't simulate anything but the look you need for your scene. 3ds Max provides two types of lights: Standard and Photometric. The different light types are available in the drop-down menu. Standard lights simulate the basic light rigs used in film and stage, and Photometric lights are used to simulate *radiosity* (bounced light) within 3D environments. You will use both kinds of lights in Chapter 10, "3DS Max Lighting," when you learn how to light and render your scenes (Figure 3.17).

Figure 3.18

**Cameras category in the Creation panel**

## Cameras

Camera objects are designed to simulate real-world still and motion cameras. They are used to record the action you animate, and they output through rendering. Just like real-world cameras, 3ds Max's camera objects allow you to use a variety of lens types. There is a standard camera and there is a camera that has a target to make it easier to follow an object or action. You'll get to use cameras a lot in Chapter 11, "3ds Max Rendering." You can see the Camera Creation category in Figure 3.18.

### Helpers

Helpers take care of the unglamorous and thankless jobs in 3ds Max. They help you construct scenes, but they aren't necessarily part of the scenes. Helpers help you position, measure, and animate a scene's renderable geometry. Figure 3.19 shows the various helpers you can create.

### Space Warps

Space warps are objects that deform or animate other objects in your scene. They are known as *deformers* in other animation packages, such as Maya. You can create ripples and waves and even blow up objects by binding them to Space Warp using the Bind to Space Warp button in the Main toolbar. The drop-down menu shown in Figure 3.20 lists the different space warps available.

### Systems

The Systems category holds some advanced functions of 3ds Max. This is where you'll go to set up Sunlight and Daylight lighting systems, or Bones systems to animate a character or object rig. Figure 3.21 shows the various systems you can create.

## Modify Panel

The Modify panel, as you saw with the Mobile project, houses all the modifiers you can apply to an object. It also houses a selected object's Modifier Stack. Using this stack, you can reorder or remove the modifiers for an object, which can be invaluable in creating precisely the right object for your scene.

This panel also allows you to change and animate the parameters for an existing object, such as the radius or length of a cylinder, even after it has been created.

Modifiers are the bread and butter of editing objects in 3ds Max. This form of workflow is terrific because you can stack modifiers on top of each other when creating an object and then go back and edit any of the modifiers in the stack (for the most part) to adjust the object at any point in its creation. This sort of workflow, where any stage of the creation process can be adjusted at any time, is akin to a *node-based* editing workflow. Figure 3.22 shows the Modify panel for a selected Sphere object.

Almost all the parameters in the Modify panel can be animated. For example, you can create a sphere and animate its radius. Then you can add a Taper modifier and animate the taper amount. You can also go into the sub-object level of a modifier, such as an FFD (free-form deformation), select the control points, and animate the points on the lattice. This can give you layer upon layer of animation. The downside of this is that editing the

Figure 3.19

**Helpers help you create your scene.**

Figure 3.20

**Creating space warps**

Figure 3.21

**Systems creation**

animation can be a nightmare. For instance, with the FFD, each control point has its own track in the Curve Editor. So, if you have a lattice with 4 × 4 × 4 tracks, you would have to edit 64 potential tracks. You will have a look into tracks and animation in Chapter 8 and in Chapter 9, "Character Studio and IK Animation."

There are two types of modifiers. World Space modifiers attach to an object but affect world space instead of local space. The object must be in proximity to the World Space modifier to be affected. Object Space modifiers affect an object's geometry in local space. Figure 3.23 shows a Bend modifier applied to a box. The Bend modifier does what it says: It bends the geometry. It is an example of an Object Space modifier because it affects the entire object as one piece.

Figure 3.23

**A Bend modifier is applied to a box through the Modify panel.**

## Hierarchy Panel

The Hierarchy panel is where you create and edit the hierarchies for your objects. As you will see in Chapter 8, creating parent-child relationships through linking allows you to create complex animations—i.e., different rotations on different parts of a mobile. The child objects—or *nodes*—travel with their parents, but retain the ability to have their own motions once they inherit their parents' motion(s).

### Pivot

In the Hierarchy panel, you can also adjust the position of an object's pivot point. The pivot point plays a critical role in how an object moves, rotates, and scales. Having control of the pivot point is important to setting up the proper animation for any given object. All objects have a *pivot point,* which is a center for all transforms. A pivot also defines the transform relationship of a hierarchy, sets the center location of an added modifier, and defines IK (Inverse Kinematics) joint locations.

In the Pivot category of the Hierarchy panel, you can adjust the pivot by moving it, centering it, or aligning it to another object or the world space, as shown in Figure 3.24.

### IK

Inverse Kinematics (IK) is a method often used in character animation; it provides an easier way to move the parts of a character's armature by using IK handles to place the limb's extremities, such as the feet. You simply animate the placement of the feet, and IK solves all the necessary rotations of the leg bones and animates the legs into the proper placement for the feet. The IK category gives you all the tools you need for adjusting hierarchical linkage between objects. The IK panel is shown in Figure 3.25. You will see how IK and bones work in Chapter 9.

### Link Info

Link Info is a great way to set limits for the motions of your objects. The Link Info category allows you to restrict the movement of objects in a hierarchy by limiting from which axes motion is inherited from parents.

Try this exercise:

1. In a new scene, create a box of any size and a teapot of similar size. You can find the teapot in the Create panel's Geometry → Standard Primitives category.

2. Click the Select and Link button ( ) on the Main toolbar. Click the teapot then drag the cursor over one of the box's edges (see Figure 3.26) and then release the mouse button. The teapot is now linked to the box so that the box is the parent of the teapot.

Figure 3.24

**Understanding the Hierarchy panel's Pivot category is a must for proper animation setup.**

Figure 3.25

**The IK category of the Hierarchy panel**

Figure 3.26

**Linking the teapot to the box**

Figure 3.27

**Setting the link
parameters**

3. Press the W hot key to activate the Move tool. Select and move the box first on the X-axis, then on the Y-axis, and then on the Z-axis. The teapot moves along with the box (assuming the link was created successfully).

4. Select and move the teapot on all three axes as you did the box. The teapot moves in all directions but the box remains stationary.

5. Select the teapot and click on the Hierarchy panel. In the panel, select the Link Info category. Under the Locks rollout, check the box in the Move section for the X-axis. In the Inherit rollout, uncheck the box for Move on the Y-axis, as shown in Figure 3.27.

6. Select and move the teapot separately on the three axes. You'll see that the teapot has been locked on the X-axis and will not move at all on X. This is what a lock does to an object, no matter where it is in a hierarchy.

7. Select the box and move it separately on all three axes. You'll see that the teapot, except along the Y-axis, moves with the box as it should. The teapot is restricted from inheriting any motion in the Y-axis from the box parent. This is what an Inherit lock does to a child under a moving parent.

## Motion Panel

The Motion panel houses all the tools for controlling animated objects using keyframe editing and animation controllers. You will have a chance to play with keyframes and controllers in Chapter 8. The Parameters category allows you to edit keyframes without using the Curve Editor, which is usually the preferred and more powerful way to edit keyframes (Figure 3.28).

The Trajectories category in the Motion panel (Figure 3.29) allows you to display the path that an object travels in its animation. This way you can actually see the movement an object takes in its animation and adjust it visually to change its course.

## Display Panel

The Display panel (Figure 3.30) allows you to choose how an object appears in your viewports. Use the Display panel to Hide/Unhide, Freeze/Unfreeze, and alter display characteristics of objects. This ability is extremely useful when you need to organize your scenes, no matter what their size.

The Hide by Category rollout allows you to turn off the display of certain types of objects to let you focus on other types of objects. For example, if you have a scene replete with geometry objects, but you

Figure 3.28

**The Parameters
category in the
Motion panel**

Figure 3.29

**The Trajectories
category in the
Motion panel**

only need to adjust your lights, you can easily hide your geometry and shapes to better see where your lights are in the scene.

Hiding objects is useful for getting parts of your scene out of the way temporarily. Similarly, freezing objects keeps them visible but prevents you from selecting them. This feature is useful when you still need to reference an object but don't want to alter it accidentally. When you freeze an object, its display in the viewports turns dark gray by default.

The larger and more complicated your scenes become, the more you can rely on the Display panel to help you with your scene.

> You can also use the Layer Manager, which is covered later in this chapter, to help you organize large scenes.

Figure 3.30

**The Display panel is important to keeping your scene organized.**

## Utilities Panel

The Utilities panel (Figure 3.31) allows you to access different utility programs, or *plug-ins,* inside 3ds Max. Some plug-ins are shipped with 3ds Max, and some are third-party applications from various software makers. One such utility is Motion Capture, which allows you to import and work with animation data captured using external devices, such as a joystick or a midi device configured to mimic puppetry animation. These utilities are all advanced and will not be covered in this book. The reactor plug-in is covered in Chapter 12, "Particles and Dynamics."

# Controls at the Bottom of the UI

Time controls, status information, animation controls, playback controls, and viewport controls are aligned at the bottom edge of the 3ds Max UI. This section covers the icons and functions.

## Time Slider and Track Bar

Running across the bottom of the 3ds Max UI are the Time Slider and the track bar, as shown in Figure 3.32.

The Time Slider allows you to move through any frame in your scene by *scrubbing* (moving the slider back and forth). By scrubbing, you can also view your animation playback in the viewports. You can move through your animation one frame at a time by clicking on the arrows on either side of the Time Slider or by pressing the < and > keys.

You can also use the Time Slider to animate objects by setting keyframes. With an object selected,

Figure 3.31

**The Utilities panel**

Figure 3.32

**The Time Slider and track bar**

a right-click on the Time Slider brings up a Create Key dialog box, which allows you to create transform keyframes for the selected object. Figure 3.33 shows the Create Key dialog box.

The track bar is directly below the Time Slider. The track bar is the timeline that displays the timeline format for your scene. More often than not, this is displayed in frames, with the gap between each tick mark representing frames. On the track bar, you can move and edit your animation properties for the selected object. When a keyframe is present, right-click it to open a pop-up menu where you can delete keyframes, edit individual transform values, and filter the Track Bar display. You will have a chance to explore using these tools in the chapters on animation in this book.

Figure 3.33

**The Create Key dialog box lets you set a keyframe for a selected object.**

The icon to the left of the track bar is the Open Mini Curve Editor icon. This toggle displays a compact version of the Track View—Curve Editor. The Track View—Curve Editor shows you your scene's animation as curves that you can edit.

## The Status Bar

The status bar in 3ds Max gives you feedback and information as you work in your scene. The status bar (Figure 3.34) runs across about two-thirds of the bottom of the screen. Check it out; you'll love it.

Figure 3.34

**The status bar is full of useful information.**

Here are the elements on the status bar.

**MAXScript Mini Listener**  This is a command prompt used for entering and viewing feedback for MAXScript. MAXScript is the scripting language used in 3ds Max to automate actions and customize functions. This line displays a single line of the actual MAXScript Listener window, which gives you easier access in a window to MAXScript.

**Status line**  Displays the number and type of objects selected in your scene.

**Lock Selection**  When your object is selected, Lock Selection lets you lock the object so you won't inadvertently deselect or select something else in your scene. The icon turns yellow when turned on. The keyboard shortcut for this tool is the spacebar.

**Relative/Absolute Transform toggle** When you enter values in the Transform Type-In boxes, 3ds Max treats the values as *absolute*. If you set the toggle to *relative*, the values you enter will be used to offset the selected object from its current state.

**Transform Type-Ins** You can enter values in these boxes (delineated as *X, Y,* and *Z* values) to transform the selected object, whether it is moving, rotating, or scaling. The Transform Type-Ins allow you to specify exact values for transforms instead of using the gizmo. When nothing is selected and you are moving the cursor around in a viewport, the Transform Type-Ins show the coordinates of your cursor.

**Grid setting** Shows the size of one grid square on the Home Grid in your viewport. To edit the size of your grid squares, go to the Grid and Snap Settings dialog box. This can be found by right-clicking the Snaps Toggle and clicking the Home Grid tab.

**Prompt line** Here, 3ds Max displays instructions that prompt you for the next action in a function, such as "Click and drag to select and move objects" when the Move tool is active. The Prompt Line gives you ongoing feedback as you work with a tool. It can be a good place to look when you're unsure of what to do next. In addition, Tool Tips are displayed here when you mouse over icons and buttons. Mousing around and checking icon names is a good way to become more familiar with the interface.

**Adaptive Degradation** This toggle helps improve performance in the viewports whenever you transform geometry, change your view, or play back an animation by decreasing the display quality of certain objects temporarily while you are making the transform or change. Only when your 3ds Max scenes become large or your system's performance is low will this toggle be truly handy. Right-click this icon to access the Adaptive Degradation priority settings.

**Add/Edit Time Tag** Add/Edit Time Tag is an animation assistant that allows you to set up tags at a certain point in your animation that you can easily jump to by selecting the tag's name.

## Animation Controls

The Animation controls are a selection of icons to the right of the status bar that are used in animation. Figure 3.35 shows the icons.

The functions of the Animation controls are covered in Chapter 8. The rundown on the icons is as follows:

**Set Keys** Sets a keyframe for the selected object(s) at the current frame for all tracks of the object. A *track* is a specific translation type (move, rotate, and/or scale, or a parameter) on a specific axis. The keyboard hot key for Set Keys is K.

Figure 3.35

**The Animation controls**

**Auto Key mode**  Toggles the Keyframing mode on and off. The icon turns red when Auto Key mode is on. Keyframes are automatically created when Auto Key icon is on and objects are transformed or parameters are changed. You don't need to set a key manually while in the Auto Key mode.

**Set Key mode**  You can create specific keyframes for a selected object by placing the object as you like and then setting a keyframe manually. This Animation mode, along with Key Filters (discussed next), allows you to control exactly which tracks are keyed while you animate. With Set Key mode off, any keys you set will be set for all tracks by default.

**Key Filters**  Clicking this icon will open the Set Key Filters dialog box shown in Figure 3.36. This is where you can pick the parameter types you want to be keyframed as you animate. This keeps your scene free of extra keyframes you may not need.

**Selection list**  Gives you quick access to named selection sets and track sets while you are working in Set Key mode. Lets you easily swap between different selection sets and track sets.

**Default In/Out Tangents for New Keys**  Shortcut for setting up tangent types for keys on curves for animation created with Set Key or Auto Key. This is only for new keyframes. Curves and keyframes are covered in detail in Chapter 8.

Figure 3.36

**The Set Key Filters dialog allows you to select the parameter types for which you want keys set.**

## Animation Playback Controls

The Animation Playback controls (Figure 3.37) are similar to the ones you would find on a VCR (how old are you?) or DVD player.

**Go to Start**  Moves the Time Slider to the first frame in the active time segment.

**Previous Frame/Key**  Moves the Time Slider back one frame or one key, depending on the Key Mode toggle.

**Play/Stop Animation**  Plays your animation in the active viewport. The icon is a flyout that lets you access another icon (an outline of a play arrow instead of the filled black arrow) to play only the animation of selected objects instead of the entire scene.

Figure 3.37

**The Animation Playback controls run your playback.**

**Go to End**  Moves the Time Slider to the last frame in the active time segment.

**Next Frame/Key**  Moves the Time Slider forward one frame or one key, depending on the Key Mode Toggle.

**Current Frame**  Also called *Go to Frame*, this field displays the current frame. It allows you to enter a frame number in the field to jump your Time Slider to that frame. There is also a spinner that you can click/drag to change the frame number.

**Key Mode** This tool allows you to jump from one keyframe to another. In order for it to work, you must enable it and then use the Previous and Next Key icons to move from one frame to the next. When active, the Key Mode icon turns dark, and the Previous Key and Next Key icons appear as shown in Figure 3.38.

**Time Configuration** A dialog box (Figure 3.39) where you control frame rates, time display, playback, and animation. You can use this to scale your animation length so it goes faster or slower, or to add more frames to the start or end of your animation. This is covered further in Chapter 8.

## Viewport Navigation Controls

The tools for viewport navigation are extensive, and many of the icons have nested flyouts that give access to multiple tools. The available tools change depending on the type of viewport you have selected, such as Orthographic, User (a 3D view that is created when an orthographic view is rotated), Perspective, Camera, or Light. Working with the UI is the best way to learn what tools are associated with each viewport.

When several of the navigation tools are is selected, they turn dark and remain selected until you choose another tool, right-click in a viewport, or press Esc.

Viewports are used for orthographic and perspective views, and also for views through cameras and lights. By setting a viewport to a view from a camera or light, you can easily position the camera or light exactly as you need it using the Viewport Navigation controls, working interactively as you watch the result in that viewport. (We will experiment with cameras and lights in later chapters in this book.)

The Navigation controls, as they appear when the Perspective viewport is active, are shown in Figure 3.40

Figure 3.41 shows how the icons appear while an Orthographic viewport is active.

Figures 3.42 and 3.43 show the default icons for a Light viewport and a Camera viewport, respectively.

In the following tables, all of the Viewport Navigation icons are laid out and briefly explained. The 3ds Max screen has a lot of icons, but experience will help you make sense of things very quickly. Take a look at these icons and click around to get a feel for how they work.

Create a few objects to have something to look at in your viewports, or open the Mobile exercise's scene file. Spend some time poking around the viewports and looking at things. Use the Viewport Navigation controls and their key/mouse combinations to get a bit more used to navigating.

Figure 3.39

**The Time Configuration dialog box**

Figure 3.40

**The Viewport Navigation icons for a Perspective viewport**

Figure 3.41

**The Viewport Navigation icons for an Orthographic viewport**

Figure 3.42

**The Viewport Navigation icons for a Light viewport**

Figure 3.43

**The Viewport Navigation icons for a Camera viewport**

The key to getting good at navigating 3ds Max, or any other 3d package, is to work on projects and get things done. You will gain the skills you need as you work toward a goal. As you will see, the exercises in the rest of this book will let you flex your muscles and give you a chance to become comfortable with 3ds Max.

The individual icons are explained in the following tables. Refer back to Figures 3.40 through 3.43 to see the icons' locations in the UI.

## Tools Available in All Viewports

Keep in mind that some of the following icons are nested icons beneath flyouts; to reveal them you will need to click and hold the flyout icon. An example of a flyout for the Viewport Navigation controls is shown here:

| ICON | NAME | FUNCTION |
|------|------|----------|
| | Zoom Extents All | Lets you zoom in your scene in all four viewports. The keyboard shortcut for this tool is Z. |
| | Zoom Extents All Selected | Works like Zoom Extents All for objects that you have selected. |
| | Maximize Viewport Toggle | Toggles between Normal and Full Screen viewport sizing. The keyboard shortcut is Alt+W. |
| | Pan View | Lets you move the view of the current viewport up, down, and side to side. The shortcut is Ctrl+P; you can also click/drag the middle mouse button. For Camera and Light viewports, this is the Truck Camera/Light that moves the respective object parallel to the viewport. |

## Tools Available in Perspective and Orthographic Viewports

These icons (refer back to Figures 3.40 and 3.41) appear available in the Perspective and Orthographic viewports. Keep in mind that some of the following icons are nested beneath flyouts.

| ICON | NAME | FUNCTION |
|------|------|----------|
| | Zoom | Zoom magnifies the objects in your viewport by moving the view in and out of 3D space in the scene. If your mouse has a scroll wheel, you can use it as a Zoom tool by placing the cursor in the selected viewport and rolling the scroll wheel to zoom in and out. |
| | Zoom All | Works like Zoom but lets you zoom all viewports at once. |
| | Zoom Extents | This flyout icon works like a Fit to Window function because it zooms all objects in your scene into the viewport. It works for only Orthographic and Perspective viewports. |
| | Zoom Extents Selected | This flyout icon is nested with Zoom Extents. It works like the Zoom Extents tool for selected objects only. |
| | Field-of-View (FOV) | This flyout icon, nested with Zoom Region, is also available in Camera viewports. FOV changes the amount of the scene that you can see in the viewport by adjusting the field of view. It increases the viewable area by increasing the angle viewed, like a camera lens. |
| | Zoom Region | This flyout icon nested with Field-of-View allows you to drag a rectangle marquee around the area you want to zoom in on. This tool is available only in Orthographic/User and Perspective viewports. |

| ICON | NAME | FUNCTION |
|------|------|----------|
| | Walkthrough | This flyout icon is nested with Pan View. This very cool tool lets you move through a viewport by pressing the arrow keys. It is similar to the Pan View tool, but you use the arrow keys instead of the mouse for navigation. When you enter the Walkthrough Navigation mode, the pointer changes to a hollow circle that shows a directional arrow while you are pressing one of the arrow keys. Walkthrough is available only for Perspective and Camera viewports. |
| | Orbit | This flyout Icon is nested with Orbit Selected and Orbit Sub-Object. Orbit lets you rotate a viewport by clicking and dragging a series of handles on the gizmo. It uses the viewport center as the center for its rotation. The shortcut is Ctrl+R and you have the same functionality, without the gizmo, using Alt+MM. Figure 3.44 shows the Orbit gizmo in action. |
| | Orbit Selected | This tool works like Orbit but uses the selected object as the center for rotation. The object remains in the same position as the viewport rotates around it. |
| | Orbit SubObject | This tool works similarly to Orbit Selected, but it rotates about the current sub-object selection. |

Figure 3.44

**The Orbit gizmo**

## Camera Viewport Controls

A camera view shows your scene through the lens of a virtual camera. The specific tools available will change depending on whether you are using a Free or Target camera. (Cameras are covered in Chapter 11.)

Again, use this section as a reference, and click along with the descriptions. You don't need to memorize it all or understand everything at once. You can come back to this chapter when you need to look up something.

To access these navigation tools, you will need to create a camera and switch a viewport to its view. To create a camera, follow these steps in a new scene or a current scene:

1. Choose Create → Cameras → Free Camera, and click in one of your viewports to place the camera. You may also click in the Create panel under the Cameras category and click the Free icon. Figure 3.45 shows a camera placed in the scene.

Figure 3.45

**A camera placed in a scene**

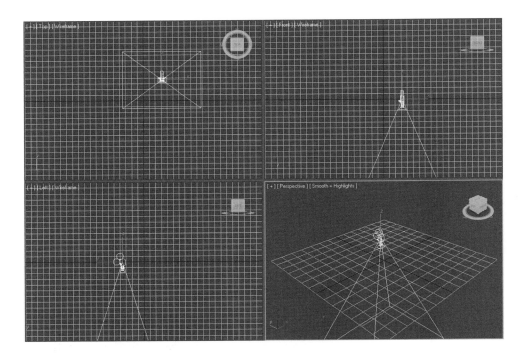

2. Click the Select Object tool to end the active tool.

3. Click a viewport name in the upper-left corner of the viewport, and select Cameras → Camera001, as shown in Figure 3.46. This will change the viewport to the camera's view. You will now be able to access the Camera Viewport Navigation tools shown in the following table.

Figure 3.46

**Set your viewport to the new camera.**

Now that you have created a Free camera in your scene, click the following icons as you explore to see how they'll help you navigate in a Camera viewport. To use these tools, select them and then click and drag in the Camera viewport. Some of these navigation icons apply to a Target camera only, and several of these icons are flyouts nested with other icons:

| ICON | NAME | FUNCTION |
| --- | --- | --- |
| | Dolly Camera | Moves the camera object toward and away from the object at which it is pointing. |
| | Dolly Target | Moves the camera's target toward and away from the object. This may not show any changes unless you use other camera tools, such as Orbit. |
| | Dolly Camera + Target | Moves the camera and target to and from the object at which it is pointing. This is available only if the camera has a target. |
| | Perspective | Adjusts Field-of-View (FOV) and lens length. |

| ICON | NAME | FUNCTION |
|------|------|----------|
| ↻ | Roll Camera | Rolls the camera around the line of sight for a Target camera or (if it is a Free camera) around the local Z-axis. |
| 🖑 | Truck Camera | Moves the camera from side to side, parallel to your scene. |
| 🜨 | Orbit Camera | Rotates the camera around the target object. This is on the flyout with the Pan Camera icon. |
| ⟩ | Pan Camera | Rotates the target around the camera. This is on the flyout with the Orbit Camera icon. |

## Light Viewport Controls

This set of tools shows your scene through the perspective of a light. This may seem a bit unusual, but it can be very useful for exact positioning of your lights. Some tools for the light objects have the same names (Dolly, Roll, Truck, Orbit, and Pan) and are used the same way as the Camera navigation tools. Therefore, their icons are not repeated here. However, the Light viewport controls that are specific to lights are listed.

You will need to create a light in your scene to access these icons in the Viewport Controls section of the UI. To create a light in the scene, follow these steps:

1. Choose Create → Lights → Standard Lights → Free Spotlight and click in one of your viewports to place the light. You may also click the Create panel, then, under the Lights category, choose Standard from the drop-down list and click the Free Spot icon. Figure 3.47 shows a light placed in the scene.

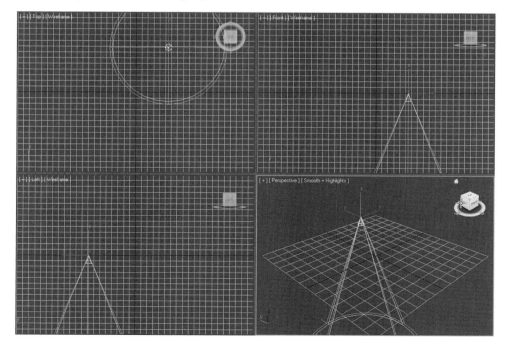

Figure 3.47

**A Free spotlight**

2. Click the Select Object tool to end the active tool.

3. Click a viewport name in the upper-left corner of the viewport, and select Lights → Fspot001, as shown in Figure 3.48. This will change the viewport to the light's view. You will now be able to access the Light Viewport Navigation tools shown in the following table:

| ICON | NAME | FUNCTION |
| --- | --- | --- |
|  | Light Hotspot | Lets you adjust the angle of the light's hotspot, which is the brightest part of the pool of light. |
| | Light Falloff | Lets you adjust the angle of the light's falloff, which is the light fading to the edges of the pool of light. |

Light viewport controls help you place your lights just the way you want them. (You'll get more hands-on experience with lights in Chapter 10, "3ds Max Lighting.")

If you are getting sick of looking at icons, remember that nearly all viewport navigation tasks can be performed using the keyboard shortcuts and the mouse buttons. This rich set of navigation tools gives you many options for moving around in 3D space, but you needn't really worry about any of them until you are comfortable just getting around—and by now this should be coming easier to you.

Figure 3.48

**Set your viewport to the new light.**

### Navigating Viewports

The easiest way to navigate the viewports is to use the keyboard/mouse combinations available in 3ds Max. Here is a review of these keyboard/mouse actions.

**Pan** Panning a viewport will "slide" the view around the screen. MM+click in the viewport and drag the mouse to move the view.

**Zoom** Zooming will move your view closer to or farther away from your objects. To zoom, use the scroll wheel or press Ctrl+Alt and MM+click in your viewport, and then drag the mouse up or down to zoom in or out, respectively.

**Orbit and Orbit Selected** Orbit and Orbit Selected let you rotate your view around your objects. To use either of the two Orbit tools, press Alt and MM+click and drag in the viewport. Use Shift+Alt+ MM for constrained rotation. By default, 3ds Max will rotate about the center of the viewport to change your perspective. However, if an object is selected, 3ds Max will revert to Orbit Selected, which will rotate about the center of the selected object instead of the center of the viewport. This way the object remains in the same position as the viewport rotates around the object.

## The Viewports

Viewports are where 3D space is simulated. Viewports in 3ds Max are initially set up with four equally sized views (Top, Front, Left, and Perspective viewports). One will have a yellow highlighted border, which shows that this viewport is the selected view. You can activate a view by working in it or by right-clicking in it. (Be careful about left-clicking, because if something is selected, it will be deselected when left-clicked.)

You can also resize your viewports by centering the pointer over the splitter bars that separate the views. The pointer will change to a two or four-sided arrow, and you can click/drag the viewports to the size desired. To switch the viewport layout back to the default, right-click over the center splitter bars the click "Reset Layout" on the pop-up menu to go back to the default.

Let's not forget the Maximize Viewport toggle in the navigation area (its hot key is Alt+W). This will change the equally sized views into one full-screen view of the active viewport.

One way to change the default look of your viewports is to use the Viewport Configuration dialog box. You can find it by choosing Views → Viewport Configuration → Layout tab and clicking the desired layout, as shown in Figure 3.49.

**Figure 3.49**

The Layout tab of the Viewport Configuration dialog box allows you to quickly change your viewport layouts.

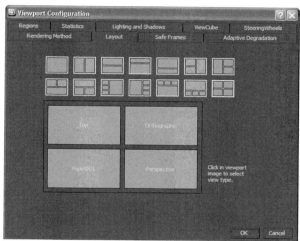

In the lower-left corner of each viewport, the axes are displayed as part of the World Space tripod. The axes are always displayed in red, green, and blue format to represent the $X$-, $Y$-, and $Z$-axes respectively, as shown in the Perspective viewport (see Figure 3.50). You have seen this familiar color scheme at work in the gizmos as well.

You've undoubtedly noticed the Home Grid in your viewports by now. This grid is a ground plane that centers around the Origin (0, 0, 0). Right-click on the Snaps toggle, then click the Home Grid tab to access the parameters that define the spacing of the Home Grid, as shown in Figure 3.51.

**Figure 3.50**

The World Space tripod in the Perspective viewport

The Home Grid is a helper for the construction of objects. When you create a new object, it is placed on the grid. The Home Grid's defaults can be edited for more effective scene creation, and they can be turned on and off in the current viewport by pressing the G key.

**Figure 3.51**

The Home Grid tab where the Home Grid parameters are set

The grid displays the units of your scene. The default is set up as Max Units, where one unit equals 1 inch. Each grid division is 10 units. The best approach is to choose a grid spacing that matches your unit of measurement. For example, if you are using centimeters, make one grid square equal 1 centimeter.

## Changing Viewport Views

As you saw earlier, the viewports are flexible and can be changed to different rendering modes by clicking on the viewport name and choosing the new viewport rendering mode from the menu (Figure 3.52).

Figure 3.52

**Selecting the viewport rendering mode**

This lets you change which view you have in a viewport. You can also use keyboard shortcuts to access any of the viewports. In an active viewport, press the hot key for the desired view. Hot keys are listed in this table:

| HOTKEY | VIEW |
| --- | --- |
| T | Top |
| B | Bottom |
| F | Front |
| L | Left |
| C | Camera |
| P | Perspective |
| U | User or Axonometric—a 3D view without perspective |

These keys are extremely helpful when one viewport is maximized and you need to access different views quickly. For scenes that have more than one camera, press the C key to bring up a pop-up menu from which you can select the camera. With so many ways to change viewport views, you'll be able to find the way that works best for your workflow.

Because the R shortcut enables the Select and Scale tool, there is no keyboard shortcut for the Right viewport.

## Viewport Rendering Modes

Viewports let you view your scene in a few different ways. For example, in the Mobile exercise, you saw how you can switch between Wireframe and Smooth + Highlights Shaded views. How you view objects in a viewport is referred to as *viewport rendering*. Again, you can access a different viewport rendering method by clicking the viewport's name. Depending on the size of your scene, your viewport may be more responsive and have a less-taxing rendering display level than the one shown here.

Each of the viewport rendering modes has specific properties.

**Smooth + Highlights** Displays scene objects with smooth shading and specular highlights from the scene lights (see Figure 3.53). This gives the best feedback for your objects.

**Smooth** Displays objects with no highlights and only smooth shading, as shown in Figure 3.54.

**Facets + Highlights** Displays scene objects with flat shading and displays specular highlights (see Figure 3.55). This is a fast way to see your solid objects with highlights when Smooth+ Highlights is too taxing with heavy scenes.

**Facets** Displays polygons as flat surfaces that are shaded, but includes no smoothing or scene highlights, as shown in Figure 3.56.

Figure 3.53

**A viewport in Smooth + Highlights rendering mode**

Figure 3.54

**A viewport in Smooth rendering mode**

Figure 3.55

**A viewport in Facets + Highlights rendering mode**

Figure 3.56

**A viewport in Facets rendering mode**

**Flat**  Displays each polygon in its raw diffuse color, disregarding any scene lighting or light sources (see Figure 3.57). This viewing method is useful when you need to see each polygon rather than to see the polygons' shading.

**Hidden Line**  A Wireframe mode that allows you to use the Wireframe mode without seeing through every object (see Figure 3.58). In this display mode only, the wireframe color is determined by choosing Customize → Customize User Interface in the Colors tab under Elements → Viewports and selecting Hidden Line Unselected rather than the object or material color.

Figure 3.57

**A viewport in Flat rendering mode**

Figure 3.58

**A viewport in Hidden Line rendering mode**

**Lit Wireframes**  Displays objects as their wireframes, with a flat shading for a sense of lighting, as shown in Figure 3.59.

**Wireframe**  Draws objects as wireframes only, as shown in Figure 3.60. This is the fastest viewing method that still lets you see an object's shape.

Figure 3.59

**A viewport in Lit Wireframes rendering mode**

Figure 3.60

**A viewport in Wireframe rendering mode**

**Bounding Box**  Displays objects as bounding boxes (see Figure 3.61). *Bounding boxes* are approximations of the volume a shape occupies. No shading is applied.

> 3ds Max 2011 will automatically degrade the display of certain objects variably (such as by using bounding boxes) when the geometry in a complex scene is too much for the display to handle when the viewport is being panned or zoomed. You probably will not encounter this feature, called Adaptive Degradation, until you begin dealing with very large scenes. You can disable Adaptive Degradation by pressing the keyboard shortcut O.

**Edged Faces**  Edged Faces draws the wireframe of an object back onto its shape when it is displayed in one of the shaded modes (Smooth, Smooth + Highlights, Facets + Highlights, or Facets). Edged Faces lets you see the wireframe lines and faces of an object for easier editing, while still seeing it shaded. Figure 3.62 shows a viewport in Smooth + Highlights mode with Edged Faces turned on.

Figure 3.61

**A viewport in Bounding Box rendering mode**

Figure 3.62

**A viewport in Smooth + Highlights rendering mode with Edged Faces**

Setting the viewport rendering modes will help you with larger scenes. More often than not, viewing your scenes with the Smooth + Highlights mode will give you the best feedback. With the Adaptive Degradation feature, you won't need to worry about which rendering level you choose. The levels are designed to automatically adapt when your system's responsiveness is slow because of a large scene.

## Gizmos

Using gizmos is a fast and effective way to transform your objects with interactive feedback. As you saw in the Mobile exercise in the previous chapter, gizmos let you manipulate objects in your viewports interactively to transform them—i.e., move, rotate, and/or scale. Coordinate Display boxes at the bottom of the screen display coordinate or angular or percentage information on the position/rotation/scale of your object as you transform it. The gizmos appear in the viewport on the selected object at their pivot point as soon as you invoke one of the transformation tools.

After you invoke the Move tool by pressing W (or accessing it through the Main toolbar), your gizmo should look like Figure 3.63.

Dragging the *XYZ*-axis handles moves an object on one specific axis. You can also click on the plane handle, the box between two axes, to move the object in that plane. Moving an object in the *XZ* plane is shown in Figure 3.64.

If you invoke the Rotate tool by pressing E, your gizmo will turn into three circles, as shown in Figure 3.65. You can click on one of the circles to rotate the object on the axis only, or you can click anywhere between the circles to freely rotate the selected object in all three axes. Click and drag the gray outer circle to rotate the object parallel with the viewport.

Invoke the Scale tool by pressing the R key, and your gizmo will turn into a triangle, as shown in Figure 3.66.

Figure 3.63
**The Move gizmo**

Figure 3.64
**Moving the object using the XZ plane handle**

Clicking and dragging anywhere inside the yellow triangle will scale the object uniformly on all three axes. By selecting the red, green, or blue handles for the appropriate axis, you can scale along one axis only. You can also scale an object on a plane between two axes by selecting the side of the yellow triangle between two axes as shown in Figure 3.67.

Keep in mind that the gizmos appear at an object's pivot point; therefore, if there is an object where you have relocated the pivot point away from the object itself, the gizmo will appear there and not on the object itself. Figure 3.68 shows the Move gizmo when the teapot's pivot is to the right of the object.

Figure 3.65
**The Rotate gizmo**

Figure 3.66
**The Scale gizmo**

Figure 3.67
**Scale along only two axes.**

Figure 3.68
**The gizmo is located at the pivot point.**

When transforming your objects, keep an eye on the Transform Type-Ins at the bottom of the UI (see Figure 3.69). These will reflect the movement distance, rotation angle, or scale percentage for the current transform. As the name indicates, you can also enter values in the fields and the object is transformed accordingly.

**Figure 3.69**

**The Transform Type-Ins**

# Managing Scene Objects

3ds Max has a few ways to organize and manage your scene elements to make you work easier. These tools include the Layer Manager, the Schematic View, two Material Editors, and the Curve Editor/Dope Sheet. The Layer Manager works with objects to organize them in layers. The Schematic View allows you to view, manage, and edit your scene's hierarchies. The Layer Manager and Schematic View windows are outlined for you here, and they are used extensively throughout this book.

The Material Editors allows you to manage your scene's materials and textures. The Material Editors are covered in Chapter 7, "Materials and Mapping." The Curve Editor manages the animation in your scene by giving you access to animation curves. The Dope Sheet manages the animation in your scene by giving you access to animation ranges or sets of keys. The Curve Editor is covered in Chapter 8, and the Dope Sheet is covered in Chapter 9.

## Layer Manager

The Layer Manager (Figure 3.70) can be accessed through the Manage Layers icon on the Main toolbar (⬛).

**Figure 3.70**

**The Layer Manager**

Layers can be used to organize scene objects. In 3ds Max, layers are organized similarly to Photoshop layers; you can organize different elements of an image in separate layers. Layers are mainly used to control object visibility, default color, selecting, freezing, and hiding. All of these functions help you organize your scene and make object management easier. You will use the Layer Manager in future exercises in this book.

The icons across the top of the Layer Manager are explained here.

**Create New Layer** Creates a new layer when you have objects selected in your scene. The selected objects are assigned to the new layer.

**Delete Highlighted Empty Layers** Deletes selected layers if they are empty.

**Add Selected Objects to Highlighted Layer** Moves currently selected objects into the selected layer.

**Select Highlighted Objects** Selects all highlighted objects, as well as all objects contained in any highlighted layers.

**Highlight Selected Objects' Layers** Highlights layers containing the currently selected objects and automatically scrolls so that highlighted layers are visible in the Layer Manager.

**Hide/Unhide All Layers** Enables the display of all layers.

**Freeze/Unfreeze All Layers** Enables the frozen state of all layers.

The columns in the Layer Manager window itself are the following:

**Layers** Displays the names of the layers/objects. To select or rename a layer, click its name. To display object or layer properties, click the object icon to open the Object Properties dialog box for all highlighted objects.

**Current Layer toggle** The unlabeled column to the right of the Layers column indicates the current layer. The check mark next to a layer means it is selected and current. This feature lets you make a different layer current.

**Hide** Hides and unhides layers. When a layer is hidden, its objects are not visible in the viewport.

**Freeze** Freezes layers. Objects on frozen layers cannot be selected.

**Render** When this feature is enabled, objects appear in the rendered scene. Nonrendering objects won't cast shadows or affect the visual component of the rendered scene.

**Color** Changes the default color on highlighted objects.

**Radiosity** When this feature is enabled, objects are included in the radiosity solution.

## Using the Layer Manager

The Layer Manager can be extremely useful for organizing and managing your scene objects. You will use the Layer Manager throughout the rest of this book. Let's take a quick look at how the Layer Manager can help you with a scene.

1. Open a new scene and create four new objects: a box, a sphere, a cone, and a torus (see Figure 3.71).

2. Open the Layer Manager by clicking the Manage Layers icon ( ) in the Main toolbar. Click the Create New Layer icon ( ) twice to create two new layers.

Figure 3.71

**The Layer Manager**

> To select more than one object in a viewport, press the Ctrl key as you click on additional objects to add to your selection. Many applications use the Shift key to add to a selection; however, 3ds Max uses Ctrl.

3. In the viewport, select the box and the sphere and assign them to Layer001 by selecting Layer001 and clicking the Add Selected Objects to Highlighted Layer icon ( ) in the Layer Manager, as shown in Figure 3.72.

4. Following the procedures in step 3, assign the cone to Layer002.

5. Select Layer001 and click in the Freeze column. The sphere and box will turn gray in the viewport and you will no longer be able to select them.

6. Click in the Hide column for Layer002, and the cone will disappear from the viewports (see Figure 3.73).

Experiment with toggling Hide and Freeze for the objects or the layers so that you can see how your scene reacts when they are on and off.

Figure 3.72

**Adding an object to the selected layer**

Figure 3.73

**Freezing and Hiding layers**

## Schematic View

The Schematic View is another way to organize and manage your scene, particularly object hierarchies. This dialog box displays the objects in your scene in a flowchart scheme, allowing you to see how objects are linked or grouped together. Parents connect down the flowchart to their children. This method of viewing hierarchies is powerful, because you get an immediate visualization of how the objects in your scene work and relate to each other. Figure 3.74 shows a scene in the Schematic View.

A scene can become so complicated that trying to select one object is impossible. The Schematic View makes editing character rigs easier, allowing you to view, create, and edit links between objects. The Schematic View simplifies the selection process by clearly displaying every object in the scene as a box with the object's name displayed in it. You can use the middle mouse button to pan in the Schematic View, or you can use any of the familiar navigation icons found in the lower right-hand corner of the window, as shown in Figure 3.74.

Figure 3.74

**A scene broken down in the Schematic View immediately tells you how the objects are organized.**

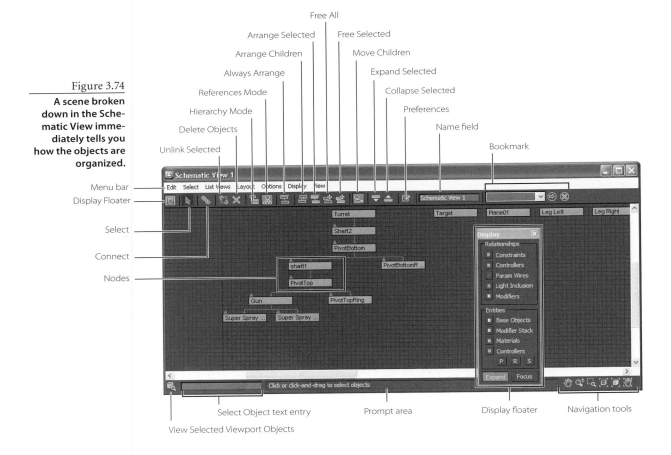

When the Modify panel is open and you select any object in the Schematic View, its parameter automatically appears in the Modify panel for easy editing. Because objects can have different states of being, different conventions are used to indicate an object's current state in the scene, with the most important states listed here:

**Red border** The object is animated.

**White fill** The object is currently selected in the Schematic View window.

**White border** The object is currently selected in a viewport.

**Collapse Selected button** Used to simplify a view. Pressing the Collapse Selected button ( ) collapses each node and its dependent child nodes up to the selected parent, putting everything into one node for simpler display. This is useful for large characters and long hierarchy chains because you don't have to see all the child nodes in a large scene. This does not remove the hierarchy; it only affects the display.

**Expand Selected button** Used to gain more information about a hierarchy of objects. Clicking the Expand Selected button ( ) expands the next child down from that node to show you its immediate child node(s).

In Figure 3.74, you can see how the Turret node is the highest parent for the hierarchy; the second row of bars hangs from the PivotBottom node as its children.

The toolbar across the top of the Schematic View is used for editing hierarchies in your scene. We will experiment with reordering the Mobile hierarchy in the Schematic View in just a moment. First, let's look at the tools as called out in Figure 3.74.

**Display floater** Enables the Display floater window, which gives you access to display toggles for certain object types in the Schematic View.

**Select** Allows you to select objects in the Schematic View. When you select an object in a viewport, its node in the Schematic View will be outlined in white. However, it will not necessarily be selected in the Schematic View. If you want to be able to select an object in either window once and have it selected in both the Schematic View and the viewports, choose Select → Sync Selection in the Schematic View window.

**Connect** To create links in the Schematic View, just as you created a link between objects earlier in this chapter, click the child object and drag it to the desired parent.

**Unlink Selected** To break links between objects, click the child to unlink and then click this icon.

**Delete Objects** Deletes the selected object(s) from the scene. If you make a mistake, you can press the Undo icon in the Main toolbar or press Ctrl+Z to get the object(s) back.

**Hierarchy Mode** Lays out the Schematic View as an outline view, as shown in Figure 3.75.

Figure 3.75

**The Schematic View in Hierarchy mode**

**References Mode** Lays out the view in the Schematic View, as shown earlier in Figure 3.74. This view is good for viewing object relationships and materials.

**Always Arrange** The Schematic View will keep the node display rigid. As you see in the References Mode, you will not be able to freely move nodes around. Turning off the Always Arrange mode allows you to arrange the nodes any way you want, as shown in Figure 3.76.

The next group of icons—Arrange Children, Arrange Selected, Free All, and Free Selected—all have to do with automatically arranging nodes when you turn off Always Arrange.

**Move Children** When you click and drag a node, all of its child nodes will follow it when this mode is enabled.

**Expand/Collapse Selected** Used to reveal or hide the child nodes of the selected node.

**Preferences** Opens the Schematic View Preferences dialog box, where you can filter certain object types (such as lights, cameras, objects, etc.) from displaying in the Schematic View.

**Name field** Lets you save certain views to recall later for easy access. When you have a heavy scene, with tons of nodes to view, getting to the right place in a complicated hier-archy can take some time. When you type a name for your current view into this text box, 3ds Max will save the view for you. To access that particular view again, in the main menu bar, select Graph Editors → Saved Schematic Views → Schematic View Name. See Figure 3.77.

Figure 3.77

**Accessing a saved Schematic View**

**Bookmark** Lets you define a selection of nodes in the Schematic View with bookmarks that you can later return to easily.

## Using the Schematic View with the Mobile

Let's take a look at the Schematic View in action, and have another whack at the Mobile scene's hierarchy.

You can start with your own Mobile scene file, or load the scene `Mobile Hierarchies.max` from the Scenes folder in the Mobile project on this book's companion web page. Just follow these steps:

1. With your Mobile scene loaded, open the Schematic View, as shown in Figure 3.78, by choosing Graph Editors → New Schematic View or by clicking the Schematic View (Open) icon ( ) in the Main toolbar.

2. Link the Star001 object to the Circle001 object. To do this, click the Connect button and then select the Star001 node and drag it to the Circle001 node, as shown in Figure 3.79. The location of the Star001 node has been moved for clarity.

Figure 3.78

**The Schematic View for the Mobile scene**

3. When you release the mouse button, notice that the Star001 node is linked to the Circle001 node. Click the Always Arrange button in the Schematic View toolbar, if necessary, and the Star001 node will relocate below the Circle001 node, as shown in Figure 3.80.

Figure 3.79

**Connecting the star to the circle**

Figure 3.80

**The star is linked under the circle.**

You can see how easy it is to restructure your scene hierarchies using the Schematic View. All the controls for viewing and arranging nodes might be a bit much for one window. You probably won't need half those icons, but knowing how to use the Schematic View is important. It is an important tool in organizing and setting up your scenes for animation. You will continue to use the Schematic View throughout this book.

## Scene Explorer

The Scene Explorer dialog (Figure 3.81) is accessed through Tools → New Scene Explorer and is an expanded version of the dialog opened with the Select by Name icon in the Main toolbar, discussed earlier in the chapter. Scene Explorer allows you to view the objects in your scene by name, as well as sort or filter them by type, view and edit their hierarchies, and generally manage the objects in your scene. Through the Scene Explorer you can rename, delete, hide, freeze, and edit some object properties en masse.

Two primary uses of the Scene Explorer are to select objects and edit their hierarchies. To select objects in your scene in Scene Explorer, enable Sync Selection by clicking its icon along the bottom of the Scene Explorer dialog box (see Figure 3.81). While it is enabled, if you select an object in your scene through a viewport, it is simultaneously selected in the Scene Explorer and vice versa.

You can link and unlink objects to edit hierarchies as well. If you drag an object's icon onto another object in the Scene Explorer dialog until you see a yellow arrow to the left of the target object, the dragged object will become a child of the target object. Figure 3.82 shows the Leg Right object being linked to the Target object. To unlink an object, drag its icon from the target object in the Scene Explorer to the Scene Root node at the top of the list.

Find       View Explorer

Display Geometry
Display Shapes
Display Lights
Display Cameras
Display Helpers
Display Space Warps
Display Groups
Display Object Xrefs
Display Bones
Display Containers
Display Frozen Objects
Display Hidden Objects
Display All
Display None
Invert Display
Enable Advanced Filter
Configure Advanced Filter
Lock Cell Editing

Selection Set     Select All         Filter Selection Set
Select None    Sync Selection
Select Invert

Figure 3.81

**The Scene Explorer dialog box**

You can have as many Scene Explorer windows open as you like, because they persist in your scene as you work. You can toggle between different views of the Scene Explorer that you have opened previously through the window's View Explorer pull-down menu.

Figure 3.82

**Linking objects in the Scene Explorer dialog box**

# The Quad Menu and the Caddy Interface

The more you can keep your eyes on the viewports, the more productive your time will be. Every time you have to move your attention to a menu, toolbar, or panel, and then back to your scene, a little more of your time is gone. 3ds Max's Quad menu and Caddy interface are part of the "on canvas" toolset designed to maximize your efficiency by minimizing the time spent looking outside of the viewports.

## The Quad Menu

The Quad menu, as the name implies, displays up to four menus, depending on the type of object(s) that are currently selected. When a primitive object, such as a sphere or box,

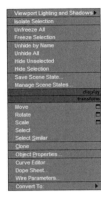

is selected, right-clicking opens two panels of the quad menu, Display and Transform, as shown in Figure 3.83.

In the Display menu, you can define how the selected object is displayed in the scene. Objects can be hidden or unhidden by name or by selection, or frozen by selection only. You can only unfreeze all frozen objects at one time using the Quad menu. The Transform panel provides quick access to the transforms (Move, Rotate, and Scale) as well as tools to select and clone objects and to access three of the graph editors. Clicking the Object Properties option opens the Object Properties dialog box (see Figure 3.84), where all of an object's properties can be edited. The Convert To option in the Quad menu expands to display a list of object types to which the current selection can be converted.

Right-clicking when a mesh object is selected brings up two additional panels, Tools 1 and Tools 2, as shown in Figure 3.85. The Tools 1 panel contains access to the sub-object levels for the mesh as well as some of the basic mesh editing tools. The Tools 2 quad only contains the Create option for creating sub-objects for the selected mesh. Meshes and sub-objects are covered in Chapter 4, "Modeling in 3ds Max: Part I."

As you've seen, the Quad menu adapts itself to the object that is selected. Sub-object selections are no exception, as you can see in Figure 3.86, which displays the quad menu when a sub-object selection is current. As you can see when compared to Figure 3.85, both the Tools 1 and Tools 2 panels are expanded to include additional, sub-object–related tools.

Figure 3.84

**The Object Properties dialog box**

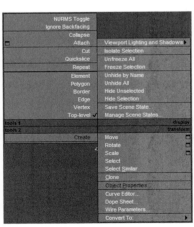

Figure 3.85

**The Quad menu when a mesh is selected**

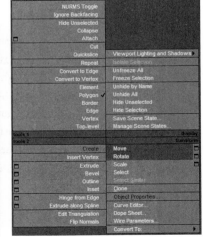

Figure 3.86

**The Quad menu when a sub-object is selected**

Quad menus are efficient, easy to open, and should be a significant component of your 3ds Max workflow.

## The Caddy Interface

Like the Quad menu, the new caddy interface is designed to keep your eyes in the view-ports while providing context-sensitive tools. The caddies replace the Settings dialog boxes available in previous versions of 3ds Max. Depending on the tool, clicking the Settings button (■) may display the tool-specific caddy directly over the selected objects or sub-objects. Figure 3.87 shows the Extrude Polygons caddy. Each tool's caddy is slightly different and may include more than one parameter.

Pausing the cursor over any of the highlighted features changes the caddy title to reflect the name of that feature. Clicking a feature with a down arrow opens a drop-down menu where you can choose an option. There are three methods for executing the changes in a caddy: OK, Apply and Continue, and Cancel. OK applies the parameter values set then closes the caddy. Apply and Continue applies the parameter values but keeps the caddy open. Cancel termi-nates the command without applying the parameter values and closes the caddy.

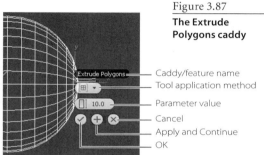

Figure 3.87

**The Extrude Polygons caddy**

Caddy/feature name
Tool application method
Parameter value
Cancel
Apply and Continue
OK

# Summary

Wow! That was a lot of information. You've learned how to navigate the menus, toolbars, icons, panels, and dialog boxes in 3ds Max. Remember, don't worry about absorbing all that information. This chapter exists to give you a unified reference guide for 3ds Max UI issues. Come back to this chapter as you work with 3ds Max in the tutorials in this book and any other 3ds Max work you have.

If you've read all the way through this chapter, you've seen the icons and buttons you will come across most often, had a taste of everything on the main 3ds Max UI screen, and found a brief description of what each feature does.

Complete understanding of how to use 3ds Max comes with time and experience. To develop that understanding, you need to work on projects that further challenge you and get you moving around inside the UI. This book begins that ride and tries to give you a good push in the right direction.

# CHAPTER 4

# Modeling in 3ds Max: Part I

*Modeling in 3D programs* is akin to sculpting or carpentry; you essentially create objects out of shapes and forms. No matter how you look at it, even a complex model is just an amalgam of simpler parts. The successful modeler can dissect a form down to its components and translate them into surfaces and meshes.

3ds Max's modeling tools are incredibly strong for polygonal modeling. The focus of this book will be on polygonal modeling because the majority of 3ds Max models are created with polygons. In addition to mechanical models, in this book you will model an organic low polygon count model—a soldier fit for a game—and use that model to animate a character with Character Studio.

In this chapter, you will learn modeling concepts and how to use 3ds Max modeling toolsets. You will also tackle two different models to get a sense of a workflow using 3ds Max.

Topics in this chapter include the following:

- **Planning your model**
- **Modeling concepts**
- **Modifiers and the modifier stack**
- **Look at the mesh you got us into!**
- **Editable Poly tools**
- **Modeling a chest of drawers**

# Planning Your Model

The most important thing to know before you begin to model is exactly *what* you are going to model. That sounds obvious, but it's true. You need to think about your model and gather as many references as you can. The best training is simply by observing the core elements and forms that make up objects in everyday life. Learn how to dissect things around you into component shapes that you can picture in a 3D window. When you look at a barbell, for example, you should see several cylinders connected to each other. When you see an office chair, you should see a few boxes and cylinders arranged and rounded at the edges. When you begin to see objects in this manner, the idea of modeling them may not seem quite as daunting.

"Yeah, but all my friends can sit down and model anything they want." Be that as it may, if you are a novice to 3D, surround yourself with references. Even if you are not new to 3D or to modeling, you should surround yourself with as many references as you can. Not having a clear picture in your head of where you need to go for your model will just aggravate the process and give you a slack result.

Take pictures all around the proposed object. Get the dimensions, sizes, angles, and slopes of the surfaces of your subject. You could even try to re-create the object in a different medium. Try sketching the subject, or grab some children's Play-Doh or a plate of mashed potatoes and make a rough sculpture. It may seem like a lot of effort to build something trivial, but it will pay off in the long run.

But enough of that old lecture.

Your first question should be, "How detailed should I make the model?" As you may have read in the first chapter, it's always a good idea to match the level of detail for a model to what is needed in the shot. If you are featuring the object up close and personal, then you should take care to build it with extra detail, adding as many polygons as it takes to make it look good and still be able to render. If, however, the object is far away and half obscured, detailing the heck out of it would be a waste of time. In Figure 4.1, on the left you can see a park bench in a far shot, compared to a view of the bench up close on the right. It would be a waste of effort and time to detail the bench to exacting levels when the bench will be seen *only* in a far shot.

You should ask yourself what the model will be used for when you are deciding how best to detail it. If you are not sure how the model will be used in the end, it's generally best to create as much detail as you think necessary. You can always prune down the details later if, for example, your scene ends up very large and will not render quickly enough.

Here's another thing to confuse you: You can always add detail to a model with texturing. Textures, when applied well, can really turn an otherwise ho-hum model into a spectacular object when rendered. You can easily add details such as grooves, dents, and engravings with special texture maps called *bump maps* or *displacement maps.* You will learn about these maps in Chapter 7, "Materials and Mapping." Don't worry about these things yet, though. Most people begin by putting all the details they can into their model, and as they gain more experience, they start to realize that some of the modeling work can be deferred until the texturing phase.

Figure 4.1

**The level of detail in a model depends on how much of the model is seen.**

## Modeling Concepts

To get a foothold in modeling, you will need to understand a number of things. If you are not new to CG or are desperate to get started, feel free to skip ahead and start modeling. However, you still might want to peruse this section for some concepts and terms that may make things easier for you in the coming exercises.

### Polygons

A *polygon* is a surface created by connecting three or more points in 3D space. This flat surface connects to other polygons to form more intricate surfaces. In Figure 4.2, you see a sphere. The facets of the sphere are polygons, all connected at common *edges* at the correct angles and in the proper arrangement to make a sphere.

The points that generate a polygon are called *vertices.* The lines that connect the points are called *edges.* If the polygon has three vertices, its surface is called a *face.* Polygons are made up of triangular faces by design. In the example of the sphere in Figure 4.2, the polygon's facets all have four vertices.

Figure 4.3 shows the same sphere with one face selected. See how the face is half of the polygon, using three of its vertices.

The more polygons you have in a model, the more detailed it becomes. However, greater numbers of polygons tax your system and take longer to render. This is where the term *low-poly modeling* originates. In computer or console games, the machine renders the scene on the fly, so its computation requirements are strict. The fewer the polygons in the scene, the faster the game can play back. Games frequently use low-poly models to maximize the effect in their game without sacrificing precious computational cycles.

Figure 4.2

**A sphere is composed of polygons.**

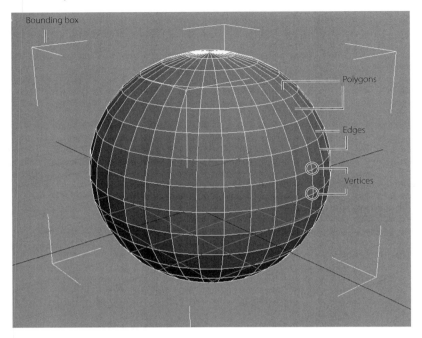

Higher-resolution models are typically used in television and film, because the scenes are all rendered beforehand and then laid off to video tape or output to film. A computational ceiling is still dictated by the machines that are used in creating the TV or film animations, however, so it is always a good idea to be smart when creating models.

Figure 4.3

**Sphere with one face selected**

## Primitives

Primitives are the basic 3D geometric shapes that are automatically generated by 3D modeling applications. As such, they do not need to be constructed from scratch. A considerable amount of modeling (perhaps most) begins with primitives, which are then edited and used with other primitives to create more complex objects. Use primitives as the core of your object. For example, to sculpt an apple, you might start out with a sphere primitive.

As you can see in Figure 4.4, 3ds Max affords you plenty of primitives to choose from for your original form. All of these primitives have their own parameters for customizing the form to your liking. You have already seen how to create some of these objects in the Mobile exercise in Chapter 2, "Your First 3ds Max Project."

Figure 4.4

**3ds Max standard
and extended
primitives**

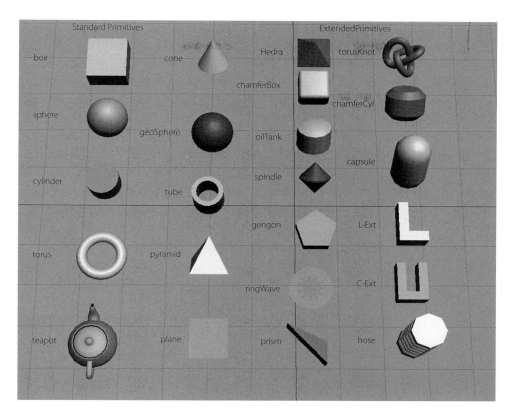

Objects such as the primitives would be useless in 3ds Max if you could not edit them
to suit your needs. For example, you could sculpt a sphere into the shape of an apple. To
sculpt a surface, you will need to convert your object (such as the sphere for the apple)
into an editable object, frequently called a *mesh,* to get to the object's component level
where you can move points and reshape faces that make up the object or primitive. We
will look at that in the next section.

## Meshes and Sub-Objects

Once you have chosen a primitive that will best work for your intended model, you begin
the modeling process by changing the primitive into a mesh object to access the components of the object with which you will edit the model (such as vertices, faces, etc.).

In 3ds Max, *mesh* objects are defined by smaller component pieces that form the object
as a whole. The smaller components (called *sub-objects*) can be manipulated to adjust the
shape of the object or to form more complex models. Once you convert your object in 3ds
Max to an editable object such as a mesh, you can edit using the sub-objects available for
that object.

For instance, mesh models break down your object into a number of individual flat
surfaces—polygons and faces. With meshes, you can select any of the sub-objects at

different component levels—such as the polygons, vertices, or faces of the mesh—to make adjustments while sculpting your model.

In 3ds Max, there are two ways to create a mesh object: by applying a *modifier* to the base object or primitive or by *converting* the primitive to a mesh. Both methods give you access to the sub-object level for editing. The one big difference, however, can be critical if you need to edit the base object—for example, if you want to change the radius of a primitive sphere after you start editing it as a mesh. Instead of converting, you are better off using the modifier method because it preserves the original primitive object intact and allows you to modify the object's original parameters (such as radius for a sphere) even after you begin to edit the mesh.

In this exercise, you will create an object and turn it into a mesh using a modifier. Follow these steps:

1. Create a sphere in a new scene using the Create panel. You will turn this object into a mesh to check out the sub-objects at your disposal.

2. With the sphere selected, switch to the Modify panel. Figure 4.5 shows the newly created sphere. Notice the Sphere heading in the Modifier Stack on the right.

3. With the sphere selected, choose Modifiers → Mesh Editing → Edit Poly. This will apply an Edit Poly modifier to the sphere, giving you access to the sub-objects that a mesh affords you.

4. The Modifier Stack will display a heading called Edit Poly. Highlight Edit Poly in the Modifier Stack. You should see something like what is shown in Figure 4.6.

Figure 4.5

**The newly created sphere, shown here with Edged Faces turned on, awaits your command.**

Figure 4.6

**You now have access to the Edit Poly's sub-object selections and parameters.**

5. Under the Selection heading in the Modify panel, select the type of sub-object you would like to begin editing. Choose the first icon ( 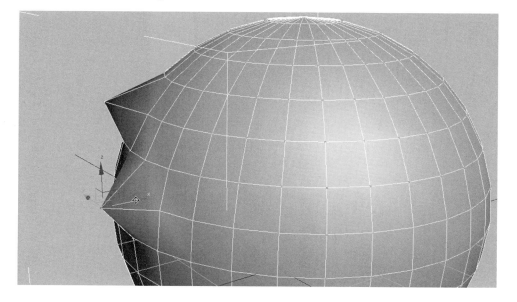 ) for Vertex.

6. As you can see in Figure 4.7, small dots appear on the sphere. They are the vertices you can now select. Choose the Move tool and select one of the vertices on the sphere. Click and drag to move the vertex anywhere to sculpt the surface of the sphere, as shown in Figure 4.7.

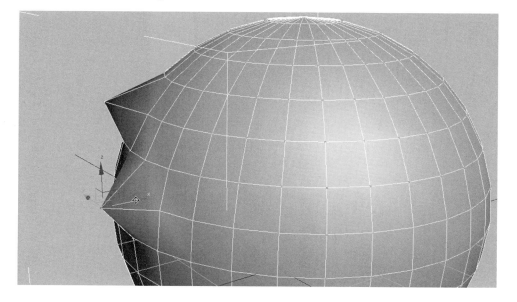

Figure 4.7

**Adjusting sub-objects such as vertices allows you to sculpt your model.**

7. Change your sub-object selection to polygons by choosing the Polygon icon (⬚) in the Modify panel. The vertices will disappear from the viewport. Change to Edged Faces display mode in the viewport either by clicking in the bracketed Smooth + Highlights label in the upper-left corner of a viewport and selecting Edged Faces or by pressing the F4 shortcut.

8. Click on a polygon to select it. Notice that the polygon turns red in the viewport. Move the selected polygon around to see how the surface of the sphere mesh changes (Figure 4.8).

Figure 4.8

**Selecting and playing around with a polygon sub-object on the sphere mesh**

9. Try selecting the other sub-object types and changing the shape of the sphere.

10. In the Modifier Stack, click on the original Sphere entry. You will see the warning shown in Figure 4.9.

As you can see, you have greater control over the shape of your model once you access the sub-object levels of an Edit Poly. You'll see quite a bit of mesh editing in the exercises throughout this book. One exercise you can do now quickly is to try to sculpt a simple cartoon head using nothing but sub-object manipulation on a base sphere.

Figure 4.9

**The topography-dependent modifier warning**

In some 3D packages, you have inherent access to a model's components (such as a vertex or face). However, with 3ds Max you will need to either convert created objects into meshes or add the appropriate modifier to create a mesh, as you did in the previous exercise, to manipulate the sub-objects. You will be modeling with meshes later in this chapter, and you will learn other ways to access sub-objects on a model.

**TOPOGRAPHY-DEPENDENT WARNING MESSAGE**

The Edit modifiers perform operations on the explicit topology of sub-object selections. When a topology-dependent modifier is present on the stack, you can adversely affect its results if you visit previous stack operations and change the number or order of sub-objects (such as polygons or vertices) in the selection. If you try to do this, a warning alerts you to the situation. This simply means some adjustments you make to a modifier before that point in the Modifier Stack may cause issues in the model. So be careful, and if you feel nervous, save your scene before continuing, just in case.

# Modifiers and the Modifier Stack

Modifiers, as you have already seen, are a way to edit your objects in 3ds Max. In almost all cases, you can apply several modifiers to an object to get the desired result. In the Modify panel's Modifier Stack, you can access any of those modifiers to change any of its parameters at any time in your modeling. This is perhaps one of the best aspects of modeling in 3ds Max.

3ds Max has tons of modifiers that accomplish any number of tasks. These tasks need not be limited to editing models, though; many modifiers work well in animation and dynamics chores as well. In this section, we will cover a few modeling-specific modifiers and, more importantly, you will see how the Modifier Stack operates.

## Applying Modifiers

Let's take a quick look at how modifiers work on editing objects. In the following steps, you will apply a few modifiers to an object.

1. In a new scene, create a tall box in the Perspective viewport, as shown here. The box should have a height of 45, with a width and length of 20, as seen in Figure 4.10.

2. With the box selected, choose Modifiers → Parametric Deformers → Twist. The box should now have an orange outline, and Twist should appear in the Modifier Stack. Go to the Modify panel to see the Modifier Stack, as shown in Figure 4.11. Click Twist in the Modifier Stack to access its parameters.

3. Click the Angle spinner and drag the mouse to increase the angle to 240 or so. As you can see in Figure 4.12, the box gets completely strange. You can see the box twist pretty nicely at first, but the higher the Angle on the Twist, the more shearing the box will undergo, to the point where it no longer resembles what a twisted box should look like.

Figure 4.10

**Box created in the new scene**

Figure 4.11

**The Twist modifier is now applied to the box. You can still access the original parameters of the box.**

4. The box is suffering from a case of low definition, meaning the box does not have enough segments to handle the twist deformation without turning inside out. You will need to add more segments to the box for a smoother twist effect. In the Modifier Stack, click Box to access the parameters for the box, before the Twist modifier.

5. To better see the effect of adding more segments to the box, enable Edged Faces in the viewport.

6. Click the Length Segs parameter spinner and increase the value to 4. Increase the Width Segs to 4 and the Height Segs to 16. As you increase the segments in the original box, the Twist modifier takes on a much nicer shape. Figure 4.13 shows the box with more segments.

7. You can increase the segments as much you prefer; however, it's best to use the fewest number of segments that will give you the desired result. Increasing the number of segments essentially increases the polygons in the surface.

8. Now add another modifier to the box. With the box selected, highlight the Box entry in the Modifier Stack. Choose Modifiers → Parametric Deformers → Spherify. Your box should look like a ball (Figure 4.14). Neat!

Figure 4.12

**The box is twisted out of shape.**

Figure 4.13

**Adding more segments to the box makes the deformation from the Twist modifier smoother.**

Figure 4.14

**Spherify the box.**

Figure 4.15

**Click the Trash Can icon to remove unwanted modifiers from stack.**

9. Play with the Spherify modifier's only parameter (Percent) to see how the twisted box can turn into a sphere. Although this is kind of a neat trick, you don't really need this modifier, so go ahead and remove it from the stack. In the Modifier Stack, click the Spherify entry and click the Trash Can icon ( 🗑 ) at the bottom of the Modifier List, as shown in Figure 4.15. This will remove the Spherify modifier without harming anything else, and it will return the box to its twisted state.

Modifiers are powerful editing and animation tools. Take some time to play around in a scene such as the one from the previous exercise. Apply different deformers to objects and see what they do. It's really best to learn by experience sometimes. The Parametric Deformer modifiers are especially fun to play with, as you can see.

You have not seen the last of modifiers in this book; they are an integral part of the 3ds Max workflow, and we will use them throughout this book. We will take another look at the Modifier Stack in the next section.

## Modifier Stack with a Side of Maple Syrup

The Modifier Stack displays the modifiers added to any objects. It gives you access to any of the parameters for the modifiers applied to the object, as well as the original parameters of the object itself. When working with the Modifier Stack, you can access several options through the icons below the stack itself, as shown in Figure 4.16.

**Pin Stack** If you want to freeze the display on the Modify panel controls on the currently selected object, click this icon. Pin Stack locks the stack and all the controls in the panel so that you can see that object's stack even while you have other objects selected in the scene.

**Show End Result On/Off Toggle** When on, it shows the effect of the entire stack on the selected object. When off, it shows the effect of the stack only up to the currently highlighted modifier.

**Make Unique** With a certain type of object duplication (instancing), making any adjustments to the instanced copy also reflects in the original object. Make Unique separates the objects and disallows a shared adjustment, so if you apply a modifier to an instanced copy, it will not reflect in the original object when Make Unique is applied.

Figure 4.16

**The Modifier Stack's controls**

**Remove modifier from stack** This deletes the current modifier from the stack, eliminating all changes caused by that modifier.

**Configure Modifier Sets** This displays a menu that allows you to configure the display of the Modify panel and choose which modifiers will be available to you directly from the Modify panel, without having to access the drop-down list.

**Sub-object icon** The plus or minus icon to the left of the modifier name signifies that you have access to the sub-object (or sub-modifier) levels.

**Lightbulb icon** This turns the effect of the modifier on and off. This is very useful for troubleshooting and verifying the effect of a particular modifier in a stack.

## Order in the Stack

Unless changed, the Modifier Stack contains a history of an object's modifiers in the order they were applied. The Modifier Stack is read and applied to the object from the bottom going up, with the original object's entry at the very bottom. As you can imagine, the order in which you stack your modifiers is very important. You can get very different results from the same objects with the same modifiers in a different order.

Fortunately, changing the order of modifiers in the stack is very easy. In the Modifier Stack, click the modifier you want to move and drag it to its new position in the stack. As you drag the mouse button, a blue line will demarcate where in the stack the modifier will be placed.

For example, you can start with a cylinder and apply the Bend modifier (Modifiers → Parametric Deformers → Bend) to the cylinder first, as shown in Figure 4.17.

Figure 4.17

**A cylinder with the Bend modifier applied**

Now if you want to pinch in or taper the bent side of the cylinder, you can add a Taper modifier (Modifiers → Parametric Deformers → Taper) to the stack and change the amount of −0.65. The results won't look the way you would expect, as you can see in Figure 4.18.

Figure 4.18

**Trying to taper the bent side of the cylinder does not work with the Taper modifier—yet.**

Now go to the Modifier Stack, click and drag the Taper modifier, and move it below the Bend modifier (Figure 4.19). These are the results you want to see. You want to bend the taper, not taper the bend. Using this principle will help you figure out how to order the modifiers in the stack.

Figure 4.19

**This is the way it's supposed to look.**

# Look at the Mesh You Got Us Into!

As you saw earlier in this chapter, to access the sub-object level of objects, you will need to turn them into a mesh. You've seen how you can add an Edit Mesh modifier to an object so you can begin to sculpt the surface using vertices and faces. There are tons of editing tools inherent in meshes.

When you create a mesh from an object, you not only have access to the sub-objects of that object, but you also have access to a host of tools to allow you to edit the surface. How do you get into a mesh? There are at least four different ways that give more or less the same result: by adding a modifier (either Edit Mesh or Edit Poly), or by converting to either an Editable Mesh or an Editable Poly. We will primarily use the Poly methods throughout the book.

## Converting versus Adding a Modifier

You can *add* the Edit Poly modifier to an object, or you can *convert* to an Editable Poly. Converting to an Editable Poly and adding an Edit Poly modifier are roughly the same; they both host the same toolset and allow you the same sub-object levels for the mesh. To experiment with the modifier method, try this exercise:

1. Create two spheres in a new scene, and place them side by side, as shown in Figure 4.20.

Figure 4.20

**Two spheres side by side**

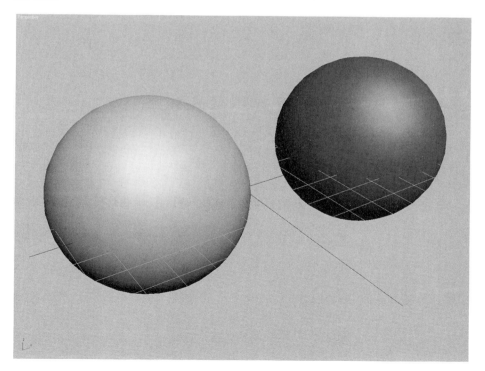

Figure 4.21

**Choosing Convert To: Editable Poly in the Modifier Stack right-click menu**

2. Select the sphere on the left and apply an Edit Poly modifier to it (choose Modifiers → Mesh Editing → Edit Poly).

3. Select the sphere on the right and convert it to an Editable Poly by right-clicking on the sphere's entry in the Modifier Stack. From the right-click menu, choose Editable Poly under the Convert To: heading, as shown in Figure 4.21.

4. Take turns clicking back and forth between the two spheres. You should notice very little difference in the toolsets in the Modify tab. Figure 4.22 shows the Modify panel for the sphere with the Edit Poly modifier, and Figure 4.23 shows the Modify panel for the Editable Poly sphere.

5. Notice that the Editable Poly sphere no longer has the same Modifier Stack entries. This sphere now displays as Editable Poly in the Modifier Stack. You should also note that the Editable Poly sphere has a rollout called Surface Properties at the bottom of the Modify panel. Aside from those two issues, the modifier and the conversion are exactly the same.

The *convert* method has its own advantages, however. Converting to an Editable Poly, as opposed to applying the Edit Poly modifier, saves memory and is more efficient because 3ds Max doesn't have to save the base object's parameter information. However, using the modifier gives you a little bit of comfort if you have commitment issues, because you can always go back to the original object and remove the Edit Poly modifier at any time. You cannot reconvert an Editable Poly back to its original object.

## Mesh versus Poly

In 3ds Max you can also edit sub-objects for a mesh as we did above by using the Edit Mesh modifier or by converting to an Editable Mesh (as opposed to the Edit Poly modifier or the Editable Poly conversion you have already seen). How do you decide which of these four

Figure 4.22

**The Modify Panel for the sphere with the Edit Poly modifier**

Figure 4.23

**The Modify Panel for the sphere that is converted to an Editable Poly**

operations to use? Well, so far you have not seen the Edit Mesh modifier or the Editable Mesh conversion because a more up-to-date toolset for sub-object tools is obtained through the Edit Poly modifier or Editable Poly procedures, and it is the preferred way to go for many 3ds Max artists.

The next question is whether to use the Edit Poly modifier or to convert to an Editable Poly in your workflow. We have shown you both because they are both good to know, and you should understand the similarities and differences in how they function. Having said that, we'll concentrate on the Edit Poly modifier and Editable Poly for this chapter's exercises.

The Edit Poly modifier gives you plenty of controls to edit an object.

The differences between mesh and poly are few. An Editable Mesh gives you a sub-object level called *faces*, which are polygons with just three edges (they have three vertices). Figure 4.24 shows you faces on a box object.

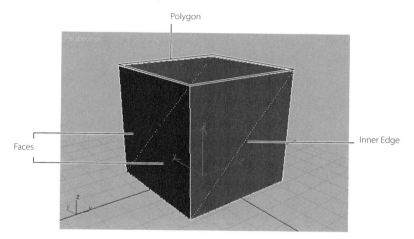

Polygon

Faces

Inner Edge

Figure 4.24

**Polygon faces on this box have three edges or sides, making them triangular. A polygon on this box has four edges or sides, making it a square.**

When modeling with an Editable Mesh (or through the Edit Mesh modifier), having faces gives you an inner edge where the faces meet along the center of the polygon. The inner edge can cause all kinds of problems even when you are working in Poly mode. An Editable Poly is similar to an Editable Mesh, but it gives you access to four-sided polygons instead of faces. It also hosts a slew of other, more refined tools and selection options.

In addition, the toolsets found in the Edit Poly/Editable Poly methods are more fleshed out than those in the Edit Mesh/Editable Mesh method and have been updated more, so they will give you slightly more options. Furthermore, the major difference between the toolsets in the Editable Poly and the Edit Poly modifier is that you have inherent access to Subdivision modeling on the Editable Poly.

In the next section, you will learn more about the Edit Poly modifier and the Editable Poly.

## Edit Poly/Editable Poly Tools

In this section, you will explore further the actual toolsets in the Edit Poly/Editable Poly world. Most of these toolsets will also apply to the toolsets you will find in the Edit Mesh/Editable Mesh world as well, although some may be used slightly differently. In either case, using an Edit Poly modifier or an Editable Poly is preferred.

Similarly, the toolset in an Editable Poly is very similar to those found with the Edit Poly modifier; here is a rundown of the rollouts and toolsets you will find for the Editable Poly. (Many cross over for the Edit Poly modifier as well.)

When you convert a primitive to an Editable Poly, you can see the controls for manipulating an object at sub-object levels in the Modify panel interface. They are very similar to the sub-objects you learned about earlier in the book with the Edit Poly modifier. In all, there are six rollouts (as shown in Figure 4.25). The main ones are Selection, Edit Geometry, and Subdivision Surface.

Figure 4.25

**The six rollouts for the Editable Poly**

## Selection Rollout

The Selection rollout contains tools used to access different levels of the object's sub-objects and their display in the viewport. You can also find information about the selected components in this rollout, as shown in Figure 4.26.

Figure 4.26

**The Selection rollout for an Editable Poly**

When you first create an Editable Poly and access the Modify tab, you are in the Object level, meaning you will edit the entire object. By clicking the different sub-object–level icons at the top of this rollout (see Figure 4.27), you can access the different selection levels as well as their relevant tools. Deselecting the icon will return you to the Object selection level.

You can also select the desired sub-object level by clicking the plus sign (+) next to the Editable Poly entry in the Modifier Stack and selecting one of the entries, as shown Figure 4.28.

Here are the different sub-object levels for an Editable Poly:

**Vertex** *Vertices* define the structure of other sub-objects that make up the poly. They are simply points in space. However, when a vertex is moved, the geometry that they form is changed accordingly. While your Editable Poly is selected, you can press 1 on the keyboard to select the Vertex level.

Figure 4.27

**The sub-object icons for an Editable Poly**

**Edge** The line connecting two vertices together is an *edge* and therefore creates the side of a polygon. Edges can be shared by only two polygons. Press 2 to enter Edge level.

**Border** A *border* is the edge of a hole. A surface's edge contains polygons that are not flanked by other polygons; in essence, they are on the edge of the surface. The row of edges on the perimeter of that surface is the border. You can invoke Border level by pressing 3.

Figure 4.28

**Editable Poly sub-object levels**

**Polygon** A *polygon* is a flat shape created by connecting three or more vertices, forming a closed shape. Polygons are what actually render when you output your scene in rendering. Press 4 to enter the Polygon level.

**Element** An *element* is one of two or more individual mesh objects (that is, groups of contiguous polygons) grouped together into one larger object. For example, if you attach one box to another, you create one mesh object from the two boxes. Each box is now an element of the object. Any function you perform on that object affects all its elements. However, you can manipulate the elements independently at the Element sub-object level. When you attach two or more meshes together, for example, the object becomes a larger single object in 3ds Max. However, the original meshes attached to each other are still accessible as elements of the larger grouped object. Press 5 to enter the Element level.

The Selection rollout has a few options that will help you quickly alter your selection to better suit your needs. The following covers a few of the important selection options:

**By Vertex** When you click the check box, you can select sub-objects by selecting the vertex they are near. This feature is grayed out when you are in Vertex mode.

**Ignore Backfacing** When you click the check box you can select only the sub-objects that are facing you. With the default, which is *off,* you can select any sub-object(s) that are facing you. Think of it like selecting a dot on an orange. With Ignore Backfacing turned on, you can select a dot only on the side of the orange you can see. With Ignore Backfacing off, you can select any dot—even if it is on the side of the orange that's away from you.

**By Angle** When you select a polygon with By Angle enabled, 3ds Max will also select the neighboring polygons based on the value given for the angle in the text box next to this check box. This value determines the maximum angle between neighboring polygons that may be selected.

**Shrink** When you have made a sub-object selection but you feel the selection is too wide, use Shrink. Shrink will deselect the outermost sub-objects to shrink your selection.

**Grow** Conversely, you can make a small selection of sub-objects and use Grow to increase the selection area outward in all available directions.

**Loop** Once you select an edge, you can propagate that selection to all the edges continuously around the mesh object by clicking the Loop button. The entire loop of edges is selected in the image on the right in Figure 4.29.

**Ring** Similar to the Loop function, Ring propagates an edge selection to the ring of edges perpendicular to the edge selected. In Figure 4.29, the left image shows a single edge selection. In Figure 4.30, the edges are selected with the Ring function.

Figure 4.29

**Selected Edge (left)
and Selected Edge
Loop (right)**

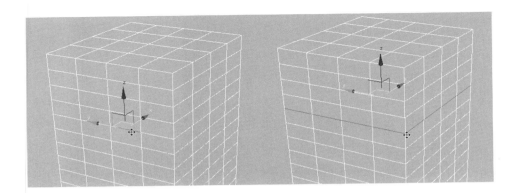

Figure 4.30

**Edges selected with
the Ring function**

Figure 4.31

**The Soft Selection
rollout**

## Soft Selection Rollout

As you already know, a regular selection selects only what you pick in the viewport for editing. You can, however, create a *soft* selection (rollout shown in Figure 4.31), where a falloff effect emanates from your selection area toward the unselected sub-objects. In this case, the unselected sub-objects gain a partial selection value that is displayed in the viewports as a color gradient on the vertices or faces. When you apply a transform—for example, if you move the soft selection—the actual selection will transform at a 1:1 ratio, while the falloff area of the soft selection will react at a lesser ratio according to the gradient falloff. This is similar to picking up a tablecloth with two fingers. The cloth between the two fingers is the full selection, while the cloth around the fingers falls off and does not lift up off the table as high as your fingers.

You can adjust the amount of falloff using the Falloff, Pinch, and Bubble parameters. In Figure 4.32, a sphere's vertices are being pulled outward with a soft selection. The area in the falloff, as you can see, is smoothly holding back as the main selection vertices are pulling out. The sphere in the back of the viewport in Figure 4.32 has a vertex pulled out without the benefit of a soft selection.

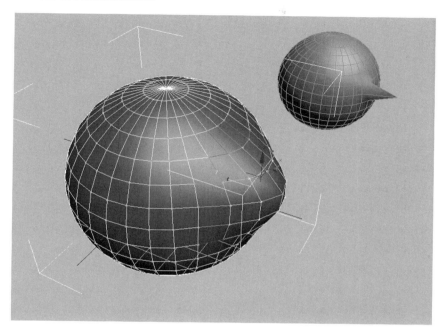

Figure 4.32

**Front sphere with Soft Selection enabled and back sphere without Soft Selection enabled**

## Edit (Sub-Object) Rollout

This rollout provides tools for editing the sub-object of your poly object. There are tools that are specific to the particular sub-object and ones that are the same for all sub-objects. The rollout heading name changes to reflect the sub-object level you are currently in and shows you the tools available for just that sub-object.

Try this exercise:

1. In a new scene, create a sphere. Convert the sphere to an Editable Poly.

2. Select the Polygon sub-object level and select a single polygon on the sphere, as shown in Figure 4.33. Make sure Soft Selection is not enabled.

3. In the Edit Polygons rollout, choose Extrude, as shown in Figure 4.34.

4. The appearance of your mouse pointer in the viewport will change when it hovers over the selected poly. Click on the polygon you already have selected, and drag the mouse up to extrude the polygon out from the sphere. If you drag the mouse down, the polygon will extrude into the sphere, creating a square tunnel. Pull the polygon out as shown in Figure 4.35 and release the mouse button.

Figure 4.33

**Selected polygon**

5. Select another polygon and extrude the face inward by dragging down on the cursor, as shown in Figure 4.36.

6. Select a third polygon on the sphere, and this time select the Bevel tool in the Modify tab. Similar to an Extrude, Bevel allows you to taper the extruded polygon. Click the polygon, and drag the mouse to pull the polygon out. When you release the mouse button, 3ds Max allows you to select the taper amount by moving the mouse up or down. When you have the desired taper, click once to exit the tool and set the bevel as you see it here (Figure 4.37).

Figure 4.34

**Extrude button selected**

Figure 4.35

**Extrude polygon by click-drag method.**

Figure 4.36

**Extrude face inward.**

Figure 4.37

**Bevel is extrude with a taper feature.**

## Edit Geometry Rollout

This rollout (Figure 4.38) is the same for all the sub-objects. These tools allow you to edit your object. You will be using many of these tools in the upcoming Chest of Drawers exercise in this chapter.

### Subdivision Surface Rollout

You have probably heard of *subdivision (SubD) surfaces* and SubD modeling. A SubD surface is a surface that has been divided to have more faces. However, the SubD surface retains the original object's general shape, which is sometimes called a *cage*. You subdivide to add more detail to a model, but you can still edit the original cage of the model to alter its overall shape and form.

The Subdivision Surface rollout lets you access tools specific to modeling with a subdivision surface, as shown in Figure 4.39. You will be modeling with subdivision surfaces later in Chapter 5, "Modeling in 3ds Max Part II."

Depending on which sub-object mode you are in, the Edit rollout will change—Edit Vertices, Edit Edges, and so on. This rollout has tools that give you access to functions such as Extrude and Bevel to help you shape your model. The next section, "Editable Poly Tools," will give you some more experience with these toolsets. You will also use many of these tools in the Chest of Drawers exercise in this chapter.

# Editable Poly Tools

Let's experiment with some of the other Editable Poly tools. Dive right into the following exercises.

## Extrude

When you *extrude* a vertex, 3ds Max moves it along a *normal*—that is, a line that is perpendicular to the surface in most cases. The extrusion creates new polygons that form the sides of the extrusion that also connect the vertex to the object.

We will start by extruding a vertex on a sphere:

1. Create a sphere by going to the Create panel and selecting Sphere. Create the sphere with about 20 units radius. Convert the sphere to an Editable Poly by right-clicking the sphere and choosing Editable Poly under the Convert To: heading in the quad menu. Go to Vertex mode, or press 1 on your keyboard. The vertices will appear as blue dots on your model.

2. Select a vertex on your sphere. The vertex will turn red. Go to the Edit Vertices rollout in the Modify tab, and press the Settings button (next to Extrude, as shown in Figure 4.40) to bring up the Extrude caddy shown in Figure 4.41. Set an exact extrusion height and base width, and click OK; this will apply your settings and close the caddy to create the extrusion. You can also click and drag to interactively pull out the vertex. Figure 4.42 shows a single extruded vertex.

Figure 4.38

**The Edit Geometry rollout**

Figure 4.39

**The Subdivision Surface rollout**

Figure 4.40

**Extrude Vertices dialog box**

Figure 4.41

**The Extrude Vertices caddy**

Extrude acts the same in three of the sub-object modes—Vertex, Edge, and Poly. Figure 4.43 shows two extruded edges; you saw what an extruded polygon looks like earlier in the chapter.

You will be able to work with more extrude options in the Chest of Drawers exercise.

Figure 4.42

**A single extruded vertex**

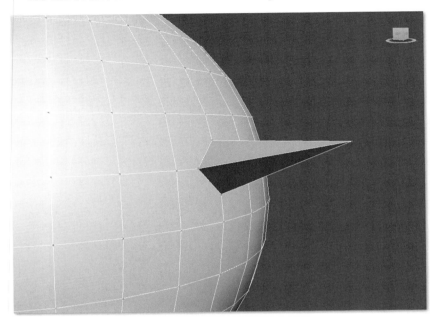

Figure 4.43

**Two extruded edges**

## Chamfer

In the following steps, you will use a different tool, called *Chamfer*, to create extra detail on an Editable Poly:

1. Undo the vertex extrusion with Ctrl+Z, or start with a fresh sphere and select a vertex. Hold down the Ctrl key and select two more vertices on either side of the one already selected. Click the Chamfer Settings button in the Modify panel to open the Chamfer caddy, as shown in Figure 4.44.

2. The new vertices are created around the ones you selected. You can dial in the exact value for your chamfer in the Chamfer caddy, as shown in Figure 4.45, then click OK. You can also simply click the Chamfer button (and not the Settings button), and click and drag in the viewport to interactively set your chamfer distance.

When you chamfer a sub-object, 3ds Max creates new faces around the area you have selected, complete with connecting edges, as you can see in Figure 4.46. Having been offset from the original vertex location, the three vertices are split into four new vertices each and arranged in a diamond formation. Chamfering, in this case, is good for creating some extra area of detail in your mesh or poly.

You can also use Chamfer to cut a hole in your surface. If you click the Open Chamfer option in the Chamfer caddy, 3ds Max will cut a hole where the Chamfer exists, as shown in Figures 4.47 and 4.48.

Figure 4.44

**Chamfer Settings button**

Figure 4.45

**Chamfer caddy**

Figure 4.46

**Chamfer three vertices next to each other.**

Figure 4.48

**Chamfer caddy**

When you are in the Edge sub-object level, you can chamfer edges. In this case, the chamfer splits an edge into more edges and offsets them from their original location. The Chamfer caddy (formally know as the Chamfer Setting dialog box), shown in Figure 4.48, has a new feature since the previous edition of this book. This feature is for adding segments. When you split an edge, you can add segments for more detail or to curve a corner. In Figure 4.49, the corner edge of a box is selected and chamfered (shown in the middle) and then four Connect Edge Segments are added (shown on right).

Figure 4.49

**Chamfering an edge in various ways**

Use Chamfer with some caution, because you can create overlapping geometry without realizing it.

## Weld

Welding vertices helps you combine vertices on a poly or mesh that should occupy the same space. It helps simplify the model by combining together nearby vertices that need not be there. Welding also can help shape your model. The following steps show you how to weld vertices together:

1. Start with a new Editable Poly sphere, in a new scene if you wish. Remember, to get an Editable Poly sphere, create a sphere and convert it to an Editable Poly by right-clicking on the Sphere entry in the Modifier Stack and selecting Editable Poly.

2. Enter Vertex mode, then select two vertices next to each other on the sphere. Select the Weld Settings button to open the Weld Vertices caddy shown in Figure 4.50.

**Figure 4.50**

**Weld Vertices caddy**

3. Using the Weld Threshold spinner, increase the value in the Weld Settings window to weld the two vertices together, as shown in Figure 4.51. The Weld tool combines selected vertices that are within the threshold you set.

**Figure 4.51**

**Welding two vertices together**

Weld is used a lot when detail is added to a model, such as with a chamfer, and some of the points need to be pulled together and combined into a single point.

## Bevel

As you saw earlier in the chapter, the Bevel tool creates a tapered edge for an extrusion. First select the polygon, and then click Bevel in the Modify panel under the Edit Polygons rollout to create bevels like the ones shown in Figure 4.52.

You can also click the Settings button next to Bevel to open the Bevel caddy shown in Figure 4.53.

Figure 4.52

**A pair of beveled polygons**

Figure 4.53

**Bevel caddy**

## Outline

Figure 4.54

**Outline caddy Controls**

The Outline function allows you to resize a polygon cleanly. Follow these steps to outline a polygon:

1. With a new Editable Poly sphere, go into Polygon level and select a polygon on the face of the sphere.

2. Open the Outline caddy and set a desired Outline amount, as shown in Figure 4.54.

   Then click OK or Apply and Continue. The polygon will change size, and the edges of the polygons around it will shift to accommodate the newly outlined polygon, as shown in Figure 4.55.

Figure 4.55

**An Outlined polygon on the sphere**

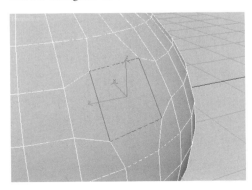

Outline lets you increase or decrease the size of the edges of a polygon. Using Outline is similar to selecting the polygon and scaling it with the Scale tool, but Outline is cleaner and easier to control.

> Clicking OK ((✓)) and clicking Apply and Continue ((+)) in a caddy are not the same. Clicking OK will perform the respective function and close the window. Clicking Apply and Continue will perform the action but keep the window open.

**Figure 4.56**
**Inset caddy**

## Inset

Similar to the Outline function for a polygon, the Inset function creates a tapered version of the original polygon that is inset from its original location. An inset is similar to a bevel, but it doesn't add any height to the polygon. Select a polygon on your Editable Poly, and click Inset on the Modify panel's Edit Polygons rollout. You can click and drag in the viewport to set the Inset size, or click the Settings button next to the Inset button to open the Inset caddy, as shown in Figure 4.56. Figure 4.57 shows an Inset polygon on a sphere.

**Figure 4.57**
**An Inset is similar to a beveled polygon, but without any height added to it.**

## Hinge from Edge

Now let's explore some of the more involved tools in the Editable Poly toolset. The Hinge from Edge tool creates a series of new polygons that rotate along an edge on the surface of an existing poly, connecting it to the original object. You can think of it as an extrusion with a rotation.

Follow these steps to see Hinge From Edge in action:

1. Create a new sphere in a new scene, and convert it to an Editable Poly. Enter into Polygon level.

2. Select a polygon and click the Hinge from Edge Settings button, as shown in Figure 4.58, to open the Hinge from Edge caddy in Figure 4.59.

3. The hinge edge is the edge about which the polygons will extrude and rotate. To select the hinge edge, click the Pick Hinge button in the caddy above the OK button. Then, in the viewport, go to the selected polygon and choose which edge you want to use.

4. Once you select the hinge edge, the polygon will hinge out, rotating about that selected edge however many degrees are cited in the Angle parameter. You can use the spinner to select or you can enter the desired angle value for the hinge.

**Figure 4.58**
**Click the Hinge from Edge Settings button**

**Figure 4.59**
**The Hinge from Edge caddy**

The model will interactively hinge the polygon as you set the Angle value. Figure 4.60 shows a small hinge. Notice the hinge is flat, as it has a Segments value of only 1.

5.  In the caddy, change the Angle value to 90, and the Segments value to 5. Press OK to complete the function. Figure 4.61 shows the results.

Figure 4.60
**A hinged polygon on the sphere, but with only one segment**

Figure 4.61
**A smoother hinge is created when you increase the Segments parameter.**

The Hinge from Edge tool is an interesting way to extrude, and it can be handy in many instances, such as when you're creating an awning or a curved overhang. Remember, the smoother you need the hinge to be, the more segments you will need to add.

## Cap

The *Cap* function creates a new polygon to fill a hole on a surface. For this function, you'll need to be in the Border-level selection. To see a cap in action, follow these steps:

1.  Create a new sphere and convert it to an Editable Poly.

2.  Select a few polys that are next to each other, side by side, and delete them by pressing the Delete key. You should now have holes in your sphere, as shown in Figure 4.62.

Figure 4.62
**A border is the edge or edges around deleted polygons**

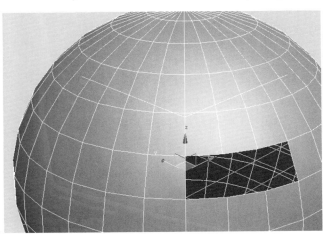

3. You may be wondering why you did that. You need to have a hole in the polygon surface for a Cap function and to check out the Border sub-object. As you may recall, a Border-level selection is the row of edges around a hole in a surface or on the edge of a surface, where only one side of the edge has a polygon. In the case of this sphere, the border is the line of edges surrounding the hole.

4. Now you need to cap the hole. Enter the Border-level selection by pressing the Border icon or pressing 3, and select the border. Under the Edit Borders rollout, select Cap. The hole should be filled with a single polygon, as shown in Figure 4.63.

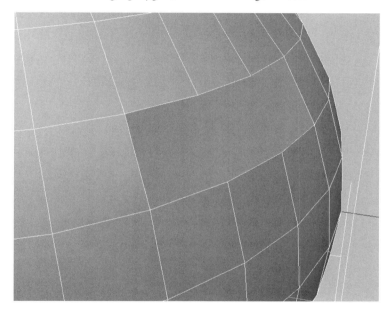

Figure 4.63

**The Cap function fills in a hole with a single polygon.**

This tool can be very convenient. If you have done something to a polygon but don't like it, you can delete that poly and use the Cap tool to create a new one. Keep in mind, however, that cap will use a flat polygon to fill the hole, so a complex surface hole will not be patched with the same surface contours as the original.

## Extrude Along Spline

The *Extrude Along Spline* function works just as it sounds. It will extrude a polygon sub-object along a spline path, which is a curve drawn in 3ds Max. Splines will be introduced later in this chapter and covered more extensively in the following chapters.

To see the Extrude Along Spline function in action, open the Path Extrude.max file found in the Chapter 4 directory's Scenes folder on the companion web page at www.sybex .com/go/intro3dsmax2011. This file has a sphere that has already been converted to an

Editable Poly, and a spline that will act as the path of extrusion. To continue, follow these steps:

1. Select the sphere and go into Polygon mode (use shortcut 4, or select the Polygon icon in the Modify panel's Selection rollout). Select a polygon; it doesn't matter which one.

2. Click the Settings button next to Extrude Along Spline to open the caddy for the tool, as shown in Figure 4.64.

Figure 4.64

**Extrude Along
Spline caddy**

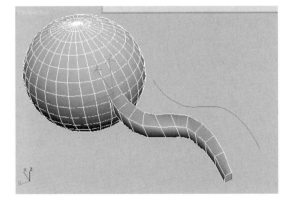

3. Click the Pick Spline button and click the spline next to the sphere.

4. Immediately, you will see an extruded element coming from the sphere. It probably doesn't look very good because you still need to work with the parameters.

5. Start by adding more segments; setting it to 20 should give you a good-looking extrusion. The extrusion in Figure 4.65 is the result of 11 segments, −0.5 Taper Amount, and 2.0 Taper Curve.

Figure 4.65

**A polygon on this
sphere is extruded
along a spline path.**

Play around with some of the settings to get a good feel for what this tool can do. As a matter of fact, it's a really good idea to play around with all of the tool settings you have seen here and some of the ones you haven't. This is a good way, if not somewhat frustrating, to learn 3ds Max—or any 3D program, for that matter. Use this sphere, or another Editable Poly you create, to experiment with the different tools available in this rollout for all the sub-object levels to get a basic idea of how things work. You can rely on the text in this book, as well as the online user-reference dialog titled "Autodesk 3ds Max Help," which you can launch from 3ds Max's Help menu from the Main Menu bar.

# Modeling a Chest of Drawers

Let's finally put some of your newfound knowledge into practice. If you skipped to this section from the beginning of the chapter or even from the beginning of the book, look at the previous sections in this chapter after you finish this model. Doing so will help fill in some of the gaps in your CG education and better explain how or why you've accomplished some of this exercise's topics.

In this section, you will model a chest of drawers (or dresser) to develop your editable-poly muscles. Why buy a chest of drawers when you can just make one in 3ds Max? Make sure you make it large enough for all your socks.

## Ready, Set, Reference!

You're so close to modeling something! You'll want to get some sort of reference for what you're modeling. Study the photo in Figure 4.66 for a look at the desired result.

Figure 4.66

**Modeling this chest of drawers**

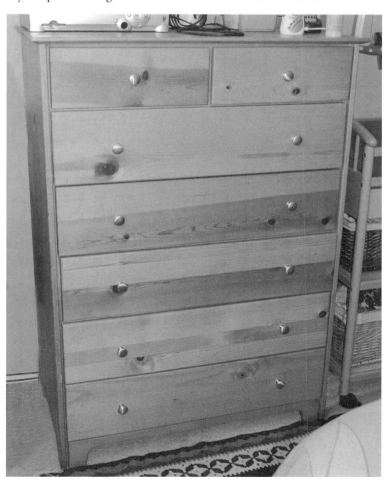

There are plenty of reference photos, and you will access them throughout this exercise to help build different parts of the chest. You may want to flip through the following pages to see the various photos to get a better idea of what you will be modeling.

Of course, if this were your chest of drawers, you could have captured tons of pictures already, right?

## Ready, Set, Model!

Create a project called Dresser, or download the Dresser project from the companion web page directly to your hard drive.

### Top of the Dresser

To begin the chest of drawers model, follow these steps:

1. Begin with a new scene (choose File → New, and click New All and then OK in the New Scene dialog box). Select the Perspective viewport and enable Edged Faces mode in the view (click the viewport mode and toggle on Edged Faces from the menu). Go to the Create panel. In the Object Type rollout, click Box. You are going to create a box using the Keyboard Entry rollout shown in Figure 4.67.

2. Using the Keyboard Entry rollout allows you to specify the exact size and location to create an object in your scene. Leave the *X*, *Y*, and *Z* values at 0, but enter these values: Length of **15**, Width of **30**, and Height of **40**. Click Create to create a box aligned in the center of the scene with the specified dimensions.

3. With the box still selected, go to the Modify panel. You can see the box's parameters here. You will need to add more height segments, so change the Height Segs parameter to **6**. Your box should look like the box in Figure 4.68.

Figure 4.67

**Keyboard Entry rollout**

Figure 4.68

**The box from which a beautiful chest of drawers will emerge.**

4. To start the process of using the new Graphite Modeling Tools, we will convert the box into an Editable Poly. Below the Main toolbar and below the Graphite Modeling Tools tab, click on the Polygon Modeling panel. This will expand and you will see the Convert to Poly button. Press it, as shown in Figure 4.69. You can always go through the Modifier Stack to convert the box to an Editable Poly instead of using the menus.

Figure 4.69

**Graphite Modeling Tools Polygon Modeling panel**

5. Press 4 on your keyboard to enter the Polygon sub-object mode. Now select the polygon on the top of the box. As you can see in the viewport, the polygon is shaded red when it's selected.

6. Now go to the Polygons panel in the Graphite Modeling Tools ribbon and select Bevel (Figure 4.70), click on the small arrow below the button, then click the Bevel Settings button, which will bring up the Bevel caddy controls (Figure 4.71). We are going to bevel several times to create the lip on the crown of the dresser shown in Figure 4.72.

7. Enter the following parameters: Height: **0.5** and Outline: **1.3**. Keep the Bevel Type set to Group. When you bevel only one polygon, the Bevel Type is irrelevant; it is only for multiple polygons. Click Apply and Continue ((+)) and 3ds Max will apply the specified settings without closing the window to give you results that should be similar to Figure 4.73.

Figure 4.71

**Bevel caddy controls**

8. In the still-open Bevel caddy, input these parameters: Height: **0.3** and Outline: **0** (as shown in Figure 4.74). Click Apply and Continue ((+)).

9. For the last bevel, input the following values: Height: **0.1** and Outline: **-0.03**. Click OK. Your dresser's top should resemble Figure 4.75.

Figure 4.70

**Polygon panel in the Graphite Modeling Tools ribbon**

10. Press 2 on your keyboard to enter the Edge sub-object mode. Select the two new edges that were created with the Bevel, as shown in Figure 4.76.

Figure 4.72

**The lip of the dresser**

Figure 4.73

**The first bevel for the crown of the dresser**

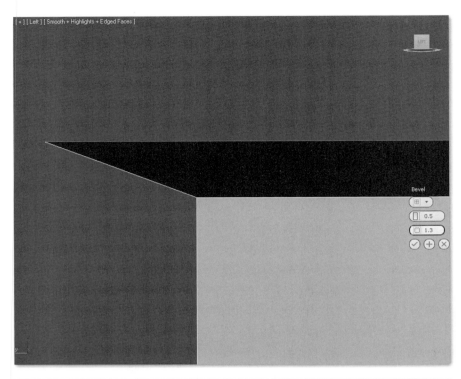

Figure 4.74

**The second bevel**

Figure 4.75

**This shows a rough version of the dresser's crown.**

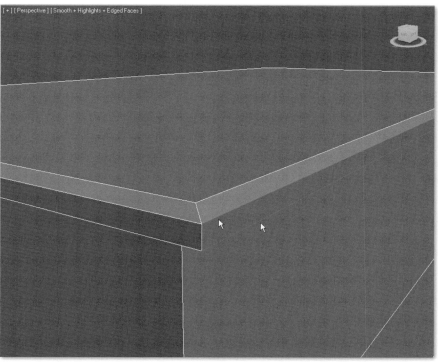

Figure 4.76

**Select these edges.**

11. Go to the Graphite Modeling Tools ribbon, and in the Modify Selection panel click on the Loop tool. This selects an edge loop based on our current sub-object selection. The loop is different from the previous version loop; you can loop in any sub-object mode (see Figure 4.77).

12. Now with the edges looped all around the top of the dresser, go to the Edges panel in the modeling ribbon. Choose the Chamfer tool and be sure to select the Chamfer Settings drop-down (arrow below the button) as shown in Figure 4.78 to bring up the Chamfer caddy.

13. In the Chamfer caddy, enter the following parameters: Edge Chamfer Amount: **0.1** and Connect Edge Segments: **2** (Figure 4.79), then select OK. Figure 4.80 shows the result.

Figure 4.77

**Loop tool in the Modify Selection panel**

Figure 4.78

**The Edges panel**

These values are not necessarily set in stone. You can play around with the settings to get as close to the image as you can or to add your own design flair. You can load the `Dresser01.max` scene file from the Scenes folder in the Dresser project from the companion web page.

Figure 4.79

**Chamfer settings**

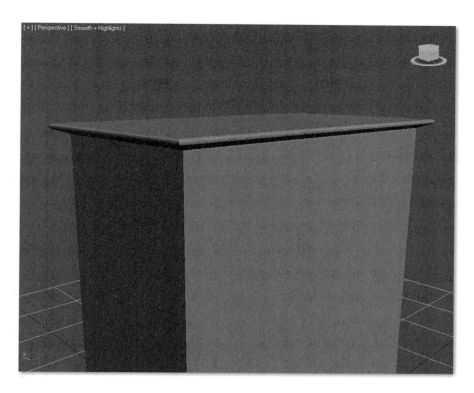

Figure 4.80

**The top of the dresser is ready.**

## I Can See Your Drawers

In the beginning of this exercise, you created a box with six segments on its height. You can use those segments to create the drawers. This is an example of thinking ahead and planning your model before you start working on an object. This was by far the easiest way to go; using another tool to add segments for the drawers after the box is made is doable, but much more laborious.

For simplicity's sake, in this exercise you will not create drawers that can open and shut. If this dresser were to be used in an animation in which the drawers would be opened, you would make them differently.

First, take a look at the drawers and see what your next steps should be. Figure 4.81 shows the drawers and an important detail we need to consider. Luckily, you needn't worry about the junk on top of the dresser.

To model the drawers, begin with these steps:

1. Create a small gap around the edge of the box. This gap will represent the space between the drawer and the main body of the dresser (Figure 4.81). Go to Polygon mode (press 4), and select the six polygons on the front of the box that represent the drawers. Remember to hold the Ctrl key while selecting the additional polygons; this will allow you to make multiple polygon selections, as shown in Figure 4.82.

Gap between drawers and dresser body

Figure 4.81

**Checking out the
real dresser drawers**

Figure 4.82

**Selected polygons
on the front of the
dresser**

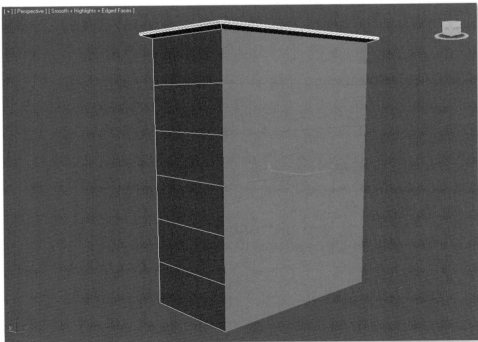

2. In the Graphite Modeling Tools ribbon, go to the Polygons panel and click the Inset Settings button to bring up the Inset caddy. Set the Inset Amount to **0.6** and keep the Inset Type set to Group, as shown in Figure 4.83. Click OK. Figure 4.84 shows the result of the Inset operation.

You can load the Dresser02.max scene file from the Scenes folder in the Dresser project from the companion web page to check your work or to begin the next series of steps.

3. Keep those newly inset polygons selected (or select them) and go back to the Polygons panel to select the Bevel Settings button to bring up the caddy. Change the Height to **−0.5**, keep Type set to Group, and press Apply and Continue (). The polygons will now extrude inward a little bit, as shown in Figure 4.85 (left). Keep those edges selected and repeat the procedure in step 2 to create another inset, as shown in Figure 4.85 (right).

Figure 4.83
**Inset Settings caddy controls**

Figure 4.84
**The inset creates the detail needed to make the drawers**

Figure 4.85
**Using Bevel to perform extrude and inset**

4. In the original reference picture (Figure 4.66), the top drawer of the dresser is split into two, so you need to create an edge vertically in that top-drawer polygon to create two drawers. Go to Edge mode and make sure you select the top and bottom horizontal edges on the top drawer, as shown in Figure 4.86.

Figure 4.86

**Select the upper and lower edges of the top drawer.**

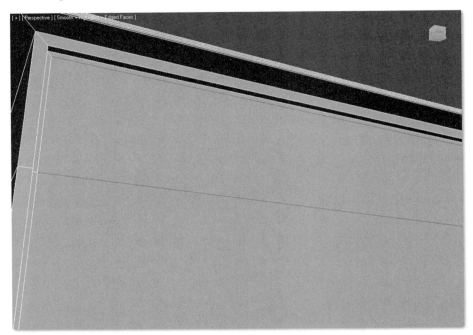

5. Go to the Graphite Modeling Tools ribbon and in the Loops panel, click on the Connect Settings button to bring up the caddy (Figure 4.87). Set the Segments to **1**, Pinch to **0**, and Slide to **0** (Figure 4.88), then click OK. The end result is shown in Figure 4.89.

Figure 4.87

**The Loops panel with arrow pointing to the Connect tool.**

Figure 4.88

**Connect Edges caddy**

Figure 4.89

**Added edge for split drawers in the dresser**

6.  Select the two polygons in the newly created top drawers. Go back to the Polygons panel and click Inset Settings. Set the Amount to **0.25**. This time we are going to change the Inset Type from Group to By Polygon, as shown in Figure 4.90.

    This setting insets each polygon individually instead of performing this operation on multiple, contiguous polygons (which is what the Group option does). Click OK to commit the Inset operation and close the caddy. Your polygons should resemble the ones in Figure 4.91.

Figure 4.90

**Inset caddy with settings for the top drawers**

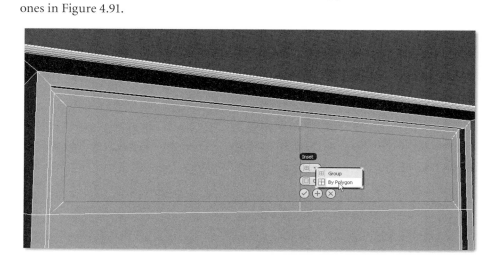

Figure 4.91

**The drawers are
inset separately.**

Figure 4.91

**The drawers are
inset separately.**

7. Perform the same inset operation on the remaining drawer polygons on the front of the box. Set the Amount to **.25**, and set the Inset Type to By Polygon. This will inset the five lower, wide drawers, as shown in Figure 4.92.

Figure 4.92

**The remaining
drawers are inset.**

8.  Select all of the drawer polygons. Go to the Polygons panel and click Extrude Settings. Set the Height to **0.7**. You don't need it to extrude very much; you just want the drawers to extrude a bit more than the body of the dresser (Figure 4.93).

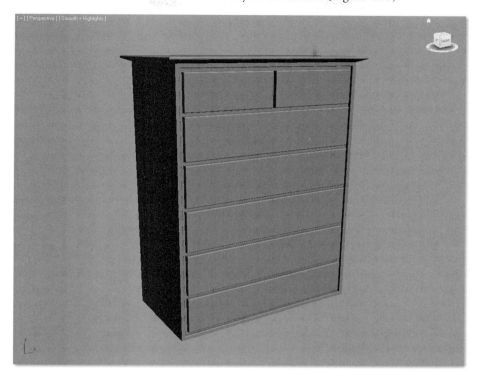

Figure 4.93

**The drawers are extruded.**

You can load the `Dresser03.max` scene file from the Scenes folder in the Dresser project from the companion web page to check your work or to skip to this part in the exercise.

### Bottom of the Dresser

Now it is time to create the bottom of the dresser. This dresser doesn't have legs, but nonetheless it has a nice detail at the bottom, as you can see in Figure 4.94 and Figure 4.95. To create this detail, you need to extrude a polygon.

1.  You should already be in Polygon sub-object mode if you are continuing with your own file, so select the polygon on the bottom of the dresser, as shown in Figure 4.96.

Figure 4.94

**An angle view of the
dresser's bottom
corner**

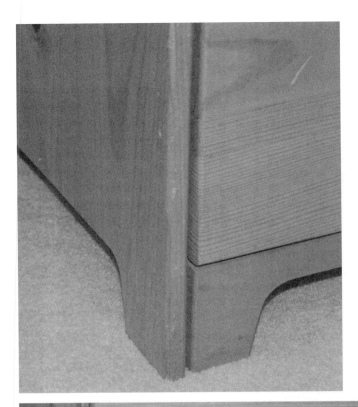

Figure 4.95

**A straight view of
the dresser's bot-
tom corner**

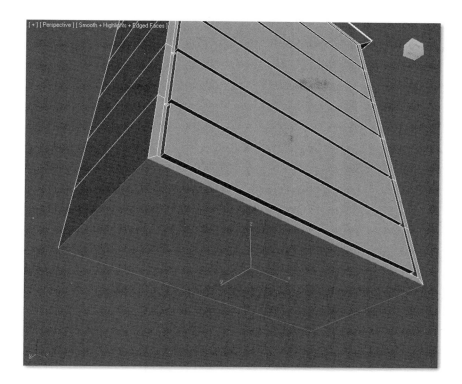

Figure 4.96

**Select the polygon at the bottom of the dresser.**

2. In the Graphite Modeling Tools ribbon, Go to the Polygon panel and select the Extrude Settings button to bring up the caddy. Change the Height to **2.5** as shown in Figure 4.97 and click OK. This will extrude a polygon out from the bottom of the dresser, essentially adding a segment to the box, as shown in Figure 4.98.

3. The polygon will still be selected, so select the Inset Settings button (  ) to bring up its caddy. Change the Amount to **0.6**, and click OK. This creates an inset poly, as shown in Figure 4.99.

4. The poly should still be selected, so select the Extrude Settings button to bring up the caddy, enter a Height of **–2.0**, and click OK. Figure 4.100 shows how the bottom of the dresser has moved up into itself slightly.

To create the detail on the bottom, you need to cut into the newly extruded polygons to create the "legs" in the corners of the dresser that you saw in Figures 4.94 and 4.95. To do this, you will use the ProBoolean tool. This method uses two or more objects to create a new object by performing a Boolean operation. Simply put, it uses the first object to create a union to, subtract from, or intersect with a second object.

Figure 4.97

**Extrude Setting caddy**

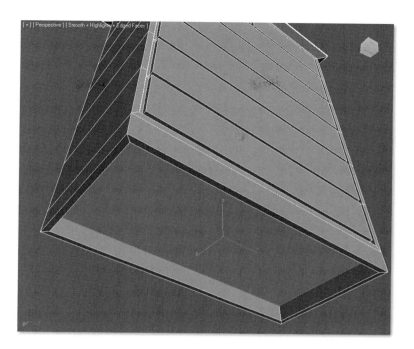

Figure 4.100

**The dresser's bottom lip**

Figure 4.101

**Select the Rectangle tool.**

To use this technique on the dresser, we will need another object to flesh out the shape to cut from the bottom of the dresser. We are going to create this object in the shape of the cutout at the bottom of the dresser (refer to Figure 4.95). It is a very specific shape starting with a simple rectangle.

5. In the Command panel, click on the Create tab, go to the Shapes button ( ), and click on the rectangle tool, as shown in Figure 4.101.

6. In a front view, make sure you can see the front of the dresser, then create a rectangle with Length: **3.0** and Width: **26.0**, as shown in Figures 4.102 and 4.103.

Figure 4.102

**Front view of dresser and rectangle**

Figure 4.103

**Rectangle parameters**

Figure 4.104

**Vertex sub-object mode**

Figure 4.105

**Fillet tool**

7. Move to the Modify Panel (  ) and add to the rectangle an Edit Spline modifier from the Modifier List drop-down menu. Click on Vertex to enter Vertex sub-object mode, as shown in Figure 4.104.

8. Select the two top vertices by clicking and dragging a selection box around them. Then under the Geometry rollout, click on the Fillet tool, as shown in Figure 4.105.

9. Click and drag on one of the two selected vertices to create the fillet (a rounded corner appears). Because both vertices are selected, they will both get the fillet, as shown in Figure 4.106. The amount of the fillet is **0.9**. You can watch the value of the fillet in the Geometry rollout.

10. From the Modifier List choose Extrude, which will then appear in the Modifier Stack above the existing Edit Spline modifier. Use an amount of **30.0** and then move the extrusion so that it penetrates both sides of the dresser.

11. Do the same to the side of the dresser:

    a. Create another rectangle but make it smaller to fit the side of the dresser.

    b. Add the Edit Spline modifier.

    c. Select the two top vertices and fillet them.

    d. Add an Extrude modifier and change the Amount to **40.0**.

    e. Place that object penetrating through the side of the dresser, as shown in Figure 4.107.

Figure 4.106

**The two vertices are filleted.**

Figure 4.107

**Objects placed for Boolean**

You can check the ProBoolean objects you just created for the bottom of the dresser against the file ProBooleanObjects.max found in the Scenes folder of the Dresser project on this book's web page.

Now for the ProBoolean operation itself. Don't get this confused with the regular Boolean operation, however. ProBoolean is the latest and greatest version, with a more advanced toolset than the regular Boolean.

1. To begin, select the object you want to keep; that is the dresser object.

2. In the Create panel under Compound Objects (selected from the drop-down menu) and at the bottom of the Object Type rollout, click the ProBoolean button.

3. In the Pick Booloean rollout, click the Start Picking button (Figure 4.108).

4. Click on both extruded rectangles placed at the bottom of the dresser. By default, ProBoolean is always set to Subtraction, so the object's shape will be subtracted from the dresser, as shown in Figure 4.109.

Figure 4.108

**Click the Start Picking button to subtract objects from the dresser.**

Go grab yourself a frosty beverage! The dresser is finished. Of course, there are many things we could do to refine the look, but this is only an introduction and we will dive in further for more modeling experience in later chapters. Go ahead and name the dresser. You can even change the color of the dresser if you'd like. Go to the Name and Color type-in box (shown in the Command panel's Modify panel to the far right of Figure 4.110), change the name of the object to Dresser, and pick a nice light color.

The finished dresser body should look like the dresser in Figure 4.110. Remember to save this version of your file. You can also load the Dresser04.max scene file from the Scenes folder in the Dresser project on the companion web page to check your work or to skip to this point in the exercise.

Figure 4.109

**Finished dresser bottom**

Figure 4.110

**The finished dresser body is named and given a color.**

### Creating the Knobs

Now that the body of the dresser is done, it's time to add the final bit of detail to make the dresser complete: knobs. We will use splines and a few surface creation tools new to your workflow. Goose bumps, anyone? Take a look at the reference for the knobs in Figure 4.111. You are going to create a profile of the knob and then rotate the profile around its axis to form a surface. This technique is known as *Lathe*, not to be mistaken for *latte*, which is a whole different deal and not really covered in this book.

Here's a quick rundown of what a *spline* is. A spline is a group of vertices and connecting segments that form a line or curve. To create the knob profile, we are going to use the Line spline, shaped in the outline of—you guessed it—a knob. The Line tool allows you to create a free-form spline.

You can use your last file from the Dresser exercise, or you can load `Dresser04.max` from the Scenes folder of the Dresser project from the companion web page. To build the knobs, follow these steps:

Figure 4.111

**A Drawer Knob**

1. Make sure you are in the Left viewport so you can see which side of the dresser the drawers are on, as shown in Figure 4.112. You are going to create a profile of half the knob, as shown in Figure 4.113. Don't worry about creating all the detail in the knob, because detail won't be seen; a simple outline will be fine.

2. Go to the Create panel and choose Shapes ( ![icon] ). Click the Line button. Use the current default values in the Creation Method rollout, as shown in Figure 4.114.

Figure 4.112

**Left view of the dresser**

Figure 4.113

**The intended profile curve for the knob**

Figure 4.114

**Line tool parameters**

3. In the Left viewport, click once to lay down a vertex for this line, starting at the bottom of the intended profile for the knob. This is the starting point for the curve. When you are creating a line, every click lays down the next vertex for the line. In essence, the vertex controls the position of a point of the line. If you want to create a curve in the line, click once and drag the mouse in any direction to give the vertex a curvature of sorts. This curve vertex creates a curve in that part of the line. You will need to follow the rough outline of a knob, so click and drag where there is curvature in the line. Once you have laid down your first vertex, continue to click and drag more vertices for the line clockwise until you create the half-profile knob shape shown earlier in Figure 4.113.

Figure 4.115 shows the profile line with the vertices numbered according to their creation order.

To create a straight orthogonal line segment between two vertices, press and hold Shift to keep the next vertex to be laid down orthogonal to the last vertex, either horizontally or vertically.

4. Once you lay down your last vertex at the top, finish the spline by either right-clicking to release the Line tool or clicking the first vertex you created to close the spline. For this example, it really doesn't matter which method you choose. Either an open or closed spline will work; however, a closed spline is shown in Figure 4.115. Drawing splines entails a bit of a learning curve, so it might be helpful to delete the one you did first and try again for the practice. Once you get something resembling the spline in Figure 4.115, you can edit it. Don't drive yourself crazy; just get the spline as close as you can.

When you are creating a line, you can click once to create a corner vertex for the line, but you need to click and drag to create a Bezier vertex if you want to put a curve into the line.

Figure 4.116

**Line sub-object modes**

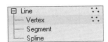

5. With the spline selected, go to the Modify panel. In the Modifier Stack window, you will see the entry Line with a plus sign in a black box next to it denoting that it has sub-object modes. Click the plus sign (+) to expand the list of sub-objects, as shown in Figure 4.116.

In some ways, a line's sub-objects are similar to the Editable Poly sub-object modes. However, when you are working with a spline, you are working with a 2D nonrendering object. A spline is made up of three sub-objects: a vertex, a segment, and a spline. As you know, a *vertex* is a point in space. A *segment* is the line that connects two vertices. The Spline mode allows you to select and/or transform a single spline or multiple splines within a spline object. To continue with the project, follow these steps:

1. Choose the vertex sub-object for the line. Make sure you are still working in the Left viewport. When you're working with 2D splines, it is always best to work in Orthographic view. Use the Move tool to click on one of the vertices. The vertex has a Transform gizmo just like an object. Use the Move tool to edit the shape to better fit the outline of the knob.

   Be sure to read the sidebar in this section entitled "A Line's Vertex Type" to learn more about the types of vertices a line can have and how it can change the curvature of a line. If needed, you can change the vertex type of your line's vertices to control the curvature.

   To catch up to this point, you can load the Dresser05.max file from the Scenes folder of the Dresser project from the companion web page.

2. The profile line is ready to turn into a 3D object. This is where the modifiers are used. Get out of sub-object mode for your line. Choose Modifiers → Patch/Spline Editing → Lathe. (You also could go to the Modifier List and choose Lathe from the alphabetical list of modifiers.) When you first put the Lathe modifier on your spline, it probably won't look anything like the knob (see Figure 4.117)—but don't panic! You need to futz with the parameters to get it right (Figure 4.118). Right now the object is turned inside out.

Figure 4.117

**Eeek! That isn't a knob at all.**

### A LINE'S VERTEX TYPE

When you center your cursor over a line's vertex and right-click to bring up the shortcut menu shown, you will have access to several vertex controls. In that shortcut menu, under the Tools 1 heading, you can choose a vertex type, as shown in the graphic below.

The vertex types are the following:

**Smooth** A Smooth vertex creates a smooth continuous curve. The actual curvature at a smooth vertex depends on the spacing of the adjacent vertices. This is a nonadjustable vertex, meaning it has no handles with which you can control the curvature directly.

**Corner** A Corner vertex is nonadjustable, which creates sharp corners.

**Bezier** A Bezier vertex is a vertex that has locked continuous handles that create a smooth curve. You can directly adjust the curvature at a Bezier vertex by manipulating its handles. Adjusting a handle on one side of the vertex will also adjust the other side's handle, as they are continuous.

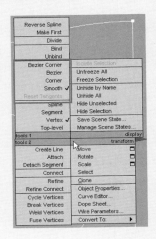

**Bezier Corner** A Bezier Corner vertex creates a sharp corner like the Corner vertex, but it has discontinuous tangent handles with which you can control the curvature of the line at that vertex. The handle on one side of the vertex will not affect the handle on the other side.

Figure 4.118

**The titillating parameters for the Lathe modifier**

3. Go to the Parameters rollout and under the Align heading click the Max button. It's a knob! Now that is more like it. You just had to change the alignment of the axis so the lathe revolution would be correct.

If step 3 does not work properly for you, try clicking Min instead of Max under the Align heading. When you are creating a line, where you begin to create that line and in what order you place the vertices (clockwise or counterclockwise) are both important. This example drew the knob's profile line in a clockwise direction.

4. Rotate the perspective view so you can see the top of the knob. You should notice a strange artifact. To correct this, check the Weld Core box under the Parameters rollout for the lathe.

That's it! Check out Figure 4.119 for a look at the lathed knob. By using Splines and the Lathe procedure, you can create all sorts of surfaces for your models. In the next section, you will resize the knob, position it, and copy it to fit on the drawers.

## Copying the Knob

Now that you have a knob, you may need to adjust it and make it the right size. If you still want to futz with the knob, go back down the stack to the line to edit your spline. For example, you may want to scale the knob a bit to better fit the drawer (refer to the reference photo in Figure 4.111). Select the Scale tool, and click and drag until the original line is about the right size in your scene. The Lathe modifier will re-create the surface to fit the new size. You can also delete the knob and restart with another line for more practice. In the following steps, you will copy and position the knob for the drawers.

Figure 4.119

**The lathe completes the knob.**

1. Position and rotate the knob to fit on to the front of a top drawer. Change its default color (if you want) and change its name to Knob.

2. You'll need a few copies of the original knob, one for each drawer. Choose Edit → Clone to open the Clone Options dialog box (Figure 4.120). You are going to use the Instance command. An instance is a copy, but is still connected to the original. If you edit the original or an instance, all of the instances change. Click OK to create an instance.

3. Position the instanced knob in the middle of the other top drawer.

4. Using additional instances of the original knob, place knobs in the middle of all the remaining drawers of your dresser, as shown in Figure 4.121.

Figure 4.120

**Using an instance to copy the knob**

As you saw with this exercise, there are plenty of tools for the Editable Poly object. Your model doesn't have to be all of the same type of modeling, either. In this example, we created the dresser with *box modeling* techniques, where you begin with a single box and extrude your way into a model, and with surface creation techniques using splines.

You can compare your work to the scene file `Dresser06.max` from the Scenes folder of the Dresser project from the companion web page.

Figure 4.121

**The dresser, knobs and all**

## Summary

In this chapter, you learned how to model with 3ds Max. Through exploring the modeling toolsets and creating a dresser, you saw firsthand how the primary modeling tools in 3ds Max operate.

You began by examining how best to plan a model. Then you learned some modeling concepts and how to use modifiers and the Modifier Stack effectively. You moved on to learning the differences between objects and meshes and how to use sub-objects to edit your surfaces before you began a series of short exercises describing some of the poly editing tools. With that under your belt, you learned how to put these tools and ProBoolean to use by making a simple dresser.

Modeling is an artful craft. It is best to know where you are trying to go in your mind's eye so you can get there with your models. Becoming a good modeler takes time and patience, so stick with it.

# CHAPTER 5

# Modeling in 3ds Max: Part II

*Building models in 3D* is as simple as building them out of clay, wood, or metal. Using 3ds Max to model something may not be as tactile as physically building it, but the same concepts apply: You have to identify how the model is shaped and figure out how to break it down into manageable parts that you can piece together into the final form.

Instead of using traditional tools to hammer or chisel or weld a shape into form, you will use the vertices of the geometry to shape the CG model. As you have seen, 3ds Max's polygon toolset is quite robust.

In this chapter, we will tackle a more complex model with a children's Red Rocket ride-on toy. We will use the Editable Poly toolset, the Lathe and Bevel modifiers, and the Loft compound object to create the toy. We will also examine the use of QuickSlice (to add detail) and Booleans (to easily create interesting indentations on an existing surface).

The topic of this chapter is as follows:

- **Building the Red Rocket**

# Building the Red Rocket

Using reference materials will help you efficiently create your 3D model and achieve a good likeness in your end result. The temptation to just "wing it" and start building the objects is strong, especially when time is short and you're raring to go. This temptation should always be suppressed in deference to a well thought-out approach to the task. Sketches, photographs, and drawings can all be used as resources for the modeling process; you can place them in a scene as backdrop images and model over them. Not only are references useful for giving you a clear direction in which to head, but you can use references directly in 3ds Max to help you model. Photos, especially those taken from different sides of the intended model, can be added to a scene as background images to help you shape your model.

## Creating Planes and Adding Materials

There are two common approaches to adding backdrop images for modeling in 3ds Max. You can use the viewport's Background Image feature or you can use the *crossing boxes* technique, which involves placing the reference images on crossing plane objects or thin boxes in the scene. In this exercise, we'll use the crossing boxes technique as the starting point to build a child's rocket ride-on toy, as shown in Figure 5.1.

Before you begin, download the Red Rocket folder from this book's companion web page (www.sybex.com/go/intro3dsmax2011) to your hard drive where you keep your other 3ds Max projects. Set your project folder to the Red Rocket project you just downloaded (Application Menu → Manage → Set Project Folder).

1. Open a new 3ds Max file by choosing Application Menu → New.

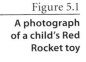

Figure 5.1

**A photograph of a child's Red Rocket toy**

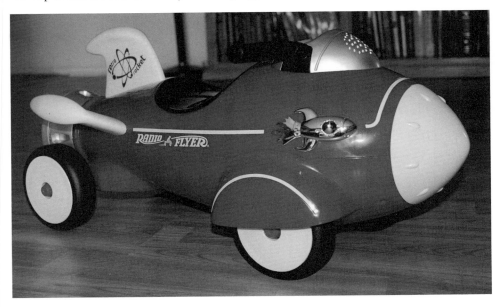

2. Go to Customize → Units Setup. In the dialog box, set the units to Generic Units and click OK. Generic units are the 3ds Max's default units—one 3ds Max unit equals one inch.

3. Go to the Create panel to create a box (click the Geometry button (  ) and, under Standard Primitives in the pull-down menu, click the Box button.

   Instead of creating the box with the click and drag method, we will use the Keyboard Entry rollout, as shown in Figure 5.2. Expand the Keyboard Entry rollout. Make sure the Perspective view is selected. Leave the *XYZ* parameters all set to 0; this will place the box at the origin point of your scene. Change the Length, Width, and Height parameters to the following and click Create:

   Length: 22

   Width: 0.01

   Height: 12

Figure 5.2

**The Keyboard Entry rollout for creating the box**

4. When you click Create, 3ds Max will create the image-plane box we'll use for the side view. Rename the Box001 object **Side View**.

5. Activate the Top viewport, then repeat step 3 to create another flat box, which you'll use for the Top View image-plane box. Use the following parameters.

   Length: 22

   Width: 12

   Height: 0.01

   Rename the box **Top View**.

6. Activate the Front viewport, and then repeat step 3 one last time to create the image-plane box for the front view of the rocket toy. Use the following parameters. Rename the box **Front View**.

   Length: 12

   Width: 12

   Height: 0.01

7. Move the Front View box up six units in the *Z*-axis to raise it so the bottom edge is directly on the Home Grid, as shown in Figure 5.3. Switch all the viewports to Smooth + Highlights (F3) and Zoom Extents All to see everything.

8. In Windows Explorer, navigate to the sceneassets\images folder in the Red Rocket directory that you downloaded to your hard drive. In this folder, you will find three reference JPEG images, one for each of the three image-plane box views we just created in the scene. Select the Top View reference image (called TOP VIEW.jpg); drag it into the Top viewport in 3ds Max, and drop it onto the Top View image-plane box. This will automatically place the image onto the box, so the image will be viewable in the viewport.

Figure 5.3

**The Front View box is moved up.**

9. Repeat the previous step to place SIDE VIEW.jpg onto the Side View image-plane box in the Left viewport and place FRONT VIEW.jpg onto the Front View image-plane box in the Front viewport. Figure 5.4 shows the image-plane boxes with the reference images applied.

   If, for some reason, the image on your Top View object seems to be the reverse of what is shown in the book, simply rotate the Top View object to line it up the way the images appear in this chapter. Also, you may notice black bars appearing in the images. They are intended to allow the images to better line up with each other.

10. If you need to, adjust the placement of the Front View image-plane box so the proportions of the rocket match up. The bottom of the wheels and the top of the handlebars should line up in all three images. Just move the box using the Select and Move tool. You will need to use the Orbit viewport navigation tool to rotate the view so that the image-plane boxes can be viewed from different sides to get them aligned.

   If the rocket images do not show up in the viewport after you drop them onto the boxes, make sure the viewport is set to Smooth + Highlights and try again.

Figure 5.4

**The image-plane boxes with the rocket views applied**

## Organizing Your Scene File

The next step is to begin organizing your scene file. We are going to use the Layer Manager (shown in Figure 5.5), which is a floating dialog window where you can organize objects into layers (something like how you can organize Adobe Photoshop layers, but for 3D objects). The objects you create have common properties for their associated layer, including color, renderability, and display settings. An object can assume these properties directly from the layer on which you create it. Using layers makes it easier to manage the information in your scenes. For example, layers are often used to control the visibility of objects in a populated scene so you can focus on certain objects without the clutter of having the entire scene all visible at once. Layers can also control the color of your objects' wireframes and the frozen and hidden state of objects to better help you organize your scene.

In the Layer Manager, when you create new layers, 3ds Max names them sequentially by default. These default names are Layer01, Layer02, and so on. After creating a layer, you should rename it something less generic so you can track your layers better. Click the layer in the Layer Manager to highlight the layer, and click again to change its name.

Figure 5.5

**The Layer Manager**

3ds Max assigns a random color to all new layers. You can accept the default settings or specify other colors by clicking on the little color swatch. For more on the Layer Manager see Chapter 3, "The 3ds Max Interface."

In the following steps, we will use the Layer Manager to organize our scene:

1. Select the image-plane boxes.

2. On the Main toolbar, click the Layer Manager icon ( ).

3. In the Layer Manager, click Create New Layer ( ) to create a new layer. Click Layer01 and enter **Image Planes** as its new name (see Figure 5.6).

4. If you create the new layer with the objects you want in the layer selected, they automatically will be added to the layer.

5. When we work in the scene, we do not want to select the image-plane boxes. There is no need to adjust them as you model. In the Layer Manager, this is made very simple. Click the icon in the Freeze column in the Image Planes layer, as shown in Figure 5.7. The layer will be frozen so its objects cannot be selected in the viewports. The frozen boxes will turn gray, and the images will disappear.

Figure 5.6

**Changing layer names**

Figure 5.7

**The Freeze icon**

6. Open the layer by clicking the plus sign. You will see the objects listed. Select all three image-plane boxes by holding down the Ctrl key and clicking the objects. Click the cube symbol next to one of the image-plane box names. This will bring up the

Object Properties dialog box for that image-plane box for that layer, as shown in Figure 5.8. In the Display Properties area, uncheck the Show Frozen in Gray box. When you press OK, the image will show up on the plane. Because all three objects were selected, this option was applied to all three.

7. Any objects you create will automatically be assigned to the selected layer, so in the Layer Manager make sure to double-click on Layer01 (default) to set it as the current layer, and then close the Layer Manager.

As you continue modeling the rocket, you will frequently use the Layer Manager to help manage the scene.

## Creating the Body

To begin the body of the rocket, you can load the scene file Rocket_00.max from the Scenes folder of the Red Rocket project that you downloaded from the web page. In the following steps, we will begin the rocket model:

1. Start in the Front viewport. In the Create panel, click the Geometry icon (  ) and select Extended Primitives in the drop-down menu. Click to activate the Capsule tool, and then create a Capsule object with Keyboard Entry values set to a Radius of 3 and a Height of 21. Remember to use the Front viewport so that the capsule is created oriented as shown in Figure 5.9.

**Figure 5.8**

Use the Object Properties list to turn on the image display for the frozen image-plane boxes.

**Figure 5.9**

Capsule in the Front viewport

2. In the Modify panel set the capsule's Sides to 8 and Height Segs to 6. Uncheck the Smooth option; we will do the smoothing later.

3. Rename the capsule **Rocket Body**. Make Rocket Body see-through in all the viewports by pressing Alt+X. This way you will be able to see the image-plane box through the geometry.

4. Line up the rocket body with the Side, Top, and Front image-plane boxes, matching the rocket body to the front end of the image as shown in Figure 5.10.

Figure 5.10

**Line up the Rocket Body object to the image-plane box views.**

Figure 5.11

**Convert to an editable poly.**

5. In the Graphite Modeling Tools ribbon, click on the Polygon Modeling panel → Convert to Poly, as shown in Figure 5.11.

6. Enter the Vertex sub-object mode and select the vertex at the very front tip of the rocket body (as shown in Figure 5.12).

7. With the vertex selected, go into the Modify panel. In the Soft Selection rollout, click on Use Soft Selection and set the Falloff to 6.0. Now switch to the Scale tool (R). We need to scale along the *XY*-axis, which is a nonuniform scale. Do the scale in the Front viewport, center your cursor over the Transform gizmo's *XY*-axis as shown in Figure 5.13, and scale while watching the Top viewport. Scale down to create a more pointed front.

Figure 5.12

**Select the vertex at the very front tip.**

8. Selecting some of the front vertices section by section in the Top viewport, scale and/or move the rest of the front to match the front of the rocket in the Top View image-plane box, as shown in Figure 5.14.

9. Using vertices with or without soft selection (using a Falloff setting if needed), shape the rest of the body to the shape in the three image-plane boxes (as shown later, in Figure 5.16). Don't worry about the back end of the rocket body just yet; we'll tackle that in the next step.

10. When you have the general shape of the body of the rocket, go into Polygon mode, select the polys at the rounded back end of your shape, as shown in Figure 5.15, and delete them by pressing Delete.

    Figure 5.16 shows the result of the deletion.

Figure 5.13

**Center your cursor over the Transform gizmo's XY-axis (shows as an angled yellow bar).**

Figure 5.14

**Select some front vertices and scale and/or move to match.**

Figure 5.15

**Select the end polys to cut off the end of the rocket body.**

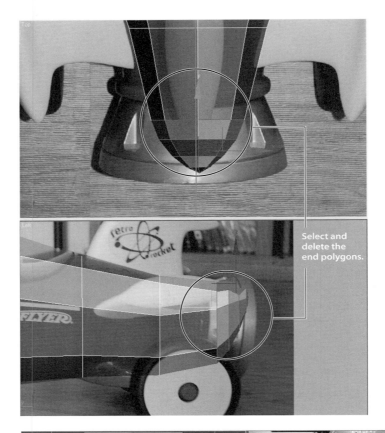

Figure 5.16

**The result of deleting the end of the capsule for the tail section of the rocket**

## Smoothing the Body

The body looks very rough and chunky right now. To smooth out the rough model, we will use Subdivision Surfaces. A subdivision surface is a surface that has been divided into more faces to create a smoother surface while still retaining the object's general shape. You subdivide to add more detail to an object or to smooth out the shape. In 3ds Max, Subdivision Surfaces is a rollout in the Modify panel for an editable poly.

The following steps will guide you through the process of smoothing out the rocket's body shape.

1. With the rocket body selected, go to the Graphite Modeling Tools ribbon, and in the Edit tab click on the Use NURMS button, as shown in Figure 5.17. This subdivides the polygons and relaxes the transition between polygons, smoothing the shape of the rocket's body. If you are still in Polygon mode, you will see the orange Subdivision Surfaces (SDS) cage appear. This cage allows you to continue editing the body's overall shape by just selecting the lower-res cage's polys and editing them. This lets you affect its broader form without having to select many more polys of the smoothed version.

Figure 5.17

**NURMS subdivides polys, and smooths.**

2. Enter Polygon sub-object mode (press 4) with the rocket's body selected, select the polygons on the rocket body's right side (as shown in Figure 5.18), and delete them.

Figure 5.18

**Select the polygons as shown.**

Figure 5.19

**Show End Result
button**

3. Go to the top level of the editable poly (press 6). Go to the Modify panel and from the Modifier list choose the Symmetry modifier. In the Symmetry parameters, choose *X* as the Mirror Axis and check the Flip box. This creates a mirrored copy of that half of the body. Using Symmetry allows you to make changes to the original side of the body and automatically have those changes mirrored to the other side.

When you go back to editing the mesh, the mirrored half of the rocket will disappear. To stop this from occurring, press the Show End Result button, which is in the line of icons below the Modifier Stack, shown in Figure 5.19.

4. In the Layer Manager, create a new layer called **Rocket**, and assign the Rocket Body object to the new layer.

### Adding Detail to the Rocket Body

The wheel wells on the front sides of the body are the first details we will add. To create the wheel wells, we need to add some more segments to the main body. To do this, we will use a new tool from the Graphite Modeling Tools, called SwiftLoop. This tool is quite popular! It places edge loops with just a click, replacing what used to take more effort. As you move the mouse cursor over your object, a real-time preview shows where the loop will be created when you click.

You will be adding edges as shown in Figure 5.20 using the following steps.

Figure 5.20

**Use the SwiftLoop
tool to add detail to
these areas on the
rocket's body.**

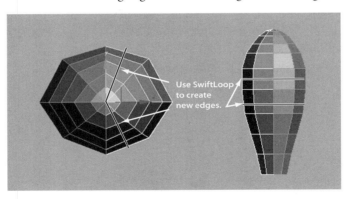

The SwiftLoop tool can be used in any of the sub-object modes or in the top level with no sub-object mode selected.

1. Go into the Layer Manager and hide the Image Planes layer. With the rocket's body selected, in the Graphite Modeling Tools ribbon, go to Polygon mode, then open the Edit panel and select SwiftLoop, as shown in Figure 5.21. Move your cursor over to the rocket, and you will see a preview of where a loop will eventually be placed. When the loop is in the correct place just click, and it will be added. You want to match placement of four new loops with those shown in Figure 5.20.

Now that the new loops are in, you will see there is a little issue. The front-end vertex of the rocket doesn't connect to the newly added SwiftLoop edge, as seen in Figure 5.22. All of those edges really need to come to a point at the tip, so we will continue the new segment to the tip manually, using the Connect vertex function in the next step.

Figure 5.21
**Select SwiftLoop.**

2. Press the 1 key to enter Vertex sub-object mode, and turn off Soft Selection. Select the two vertices shown in Figure 5.23.

Figure 5.22
**Incomplete edge loop**

Figure 5.23
**Select the two vertices.**

3. Go to the Graphite Modeling Tools ribbon, and in the Loops panel click on the Connect tool as shown in Figure 5.24. This will complete the loop.

Figure 5.24
**Connect tool**

4. Repeat the same with the vertex on the lower side of the rocket. The completed loops are shown in Figure 5.25.

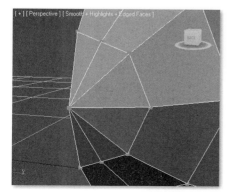

Figure 5.25
**Completed vertex connection**

### Creating the Wheel Well

Now that we have created more detail on the mesh, we can mold the wheel wells as shown on the actual rocket in Figure 5.26.

Figure 5.26

**The rocket's wheel wells**

You can continue with your own scene file (just make sure to turn off NURMS smoothing before you continue), or use the scene file Rocket_01.max from the Scenes folder in the Red Rocket project that you downloaded to your hard drive.

Here are the steps to follow.

1. Select the rocket and change to Polygon sub-object mode (press 4), and from the Left viewport select the three polygons in the middle of the body, as shown in Figure 5.27.

Figure 5.27

**Change to the Polygon sub-object mode and select these three polygons.**

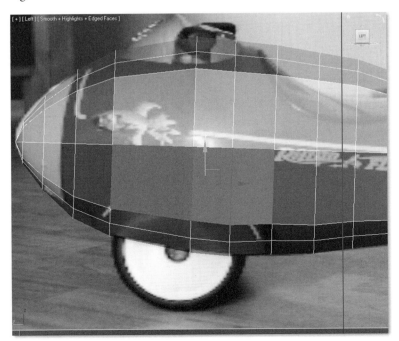

2. In the Graphite Modeling Tools ribbon in the Polygons panel, click the Extrude Settings button, as shown in Figure 5.28, to bring up the caddy.

   In the Extrude Polygons caddy, set Extrusion Type to Group and Height to 0.8, as shown in Figure 5.29. Click OK.

3. Now select all the polygons that were created with the extrude operation, shown in Figure 5.30 (on the left). If you don't have the back view already visible, right-click in the Front viewport to activate it, press the V key, and select Back View to switch to the Back viewport. Turn on the Image Plane layer in the Layer Manager to see the image-plane boxes. Then, in the Back viewport, use the Rotate and Move tools to align the polygons so that they line up with the wheel well in the Front View image-plane box, as shown in Figure 5.30 (on the right).

4. Switch to Vertex mode. Use a window selection to select and move the second row of vertices from the bottom of the rocket body out to the right and slightly down, as shown in Figure 5.31. This evens out the bottom part of the body to give it a more rounded look. If we left those vertices where they were, that part of the body would appear lopsided. And who wants that?

Let's apply Subdivision Surfaces to the model again to see how the wheel wells looks when smoothed. There are still several things that we need to do to improve the look of the body.

First, the wheel well polygons need to be moved down and reshaped to have an arch on the top.

Figure 5.28

**Click the Extrude Settings button in the Graphite Modeling Tools ribbon.**

Figure 5.29

**Setting the extrusion parameters in the caddy**

Figure 5.30

**Use the Rotate and Move tools.**

Figure 5.31

**Round out the bottom of the rocket's body.**

Exit sub-object mode and select Rocket Body, and in the Graphite Modeling Tools ribbon click the Use NURMS button in the Edit panel. Now, when it is subdivided it looks a bit better. Figure 5.32 shows the rocket after NURMS has been enabled for the mesh.

Now we need to hollow out the wheel well. Follow these steps.

1. Disable NURMS smoothing by clicking on the Use NURMS button again.

2. Enter Polygon sub-object mode. Select the polygons at the bottom side of the wheel well, as shown in Figure 5.33.

3. In the Graphite Modeling Tools ribbon go to the Polygons tab and click the Bevel Settings button. Set the Outline to −0.1 and the Height to 0, then click Apply and Continue. Reset Outline to 0.0, then set Height to −0.7 to push in the area, then click OK. Finally, delete the inside polygon as shown in Figure 5.34.

We don't need to create the inside of the wheel well because we are not going to see it. We extruded into the wheel well in step 3 to make a solid lip at the wheel well, but it only needs to go halfway up.

4. Check to make sure that the new edges don't poke through the mesh (see Figure 5.35). If any do, select the vertices and move them inward.

Figure 5.32

**After Use NURMS is applied, the smoothed rocket looks better (shown here without the background reference image planes).**

Figure 5.33

**Select the polygons at the bottom of the wheel well.**

Figure 5.34

**The wheel well after polygons are deleted. You may see some geometry poking through the side, as shown here.**

Figure 5.35

**The geometry is poking through the outside!**

5.  Enable NURMS smoothing, and your rocket body should resemble the one in Figure 5.36. Make sure to disable NURMS smoothing before you continue with the rest of the exercise.

6.  Save your work.

Figure 5.36

**The smoothed wheel wells look pretty good.**

## Creating the Control Panel

We'll now create the control panel for the rocket, as shown in Figure 5.37. You can continue with your own scene file or use the scene file Rocket_02.max from the Scenes folder in the Red Rocket project you downloaded from the web page.

Figure 5.37

**The control panel**

1.  To create the control panel, we need to add one more segment along the top of the body for extra mesh detail, as you can see in Figure 5.38. To Create the new edge, we will try another method of segmenting new polygons: Connect.

    Connect creates new edges between pairs of selected edges. In the Connect Edges caddy, shown in Figure 5.39, you can specify the number of edges to be created. Using the Pinch and Slide values, you can define the spacing between those new edges.

2.  Switch to Edge sub-object mode (press 2). In the Top viewport, select the edge at the top center of the Rocket, as shown in Figure 5.40. Go to the Graphite Modeling Tools ribbon, and in the Modify Selection panel click on the Ring button. This selects all the edges from top to bottom.

[ + ] [ Top ] [ Smooth + Highlights + Edged Faces ]

Location of
the new segment

Figure 5.38
**Add a segment line using the Connect tool to create extra mesh detail for the control panel.**

Figure 5.39
**The Connect Edges caddy**

Figure 5.40
**Select the edge at the top center.**

[ + ] [ Top ] [ Smooth + Highlights + Edged Faces ]

Select this edge.

3. Stay in Edge mode, and in the Graphite Modeling Tools ribbon → Loops tabs select the Connect button. This adds a single new edge.

4. Now we are going to create a new segment line vertically down the length of the rocket body, as shown in Figure 5.41, using the same technique as in the previous exercise (the Connect tool).

Figure 5.41

**Add a lengthwise cut line to the rocket body.**

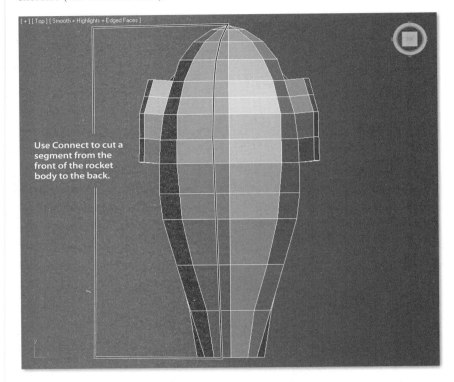

5. This time, select one of the horizontal edges at the top of the rocket (as shown in Figure 5.42). Then in the Modify Selection panel in the Graphite Modeling Tools ribbon, select Ring to automatically select all the horizontal edges above and below your initial selection. Go to the Loops panel and click Connect to create the new cut line shown in Figure 5.41.

   Now we see the same problem at the tip of the rocket that we saw in the last exercise. Going back to Figure 5.23 and reading from there will guide you through connecting these two vertices.

6. With the new vertices along this lengthwise cut line, in the Top viewport move the vertices to fit the shape of the control panel, as shown in the Top View image-plane box. See Figure 5.43.

**Figure 5.42**

Select one of the horizontal edges at the top.

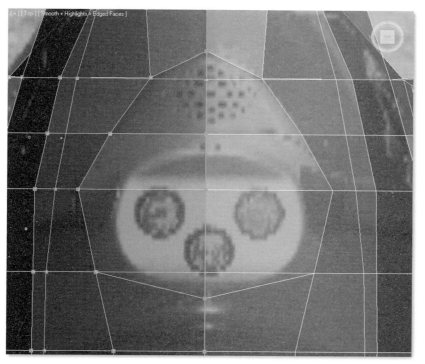

**Figure 5.43**

Shape the new vertices around the control panel in the Top viewport.

7. Switch to Polygon sub-object mode and select the control panel polygons shown in Figure 5.44.

Figure 5.44

**Select the control panel polygons.**

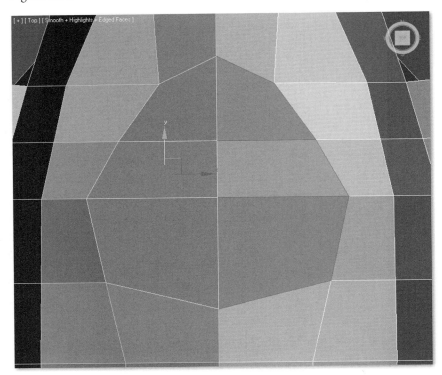

8. Go to the Graphite Modeling Tools ribbon and click the Extrude Settings button in the Polygons panel. Extrude the polys with an Amount of 1.0 and with the Extrude Type set to Group, and click OK.

If you look at the top view of the rocket, you will see the new extrusion where it meets the reference half of the rocket body, as shown in Figure 5.45.

The two sides where you extruded should split away from each other. Remember that the two sides are being stitched together to form the whole body using the Symmetry modifier, so all we need to do is make sure that all the vertices of the original side are aligned in the middle. For the original rocket half, you'll need to delete the polygons along the middle and move the vertices together. We'll do this in the following steps.

9. Select the middle inside polygons, as shown in Figure 5.46, and delete them.

10. Switch to Vertex mode and select the vertices shown in Figure 5.47. Move them along the X-axis to the middle, where the original and the reference halves meet, as shown in Figure 5.48. The problem is fixed! When the body halves are stitched together later, the body mesh will look seamless.

Figure 5.45

The top view of the rocket.

Figure 5.46

Select the middle inside polygons.

Figure 5.47

**Select the vertices shown here.**

Figure 5.48

**Line up the vertices to fix the split in the control panel between the two halves of the rocket body.**

11. Make sure you are in Vertex mode. Using the Front, Side, and Top viewports, move the vertices of the control panel to line up with the real rocket's control panel in the image-plane boxes, as shown in Figure 5.49.

Figure 5.49

**Shape the vertices of the control panel to the outline shown in the image-plane boxes.**

12. Let's look at this rocket body smoothed. Go to the Edit panel in the Graphite Modeling Tools ribbon and click on the Use NURMS button to smooth the model again. It should look like Figure 5.50.

Figure 5.50

**Use NURMS subdivision.**

13.  Use the cage to further edit the control panel to better fit the real control panel in the reference image-plane boxes.

You will see the Subdivision Surfaces cage as long as you are in Polygon mode.

When you disable NURMS, the polygons for the control panel will seem exaggerated, as shown in Figure 5.51, and will go beyond the outlines of the real control panel in the image-plane boxes.

That is because the lower-resolution cage model is a rough shape before smoothing is applied to it. Once NURMS is enabled, it will smooth the detail down, shrinking it back from the cage's shape a little. With NURMS smoothing enabled, the control panel will look like Figure 5.52 and will fit the real model.

[ + ] [ Left ] [ Smooth + Highlights ]

Figure 5.52

**The smoothed control panel as seen in profile**

## Creating the Back Wheel Axle Assembly

Let's turn our attention to the back wheels. In the following steps, we will create the back axle assembly shown in Figure 5.53. You can use your own scene file or load the scene file Rocket_03.max from the Scenes folder in the Red Rocket project.

1. Disable smoothing by clicking the Use NURMS option and switch to Polygon sub-object mode. Change your Top viewport to a Bottom viewport. Also, hide the Image Planes layer in the Layer Manager to get them out of the way.

2. Select the two polygons at the back bottom of the body, shown in Figure 5.54, and extrude them with an Amount of 0.6.

3. The extruded polygons will split at the middle where the original and mirrored reference halves of the body meet, as they did with the control panel earlier in this exercise. Move the vertices and fix the seam in the center the same way you did for the control panel. Make sure to delete the unneeded inside polygons as you did with the control panel. You can see the result in Figure 5.55.

Figure 5.53

**The back wheels**

Figure 5.54

**Select the two polygons at the back bottom of the body.**

Figure 5.55
**The result**

4. Go into Vertex mode and adjust the extruded polygons of the back axle so that they have the shape of the axle from the Side View image-plane box, as shown in Figure 5.56.

Figure 5.56
**Adjust the extruded polygons to better fit the shape of the back.**

5. Select the polys on the side of the extruded polygons and extrude them with an Amount of 0.6, as shown in Figure 5.57.

Figure 5.57

**An extrusion with an Amount of 0.6**

6. Rearrange the vertices to create a small delta wing coming off the bottom/side of the body, as shown in Figure 5.58.

Figure 5.58

**Create a small delta wing.**

7. Turn on NURMS again to see the smoothed results shown in Figure 5.59.

Figure 5.59

**The rocket body is taking shape.**

8. While still in NURMS, try moving the cage vertices to sculpt the back wheel axle. Save your work.

The body is finished for now. Later we will create the seat and add the small lip that connects the thruster to the back.

## Creating the Fins

In this section, we will create the top and side fins for the rocket body, shown in Figure 5.60. Load the scene file Rocket_04.max from the Scenes folder in the Red Rocket project you downloaded from the web page, or continue to work with your own scene file.

Figure 5.60

**The top and side fins**

The fins have specific features—rounded corners and edges—that require us to create them as a modified primitive. There is a nice dip in the wing and a bulbous rounded end, so we will need extra segments across the top. Follow these steps to create the fins.

1. In the Create panel, click the Geometry icon and select Standard Primitives from the drop-down menu. Click to create a Box primitive. Switch the Bottom viewport back to the Top viewport if you need to. In the Top viewport over the wing on the image-plane box, click and drag to create a box with the following parameters: Length: 4.5, Width: 3.2, Height: 0.4, Length Segs: 4, Width Segs: 4, and Height Segs: 2.

2. Press Alt+X to make the model see-through (if it isn't already). Now you should be able to see the image-plane box under the box you just created for the side fin.

3. Select and rotate the box –15 degrees on the Z-axis to line up with the side fin. Convert the box to an editable poly and enter Vertex mode.

4. Using the Top viewport, move the vertices to match the fin in the Top View image-plane box, as shown in Figure 5.61.

Figure 5.61

**Move the vertices to match the fin.**

5. On the side of the fin model, select the center row of vertices, then go to the Edit panel of the Graphite Modeling Tools ribbon and click the Constrain to Normal button as shown in Figure 5.62. Move the vertices, which are now constrained along their individual normal (meaning they will move only perpendicularly out from their current surface location), to create the nice round edge shown in Figure 5.63.

6. Select the vertices along the top and bottom rows at the edge of the fin model. The Constrain to Normal setting is still turned on. Now move the vertices up along the Z-axis, and they will move away from the center to create the bulbous rounded end of the fin (Figure 5.64).

7. Choose the row of vertices shown in Figure 5.65. (Make sure you select both rows on the top and bottom sides of the box.)

8. With Constrain to Normal in the Edit panel still turned on, move this set of vertices along the Z-axis, as you did in step 6 to increase the bulbous end of the fin, as shown in Figure 5.66. Move that row of vertices on the X-axis a little closer to the tip of the fin. Figure 5.67 shows how you can adjust the next row of vertices down a little bit into the fin to further accentuate the bulbous part of the fin.

**Figure 5.62**

The Constrain to Normal button in the Edit panel of the Graphite Modeling Tools ribbon

**Figure 5.63**

Move the vertices to create a nice round edge.

Figure 5.64

**Create the rounded end of the fin.**

Figure 5.65

**Choose the row of vertices here.**

Figure 5.66

**Move up more vertices to create the rounded tip of the fin.**

Figure 5.67

**Adjust vertices to achieve the bulbous shape of the fin's edge.**

Figure 5.68

**Set the constraint
back to None.**

9. In the Edit panel turn the Constrain setting back to None, as shown in Figure 5.68. Then select the row shown in Figure 5.69, and move the vertices closer to the tip of the fin to slightly narrow the bulbous end.

10. Enable Use NURMS to smooth the fin as you did for the Rocket body, and check your work against the fin shown in Figure 5.70 . Remember to disable smoothing when you're done.

> To set up a hot key for NURMS, go to Customize → Customize User Interface → Keyboard tab → Main UI group → All Commands → NURMS toggle (Poly) and assign a hot key combination such as Ctrl+Alt+Y. (We personally used Ctrl+Alt+Y.) As a general rule, it is best to learn the default UI before assigning any hot keys.

11. Exit sub-object mode, select the fin, and select the Move tool. Press and hold the Shift key and move the fin to create a copy of the fin. In the Clone Options dialog that opens when you release the mouse button, click Copy in the Object area. You now have two fins. Clone one more fin so you have three fins. Select the fins and add them to the Rocket layer in the Layer Manager.

12. Select the first fin and line it up to the body of the rocket on the side on which you are currently working. Select a copied fin, and orient it to line up with the fin on the other side of the body.

Figure 5.69

**Refine the shape of
the fin's bulbous tip.**

13. Select the third fin and place it on top of the rocket body as the vertical fin. Line it up with the images of the real rocket. Figure 5.71 shows you the fins placed on the rocket.

14. Save your work.

Figure 5.70

**Smoothing makes the fin look more like the real fin on the red rocket.**

Figure 5.71

**The fins are in place.**

The Scenes folder of the Red Rocket project has a completed fin model. The "Merging Objects into a Scene" sidebar discusses how to import a finished model into an existing scene and merge it with the current objects.

**MERGING OBJECTS INTO A SCENE**

Let's try to merge an external model into this scene. Pretend that you have created a fin model for the red rocket in a different scene file. You can import that fin into your current scene with the rocket body instead of creating a whole new Fin object in this scene. In 3ds Max, this procedure is called *merging*.

1.  Save your work.

2.  Delete the three fins you've already created for your rocket.

3.  Click the Application menu → Import → Merge and navigate to the Fin.max file in the Scenes folder in the Red Rocket project.

4.  Click Open. The Merge dialog window opens, as shown here.

5.  Select the Fin object from the dialog window and click OK. The Fin object will appear in your scene as the top center fin of the rocket.

Instead of creating the fins from scratch, you can clone and position the fin to create the side fins, or you can load your previous scene file and continue with the Red Rocket exercise. If you keep the merged fins, make sure to add them to the Rocket layer in the Layer Manager.

## Creating the Thruster

The back end of the rocket toy is the round thruster shown in Figure 5.72. You can continue with your own scene file or load `Rocket_05.max` from the Scenes folder in the Red Rocket project you downloaded from the web page.

Top view

Bottom view

**Figure 5.72**

**The thruster seen from above and below**

You will create the thruster using the Lathe modifier technique, which you used to create the knobs for the dresser model in Chapter 4, "Modeling in 3ds Max: Part I." Using Lathe works only when the object to be modeled is round and has the same look and detail all the way around. Like we did with the dresser knob we created in Chapter 4, we will use splines—more specifically the Line tool—to fashion the profile of the thruster. The Line tool in 3ds Max is like the Pen tool in Photoshop or the Mask tool in After Effects: It creates a 2D shape with no depth. The Lathe modifier then creates a 3D object by rotating that shape about one of the three axes ($X$, $Y$, or $Z$).

### Using Lathe for the Thruster Shape

We need to identify the profile and draw it with the Line tool.

1. The profile shape we need to use is laid out in Figure 5.73. In the Create panel, click the Shapes icon. There you will find the Line tool button. Click Line, and in the Front viewport lay out a profile similar in shape to Figure 5.73. The shape will make more sense once you see it lathed.

If you prefer not to create the shape, you can merge in an existing shape for the thruster's profile. Click the Application menu → Import → Merge, navigate to the Scenes folder of the Red Rocket project, and open the file called ThrusterProfile.max. Select the Exhaust Profile Line object and click OK. The profile shape will merge into your scene.

Figure 5.74

**The lathe is rotating about the wrong axis.**

2. Once you have created the spline or merged the existing one into the scene, select the spline, go to the Modify panel, and add the Lathe modifier to the line.

   Don't worry if you get something like the lathe shown in Figure 5.74, which is rotating about the wrong axis. Currently, the profile line is rotating about the axis at the center of the line shape. We need the axis of rotation to be at the inside edge of the profile shape.

3. Go to the Modify panel and make sure the lathe is selected. Under the Parameters rollout, in the Align section click the Min button (shown in Figure 5.75). This moves the rotation axis for the profile to the inside edge.

The lathed object should look more like the thruster but will have a big hole in the middle (Figure 5.76). This is also an axis issue. You need to adjust the lathe's axis of rotation to get rid of the hole.

4. Go to the Modifier Stack, expand the Lathe modifier (click the plus sign to the left of the Lathe entry in the Modifier Stack), and select Axis. We now are in the lathe's sub-object mode. Go to the Perspective viewport and move the Transform gizmo to the left (or right, depending on your orientation) along the X-axis until the hole is closed to the naked eye.

> Be cautious with step 4. You can't actually close the hole this way; you can only make it smaller. If you cross over the line, the normals will flip on the entire object. Get the hole as small as you can; when the thruster is finished, you can add a Cap Holes modifier from the Modifier List.

5. Go back to the Lathe parameters and change Segments to 20. This will help the thruster look less faceted than it does right now, but it will look a bit chunky on the edges. Don't be too concerned with that; the thrusters will not be seen close up in this scenario. Use the Segments parameter to make your lathes look only as smooth as needed for your shot.

6. Name your thruster geometry **Thruster**, and add it to the Rocket layer in the Layer Manager.

7. Move it to the back of the rocket body, according to the reference images.

## Using Booleans for the Thruster Detail

Take another look at Figure 5.72. The thruster has indented detail running around the side. We will create this in our model using a Boolean operation. A *Boolean operation* is a geometric operation that creates a shape from the addition of two shapes, the subtraction of one shape from another, or the common intersection of two shapes.

In theory, we will need to subtract the indented shape from the thruster mesh we have created so far. We'll start by creating the shape we need to use by cutting it out of the thruster mesh. In Figure 5.72, you can see that the top of the shape indented into the thruster side has flat corners, the bottom corners are rounded, and the whole rectangle shape tapers.

Figure 5.75

**Click the Min button.**

Figure 5.76

**The lathe is starting to look more like the thruster.**

You can continue with your own work or open `Rocket_06.max` in the Scenes folder of the Red Rocket project to catch up to this point.

> If you don't want to spend time creating the thruster detail objects, you can merge the premade model from the scene file `Thruster Detail.max` in the Scenes folder of the Red Rocket project.

1. Let's make the work area a little easier to navigate by hiding some of the rocket parts. Open the Layer Manager and click to hide the Image Planes layer, then expand the Rocket layer, and click in the Hide column to hide the three fins and the rocket body. You can unhide them from the Layer Manager at any time.

> If you don't want to create the splines, you can merge an already created spline from the scene file `Thruster Detail Spline.max` in the Scenes folder of the Red Rocket project. If you merge in this file, you can skip to step 3.

2. Go to the Create panel and, under Shapes, select Rectangle. Click and drag in the Top viewport to create a rectangle with Length 0.74 and Width 0.42. Move the rectangle above the thruster geometry we just lathed, as shown in Figure 5.77.

Figure 5.77

**Move the rectangle above the thruster geometry.**

3. Center your cursor over the wireframe of the rectangle and right-click; choose Convert To → Convert to Editable Spline, as shown in Figure 5.78. Converting to an editable spline will give you access to the sub-object modes, as you saw in the previous chapter, and it will let you edit the shape for the detail you need in the thruster.

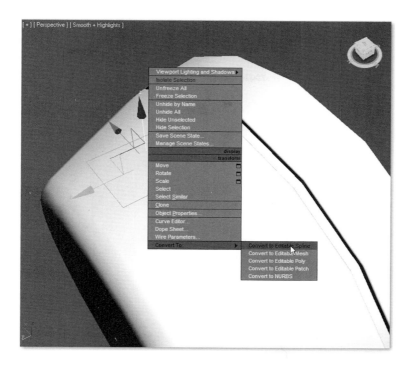

Figure 5.78

**Convert the rectangle to an editable spline.**

4. Go into Vertex mode for the rectangle spline and select the bottom two vertices. Go into the Geometry rollout, enter a value of 0.04 for Chamfer, and press Enter (Figure 5.79).

5. Select the two top vertices individually and move them closer together so that the rectangle tapers at that end. Select both of the top vertices, and in the Geometry rollout enter a value of 0.1 for Fillet. Click the Fillet button to round out the top of the spline, as shown in Figure 5.80.

Figure 5.79

**Enter a value of 0.04 to get the resulting chamfered corners at the bottom.**

Figure 5.80

**Click the Fillet button to round out the top of the spline.**

Watch carefully to make sure the chamfer and fillet in steps 4 and 5 don't create overlapping vertices. Too much of a good thing can cause trouble.

6. Exit Vertex mode by clicking on Editable Spline in the Modifier Stack.

7. With the spline selected, go into the Modifier List and choose Extrude. Set the Amount to 0.4. We will use this to indent into the thruster sides.

8. Line up the thruster detail object with the thruster as shown in Figure 5.81. Center the object on top of the thruster for best results in the following steps.

Figure 5.81

**Center the thruster detail object on the thruster.**

There are eight indentations all around the thruster, so we are going to copy one and array the indentation around the thruster eight times. To make it easier, move the pivot point of the Boolean object to the center of the thruster; this will enable the object to be copied nicely around the thruster.

9. With the thruster selected, go to the Hierarchy panel (⊞) and click Affect Pivot Only.

10. We want to make sure the pivot is in the center of the exhaust. Select the thruster, and in the Main toolbar select the Align tool (⊞), making sure that Affect Pivot Only is active. Leave the dialog box settings at their default values and press OK.

The pivot should be the only thing that moves. If the object moves, Undo (Ctrl+Z) and try the step again.

Figure 5.82

**Clone Options dialog box**

11. Click Affect Pivot Only again to disable it. Press the A key to turn on Angle Snap, then change to the Rotate tool. While holding down the Shift key, rotate the thruster detail object 45 degrees in either direction around the thruster dish. When you release the mouse button, the Clone Options dialog box should open. Select Copy, enter a value of **7** for Number of Copies (Figure 5.82), and press OK. This will place seven copies of the object, each at 45 degrees of rotation around the thruster, making a total of eight objects that are 360 degrees around, as shown in Figure 5.83.

Figure 5.83

**Seven copies of the object**

12. Select the thruster, go to the Create panel, and select Geometry. Choose Compound Objects from the pull-down menu and then click the ProBoolean button. Click the Start Picking button, as shown in Figure 5.84. Move to the thruster detail objects and click on each one to subtract from the thruster.

Your thruster should now have the indentations shown in Figure 5.85.

13. Click Start Picking to turn the feature off. Then unhide the other parts of the rocket to see how everything looks so far. You can do this through the Layer Manager window. Save your work.

Figure 5.84

**Using Start Picking to add detail to the Thruster object**

Figure 5.85

**The thruster with its indentation detail**

## Further Body Work

We need to add some finishing touches to the body of the rocket. You can continue working with your own scene file or load `Rocket_07.max` from the Scenes folder in the Red Rocket project.

You should see a seam running along the top middle of the body (Figure 5.86). To fix this, we need to bring those vertices in toward the center of the body until the seam disappears.

Figure 5.86

**A seam runs down the middle of the rocket body.**

1. Select the rocket, then in the Modifier Stack select Vertex mode. The mirrored side of the body will disappear because we are lower in the Modifier Stack. If you want the Symmety to remain, click on the Show End Result button ( I ), which you will find in the row of icons below the Modifier Stack.

2. Select the vertices that run along the middle. Select and move a few at a time. From the side view, you can see that those vertices stick up farther than the row below; this is what causes the ridge. Make the vertices level with the row of vertices below them by moving them along the Z-axis, as shown in Figure 5.87. (This step will be easier if you turn off Use NURMS in the Subdivision Surface rollout.)

Figure 5.87

**Make the vertices level with the row of vertices below them.**

3. Go to Symmetry up in the Modifier Stack to view the whole body without the seam. Turn smoothing back on if necessary (Figure 5.88).

The next detail to manage is a small lip at the back end of the body (shown in Figure 5.89). We are doing the lip after we complete the body because this detail is easier to create after the body is stitched together.

1. Turn off Use NURMS if it's currently enabled. Also, hide the fins and the thruster.

2. Make sure the body is selected (with the Symmetry modifier). Go to the Graphite Modeling Tools ribbon, and in the Polygon Modeling menu click on Collapse Stack.

3. In the Polygon Modeling panel, click on Border mode and select the edge in the back of the body, as shown in Figure 5.90.

4. Go to the Geometry (All) panel in the Graphite Modeling Tools ribbon and click Cap Poly, as shown in Figure 5.91. This will create a poly where the hole was.

Figure 5.88

**The seam is gone!**

Figure 5.89

**The lip between the thruster and the rocket body**

Figure 5.90

**Select the edge in the back of the body.**

Figure 5.91

**Click Cap Poly
in the Geometry
(All) panel.**

Figure 5.91

**Click Cap Poly
in the Geometry
(All) panel.**

5. Switch to Polygon sub-object mode and select the new polygon. Go to the Polygons panel of the Graphite Modeling Tools ribbon and click the Bevel Settings to open the Bevel caddy. We will do four bevels through the open Bevel caddy. Between each bevel, make sure you click Apply and Continue, not OK. This will apply your bevel but keep the caddy open for more.

6. Make four bevels with the following values:

| BEVEL NO. | HEIGHT | OUTLINE AMOUNT |
|-----------|--------|----------------|
| 1 | 0.05 | 0.3 |
| 2 | 0.2 | 0.1 |
| 3 | 0.2 | −0.1 |
| 4 | 0.05 | −0.3 |

7. Click on the Poly button to go to the top level of the Edit Poly modifier.

Now you can unhide the thruster and the fins. Make sure everything lines up, and render if you'd like (Figure 5.92). (See Chapter 11, "3ds Max Rendering," for more about rendering.)

Figure 5.92

**The finished
rocket body**

## Making the Wheels

We are in the home stretch. The wheels, the handlebars, and the buttons for the control panel are all that are left to model. In this section, we will model the wheels shown in Figure 5.93.

You can continue with your own scene file or load `Rocket_08.max` from the Scenes folder in the Red Rocket project.

Figure 5.93

**The wheels of the rocket are next.**

If you don't want to create the wheels, you can merge the wheels using an already created model from the scene file Wheel.max in the Scenes folder of the Red Rocket project.

## Creating the First Wheel

The wheels are created using the same general technique as the body and fins: Select the polygons of a standard/extended primitive and edit them. This time we are going to use a chamfer cylinder.

1. If the image planes are hidden, unhide them for the side view. In the Layer Manager, make sure the default layer is checked. This will ensure that the object you create for the wheel will not be in the layer that has the hidden Rocket objects.

2. Go to the Create panel. In the drop-down menu, select Extended Primitives and click to create a chamfer cylinder.

3. To get the side of the wheel to finish, click and drag to create the circle of the cylinder, then release the mouse button. Drag and click the mouse again to set the depth of the cylinder, and finally drag the mouse a third time to set the amount of the chamfer. Click to set the final shape in the Left viewport. Go to the Modify panel and set the Chamfer Cylinder parameters shown in Figure 5.94.

| PARAMETER | VALUE |
|---|---|
| Radius | 2 |
| Height | 1.2 |
| Fillet | 0.2 |
| Height Segs | 1 |
| Fillet Segs | 3 |
| Sides | 30 |
| Cap Segs | 1 |
| Smooth | Checked |
| Slice On | Unchecked |

4. Go to the Graphite Modeling Tools ribbon, and in the Polygon Modeling panel click Convert to Poly. Go into Vertex mode and select the vertex on the front in the center, as shown in Figure 5.95.

5. Go to the Graphite Modeling Tools ribbon's Vertices panel and click on the Chamfer Settings button. Set the Vertex Chamfer Amount to 0.4 and click OK.

6. Switch to Polygon mode and select the new center polygon, as shown in Figure 5.96.

7. Go to the Polygons panel and open the Bevel Settings caddy. Set Height to −0.4 and Outline to 0.0, and click Apply and Continue to create one bevel. Then set Height to 0.5 and Outline to −0.12 and click OK to create a second bevel.

8. Now change the viewport so you can see the back of the wheel.

9. Go back into Vertex mode and select the center vertex. Go to the Vertices panel and click the Chamfer Settings button. Set the Vertex Chamfer Amount to 0.2 and click OK.

10. Switch back to Polygon mode and select the new center polygon. In the Polygons panel, extrude the polygon with an Amount of 3.0. You can see the completed wheel in Figure 5.97.

Figure 5.94

**Set the Chamfer Cylinder parameters as shown.**

Figure 5.95

**Select the vertex on the front in the center.**

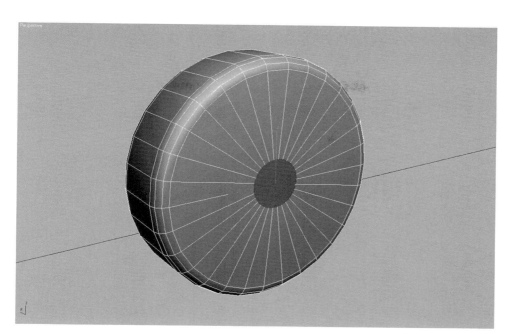

Figure 5.96

**Select the new center polygon.**

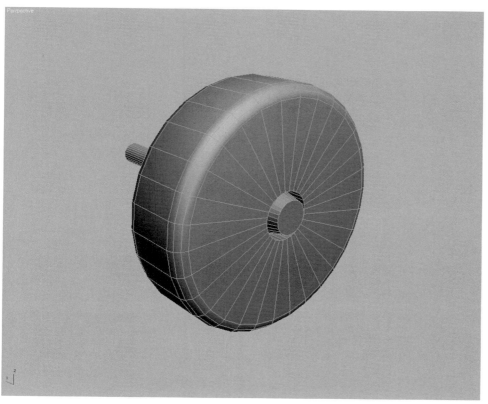

Figure 5.97

**The completed wheel**

### Placing the Wheels

One wheel is done! Now exit the Polygon level and make three clones for the front and back wheels. Unhide the rocket body and place the wheels at the wheel wells. Don't worry if the front wheels don't fit perfectly and happen to penetrate the body's geometry. It was hard to tell how big to make the wheel wells until we had the wheels. We will fix that here:

1. Select the rocket body and, in the Edit menu of the Graphite Modeling Tools ribbon, click Use NURMS to turn it off.

2. The body of the rocket will appear low poly again, as you can see in Figure 5.98. It's usually easier to model in the low-poly version rather than the smoothed one.

3. Go into Vertex mode.

4. Change any viewport to a bottom view. Select the vertices on the inside of the wheel well and move them to make the opening larger so the wheels can fit, as shown in Figure 5.99.

5. Click the Use NURMS button to turn it back on. See if the wheels fit with the body when it is smoothed as shown in Figure 5.100.

Figure 5.99

**Select the vertices on the inside walls of the wheel well and move them in closer to the centerline of the rocket body to give the wheels room.**

Figure 5.100

**Make sure the wheels fit into the wheel wells.**

One last thing you can do is to give your new wheels proper names (we used Wheel01, Wheel02, Wheel03, and Wheel04) and place them in the Rocket Layer by selecting all the wheels, clicking on the Rocket layer, and then clicking on the plus sign (+) in the Layers toolbar.

## Getting a Handle on Things

The red rocket has a set of handlebars just as a bike does. They help keep the driver (usually a child) from face planting every time he or she gets on it. As funny as that may be, a parent can watch it only so many times. This is why most grownups find the handlebars (shown in Figure 5.101) to be the most important part of the rocket. We will model them now.

Figure 5.101

**The handlebars help prevent calamities of the falling kind.**

The handlebars will be created using a modeling technique called *lofting*, which creates a shape that is extruded along a path. Each handlebar is a compound object that uses one shape as a profile and another as the path to form a 3D surface or object.

### LOFTING

The Loft compound object has many features and only a few restrictions. The Shape object can be complex, consisting of several noncontiguous splines and even nested splines. A new Shape object can be selected at any point along the path, and the cross-section will automatically transition from one shape to the next. Any 2D shape can be used as the Shape object, but only a shape that consists of a single spline can be used as the Path object.

### Creating the Path

Take another look at Figure 5.101 and imagine a straight line passing through the middle of one of the handlebars. This is the path we want to create.

You can continue with your own scene file or load `Rocket_09.max` from the Scenes folder in the Red Rocket project. You can hide the objects in the scene at this point to help keep an uncluttered workspace.

> Merge the scene file `Handle Bar Spline.max` from the Scenes folder of the Red Rocket project if you don't want to create the path yourself.

1. Start by going to the Create panel. Click the Shapes icon and select the Line tool.

2. In the Back viewport, against the image of the front view of the rocket, click to place the line's first point where the handlebar meets the control panel. Move the cursor to where the handlebar bends, and create another point. Place a final point where the handlebar ends, as shown in Figure 5.102, and right-click to create the line. You may need to move the line forward in the Top viewport to get the proper alignment shown in Figure 5.102.

Figure 5.102

**Place a final point where the handle ends.**

3. Move to the Modify panel and enter Vertex mode for the line, as shown in Figure 5.103. Select the middle vertex, go to the Fillet parameter in the Geometry rollout, and enter **0.1**. This will add a smooth corner to the bend.

Figure 5.103

**Enter Vertex mode for the line.**

### Creating the Shape

Now that we have the path for the loft, we need the profile shape, which is a cross-section of the handlebar. This shape is an oval with a flat top, as shown in Figure 5.104.

To create this shape, follow these steps:

1. Exit Vertex mode. Create a Circle shape from the Create panel and convert it to an editable spline.

Figure 5.104

**An oval with a flat top**

2. Go into Vertex mode, select the top vertex, and delete it to flatten the top.

   Next, we will create the Loft object.

3. Exit Vertex mode then select the path spline for the handlebar and go to the Create menu. Click Geometry → Compound Objects → Loft.

4. Because we started the lofting process with the handlebar's path line, we only need to let 3ds Max know which shape to use. In the Modify panel go to the Creation Method rollout (Figure 5.105), and select Get Shape.

5. Select the handlebar shape in a viewport to use as the loft's shape.

Figure 5.105

**Select Get Shape from the Creation Method rollout.**

## Editing the Loft Object

In Figure 5.106, you can see the loft's path and cross-section shape as well as the resulting Loft object.

Figure 5.106

**The loft lives!**

In this example the shape is rotated 90 degrees along the path, putting the handle on its side, as you can see in Figure 5.107.

The shape needs to be turned to make the broad flat side point up, as shown in Figure 5.108.

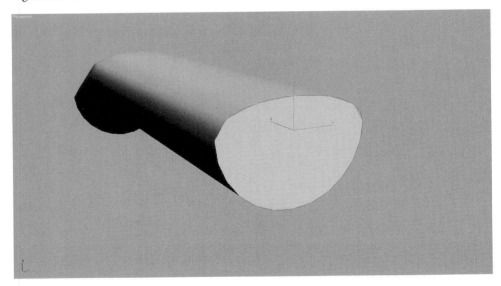

To edit the loft, we will go into its sub-object mode. The sub-objects of a loft are the path and the shape.

> The original splines were instanced when the loft was created, so they are still connected to the loft. This means changes made at the sub-object level on the splines will be transferred to the lofted object. If necessary, you can alter the shape of the path line or shape splines and the loft will change accordingly. You cannot, however, move or rotate the path or shape splines to affect the shape of the loft. You must use Move or Rotate at the sub-object level of the loft instead.

1. Go to the Modify panel and expand the Loft object in the Modifier Stack.

2. Go into the Shape sub-object mode (Figure 5.109).

3. In a viewport, select the loft's shape at the end of the Loft object. The shape will turn red when it is selected, as shown before in Figure 5.107. The shape spline is the thin, smoother line in this grayscale figure.

4. Select the Rotate tool and rotate the shape on the loft −90 degrees. The entire loft will be updated, as shown earlier in Figure 5.108.

Figure 5.109

**The Shape sub-object mode**

## Adding Detail

The next step is to create the subtle curves and dips of the handlebars. The outside end of the real handlebar is curved. There is a groove toward the middle, and the handle tapers up where it meets the control panel. To look this good, the handlebar we've created needs more than one cross-section. With a Loft compound object in 3ds Max, you can have any number of cross-sections for your loft, and they can be of varying shapes.

To edit a loft for these details, we are going to add more shapes along the path, and then edit those shapes to taste.

Figure 5.110

**Reduce the Path Steps.**

1. Go back to the top level of the Loft object in the Modify panel, and go to the Skin Parameters rollout. This is where you can manage the Steps (subdivisions) in the loft. By default, there is a value of 5 for both the Shape Steps and the Path Steps. The Shape Steps here are fine, but the Path Steps value is too high. To fix this, turn Path Steps down to 1, as shown in Figure 5.110. If there are too many steps in your loft, it will get too heavy and dense to model.

> If you prefer, you can merge the scene file Handle Bar.max from the Red Rocket project to complete the one handlebar or to check your own work.

Figure 5.111

**Make a copy of the loft shape.**

2. Go back to Shape mode and select the shape. Using the Move tool, center the cursor over the *Z*-axis wire of the Transform gizmo that is connected to the shape.

3. We need to make copies of the Shapes so we can taper down the end of the handlebar. Shift+click and drag the gizmo to move the shape just a little bit up the body of the handlebar to make a copy of the loft shape, as shown in Figure 5.111. The loft shape is shown as a dashed red line.

4. In the Copy Shape dialog box, choose Copy, then click OK. Repeat these steps twice to end up with three copies, and place them close to the end of the handle, as shown in Figure 5.112. Switch to the Scale tool, and scale the outside shape down 30 percent and the middle shape down 10 percent. Leave the last inside shape alone, which should create a nice curved taper at the end of the handlebar.

5. Select the inside shape on the loft, and make four more copies in a row close to where the bar curves (Figure 5.113). Select the two inside copies and scale them both down 20 percent. This will create the groove toward the center of the handlebars.

6. Select the shape closest to the bend, and make a copy. Move it all the way to the other end of the object, away from the tapered tip. This is where it will meet the body of the rocket. Select the Scale tool, and scale this end shape up 50 percent. Exit the Loft's sub-object mode.

7. If any parts of the rocket are hidden, unhide them and see how the handlebars line up. You will probably agree that there is room for improvement (Figure 5.114).

Figure 5.112

**Place copies of the loft's shape close together at the end to taper them down.**

Figure 5.113
**Creating the groove**

Figure 5.114
**The handlebars will probably not line up with your rocket body right away.**

8. Instead of rotating the Loft object, rotate the last shape at the end of the loft. Go back to sub-object mode and select the last shape to rotate to line up with the body, as shown in Figure 5.115.

9. Select the handlebar, and in the Main Toolbar click the Mirror icon (🔲) to mirror a copy of the handle for the other side of the rocket. Place it as needed. Figure 5.116 shows the rocket with its handlebars.

Figure 5.115

**Rotate the end shape object to line up with the rocket body.**

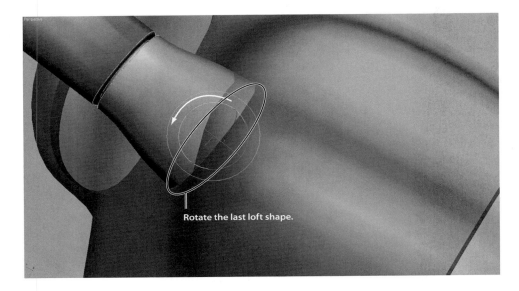

Figure 5.116

**The rocket with the handlebars in place**

## Hold onto Your Seat

Figure 5.117

**The Parameters rollout**

What fun would it be to ride a rocket standing up? Speaking from experience, it's not fun. So let's give our rocket model a nice comfy seat. Then we'll be finished with the model!

You can continue with your own scene file or load `Rocket_10.max` from the Scenes folder in the Red Rocket project.

1. Using your own scene file or the provided `Rocket_10.max` scene, in the Left view create a cylinder with the following parameters shown in Figure 5.117.

| PARAMETER | VALUE |
| --- | --- |
| Radius | 3 |
| Height | 8 |
| Height Segments | 1 |
| Cap Segments | 1 |
| Sides | 40 |
| Smooth | Checked |

2. From the side view, line up the cylinder so it is over the part of the rocket body where the seat would be (as shown in Figure 5.118).

Figure 5.118

**Line up the cylinder with the seat area.**

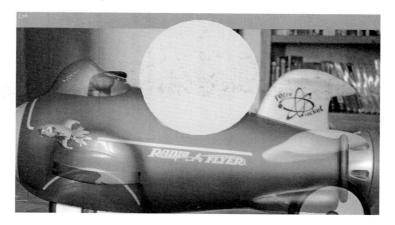

From the top view, the cylinder should be evenly spaced on both sides of the rocket (Figure 5.119).

3. Select the rocket body and before performing the Boolean operation, turn on Use NURMS as needed from the modeling ribbon. Then go to the Create menu → Geometry → Compound Objects → ProBoolean. Choose Start Picking from the Pick Boolean rollout, and then select the cylinder in a viewport. The cylinder will cut a seat into the rocket body as shown in Figure 5.120.

Figure 5.119

**The top view of the cylinder**

Figure 5.120

**The seat is almost done.**

Because the Boolean operation will collapse all the modifiers on the body, it is important that it be the last operation we perform on this model. We won't want to make any changes to the body that would require access to its modifiers. Once any modifiers are collapsed, editing becomes difficult.

4. Convert the rocket body to an editable poly by right-clicking on the Rocket Body object and choosing Convert To: Convert to Editable Poly from the Quad menu.

5. Unhide any parts of the rocket that you may have hidden to clear your workspace.

6. The control panel of the rocket needs some buttons. To add them, create a few chamfer cylinders and place them there. Now you're really done! Figure 5.121 shows the completed red rocket with buttons in the control console.

7. Save your work; that is second nature to you by now—right?

Figure 5.121

**The completed
rocket!**

Take it all in. As you can see, a fairly complex object is nothing more than a collection of simple shapes hammered, chiseled, cut, poked, and prodded into place. By learning how to dissect a complex object into its component shapes and learning how to view modeling an object as a series of steps, you will grow as a modeling artist.

## Summary

When you built the red rocket, you employed several of the Editable Poly tools and ProBoolean functions you learned about in the previous chapter. The more you use these tools, the faster they will become an instinctive part of your workflow. You also used the very handy Symmetry modifier to cut your work on the body in half.

After setting up the scene with background images, you were able to line up model parts and build them to fit the actual object as you worked in the scene.

In the next chapter, we will continue exploring the Editable Poly tools while creating a lower polygon count character model, a commando soldier like you may find in a game.

# CHAPTER 6

# Character Poly Modeling

*Organic modeling* is typically used when you create natural objects, such as a tree trunk, a hilly landscape, or a character. These models are generally of a higher polygon count than most because organic models require smooth surfaces and need to be seamless. With a more mechanical model, such as the dresser you modeled in Chapter 4, "Modeling in 3ds Max: Part I," there is little to no need for highly detailed, high-polygon-count surfaces. A human head model for a character, however, needs finely detailed surfaces because an organic model's parts need to flow together seamlessly. With the human head model, there should be no clear distinction between where the geometry of the lower lip stops and the jaw starts, or where the top of the nose ends and the forehead begins. A basic knowledge of anatomy and an understanding of balance and proportion are important when you're designing a character that needs to be appealing and believable.

Realistic computer-generated (CG) characters are already very common in television and films; they appear as stunt doubles, as vast crowds of people, and even as primary characters to the scene or even the entire show. There are several situations where using a CG character works better for a show than using a real person. For example, CG stunt doubles are safer and sometimes cheaper than using an actual stunt person. Another opportunity for organic character modeling arises when a storyline calls for an unusual or nonhuman character. Weird creatures can be created with better clarity using CG than using puppetry or special makeup effects.

This chapter introduces you to character modeling, focusing on using the Editable Poly toolset to create a relatively low polygon count soldier model suitable for character animation and for use in a game engine (though that is not covered in this book). The model of a special operations soldier character frequently seen in a game will finish as a single object created from very basic forms. However, the concepts and practices talked about in this chapter will give you a solid foundation for any kind of character modeling.

Topics in this chapter include the following:

- ■ **Setting up the scene**

- ■ **Creating the soldier**

# Setting Up the Scene

As mentioned throughout the previous chapters, acquiring and utilizing good reference material is essential for creating a successful character. At the minimum, sketches of the character's front and side features are necessary. You can import and use these views as background images as you create the character in 3ds Max. Additional perspective sketches of your intended character from several points of view and sketches of specific features, such as headgear, weapons, or other devices, can be very helpful during the modeling process for quick reference to your goal.

---

**HIGH- AND LOW-POLY MODELING**

High polygon count models are used when a model's level of detail needs to be impeccable, such as when the model is used in close-ups. In such a case, detail is favored over efficiency.

Low polygon count modeling, also called low poly modeling, refers to a style of modeling that sacrifices some detail in favor of efficient geometry that places a very low load on the system on which it is being created or rendered. Because they require less memory, can be easier to animate, and can render quickly, low-poly models are especially useful in games, as well as for filling in a scene's background without overly taxing the scene.

---

## Creating Planes and Adding Materials

Like the toy rocket exercise in Chapter 5, "Modeling in 3ds Max: Part II," this exercise begins by creating crossed boxes and applying reference images to them.

1. In a new scene, go to the Front viewport and create a plane.

2. In the Parameters rollout of the Command panel, set the Length to 635 and the Width to 622. The units are in inches, which is the default in 3ds Max. The size of the image planes in units is the same size as the reference images in pixels. Thus, when we apply the image to the plane it will be proportional, maintaining its width and length with no stretching or squeezing of the images.

3. Rename this box **Image_Plane_Front**.

4. With the plane still selected, click the Move tool ( ) in the Main toolbar. In the Transform Type-Ins at the bottom of the user interface, move the plane to these coordinates: (0.0, 80.169, -5.228), as shown in Figure 6.1

Figure 6.1

**Use the Transform Type-ins to move the image plane to the given coordinates.**

1 Object Selecte  X: 0.0  Y: 80.169  Z: -5.228  Grid = 10.0

5. Click the Z key on the keyboard; it is the shortcut for Zoom Extents All. Then, in the Main toolbar, turn on the Angle Snap toggle ( ). This will snap your rotation to every 5 degrees. This will make getting an exact rotation easier. Select the Rotate tool

and hold down Shift on the keyboard, then in the Front viewport rotate the image plane along the Y-axis -90 degrees. Using Shift activates the Clone tool, as shown in Figure 6.2.

Figure 6.2

**Clone Options dialog box**

6. In the Clone Options dialog box, under Object, select Copy, then name it **Image_Plane_Side** and hit OK.

7. Switch to the Move tool and move the plane to these coordinates: (-159.85, 80.169, -5.228), as shown in Figure 6.3.

Figure 6.3

**Image plane coordinates**

8. Now that both image planes have been created and positioned, open the Layer Manager. Select both image planes, and in the Layer Manager click the Create New Layer. Because the image planes were selected when you created the new layer, the image planes were automatically added to the new layer. Rename the layer **Image Planes**, and check the Current Layer column next to the 0 (default) layer, as shown in Figure 6.4.

Figure 6.4

**The current Layer toggle in the Layer Manager. Check the box next to the 0 (default) layer.**

9. In the Layer Manager, click on the Layer icon for the Image Planes layer to open the Layer Properties dialog box, as shown in Figure 6.5.

10. Uncheck the Show Frozen in Gray box. This will allow you to freeze the image planes and still see the images on the planes.

11. Click OK then click the Freeze column next to the Image Planes layer.

Figure 6.5

**Click the Layer icon to open the Layer Properties dialog box.**

## Adding the Materials

The reference materials are then texture mapped onto the planes to provide reference inside the scene itself while you model the character. Therefore, it's critical to ensure that the features of the character that appear in both reference images (the front and the side) are at the same height. For instance, the top of the head and the shoulders should be at the same height in both the front and side views to make the modeling process easier, eliminating as much guesswork as possible.

1. In the Front viewport, change the viewport shading to Smooth + Highlights (F3). Change a viewport so it is a Right view, press the V key on the keyboard, and select Right View from the list. Change the shading in the Right viewport to Smooth + Highlights.

2. Open an Explorer window and navigate to the Soldier/sceneassets/images folder on your hard drive from the Soldier project you downloaded from the web page at www.sybex.com/go/3dsMax2011. Drag ImagePlane_Front.jpg from the Explorer window to the image plane in the Front viewport.

3. Drag ImagePlane_Side.jpg onto the image plane in the Right viewport. The image planes should have the two images mapped on them, as shown in Figure 6.6.

### SEEING QUALITY BITMAPS IN THE VIEWPORTS

The Show Map in the Viewport toggle (  ) in the Material Editor determines whether the maps in a material are displayed in all viewports set to the Smooth + Highlights display mode. In many cases, the quality of the images displayed is high enough to allow you to line up major features in the reference image to the model's corresponding feature, but not high enough to have a very effective reference. The quality level of the bitmap display can be set in the Preference Settings dialog box. The following steps explain how to change the bitmap viewport quality when using the DirectX video driver. The steps to follow when using the OpenGL or Software drivers are similar.

1. From the main menu, select Customize → Preferences.

2. Click the Viewports tab, and then click the Configure Driver button in the Display Drivers section, as shown here.

3. In the Configure Direct3D dialog box that appears, select a resolution in the Download Texture Size section or select the Match Bitmap Size as Closely as Possible option. This allows you to increase the displayed resolution of any maps shown in the viewports. This does not affect the actual size of the images used in the scene, only how they are shown in the viewports.

4. If necessary, repeat step 3 to increase the resolution of the background image in the Background Texture Size section.

5. Click OK in both dialog boxes to accept the changes. You must close and then reopen 3ds Max for the changes to take effect, however.

Beware that increasing the displayed resolution can decrease viewport performance and increase the system resources required to manage the scene.

Figure 6.6

**Mapped image planes in viewports**

# Creating the Soldier

The soldier character we are modeling here is pretty common: one head, one neck, two arms, a torso, and two legs—a typical, bipedal human 3D character.

When you create an organic character, you might be tempted to model one piece of the final product, such as the head or hands, to completion *before* you begin modeling another piece of the character. This is rarely a good idea, because the scale and balance of the components must be built together from the beginning. A better practice is to block out the basic form of the character and focus on the size and crucial shapes of the major elements, and then add detail for the finer features. The following exercises describe the steps required to block out the soldier's major features. When you have gained enough confidence, we encourage you to step back into this soldier exercise and redesign the soldier with more intricate features, or even add an additional set of arms to the torso. Go wild!

## Forming the Torso

The basic structure for the torso will begin with a simple box primitive. After converting the box into an Editable Poly, you will use the Mirror tool on the object so that any manipulations performed on one side are also performed on the other. You will begin forming the basic shape of the torso by moving the Editable Poly's vertices and extruding its polygons in the following steps.

Continue with the previous exercise's scene file, or open the Soldier_V01.max scene file in the Scenes folder of the Soldier project downloaded from this book's companion web page at www.sybex.com/go/intro3dsmax2011.

1. Select each viewport and press F3 and F4 so that Smooth + Highlights with Edged Faces is the display mode.

2. Start by creating a box primitive in the Perspective viewport with these parameters: Length: 25, Width: 16, Height: 53, Input Height Segs: 8. Leave the Width and Length Segs at 1 (see Figure 6.7). This is a starting point for the detail needed to create the form of the body. Position the box as shown in Figure 6.8. Press Alt + X to make the box see-through. Change the box's name to **Soldier**.

Figure 6.7

**Box parameters**

Figure 6.8

**Box position from the front and side views**

3. In the Graphite Modeling Tools ribbon, click Polygon Modeling → Convert to Poly (as shown in Figure 6.9).

4. Enter the Vertex sub-object level. In the Right viewport, position the vertices on the right side of the box to match the side outline of the character on the image plane, as shown in Figure 6.10.

5. In the Graphite Modeling Tools ribbon, click Edit → Swift-Loop. Use the SwiftLoop tool to create two new edge loops that run vertically from the front of the model to the back, as shown in Figure 6.11. The dashed lines show the loop running in the back and bottom of the model.

**Figure 6.9**

**Convert the soldier box to an editable Polygon.**

**Figure 6.10**

**Move vertices to match the soldier image in the Right viewport.**

6. Repeat step 5 but create a single new edge on the side of the model running from the left side to the right side, as shown in Figure 6.12. The dashed lines show the loop running across the bottom of the model.

**Figure 6.11**

**Create two new edge loops using SwiftLoop.**

7. Now round the side of the torso. Switch to Edge mode and select one of the edges running vertically on the side of the torso box. In the Graphite Tools Modeling ribbon go to the Modify Selection tab and press Loop to select the loop of edges running along the side of the torso (Figure 6.13). Move the loop of edges toward the back of the model to begin rounding that edge. Then select the loop of edges to the left of the previous loop with the Loop tool and move them back to form a more rounded front to the torso, as shown in Figure 6.13.

Figure 6.13

**Select and move edges toward the back of the model.**

First select this loop of edges and move them back.

Next select this loop of edges and move them back.

8. Switch to Vertex mode and select the vertex on the left side below the top edge, as shown in Figure 6.14. In the Graphite Tools Modeling ribbon's Vertices tab, select Chamfer Settings by clicking the tool's name under the icon. This opens the tool caddy shown in Figure 6.15. Use a Vertex Chamfer Amount value of 4.808 as shown, and click the green checkmark button (OK) in the caddy to commit the action. This is where the arm will be positioned.

Figure 6.14

**Select the vertex right above the mouse cursor shown here.**

Figure 6.15

**Use Chamfer to create a new polygon where the arm will be positioned.**

9. Switch to Polygon mode, select the new diamond-shaped polygon in the middle, and press Delete to delete the polygon. A hole appears where the arm will be positioned.

10. Switch to Edge mode and select the four diagonal edges of the diamond-shaped hole and the four edges shown in Figure 6.16.

11. Select the Graphite Modeling Tools ribbon → Modify Selection → Ring to select the ring of edges running across the top of the chest. Select Modeling ribbon → Loops → Flow Connect to create more horizontal divisions for the upper chest. The newly created edges are illustrated in Figure 6.17. The diamond-shaped hole in the shoulder is now more rounded (the hole is now an octagon) as well, since more edges were created at the hole, too. The dashed lines show the loops running behind the model.

12. Select the two horizontal edges under the armhole (left image in Figure 6.18), and select Modeling ribbon → Modify Selection → Ring to select the horizontal edges running down the side of the torso. Select Modeling ribbon → Loops → Flow Connect to create two new loops of edges, shown on the right in Figure 6.18.

Select these eight edges.

**Figure 6.16**

**Select these eight edges.**

**Figure 6.17**

**Use Flow Connect to create two new edges around the model.**

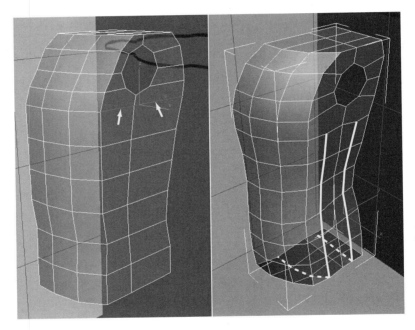

**Figure 6.18**

**Select the two horizontal edges under the armhole (left) and use Flow Connect to create more edges (right).**

13. The new edge ring, as you can see in Figure 6.18, does not reach all the way up to the octagon armhole. You will need to cut an edge from the top of the new edges you just made, to the bottom of the armhole. Select Modeling ribbon → Edit → Cut to enter the Cut tool. Click on the first vertex under the armhole in Figure 6.19, then click on the second vertex above at the armhole to create the first new edge. Right-click to commit the edge. You will still be in the Cut tool, so click on the third vertex shown in Figure 6.19 and create the second new edge up to the fourth vertex shown in Figure 6.19. Right-click to commit the second edge.

Figure 6.19

**Use the Cut tool to add two edges to the armhole.**

Fourth vertex

Second new edge

Third vertex

First vertex

First new edge

Second vertex

14. The armhole isn't great right now; it will be easier to start from a circular shape rather than the uneven octagon form we have now. Enter Border sub-object mode, select the armhole's border, and in the Graphite Modeling Tools ribbon's Geometry (All) tab, click the Cap Poly tool to create an NGon (a polygon with more than four sides) cap to fill the hole.

15. Go to Polygon mode and select the new NGon. Go to the Graphite Modeling Tools ribbon's Polygons tab and click the GeoPoly tool to create a symmetrical polygon from the previous shape, as shown in Figure 6.20. GeoPoly untangles a polygon and organizes the vertices to form a perfect geometric shape. This will make it easier for us when we create the arm later.

16. Select the new NGon cap you created in step 14 and press Delete to delete the NGon. Also select and delete the top and bottom polygons on the model as shown in Figure 6.21 (left).

17. Under the Graphite Modeling Tools Ribbon tab, under the sub-object mode buttons, turn on Ignore Backfacing (⊞). Then select the left-side polygons as shown in Figure 6.21 (right) and delete them as well. Your torso should now have only a front, side, and back.

18. Now, select the edge loops on the right of the model and move them closer toward the left, and closer to the center of the model (Figure 6.22). You might want to translate them on the *Y*-axis as well. Your goal is to round out the character for a more organic feel.

Figure 6.20

**Use GeoPoly to create a symmetrical shape for the armhole.**

Figure 6.21

**Delete the NGon as well as the topmost and bottommost polygons of the model.**

Delete these polygons.

Figure 6.22

**Select the edge loops and move them to create a more rounded look to the model.**

19. Notice how the armhole's circle looks neat, but the edges on the right and top are a bit awkward. Enter Vertex mode and move the edges to give the armhole a more rounded feel as in Figure 6.23. Try to match the relative size of the hole shown in Figure 6.23, as well.

Figure 6.23

**Adjust the Editable Poly's vertices to match the background image.**

Figure 6.24

**Move the selected edge toward the front of the torso to round out the back.**

Figure 6.25

**Line up the extruded border with the arm in the image plane.**

20. Go into Edge mode and select the edge running vertically on the right side of the model's back (as shown in Figure 6.24) and move it toward the armhole. This will make the back rounder.

Now we are starting to see some shape in the torso. Let's move on to the arms.

## Creating the Arms

Continue with the previous exercise's scene file, or open the Soldier_V02.max scene file in the Scenes file of the Soldier project on the companion web page.

1. In Border mode, select the armhole's border, then hold down the Shift key, and with the Move tool, drag out from the body on the *X*-axis, extruding polygons as you drag. This method is a form of Border Extrude. This method gives you more control over the extrude process because you can more easily choose the axis along which to extrude. Release the mouse button and view your model in the Front viewport to line up the border to the wrist of the arm in the image plane, as shown in Figure 6.25.

2. Select Modeling ribbon → Edit → SwiftLoop to create three edge loops on the arm, as shown in Figure 6.26.

Figure 6.26

**Use SwiftLoop to create three new edges on the arm.**

3. Switch to Vertex mode and move the newly created vertices on the Y-axis to fit the form on the image plane, as in Figure 6.27. It is OK to select a group of vertices and scale on the Y-axis to taper that part of the arm to create the wrist.

4. In Edge mode, select and use Loop selection (Graphite Modeling Tools Ribbon →
Modify Selection → Loop) on the horizontal edge running around the body
under the arm and move the edges down.
Repeat the same process with the loop of
edges under the previous loop, as shown
in Figure 6.28. This ensures the underarm
area geometry is lined up properly, as
shown later in Figure 6.30.

Figure 6.27

**Edit vertices to match the shape of the arm.**

5. In Edge mode, select and use Loop
(Graphite Modeling Tools Ribbon → Modify Selection → Loop) on the horizontal edge
running directly at the underarm and move the loop down, as shown in Figure 6.29.

6. In the Front viewport, in Edge mode, select the middle edge on the arm, then Select
Modeling ribbon → Modify Selection → Loop. Then select Modeling ribbon → Edges →
Chamfer → Chamfer Settings and enter an Edge Chamfer Amount of 2 and a Connect
Edge Segments value of 2.

Figure 6.28

**Move these looped edges down.**

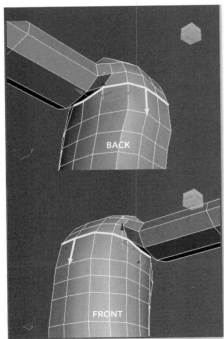

Figure 6.29

**Select and Loop these edges to move them down.**

7. Then Chamfer the edges to the right and left, using an Edge Chamfer Amount of 3, with a Connect Edge Segments value of 1 (Figure 6.30). Keep the middle edge a bit tighter together. Since this is the area where the elbow bends, it is a good idea to include more detail there for deformations at the elbow. Your model should have the vertical edges you see in Figure 6.30.

8. In Border mode, select the wrist border and, while holding down the Shift key, use the Scale tool to scale the wrist border down on the $Z$- and $Y$-axes into the center, as shown in Figure 6.31 (left). Using Shift while performing a Scale operation clones the selected objects much like an extrusion with the Shift + Move method used before. In this case, it makes a copy of the border, effectively closing the open end of the wrist.

9. Then switch to Vertex mode, select the vertices of the smaller wrist hole, and select Modeling ribbon → Vertices → Weld → Weld Settings (✏) to open the Weld tool caddy (Figure 6.31 (middle). Use a Weld Threshold of 3.39, as shown. This creates a completed cap at the end of the arm shown in Figure 6.31 (right). We will continue with the hand in a later section.

Figure 6.30

**Chamfer the arm to add more edges for detail.**

Figure 6.31

**Fuse the wrist edge in toward the center.**

Shift + Scale edges          Weld vertices to fuse in center                    Completed

## Creating the Legs

Continue with the previous exercise's scene file, or open the Soldier_V03.max scene file in the Scenes folder of the Soldier project downloaded from the companion web page.

1.  In Edge mode, select the bottommost loop of edges on the model's torso and Shift + Move (hold down the Shift key while moving with the Move tool, as you did in the previous set of steps) to create a new extrusion all the way down to the groin of the reference illustration. You will extrude and move down on the *Y*-axis as shown in Figure 6.32.

2. We are starting to prepare the model for the legs and groin area. Use the Cut tool (Graphite Modeling Tools Ribbon → Edit → Cut), and cut an edge from about 25 percent to the right from the corner of the bottommost edge of the model, to the top corner on the polygon closest to the groin, as shown in Figure 6.33 (left). Do the same for the polygon at the back of the model in the corresponding corner.

Figure 6.32

**Select the edge loop at the bottom of the model and Shift + Move down.**

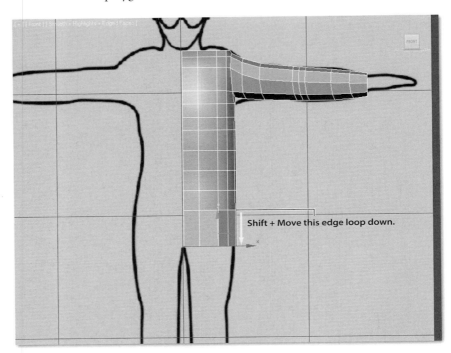

Shift + Move this edge loop down.

Figure 6.33

**Cut the polygon and raise the corners.**

Use the Cut tool to cut the edge.

Select this vertex and move it up.

3. In Vertex mode, select the lowest inside vertices and move them up a bit to create a diagonal edge. Do this for both the front and back of the model, as in Figure 6.33 (right).

4. In Edge mode, select both of the new diagonal edges (front and back), then choose Modeling Ribbon → Edges → Bridge → Bridge Settings. Use four segments to create a bridge, as shown in Figure 6.34. This will create a bridge between the front and back.

Figure 6.34

**Bridge between two edges to create the groin area.**

With the bridge in place, the border edge on the bottom of the torso resembles a capital letter *D* (Figure 6.34). If we extrude the leg down from here, the inner thigh will be flat. For a better starting point to form the leg, we need to cap the hole as we did with the arm previously. If you wish to review these steps before continuing with the thigh, refer back to steps 14 and 15 of the "Forming the Torso" section.

To begin the upper thigh extrusion, continue with the following steps to cap the D shape:

5. Select the D-shaped border edge and Shift + Move down on the *Z*-axis to extrude the upper thigh downward to right above the knee pad, as in Figure 6.35 (left). The knee pad's position can be better seen in the side reference image plane shown later in Figure 6.37. Don't worry; you will adjust the shape to fit the thigh later.

6. With the D-shaped border still selected, choose Graphite Modeling Tools Ribbon → Geometry (All) → Cap Poly to cap the end of the thigh stump. Select the new poly and choose Graphite Modeling Tools Ribbon → Polygons → GeoPoly to make the end of the thigh a more even shape; see Figure 6.35 (middle).

7. Select the thigh's end polygon, and scale on the *X*-axis as shown in Figure 6.35 (right) to create a more oval shape. Then delete the cap so the bottom of the leg is open once again.

Figure 6.35

**Creating the upper thigh**

8. In the Front viewport, switch to Vertex mode, and scale and move the vertices on the leg to match the image plane. Check the Side viewport and shape the thigh as needed. Notice the bottom of the geometry should be located at about the top of the knee pad. Pop back into the Perspective viewport often as you work on these vertices to make sure some of the vertices are not being accidentally moved where they should not be. Figure 6.36 shows the front of the leg and Figure 6.37 shows the side of the leg.

Figure 6.36

**Front view of leg**

**MAKE ADJUSTMENTS AS YOU GO**

Feel free to adjust and smooth out your model by moving vertices as you progress through the tutorial. Little tweaks here and there may be necessary to keep the form fitting the intended character; use the image planes as guides to fit the geometry.

9.  On the inside of the groin area where you created the four-segment bridge in step 4, move the edges as needed to make sure the segments are evenly spaced, as shown in Figure 6.38. This step should be repeated throughout the tutorial; keeping edges evenly spaced ensures that the model is organized and clean, and prevents polygons from penetrating each other.

10. Switch to Border mode and select the border opening at the bottom of the leg. Then use the Extrude Border method (hold Shift + Move), to extrude the leg down to the ankle as shown in Figure 6.39 (left).

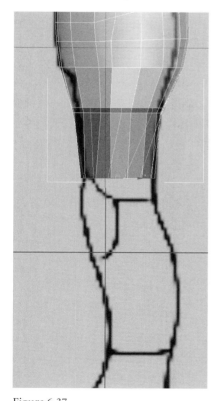

Figure 6.37
**Side view of the leg**

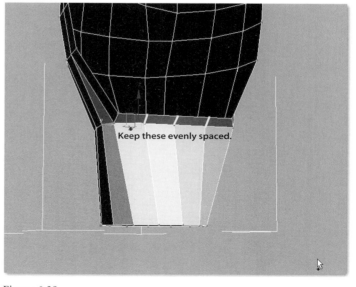

Figure 6.38
**Keep the edges in the groin area evenly spaced.**

11. Choose Graphite Modeling Tools Ribbon → Edit → SwiftLoop and create three new horizontal segments around the leg as shown in Figure 6.39 (middle). Then fit the vertices to the shape of the soldier's leg in the side image plane in the Right viewport, as shown in Figure 6.39 (right). Go into the Front viewport and do the same to shape the leg properly.

12. In Border mode, select the ankle border as shown in Figure 6.40 (left) and Shift + Scale the border down on the Z- and Y-axes and in toward the center of the ankle, leaving a small hole; see Figure 6.40 (middle). Then switch to Vertex mode and select the vertices around the resulting small hole, and use Weld (Graphite Modeling Tools Ribbon → Vertices → Weld) to bring the vertices together; see Figure 6.40 (right). Adjust the Weld Threshold setting as needed to weld these vertices together.

Figure 6.40

**Closing the ankle's hole**

Select the border.          Shift + Scale down.          Weld the vertices.

## Fixing Up the Body

Continue with the previous exercise's scene file, or open the Soldier_V04.max scene file in the Scenes folder of the Soldier project from the companion web page.

1. The pelvis looks a bit funky. We need to streamline the mesh by combining some edges together. Select the vertical edges at the waist (select a single vertical edge and use Graphite Modeling Tools Ribbon → Modify Selection → Ring); see Figure 6.41.

2. Right-click to bring up the Quad menu. In the upper-left Quad, in the Tools 1 section, use Collapse, as shown in Figure 6.42. This will bring the two horizontal edge loops at the top and bottom of the selected vertical edges together into one edge loop.

3. In the Perspective viewport, use Orbit (use the ViewCube or Alt + MMB) to adjust the view to see under the groin area. In Edge or Vertex mode, move the segments to round that section out, as shown in Figure 6.43.

Figure 6.41

**Select waist edges and use Ring to prepare for Collapse.**

Select the ring of vertical edges.

Round out these edges so they're not so boxy.

Figure 6.42

**Use the right-click Quad menu to access Collapse.**

Figure 6.43

**Round out the edges in the groin area.**

Figure 6.44

**The leg with good edge spacing**

Figure 6.45

**Affect Pivot Only**

4. In the Perspective viewport, use Orbit again around the leg and look for any spikes or pinches that may have occurred in the model. The goal is to split the difference between edges so that they're as close to 50 percent from another edge as possible.

Keep in mind that a joint edge, such as the edges that make up the knee or elbow, need to stay where they are. Figure 6.44 shows the leg with good edge spacing. Take a moment to go back through the model and tweak the rest of it until you feel it is right. When modeling for animation, the mesh flow is an important factor.

## Completing the Main Body

Continue with the previous exercise's scene file, or open the Soldier_V05.max scene file in the Scenes folder of the Soldier project from the companion web page.

To create the other half of the model we are going to use the Mirror tool. The Mirror tool works off your character's current pivot point. We want to mirror on the X-axis, so the gizmo needs to be in the dead center of our to-be-completed character (at the left side of the half model in the Front viewport); you will take care of that in step 1 of the following exercise.

In Chapter 5, when we built the Red Rocket, we used a modifier called Symmetry. This mirror technique gives the same results but in a different way. We will mirror the soldier's body in the following steps:

1. In the Front viewport, select the model. Go to the Command panels to the right of the interface and, under the Hierarchy tab, select Affect Pivot Only (Figure 6.45). If you cannot find the gizmo, click on Center to Object under Alignment in the Command panel. This will pop the gizmo to the center of the model. We want the pivot on the left edge of the model so it's in the center of the torso when it's mirrored. With Affect Pivot Only, use the Move tool to move the gizmos to the left edge of the geometry, as shown in Figure 6.46.

2. Toggle off Affect Pivot Only. Select all the inside vertices and go to the Modeling ribbon → Align → X, this will move all the vertices to line up along the X-axis.

3. In the Main toolbar, click the Mirror button ( ) to bring up the Mirror dialog box. Select Mirror Axis X and Instance under Clone Selection, shown in Figure 6.47. Then click OK.

Figure 6.46

**Move the pivot point to the edge of the geometry.**

Figure 6.47

**Mirror dialog box**

With the mirror set to Instance, we can make some minor changes to the model before we combine the two sides more permanently. For example, in the next step we will move to the neck area where we will extrude out edges on one side, and see the mirrored side do the same on the other side.

4. In Edge mode, select the edges at the top of the right side of the torso geometry as shown in Figure 6.48 (left image) and Shift + Scale them on the *X*- and *Y*-axes to extrude the top of the shoulders toward the neck. With those edges still selected, Shift + Scale again to extrude another set of polygons toward the center neck as shown in Figure 6.48 (middle image). The edges all scale in toward the middle of the shoulder area and not the center of the neck at the spine, so switch to Vertex mode and move the vertices to better match the shape shown in Figure 6.48 (right image).

Figure 6.48

**Drag out the edges around the neck.**

5. Go back to Edge mode and select the same inner neck edges again, and extrude-move them (Shift + Move method) down to create a lip downward into the torso. Release the mouse, and then click again to Shift + Move in toward the center of the model to create a cap at the neck area (as shown in Figure 6.49). You can see the original model half is in X-Ray mode (Alt + X), while the mirrored instanced half mimics what you do to the original part.

Now, go through one last time and fix any edge spacing issues or wonky geometry you may have. It's easier to do it now since your actions will be mirrored to the other side. You can always fix things later, but then you'll just have to do them twice, once for each side of the model. When you're ready we are going to combine and weld the two parts of the model together.

To un-instance the instanced side of the model, select it and go to the Modify panel. In the toolbar under the Modifier Stack, click on the Make Unique icon ( ![icon] ). Now the two instances are two copies and are no longer mirroring each other.

6. Select the right half, and then select Modeling ribbon → Geometry (All) → Attach and select the other side of the model; this will combine both halves.

We are not done, however; the vertices in the center of the model are not welded together yet! They might look like it, but they are indeed separate sets of vertices running down the seam where the two halves attach. We need to keep this model solid to prevent the mesh from tearing apart during animation:

7. Enter the Front viewport and switch to Vertex mode. Marquee a selection box down the center of the torso model to select the vertices along the seam of the two halves. Make sure Ignore Backfacing is off, then select Modeling Ribbon → Align, and click on the X. This will align vertices along the X-axis.

8. With the vertices selected, choose Modeling ribbon → Vertices → Weld → Weld Settings (  ) to open the Weld caddy. Notice that there is a before and after count on the Weld caddy that pops up in the viewport. Increase the Weld Threshold setting until something visibly changes in the viewport, then reduce the value slightly to undo the change. Feel free to go into the Perspective viewport to check this. Weld the vertices together by pressing the OK (check mark) button.

## Creating the Accessories

Continue with the previous exercise's scene file, or open the Soldier_V06.max scene file in the Scenes folder of the Soldier project from the companion web page. Most of the smaller detail in the model will be added through textures; however, it helps tremendously to add detail, such as pouches and elbow and knee pads, into the actual geometry. This creates a better silhouette for your character. These details are further enhanced with textures in Chapter 7, "Materials and Mapping."

1. To create the belt we're going to chamfer and extrude an edge loop that's located closest to the belt line on the model. Select an edge at the belt line, then choose Graphite Modeling Tools Ribbon → Modify Selection → Loop, as shown in Figure 6.50.

2. With the edge loop selected, select Modeling ribbon → Edges → Chamfer → Chamfer Settings with an Edge Chamfer Amount of 1.5, as shown in Figure 6.51.

Figure 6.50

**Select and then Loop the edges at the belt area.**

Select this edge loop.

Figure 6.51

**Chamfer setting for the belt**

3. With the two edges from the chamfer still selected, hold Shift and click Graphite Modeling Tools Ribbon → Polygon Modeling → Polygon icon (□). This will select the polygons associated with the two selected edges. Next, choose Graphite Modeling Tools Ribbon → Polygons → Extrude → Extrude Settings, and make sure you extrude by local normal with a Height of 0.5, as shown in Figure 6.52.

Figure 6.52

**Extrude polygons for the belt.**

4. Next we're going to block out a pouch on the belt. Delete two sections of the belt on the body's left side, as shown in Figure 6.53.

5. Select the four polygons above and below the deleted area (also shown in Figure 6.53). Select Modeling ribbon → Polygons → Extrude → Extrude Settings, set an amount of 0.5, then click + to apply one extrusion, and then press OK for a second extrusion and to exit the caddy. The pouch is now extruded twice for a total extrusion depth of 1, as shown in Figure 6.54

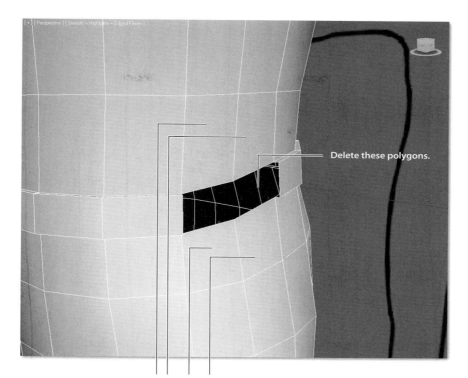

Delete these polygons.

Select these polygons.

Figure 6.53

**Delete the belt polygons on the left side of the belt. Then select the indicated polygons for the next step.**

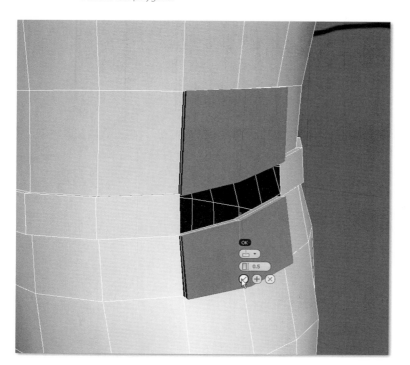

Figure 6.54

**Extruded pouch polygons**

6. Select the four polygons on top of the bottom half of the pouch, and the four polygons on the bottom of the top half of the pouch, as shown in Figure 6.55, and delete them. The figure shows the model in See-Through mode (Alt + X) to see all eight polygons to be selected and deleted.

Figure 6.55

**Select and delete polygons.**

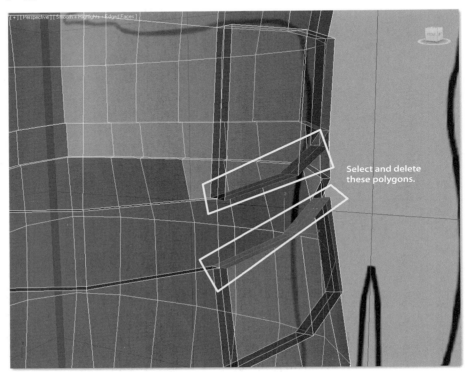

7. In Edge mode, select the top and bottom edges around the newly deleted areas and use Bridge to create polygons in between (Graphite Modeling Tools Ribbon → Edges → Bridge) to close the gap between the two pouch halves.

The pouch should look like a box; if it doesn't, move vertices around so it does. Once the pouch has the correct shape, move the top level of polygons further out away from the belt to give the pouch more depth. It should look something like the model in Figure 6.56.

8. To create some depth to the vest that our character will be wearing, you will want to cut out a level of clothing under the arms. Select two columns and three rows of polygons directly underneath the armpit, as shown in Figure 6.57.

9. Choose Graphite Modeling Tools Ribbon → Polygons → Bevel → Bevel Settings and, in the caddy, use a Height of -0.5 and an Outline of -1.0, as shown in Figure 6.58.

Figure 6.56

**Finished pouch**

Figure 6.57

**Select the polygons directly under the armpit.**

Figure 6.58

**Bevel the selected polygons.**

Adjust any vertices as necessary for an even and smooth look. Do the same for the other side of the model. The final appearance of the area underneath the armpit is seen in Figure 6.59.

10. Next, we're going to add a leg strap to hold a gun holster. Choose Graphite Modeling Tools Ribbon → Edit → SwiftLoop, and add a new horizontal loop of edges below the groin area on both legs. When the loop is created it is crooked, but we need the new edges to be straight. So, after you create the edge, hold Ctrl + Alt and click and drag on the new edge to straighten it. The SwiftLoop tool should still be active, as shown in Figure 6.60.

11. On the right leg, in Edge mode, select one edge of the new edge loop you created in the previous step. Select Modeling ribbon → Modify Selection → Loop, then Graphite Modeling Tools Ribbon → Edges → Chamfer → Chamfer Settings and enter an Edge Chamfer Amount of 1.5 and press OK.

12. Then in Polygon mode, select the loop of new polygons (hold Shift and click on the polygon icon in the Graphite Modeling Tools Ribbon → Polygon Modeling) and select Modeling ribbon → Polygon → Extrude → Extrude Settings, using a Height of 0.4, as shown in Figure 6.61, to pull out the strap.

Figure 6.59

**Final appearance of the area under the arm**

Figure 6.60
**SwiftLoop**

Use SwiftLoop, then
Ctrl + Alt and drag
on the new edge to
straighten out the line.

Figure 6.61
**Extrude polygons.**

Figure 6.62
**Delete polygons.**

13. In Polygon mode, select a strip of polygons that goes from the top of the leg strap to the bottom of the belt, and delete them. This is shown in Figure 6.62.

14. Select the edge at the leg strap and at the belt, and use Bridge to create the polygons needed to fill out the strap, as shown in Figure 6.63. The sides of the holster are still open.

15. Now select the edges between the new bridged polygons and the model's hip, then use Bridge again in this area, as shown in Figure 6.64. Make sure to repeat this on the other side of the holster also.

16. To finish the gun holster, go into the Right viewport and create a plane with these parameters as shown in Figure 6.65—Length: 20, Width: 7, Length Segs: 4, Width Segs: 1.

17. Convert the plane to an Editable Poly. Position the place where the holster will be and in Vertex mode, shape it as shown in Figure 6.66.

18. In the Modify panel → Modifier List, add a Shell modifier to the plane and give it the following parameters (seen in Figure 6.67): Inner Amount: 1.2, Outer Amount: 1.2, Segments: 1. Fit this piece in place on the vertical leg strap you created.

19. Select the body now and select Modeling ribbon → Geometry → Attach and click on the gun holster.

Whew! Now it is time to work a bit on your own. Follow the previous steps to create any additional pouches or straps you may want on your model. We added one more pouch, about half the size of the first one, on the front right side of the model. Keep in mind, any changes you make to the design of the book's model will make your model differ from the one we use for texturing in Chapter 7.

Figure 6.63
**Use Bridge to create polygons to fill out the strap.**

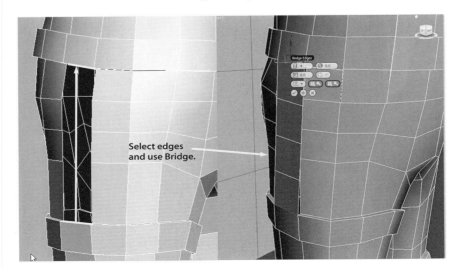

Select edges and use Bridge.

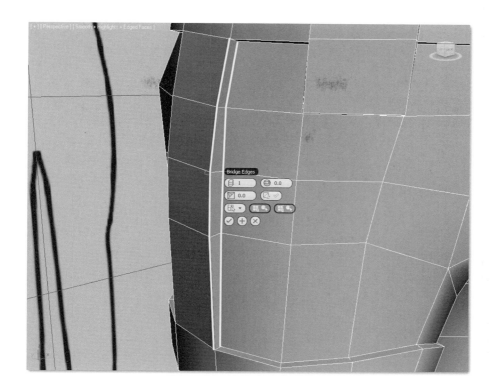

**Figure 6.64**

Use Bridge to fill the gap on the side of the strap.

**Figure 6.65**

Plane parameters for the gun holster

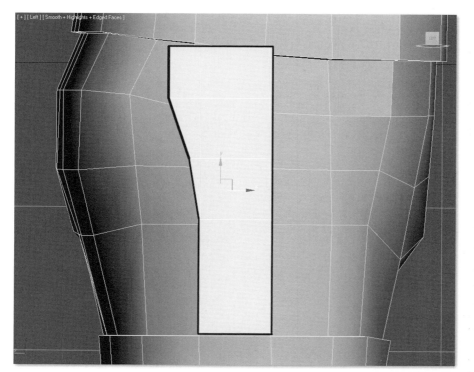

**Figure 6.66**

Shape the plane into a holster shape.

**Figure 6.67**

Shell modifier parameters

Using the tools to create the belt and pouches, you can easily create geometry for knee pads and elbow pads. Refer to the beginning of the "Creating the Accessories" section if you need a refresher on how to do this. You can see the completed body in Figure 6.68.

## Putting On the Boots

Continue with the previous exercise's scene file, or open the Soldier_V07.max scene file in the Scenes folder of the Soldier project from the companion web page. At this point in the tutorial, you are probably feeling more comfortable with the tools and interface. For this next part of the tutorial we are going to be more efficient with the descriptions and directions given unless the procedures are new to this chapter.

Figure 6.69

**Cylinder parameters**

1. To create the boots start by creating a cylinder in the Perspective viewport. Select the Create panel → Geometry → Cylinder. The parameters are shown in Figure 6.69. Select the cylinder and Convert to Poly, then position it under the left leg to be the top part of the boot.

2. Using the Right viewport, move vertices on the cylinder so the shape mimics the form of the boot in the image plane. Delete the topmost and bottommost polygons that were created with the cylinder.

3. Ignore the two bottom front edges of the cylinder where the top of the foot would be, and select the bottom U-shaped edges of the cylinder. Extrude (Shift + Move method) the edges of the back half of the boot top to the bottom of the foot in the image plane, as shown in Figure 6.70.

4.  Select the two bottom-front edges that you ignored previously, and extrude-move them (Shift + Move method) four times to form the extruded polygons to the image plane as shown in Figure 6.71. You will need a total of four rows of polygons for the top of the foot. As you extrude, you can simply release the mouse button after one extrusion, and then Shift + Move again for the next extrusion. Repeat for a total of four new strips of polygons, as shown in Figure 6.71. Form the new polygons as needed to fit the top of the foot.

Using the Extrude Edge (Shift + Move) method

Figure 6.70

**Using Extrude Edge to create another set of polygons for the U-shaped back and side part of the boot**

5.  In Edge mode, select the vertical edges on either side of the gap as shown in Figure 6.72 (left). Then choose Graphite Modeling Tools Ribbon → Edges → Bridge → Bridge Settings and enter three segments and bridge the gap. Repeat the same on the opposite side of the foot.

6.  Then switch to Vertex mode, and choose Graphite Modeling Tools Ribbon → Vertices → Weld to fuse together the vertices, also shown in Figure 6.72 (right).

7.  Select Modeling ribbon → Edit → SwiftLoop, and create a new horizontal edge loop around the foot from heel to toe on the side of the foot, as shown in Figure 6.73.

Figure 6.71

**Using Extrude Edge to create three new polygons that form with the image plane for the top of the foot**

**Figure 6.72**

Use Bridge to fill the gap and Weld to close the gaps.

Select edges; use Bridge with three segments.

Select the vertices and weld them.

**Figure 6.73**

Use SwiftLoop to add a horizontal loop around the boot.

The eight segments we defined on the original boot cylinder are not enough, so we need to create more segments for the cylinder.

8. In Edge mode, select the middle vertical edge of the foot, and use Loop. Then select Modeling ribbon → Edges → Chamfer → Chamfer Settings, and enter the caddy parameters shown in Figure 6.74.

9. Follow the same process to chamfer the very back vertical edge on the boot (running just below the calf) and use the added vertices to round out the heel. The top of the foot is a bit boxy, so scale in the vertices and smooth out the sides as in Figure 6.75.

**ADJUSTING AS YOU GO**

Remember to always adjust vertices to fit the form on the image plane, or use your own artistic license as to what you think looks best. If you do make your own modifications, keep in mind that we will texture this soldier in the next chapter, and the UV layout and painted maps we use may not fit any adjustments you make to your own design of the model.

When you are happy with how this looks, center the pivot to the boot model and mirror it on the *X*-axis as a copy (not an instance). You can then attach the boots to the rest of the body, as you did with the gun holster. The two completed boots, now attached to the body, can be seen in Figure 6.76.

Figure 6.74
**Chamfer the middle edge loop.**

Figure 6.75
**Smooth out the sides of boot.**

Figure 6.76
**Boots completed and attached to the body**

## Creating the Hands

Continue with the previous exercise's scene file, or open the Soldier_V08.max scene file in the Scenes folder of the Soldier project from the companion web page. In this section, we will create simple hands for the soldier. For this model we don't need finger manipulation, so any hand detail will be taken care of in textures. Instead, we're going to create a mitten for the soldier's hand.

Figure 6.77

**Box primitive parameters**

1. To create one of the hands, start with a box. Create a box primitive in the Perspective viewport, and then in the Modify panel, change its parameters, as shown in Figure 6.77. Position the box in your Top viewport over the wrist. Finish positioning it in the Front viewport and convert it to an Editable Poly.

2. In the Top viewport, use SwiftLoop to create two segments vertically and two segments horizontally. Then, in Vertex mode, move the vertices to create a mitten arc as shown in Figure 6.78.

3. With the hand selected, go into Polygon mode and select the polygons on the hand where the wrist and the arm meet, and delete them. Figure 6.79 shows the hollow hand.

4. In Edge mode, select the outer edge loop on the top and bottom of the hand. Then go to Graphite Modeling Tools Ribbon → Edges → Chamfer, with an amount of 0.7 as shown in Figure 6.79.

5. Use SwiftLoop to create an edge up from the wrist, as shown in Figure 6.80.

Figure 6.78

**Reshape vertices to create a mitten shape.**

[ + ] [ Perspective ] [ Smooth + Highlights + Edged Faces ]

Select Edges and Chamfer.

Figure 6.79

**Chamfer the top and bottom edge of the hand.**

Using SwiftLoop to create a new edge.

Figure 6.80

**Use SwiftLoop to create an edge at the wrist.**

6. In Polygon mode, select the three polygons just up from the newly created edge on the side of the hand, where the thumb should be. Select Modeling ribbon → Polygons → Extrude → Extrude Settings and use a Height of 0.8 to start pulling out the thumb. With those polygons still selected, go to the Align icon in the Main toolbar (📂), and click the Y-axis option in the Align orientation (Local) area and click OK. Then move the corner edges in to round out the beginning shape of the thumb (see Figure 6.81).

Figure 6.81

**Begin to shape the thumb.**

7. Now bevel the polygons at the end of the thumb for the knuckle. Select Modeling ribbon → Polygons → Bevel → Bevel Settings, using the values shown in Figure 6.82.

8. Repeat step 7 at the tip of the thumb geometry to create another segment for the thumb from the knuckle to the tip of the thumb, as shown in Figure 6.83. Adjust the polygons, vertices, and edges to get the thumb to look like Figure 6.84.

9. Select the polygon at the ends of the thumb and fingers. Turn on Use Soft Selection—Graphite Modeling Tools Ribbon → Polygon Modeling - Soft Selection icon ( ⊚ )—and in the Front viewport, move down the thumb and fingers to give them a slight slope, as shown in Figure 6.85.

10. In the Perspective viewport, scale the wrist down to fit within the sleeve if necessary. Center the pivot to the model, and mirror it as a copy for the other side. Place the hands at the wrists and attach them to the rest of the model. The final gloved hand is shown in Figure 6.86.

Figure 6.82
**Bevel settings**

Figure 6.83
**Move, rotate, and scale the polygons to shape in the thumb.**

Figure 6.84

**Thumb with all
its joints**

Figure 6.85

**Give the thumb and fingers a slight slope downward.**

Figure 6.86

**Final glove**

## Creating the Head

Continue with the previous exercise's scene file, or open the Soldier_V09.max scene file in the Scenes folder of the Soldier project from the companion web page.

The soldier's head will consist of four parts: a helmet, goggles, a face mask, and a head shape for them to sit on. The easiest way to create and fit these components is to start with the head shape. First, though, we need to adjust the body's neck line so it's a bit better to work with. Right now the neck area is close to a circle shape. We want this to be closer to an oval that follows the contour of the rest of the model.

1. In Polygon mode, select the front of the neck line, turn on Use Soft Selection—Graphite Modeling Tools Ribbon → Polygon Modeling → Use Soft Selection (  ). Then adjust the falloff of the soft selection in the Graphite Modeling Tools Ribbon → Soft tab, and change the Falloff value to 4.0. Now move the polygons down on the *Y*-axis as shown in Figure 6.87. Do the same for the back of the model, as in Figure 6.88. These actions will smoothly create a lower neck line, giving more definition to the shoulders as well.

2. Create a Cylinder with the parameters shown in Figure 6.89. Convert it to an Editable Poly and position the cylinder inside the neck line as shown in Figure 6.90.

3. Once again we will model half of each part and then mirror it to save time. Delete the left half, the top, and the bottom of the cylinder, and move the edges and vertices so it's formed better within the neck line, as shown in Figure 6.91.

Figure 6.89

**Cylinder parameters**

Figure 6.87

**Soft select the polygons at the front of the neck and move them down.**

Figure 6.88

**Repeat on the polygons on the back of the neck.**

4. Now select the top edges of the cylinder and use the Extrude Edge (Shift + Move method) method to create another level of polygons. The neck now has two rows of polygons. Then, select the first edge on top nearest where the Adam's apple would be, and use Extrude Edge (Shift + Move method) to create a new polygon. Move the edge up along the *Z*-axis, as shown in Figure 6.92.

Figure 6.90

**Position the cylinder inside the neck area.**

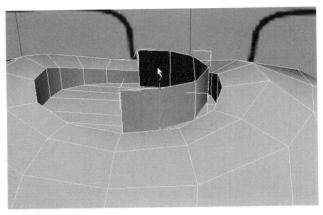

Figure 6.91

**Delete half of the cylinder and its top and bottom.**

— Use Extrude Edge (Shift + Move method)

Figure 6.92

**Begin the creation of the neck with Extrude.**

## Outlining the Head

In the following steps, we will create an outline of the head by creating one strip of polygons and then forming them to the side image plane. We will extrude 15 times total, and move the edges to create the general form of a head. Be sure to keep the outer edge of the head inside the edges of the image plane; this allows room to fit the head accessories.

5.  You should still have the edge selected from the last step. Use Extrude Edge (Shift + Move method) from the previous step, but when you finish one polygon, release the mouse button, then click again and move the edge to create another extruded polygon. You will do this 14 more times, following the form of the head in the image plane, as shown in Figure 6.93.

6.  In the Front viewport, select the edge on the top base of the neck about where the ear might be. Use Extrude Edge (Shift + Move method) and position a polygon strip as we did in Step 5, but this time for the side of the head. Extrude a total of five segments up from the neck. Also in Edge mode, use Bridge (Graphite Modeling Tools Ribbon → Edges → Bridge) to fill the gap between the side of the head and the nearest edge on the top of the head, as shown in Figure 6.94.

Figure 6.93

**Create the head outline using the Shift + Move method, following the image plane.**

Use the Extrude Edge (Shift + Move method). Do this 15 times, following the form of the head in the image plane.

Bridge this gap.

Extrude from here... ...to here.

Figure 6.94
**Creating polygons for the side of the head**

Extrude these.          Weld these.

Figure 6.95
**Extrude edges to the right and weld the neck vertices.**

7. To build out the front of the face, start by selecting the two edges just under the chin and use Extrude Edge (Shift + Move method) to extrude them out to the right, as shown in Figure 6.95. In Vertex mode, select Modeling Graphite Modeling Tools Ribbon → Vertices → Target Weld. To use Target Weld you click on one vertext and drag a line to the other to fuse the vertices together. So first click the vertex on the new polygon closest to the neck, and then click on the neck vertex, shown in Figure 6.95. This will fuse the new polygons for the jowls to the neck.

8. Back in Edge mode, select the two rightmost edges of the polygons we just created for the jowls, then use Extrude Edge (Shift + Move method) to extrude those edges up on the $Z$-axis. Match the number of segments with the segments on the outer head strip we already created. This is shown in Figure 6.96.

9. Select the edges shown on the left side of Figure 6.97. Use Bridge (Graphite Modeling Tools Ribbon → Edges → Bridge) to curve the strip toward the forehead, as shown in Figure 6.97.

Figure 6.96
**Extrude a new strip; match the segments.**

Select these edges and use Bridge.

Figure 6.97
**Use Bridge to close the gap.**

10. As we did in step 9, in Edge mode, use Extrude Edge (Shift + Move method) to extrude another row of polygons in toward the front of the face. Then in Vertex mode, use Target Weld on either side of the front face strip, as shown in 6.98.

11. Looking at the ring of edges from the front of the strip of the head to the side of the head, it's clear we don't have enough horizontal edges. Select the edge closest to where the bridge of the nose would be, then use Chamfer (Graphite Modeling Tools Ribbon → Edges → Chamfer Settings → Chamfer Settings) with an amount of 1.346, then press OK. Try to keep the edges equally spaced, as shown in Figure 6.99.

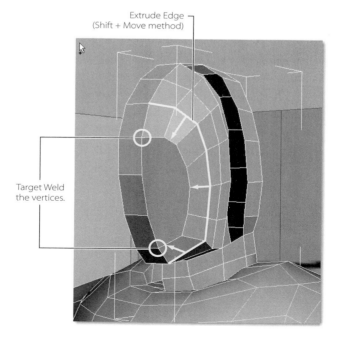

Extrude Edge
(Shift + Move method)

Target Weld
the vertices.

Figure 6.98
**Use Extrude Edge, then Target Weld the vertices.**

Figure 6.99
**Chamfer the edge that falls at the bridge of the nose.**

12. Select the four edges from the front of the face to the side of the face, and then use Bridge, as shown in Figure 6.100. Notice that there is nowhere to weld to on the vertical edge on the top of the head. We need to create another edge running down the front of the face and then weld the vertices together to close the head.

13. Choose Graphite Modeling Tools Ribbon → Edit → Cut to enter the Cut tool. Then cut from the dead end edge at the top of the head down to the bottom of the neck, as shown in Figure 6.101. Make sure you start and end the cut directly on the vertices.

14. Then, in vertex mode, select the two vertices at the top of the cut, go to Graphite Modeling Tools Ribbon → Vertices → Weld and change the Weld Threshold setting until the two vertices are welded together.

Figure 6.100
**Select edges and use Bridge.**

Use the Cut tool.

Figure 6.101
**Cut the new edge.**

## Rounding Out the Face

Take some time to round out the face a bit as shown in Figure 6.102. The face doesn't have to be perfectly round, but it will help if the face is close to a round shape. The majority of the head mesh we will create will be covered with the goggles, helmet, and face mask. However, we can use the geometry we create to fit and form those accessories.

Figure 6.102

**Take some time to round out the face.**

15. In Edge mode, select the edges around the ear and use Bridge (Graphite Modeling Tools Ribbon → Edges → Bridge) as shown in Figure 6.103.

16. Looking at the back of the head, you can see an edge open on the bottom. Use the Cut tool to add another vertical edge, as shown in Figure 6.104.

17. Select the edges on the inside of the gap closest to the back of the head and use Extrude Edge (Shift + Move method) to extrude more faces toward the ears as shown in Figure 6.105. Then switch to Vertex mode and use Target Weld to weld the loose vertices at the top and bottom, also shown in Figure 6.105.

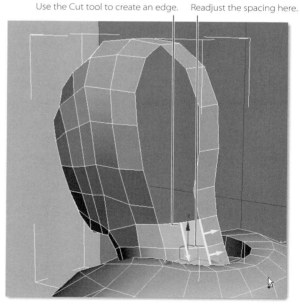

Use the Cut tool to create an edge.    Readjust the spacing here.

Figure 6.103

**Bridge edges.**

Figure 6.104

**Create a new edge for the back of the head/neck using the Cut tool.**

Figure 6.105

**Extrude edges and use Target Weld on the loose vertices.**

Target Weld

### Creating the Back of the Head

We have the same problem with the back of the head as we did with the front of the face. There are not enough horizontal edges.

18. Chamfer a horizontal edge near the top of the back of the head, as shown in Figure 6.106. In Figure 6.106, we can visualize how the polygons will bridge over. In this case, after we create the chamfer, we will have five segments that can bridge in the next step.

19. Bridge the vertical edges of the hole; you can see that completed in Figure 6.107. This time we have the exact amount needed to create a solid head shape.

20. Go into the Right viewport and notice how the edges are closer to the front of the head than the back of the head, as shown in Figure 6.108 (left). Select and move edges or vertices until the vertices are more evenly spaced, as shown in Figure 6.108 (right).

Newly chamfered edges

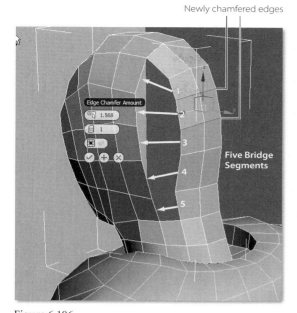

Figure 6.106
**Chamfer edges.**

Figure 6.107
**Bridge the vertical edges to fill the last hole.**

This geometry needs fixing.   Evenly space these.

Figure 6.108
**Move edges or vertices to evenly space the edges.**

**Mirroring the Head**

Now make any necessary adjustments to your mesh to get it just right. Again, it's not terribly vital that this part be perfect because we will cover it up with accessories in the steps ahead. Once you're satisfied continue with the following steps:

21. Adjust the head's pivot to the left edge of the geometry and mirror the half over on the *X*-axis as a copy, as shown in Figure 6.109.

22. Select Modeling ribbon → Geometry → Attach, and then select the other side of the head to attach them together. Now in Vertex mode, select all the vertices in the center vertical seam of the head, and choose Graphite Modeling Tools Ribbon → Vertices → Weld → Weld Settings. Turn the Weld Threshold up a bit to be sure all the vertices are welded when you click OK.

23. Going into the Front viewport we can see our head is a little wide compared to the image plane. Scale it just a bit to fit on the *X*-axis so we have room to put on the helmet. (See Figure 6.110.) Our base head is complete; now we can add the details.

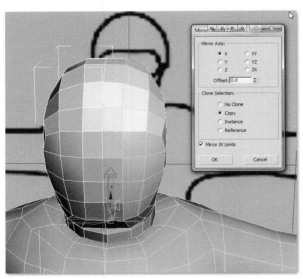

Figure 6.109
**Mirror the head halves.**

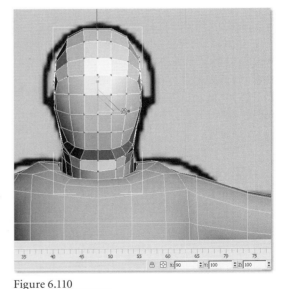

Figure 6.110
**Scale the head on the *X*-axis to make room for the helmet.**

## Merging in and Attaching the Head's Accessories

The remaining accessories for the soldier are the helmet, goggles, and face mask. To create these we would repeat the same methods we have already covered, so we'll cut a little time and merge in the finished pieces.

The finished models for the helmet, goggles, and face mask have been created separately and can be merged into your final model. The process is the same as the one used in Chapter 5 for the Red Rocket project. Keep in mind that if you changed the design of the soldier as you built him in your scene, the accessories for the head may not fit perfectly. If this is the case, you may wish to use the scene file provided.

Continue with the previous exercise's scene file, or open the `Soldier_v10.max` scene file in the Soldier project's scenes folder from the companion web page.

1. Click the Application button → Import → Merge and, from the Merge File dialog box, choose the file `Soldier_Accessories.max` in the Scenes folder of the Soldier project from the web page, then click Open. From the Merge dialog box (see Figure 6.111), select all the objects in the list, and click OK. You might see a warning about materials (see Figure 6.112), so just click Use Scene Material. The object will appear in the scene, lined up with the model.

The next step is that we need all the accessories to be attached to the main body. This means the entire soldier model is a single mesh and is for the purpose of creating the UVW mapping for the model in Chapter 7.

**Figure 6.111**

**Merge dialog box**

2. Select the body and Select Modeling ribbon → Geometry (All) → Attach → Attach from List to open the Attach List dialog box. This makes it easier to attach when you have multiple objects to attach.

3. Because we selected the body when we went into the Attach List dialog box, the window won't show the body as an object that we can select. Select the four objects in the list and click Attach.

**Figure 6.112**

**Warning**

The soldier is complete! Well, at least the model. Now that the head objects are attached to the body, they cannot be selected individually. As a matter of fact, the entire soldier is one object, from the boots to the helmet. You have to select the boots, hands, or any accessories we added to the model by using Element mode from the Modifier Stack. We will see this point in action in the next chapter as we lay out UVs for the soldier.

Go grab a beverage; you've earned it!

## Summary

By now you have had a lot of exposure to, and a lot of experience with, modeling with 3ds Max. You will find that the more you model, the easier the process becomes, and the more detailed and finessed your models will turn out.

This chapter explored and explained several tools used in modeling, organic or otherwise. From a simple box, a torso was formed to match the general shapes shown in the reference images. The arms and legs were extruded and shaped. Using Mirror required you to model only half of the soldier character at a time. The head modeling came next and then you merged in already completed accessories from another scene file to add detail to the model's head.

Although we used a fairly low-polygon count soldier character here, this toolset can be utilized for any type of model.

# CHAPTER 7

# Materials and Mapping

*Applying materials* is the phrase used in 3ds Max to describe applying colors and textures to an object. A material defines an object's look—its color, tactile texture, transparency, luminescence, glow, and so on. *Mapping* is the term used to describe how the textures are wrapped or projected onto the geometry (for example, adding wood grain to a wooden object). After you create your objects, 3ds Max assigns a simple color to them, as you've already seen. This allows them to render and display properly in your viewports.

How you see an object in real life depends on how that object transmits and/or reflects light back to you. Materials in 3ds Max simulate the natural physics of how we see things by regulating how objects reflect and or transmit light. You define a material in 3ds Max by setting values for its parameters or by applying textures or maps. These parameters define the way an object will look when rendered. As you can imagine, much of an object's appearance when rendered also depends on the lighting. Applying materials and lighting go hand in hand. In this chapter and in Chapter 10, "3ds Max Lighting," you will discover that materials and lights work closely together.

Topics in this chapter include the following:

- **Materials**
- **The Material Editor**
- **Mapping a pool ball**
- **Mapping, just a little bit more**
- **Exploring the various map types**
- **Using opacity maps**
- **Mapping the rocket**
- **Mapping the soldier**

# Materials

Materials are useful for making your objects appear more lifelike. If you model a table and want it to look like polished wood, you can define a shiny material in 3ds Max and apply a wooden texture, such as an image file of wood, to the diffuse channel of that material.

> The first half of this chapter shows you the parameters and functions of the materials and the Material Editor. If you want to skip ahead to work on a mapping exercise, go to the "Mapping a Pool Ball" section later in the chapter. Make sure you come back to skim over the hows and whys in the first half of the chapter.

Materials also come in handy when you want to add the appearance of detail to an object without actually modeling it. For instance, if you want a brick wall to look like real brick, but you don't want to model the bricks in the wall, you could use a brick texture. Using a texture would be a time-saving alternative. You can plainly see a brick wall in Figure 7.1.

However, in Figure 7.2, the wall shows the appearance of detail in each line of bricks using a texture map (called *bump mapping*). This texture map renders the appearance of dimension for each brick and the inset grooves between each of them, without the hassle of actually modeling the surface of the wall with that level of precision.

This shortcut is an easy trap to fall into. Using texture maps to accommodate too much detail can make your scene look fake and primitive. Don't depend on textures to do the work for you. A model that is not detailed enough for a close-up shot more than likely will not be saved by a detailed texture map. In the end, the level of detail that is needed boils down to trial and error. You have to see how much texture trickery you can use to keep a model's detailing at bay before the model no longer works in the shot. In the beginning, it's safe to assume you should model and texture as much detail as you can. You can work toward efficiency as you learn more about 3ds Max and CG.

Figure 7.1

**A brick wall**

Figure 7.2

**The same brick wall shown from an angle. The detail in the wall was created with bump mapping.**

Like a model, a texture map needs to be as detailed as the scene calls for. You will want to gauge the detail of your texturing based on the use of the object in the scene. A far-away object won't need to have a massive texture map applied to its material. Textures mapped onto a material often add the final element of realism to a scene, and it takes a lot of experience to determine how detailed to make any textures for mapping. You'll start gaining some of that experience now.

## Material Basics

What makes a material look the way it does? The primary force in a material is its color. However, there are several ways to describe the color of a material. In 3ds Max, three main parameters control the color of a material: ambient color, diffuse color, and specular color.

**Ambient color** is the color of a material when it is exposed to ambient light. This essentially means that an object will appear this color in indirect light or in shadow. Ambient gives you the very base color of the object, upon which you add the diffuse and specular colors.

**Diffuse color** is the color of a material when the object is exposed to direct light. Typically, ambient and diffuse colors are not too far apart. As a default they are locked together in the Material Editor.

**Specular color** is the color of a shiny object's highlight. The specular highlight on an object can be controlled by factors other than its color—for example, its size and shape. The color, however, sets the tone of the object and, in some cases, the degree and look of its shine.

For example, in a new scene, open the Material Editor by choosing Rendering → Material Editor → Compact Material Editor. The spheres you see in the Material Editor are sample slots where you can edit materials.

Each tile, or slot, represents one material that may be assigned to one or more objects in the scene. As you click on each slot, the material's parameters are displayed below. You edit the material through the settings you see in the Material Editor.

Select one of the material slots. Let's change the color of the material. In the Blinn Basic Parameters rollout, click on the gray color swatch next to the Diffuse parameter. This opens the Color Selector dialog box, as shown in Figure 7.3.

Use the sliders on the right to set the red, green, and blue values for the color, or control the color using the Hue, Sat (Saturation), and Value levels.

You can also very easily select the desired color from the gradient on the left by dragging your mouse pointer over the colors until you find one you prefer. It's best to pick the general color you need from the swatch on the left and then tweak the exact color by

**Figure 7.3**

**Color Selector**

using either the RGB or the HSV controls on the right. The Hue of a color represents the actual color itself. Saturation defines how saturated that color is. Value sets how bright the color will be.

Once you have a color you like, click OK. If you want to restart the color, press Reset to zero out any changes. You'll notice that the ambient color has changed as well as the diffuse color. You will see why in the next section, on the Material Editor itself.

In addition, you can add textures to almost any of the parameters for a material. Notice the blank square icon next to the Diffuse color swatch. Click that icon, and you will get the Material/Map Browser, which will be discussed later in the chapter.

## The Material Editor

The Material Editor is the central place in 3ds Max where you do all of your material creation and editing. You create materials to assign to any single object or group of objects in the scene. You can also have different materials assigned to different parts of the same object. In a full scene, it's customary to have many different materials.

In 3ds Max 2011, there are two interfaces to the Material Editor: the Slate Material Editor (or Slate) and the Compact Material Editor.

### Slate Material Editor

The Slate is a dialog box in which materials and maps appear as graphical nodes that you can connect or "wire" together to create material trees. In general, the Slate is more versatile than the Compact Material Editor when designing materials, while the Compact interface is more convenient when applying materials that have already been designed. If you are designing new materials, for example, the Slate is especially powerful since it gives a graphical view into how maps and materials are connected. The Slate (Figure 7.4) also includes search tools to manage scenes that have a large number of materials.

Get to know how the Slate works first, then get to know the types of materials and shaders in 3ds Max. Open the Slate by choosing Rendering → Material Editor → Slate Material Editor or by pressing the hot key M.

The main elements of the Slate are described in the following sections:

#### Material/Map Browser

Running vertically on the left of the Slate is the Material/Map Browser shown in Figure 7.5. The Material/Map Browser interface is a list of materials, maps, and controllers, organized by libraries and groups that you can use in your scene. As shown in Figure 7.5, each library and group has a rollout to expand and contract the list, organizing the various material elements you can create.

Toolbar    Menu bar    Material/Map browser                              Navigator

Figure 7.4

**The Slate Material Editor**

Parameter Editor

Sample slots    Status    Active View    View navigation

## MATERIAL/MAP BROWSER DISPLAY

The Material/Map Browser is not only a part of the Slate, but can also be its own dialog box. Simply click and drag the top of the Material/Map Browser to undock it from the Slate. You can double-click its title bar to dock it. Additionally, the Material/Map Browser displays only materials and maps compatible with the currently active renderer. When using the Default Scanline Renderer for example, only Standard materials and maps are available. When using the mental ray renderer, more material and map options are available.

## MATERIALS

Materials are assigned to objects in the scene and give the geometry renderable qualities, such as color, transparency, and shininess. How you create your materials defines what the scene's objects will look like when lighted and rendered. Different materials have

Figure 7.5

**The Material/Map Browser**

different uses. You can even combine the effects of different materials using a material node called Blend. For example, a Blend material will mix together the results from two different materials for a compound effect, giving you incredible power in creating the surface look of your objects.

The Standard material types are shown in Figure 7.6.

### MAPS

Maps allow you to apply *bitmap* image file textures or *procedural textures* to almost any parameter of a material. Maps create interesting looks by affecting color, transparency, bumpiness, and reflection.

Bitmap images are images and pictures on your computer, such as a JPEG photo, while procedural textures are texture maps created and easily edited within 3ds Max, such as a checker pattern. Maps are shown in Figure 7.7.

### CONTROLLERS

Controllers are nodes that control animation values on any given parameter for a material or map. For instance, if you wish to show an object slowly fade away, you can animate the value for the material's transparency. These nodes make it possible for 3ds Max to have animated parameters and are only shown in the Slate.

### SCENE MATERIALS

The Scene Materials rollout lists the materials (and sometimes maps) that are already being used in the scene (i.e., they have been assigned to an existing object in the scene). By default, it is always updated so it shows the state of the current scene. This is the best place to find and edit the materials in your scene.

### SAMPLE SLOTS

The Sample Slots rollout (Figure 7.8) is a sampling of the materials with which you can work. The Slate's Sample Slots section is a smaller version of the one seen in the Compact Material Editor, which you will see later in this chapter. This is a sort of "scratch pad" area where you can work on materials that are not yet part of the scene.

Figure 7.6

**Standard material types**

Figure 7.7

**Maps**

## Active View

The Active View (shown in Figure 7.9) is where you design materials and lay out material node trees for the materials you want assigned to your scene objects. You construct material trees by double-clicking on a material in the Material/Map Browser section, such as a Standard material. You can also drag a material or map from the Material/Map Browser directly into the Active View.

Figure 7.8

**Sample Slots rollout**

In Figure 7.9, we've created an oak material to assign to a CG surface in the scene. First we created a Standard material. Then we dragged a bitmap node (from the Maps Standard rollout) from the Material/Map Browser directly onto the little dot to the left of the Diffuse Color parameter on that Standard material. We chose the Oak Wood image file from 3ds Max's installed library, giving the material its wood texture and color. This is called making a connection, or *wiring*; the bitmap (picture of the oak wood) is wired to the Diffuse Color parameter. Next we wired a Noise texture node to the Bump parameter to give the material some bumpiness.

Figure 7.9

**The Active View shows a Standard material with maps wired to several parameters.**

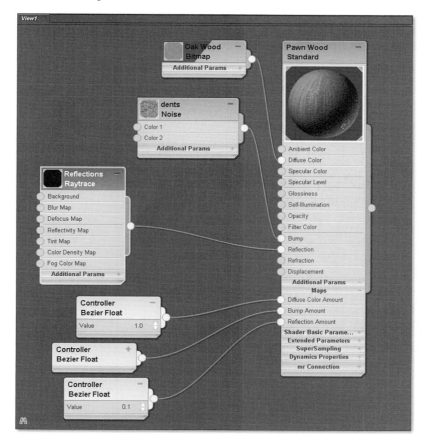

Finally we wired a Raytrace node to the Reflection parameter of the Standard material so 3ds Max would render reflections of the rest of the scene in the surface of this material's object (for instance, a table top). As you can see in Figure 7.9, these nodes show clear connections so you can graphically see how the material works. The three nodes called Controller are created by 3ds Max by default and always appear as soon as you wire any maps to a material's parameters. They are for creating animations of the settings for the maps and are otherwise ignorable.

The node display for the Standard material in Figure 7.9 shows a listing of parameters under the title of the node, such as Ambient Color, Diffuse Color, and Specular Color. Each of these entries is called a *Nodeslot* or simply *slot*. When a map is connected to a parameter, you see a red curved line from the texture's output slot to the material's input slot, turning the slot's dot yellow.

This is merely an introduction to the Slate; we will cover in much more depth how to create and edit materials using the Slate later in the chapter.

Figure 7.10
**Parameter Editor**

The keyboard and mouse controls for navigating the Active View are the same as those for navigating in the viewports. Furthermore, navigation tool icons are located at the bottom-right corner of the Slate. There is also a Navigator window in the Slate similar to the one used in Adobe Photoshop when you have a large number of nodes in the Active View.

You can also have multiple views to organize sets of material trees. Simply right-click by the tab named View1 in the Active View and choose Create New View from the context menu. We will use multiple views later in the chapter.

### Parameter Editor

This is the area where you change the parameter values for your materials and maps. This will be explained further below and is shown in Figure 7.10.

### Toolbar

You will find access to a variety of commands in the Slate's toolbar. Many of these commands can be accessed through the Slate menu bar as well. The toolbar also has a drop-down list on the far right that lets you choose among multiple views.

**Select Tool (  )** Speaks for itself—it selects! The hot key is S.

**Pick Material from Object (  )** An eyedropper cursor is displayed in the viewports when the tool is active. Click on an object in a viewport, and its corresponding material is displayed in the current Active View for editing.

**Assign Material to Selection (  )** Use this button to assign the selected material in the Slate to the object(s) you already have selected in a viewport. Also, you can drag a material's output dot from the Slate to an object directly in a viewport.

**Delete Selected** ( ) This deletes any material or map nodes that you have selected in the Active View and removes them from the Active View. It does not delete them from the scene. You may also press the Delete key.

**Move Children** ( ) When Move Children is on, moving a parent node moves the child nodes along with the parent. This means any materials with wired connections to maps, for example, will move the entire tree when you click and drag the material node, not just the material. This is similar to the animation exercise of the mobile and its hierarchy from Chapter 8, "Introduction to Animation." The default is off and the hot key is Alt+C.

**Hide Unused Nodeslots** ( ) When a node is selected, this icon toggles how many of the slots for that node are displayed. When off, all of the node's parameter slots are visible. When on, any slot that is not wired to another node is hidden. Default is off and the hot key is H.

**Show Standard Map in Viewport** ( ) This will display a material's texture map in the viewport that is set to display Smooth + Highlights, so you can see the map on your model as you work in the scene. This is extremely helpful in positioning and sizing textures, as well as viewing your objects' textures without rendering them. Lighting, however, is not taken into account here, so rendering is still the best way to see exactly how your scene will come out.

**Show Background in Preview** ( ) When you are working with transparent materials, turning on Show Background in Preview will place a multicolored checkered background in the Preview window for that material.

**Layout All flyout** ( ) This flyout icon lets you choose between a vertical or a horizontal layout for the nodes in your view. Hold down the mouse button to access the other icon under the flyout.

**Layout Children** ( ) When you have a complicated material tree, this button automatically lays out all the child nodes for the material in an easy-to-read fashion. The hot key is C.

**Material/Map Browser** ( ) Toggles display of the Material/Map Browser. The default is on and the hot key is O.

**Parameter Editor** ( ) Toggles display of the Parameter Editor. The default is on and the hot key is P.

**Select by Material** ( ) When you have a selected material in the Slate and you click this button, all the objects assigned to that material are selected for you in the viewports.

## Compact Material Editor

The Compact Material Editor is the interface you are ready familiar with if you have used the program before this current version. This is a smaller dialog box than the Slate that gives you quick previews of various materials, without the node display (Figure 7.11.).

You can open the Compact Material Editor by opening the Slate and then in the Slate's menu bar, selecting Modes → Compact Material Editor. You can switch back to the Slate through the same Modes menu.

Figure 7.11

**The Compact Material Editor**

Figure 7.12

**Sample slot number options**

**Sample Slot** The sample slot provides you with a quick preview of your material. Each material is displayed on a sphere in one of the tiles (or slots) in the Material Editor dialog. Right-clicking on any of the materials will give you a few more options, including the ability to change how many sample tiles you can see in the Material Editor (as shown in Figure 7.12). The fewer the samples, the quicker the Material Editor will load.

**Get Material** This button brings up the Material/Map Browser. Here you can browse from the scene or from a Material Library. The Material Library stores a collection of saved materials that you can bring into the current scene. You can use 3ds Max's default materials or create your own and store them in your own custom library.

**Assign Material to Selection** You can use this button to assign the material to the selected object(s) in the scene. You can also apply materials by clicking and dragging the sample sphere from the Material Editor directly onto the object in the viewport; however, this can be less accurate, especially if you have a lot of objects.

**Reset Map/Mtl to Default Settings** This function resets the values for the map or material in the active sample slot.

**Put to Library** You can save your material to a library using this function. Building up a library of useful materials can save time, especially when you're trying to re-create complex materials. Once you've gotten a material just right, there's no reason you shouldn't save it to your library by using this button.

**Material ID Channel** Here you can assign an effect ID to the material. Effects are used in the video post or the Combustion plug-in for things such as glow, highlights, and so on. Some of these effects will be covered in Chapter 11, "3ds Max Rendering."

**Show Standard Map in Viewport** This will display your texture map in the viewport. This means that you won't have to render every time you want to see how your material appears on a 3D object. However, displaying your map in a viewport has limitations. The limitations are basically those of your graphics card and your chosen method of displaying 3D in the viewport (Open GL, Direct3D, or Software). The difference between viewing the map in the viewport and in its final rendered state may be quite different. However, seeing a map in the viewport is useful on many levels.

**Go to Parent** Just as you created objects that related to each other, materials in 3ds Max may have several components to them (such as texture maps) that work in a hierarchy, where information from one node is fed upstream into the parameter for the material. When you are working with sub-maps, this option will take you back to the base material. This makes it easier to navigate in the Material Editor when you are editing your materials.

**Go Forward to Sibling** This option will take you into the next map channel; a lateral move from map to map.

**Preview type** Sometimes the default sphere won't give you an adequate preview of the material. You can change the preview to a cube, a cylinder, or an object.

**Pick Material from Object** When you need to edit a material on an object, you can use this button to select the material from an object in the scene. The material is placed in the active sample slot.

**Material name** This is the name you give a material. This should be a descriptive name for the material that will instantly tell you what the material is for. 3ds Max will automatically give new materials a default name, such as the name 03, but it's recommended that you change the material name from the default. You should do this before you apply it to an object, when you are adjusting the parameters (color, etc.) to suit your needs.

**Material type**  Different materials have different uses. When called on to create a more complex material, for example, you can change the material type to Blend. A Blend material will mix the results from two different materials together for a compound effect. The default material type is Standard. Material types are explained later in this chapter.

**Shader type**  Shader types describe how the surface responds to light. How an object looks depends on how its surface reacts to light, so the shader type for a material is very important. Shaders provide different options for specific materials. The default shader is Blinn. Shader types are covered later in this chapter. Not all material types let you specify different shaders.

**Miscellaneous settings**  These are fairly basic settings used to change the appearance of the material. Here are two important settings.

**Wire**  When you turn Wire on, the object attached to this material will render as a Wireframe object, as shown in Figure 7.13. This simple setting is very powerful; it's used when you need to render line art or wireframe views.

Figure 7.13

**The render as a Wireframe object (Wire on)**

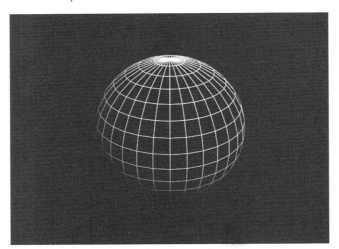

**2-Sided**  This setting enables you to render both sides of a single surface. By default, only one side of a surface will render, and that is typically all you need. Sometimes, however, when you penetrate through a surface, you will have to see the other side. In Figure 7.14, a hemisphere is rendered without 2-Sided turned on. In Figure 7.15, 2-Sided has been enabled. Notice the inside of the hemisphere.

**Locks**  Here you can lock the Ambient parameter to the Diffuse parameter and lock the Diffuse to the Specular. Any changes made to one while the locks are enabled affect both.

Figure 7.14

**The render without 2-Sided enabled**

Figure 7.15

**The render with 2-Sided enabled**

**Ambient, diffuse, and specular color**  Changing the ambient color will affect the way the material appears for ambient light. Changing the diffuse color affects the overall color of the material. Changing the specular color changes the color of the highlighted light. You change the color by clicking on the color swatch next to the parameter.

**Diffuse and specular maps**  These buttons provide shortcuts to the maps for diffuse color and specular color. A map applied to diffuse color (for example: bitmap, which is an image file) will affect the base appearance of the material. A map applied to specular color will use the mapped image to define the location of the shine. Mapping is covered in the Pool Ball exercise later in this chapter, as well as in the rocket that we'll texture.

**Specular level map**  This setting determines how shiny the material appears. For something such as a metallic surface, the setting will be up around 180 to 220. You can also map a grayscale texture to determine which areas will appear shiny and which will appear dull.

**Glossiness level map**  This setting determines the spread of the specular shine. A higher value means that it will look more plastic (high gloss across the surface of the model).

**Self Illumination level map**  This slot creates the illusion of being lit from within. The more self illumination it is given, the less the material is affected by lighting, but the flatter it will appear.

**Opacity level map**  A material's opacity determines how transparent it appears. If it is set to 100 (the default), then the material is 100 percent opaque—that is, it's solid. If it is set to 0, then it is completely invisible. You can apply a grayscale opacity map here that uses a bitmap (or other map) to define which portions of the material are transparent.

Areas of white on the map will be opaque, whereas the black areas will render transparent; the intermediate values of gray will have different levels of transparency.

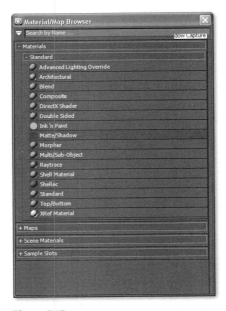

**Maps rollout** Maps allow you to apply bitmap or procedural textures, which help define the material beyond simple color and opacity settings. Common maps include bump maps (use grayscale values to simulate bumps and dents), displacement maps (use grayscale maps to mathematically calculate depth and height and redefine the mesh accordingly), reflections, glossiness, and so on, as shown in Figure 7.16.

## Standard Material Types

Now that you've seen how the Slate and the Compact Material Editor work, let's look at the different materials in 3ds Max. Different materials have different uses. The Standard material is fine for most uses. However, when you require a more complex material, you can change the material type to one that will fit your needs. To change a material type in the Slate, just choose from the list under the Materials rollout. By default, you will see a rollout for Standard. If you switch to a different renderer, for example mental ray, you will have other material type options. For example, using mental ray will give you access to a rollout for mental ray and MetaSL materials, as shown in Figure 7.17. The list is extensive, so we will touch on some of the best for an introduction here. We will also be showing examples using the Slate.

### Standard

Standard material is the default type for the materials in the Material Editor. This material has values for ambient, diffuse, and specular components. With it, you can imitate just about any surface type you can imagine. The more advanced surface types (see the following discussions) combine elements of different shaders for more complex effects (Figure 7.18).

Figure 7.17

**Choose the material type from the Material/Map Browser.**

Figure 7.18
**Standard material**

## Blend

Just as it sounds, this material type blends two materials together. Figure 7.19 shows the parameters for a Blend material type. Notice the controls for mixing two different materials. You assign the materials through the Material 1 and Material 2 parameters.

## Composite

Similar to the Blend, a Composite material combines up to 10 materials, using additive colors, subtractive colors, or opacity mixing (Figure 7.20).

Figure 7.19

**The Blend material type allows you to mix two different materials together.**

## Double Sided

The Double Sided material type divides the material into two sub-materials, one for the outward face (Facing) and one for the inner face (Back). Figure 7.21 shows the parameters for the material.

In Figure 7.22, one material is assigned to the outer face of an object and another one is assigned to the back of the surface. Here, a bowl has a solid blue material mapped to the outside, and the inside face is a checker pattern map.

Figure 7.22

**One material is assigned to the outer face and another material is assigned to the back.**

Neither the facing nor the back material need to have 2-Sided enabled for the Double Sided material to render both sides of the surface.

### Ink 'n Paint

Ink 'n Paint is a powerful Cartoon material that creates outlines and flat cartoon shading for 3D objects based on falloff parameters. Figure 7.23 shows the parameters for an Ink 'n Paint material.

Figure 7.24 shows you a sample render with the Cartoon shading material applied to a bowl and a cone.

Figure 7.23

**The Ink 'n Paint material's parameters**

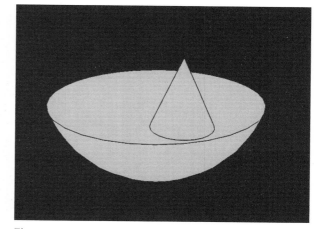

Figure 7.24

**A Cartoon-shaded render using the Ink 'n Paint material**

## Matte/Shadow

Use Matte/Shadow material when you want to isolate the shadow. The material will receive shadows, but it will remain transparent for everything else. It is useful for rendering objects onto a photo or video background because it creates a separate shadow that you can composite on top of the background. Rendering in separate passes, such as a separate shadow, is very useful because you can have total control of the image by compositing just the right amount of any particular pass. The Matte/Shadow material is unavailable when mental ray is active; instead, use the Matte/Shadow/Reflection mental ray material.

## Multi/Sub-Object

Use this material when you need to apply different materials to polygons of a 3D object. Material IDs are assigned either manually or automatically, depending on how you create the material. (This is covered later in the chapter.) Material IDs determine which sub-material is applied to which polygon. This lets you assign different surface treatments to a single object. This keeps modeling simpler because you do not have to make separate objects for everything that needs a different material.

## Raytrace

The Raytrace material is a powerful material that expands the available parameters to give you more control over photo-real renderings. The material uses more system resources than the Standard material at render time, but it can produce more accurate renders—especially when true reflections and refractions are concerned (Figure 7.25).

Figure 7.25

The Raytrace material node gives you true reflections and refractions.

## Shellac

The Shellac material superimposes one material on another using additive composition. This allows you to create a material that is highly glossy, such as a finely varnished wood surface (Figure 7.26).

## Top/Bottom

Top/Bottom divides the material into a top material and bottom material with an adjustable position (Figure 7.27). This material is useful for creating an object that has two different materials on either side, such as a cookie with chocolate on the top.

Figure 7.26

**The Shellac material allows you to super-impose a shiny layer on top of another material.**

Figure 7.27

**The Top/Bottom material type**

## mental ray Material Types

3ds Max comes with several materials that are created for use only with the powerful mental ray renderer. These materials are visible in the Material/Map Browser only when mental ray is the active renderer. In Chapter 11, we will further cover one of the mental ray materials, the Arch & Design material. Brief descriptions of a few mental ray materials are provided here.

### Arch & Design

The mental ray Arch (architectural) & Design material is a material with a refined and high quality feel. Made for architectural renderings, this versatile material provides great glossy surfaces, such as polished floors, ceramics, enamel, and metals This material has special features, including advanced options for reflectivity and refractive transparency (Figure 7.28).

Figure 7.28

**Arch & Design material node and parameters**

## Car Paint

This material simulates the look of a car's surface when it is lighted properly. The material itself has a tremendous number of options and parameters, and is a an advanced material. In addition to the material, there are several lighting considerations to be made when rendering an object with the Car Paint material.

## Subsurface Scattering Fast Material

The Subsurface Scattering (SSS) materials, including the Fast Material, simulates surfaces that absorb and diffuse light, such as wax, skin, or a sponge. These objects take in a certain amount of light and scatter the light through the surface for a definitive look. For example, a leaf that is backlit would use a Subsurface Scattering material. 3ds Max's Subsurface Scattering Fast Material does a good and quick job of rendering such surfaces compared with the other SSS materials. The SSS materials are advanced materials that require quite a bit of rendering and lighting experience.

# Shader Types

The way light reflects from a surface defines that surface to your eye. In 3ds Max, you can control what kind of surface you work with by changing the shader type for a material. In either the Compact Material Editor or the Slate Material Editor, you will find Shader Types as a pull-down menu in a material's Shader Basic Parameters rollout, as shown in Figure 7.29. This option will let you mimic different types of surfaces, such as dull wood or shiny paint or metal. The following descriptions outline the differences in how the shader types react to light.

Figure 7.29

**Shader types define the surface of the material.**

## Anisotropic

Most of the surface types that you will see in this section typically create rounded specular highlights that spread evenly across a surface. By contrast, *anisotropic* surfaces have properties that differ according to direction. This creates a specular highlight that is uneven across the surface, changing according to the direction you specify on the surface. The Anisotropic shader (Figure 7.30) is good for surfaces that are deformed, such as foil wrappers or hair.

Figure 7.30

**The Anisotropic shader**

Figure 7.31 shows the Material Editor for an Anisotropic material. Notice the extra controls for the specular highlights. These allow you to control how the specular highlight will fall across the surface.

Figure 7.31

**The Material Editor for the Anisotropic shader**

### Blinn

This is the default shader in 3ds Max because it is a general-purpose, flexible shader. The Blinn shader (Figure 7.32) creates a smooth surface with some shininess. If you set the specular color to black, however, this shader will not display a specular highlight and will lose its shininess, making it perfect for regular dull surfaces, such as paper or an indoor wall. Figure 7.33 shows the Blinn shader controls in the Material Editor.

Figure 7.32

**The Blinn shader**

Because this is the most-often used shader, let's look at its Material Editor controls. The ambient color, and specular colors all work as you read previously in this chapter. You can set the color you want by clicking the color swatch, or you can map a texture map to any of these parameters by clicking the Map button and choosing the desired map from the Material/Map Browser.

#### SPECULAR HIGHLIGHT CONTROLS

The parameters in the Specular Highlights section of the Blinn Basic Parameters rollout are interesting in this shader. The specular color, which defaults to white, controls the color of the highlight. Decreasing the brightness of that specular color, whatever the color may be, will decrease the brightness of the specular highlight on the object, making it seem less shiny. Changing the specular color to black will negate any surface shine.

The surface shine is also regulated by the Specular Level parameter. The higher the value, the hotter the specular highlight will render on the object. Figure 7.34 shows a sphere with a Blinn with a Specular Level of 0 on the left, 35 in the middle, and 100 on the right.

Figure 7.33

**The Material Editor for the Blinn shader**

The Glossiness parameter controls the diameter of the specular highlight. With the same sphere with a Specular Level of 35, Figure 7.35 shows you a Glossiness of 0 on the left (which creates a broad specular highlight), a Glossiness of 35 in the middle (which creates a fairly tight, shiny specular highlight), and a Glossiness of 75 on the right (which creates a high gloss pinpoint specular highlight). The higher the value, the glossier the surface will appear.

Figure 7.34

**The Specular Level parameter of the Blinn shader controls the amount of highlight on the surface.**

Figure 7.35

**The Glossiness parameter controls the diameter of the specular highlight.**

Finally, the Soften parameter controls the softness of the specular highlight. Figure 7.36 shows a sphere with a Blinn material assigned with a Specular Level value of 55, a Glossiness value of 10, and a Soften value of 0 on the left and 1 (the max) on the right.

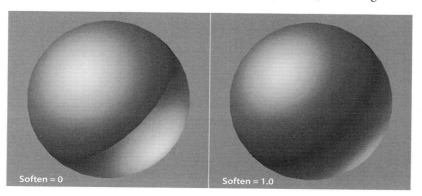

Figure 7.36

**The Soften parameter helps rein in broad specular highlights by softening their edges.**

Soften controls the specular breadth on specular highlights that are already broad—that is, they have lower Glossiness values. You may want to look at these parameters at work in a 3ds Max scene, as your monitor will display the specular highlights better than a printed page.

You've probably noticed the graph (shown in Figure 7.37) in the Material Editor when you work with the Specular Level, Glossiness, and Soften parameters. This graph shows

Figure 7.37

**The Specular Highlights level graph shows the falloff of the specular highlights.**

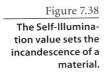

you the falloff of the specular highlight you are editing for the material. The shorter the graph, the lower the level of specular highlight. The rounder the graph, the broader and softer the specular highlight.

For shiny objects, you will need to use a fairly sharp specular highlight. For extremely shiny objects, such as polished metals, a pinpoint specular highlight is best. Plastic objects will work best with a broad, diminished specular highlight. Matte objects, such as paper or cloth, work great without a specular highlight, or at least a very darkly colored one.

### SELF-ILLUMINATION

The Self-Illumination parameter creates the illusion of incandescence on an object, meaning the object seems to be self-lit. The object's darker areas (where it is not receiving direct light) will essentially take on the color specified for the Self-Illumination parameter.

The higher this value, the flatter the object will appear, because Self-Illumination will essentially negate any shadowing or ambient falloff on the material. The specular highlights on the material will still show up on a material with Self-Illumination turned all the way up to 100. You can also change the color of the Self-Illumination by clicking the Color check box and choosing a color in the swatch that appears when Color is enabled. This allows you to have a different self-illumination color than the color of the material itself. Figure 7.38 shows a Self-Illumination value of 0 on the left and a Self-Illumination value of 1.0 on the right. Notice how the sphere flattens out as Self-Illumination helps keep the shadow areas as bright as the diffuse areas.

Figure 7.38

**The Self-Illumination value sets the incandescence of a material.**

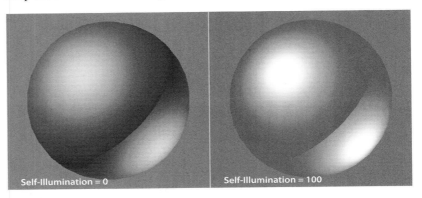

Self-Illumination = 0          Self-Illumination = 100

A Self-Illumination value does not emit a light in the Default Scanline Renderer—that is, the object will not illuminate other objects in the scene. For such an effect, you will need to use more advanced rendering techniques with mental ray, for example.

## OPACITY

The Opacity setting sets the transparency of an object. The higher the Opacity value, the more solid it renders. The lower the Opacity value, the more see-through the object will render.

## Metal

The Metal shader is not too different from the Blinn shader. Metal creates a lustrous metallic effect, with much the same controls as a Blinn shader, but without the controls for specular highlights. When you are first starting, it's best to create most of your material looks with the Blinn shader until you're at a point where Blinn simply cannot do what you need. Figure 7.39 displays a sphere with a Metal shader with a Specular Level of 120 and a Glossiness of 60.

The dark areas of the shader may throw you off at first, but keep in mind that a metallic surface is ideally black when it has no light, meaning there's nothing to reflect. Metals are best seen when they reflect the environment. Given that, this shader requires a lot of reflection work to make the metal look just right.

## Multi-Layer

With some surfaces, you need complex highlights. In some cases, while an Anisotropic shader might be useful, you may need further control in the complexity of your specular shape and falloff. A Multi-Layer shader will stack two Anisotropic highlights together to give you increased control over the highlights you can create.

Here you can see a material with the Multi-Layer shader assigned to a sphere (Figure 7.40).

The two layered specular highlights are created in such a way, as shown in Figure 7.41, to create an "X" formation for the highlights.

## Oren-Nayar-Blinn

The Oren-Nayar-Blinn shader (Figure 7.42) generally creates good matte surfaces such as cloth or clay. The shader has specular highlight controls very similar to those of the Blinn shader.

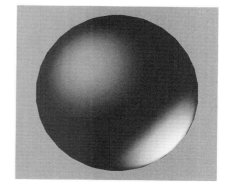

Figure 7.39

**A sphere with a Metal shader**

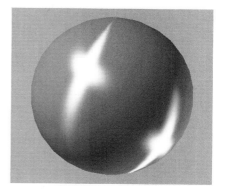

Figure 7.40

**A material with the Multi-Layer shader assigned to a sphere**

Figure 7.41

**The Multi-Layer shader lets you create complex highlights.**

## Phong

The Phong shader (Figure 7.43) is a legacy shader that was created before the introduction of the Blinn shading model. The Phong shader looks very similar to the Blinn shader, and it has the same controls. Phong creates smooth surfaces with some amount of shininess, just as Blinn does. However, Phong does not handle highlights as well as Blinn. This is especially true for glancing highlights, where the edge of a surface catches the light. Phong is good for creating plastic objects, as well as many other surfaces.

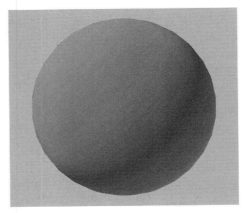

Figure 7.42

**The Oren-Nayar-Blinn shader**

Figure 7.43

**The Phong shader**

## Strauss

The Strauss shader (Figure 7.44) can create metallic and nonmetallic surfaces. Its main controls are Color, Glossiness, Metalness, and Opacity. The specular highlights, for the most part, are governed by the Glossiness setting of the material. The higher the Metalness value, the darker the unlit portions of the surface become, again relying on reflections for the metallic look.

## Translucent Shader

*Translucence* is the degree to which light is scattered as it passes through the material—for example, when a flashlight shines behind a sheet of parchment. The Translucent shader (Figure 7.45) is very similar to the Blinn; however, this shader adds a touch of translucency to the material.

You can also simulate frosted and etched glass by using translucency. Figure 7.46 shows the Translucent Basic Parameters rollout for a Translucent shading material.

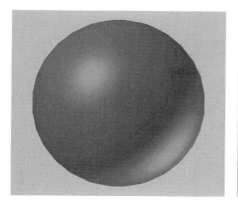

Figure 7.44

**The Strauss shader**

Figure 7.45

**The Translucent shader**

Figure 7.46

**The Translucent shader allows light to scatter through the object.**

# Mapping a Pool Ball

Let's put some of that hard-earned knowledge to work and map an object. You will be creating and texturing a pool ball. Although this may not seem the most exotic thing to texture, you can learn a lot about surfaces, shading, and mapping techniques by texturing it. You'll be able to flex your mapping muscles even more in exercises later in the chapter.

## Starting the Pool Ball

If you have skipped to this section from the beginning of the chapter, have a run through and get a good taste of texturing in 3ds Max. Feel free to look at the earlier parts of the chapter for some of the hows and whys of what you will accomplish in this exercise. Otherwise, roll up your sleeves and follow along with these steps to texture a pool ball.

You can begin with your own project, or you can copy the Pool Ball project you have downloaded from the web page at www.sybex.com/go/intro3dsmax2011. It contains texture image files you'll need for this exercise.

1. In a new scene, create a sphere. The size doesn't matter here. How's that for fast modeling?

2. Open the Material Editor by pressing the hot key M or clicking the Slate Material Editor icon () in the Main toolbar. If the icon isn't visible, click and hold down on the Compact Material Editor icon to bring up a flyout, then choose the Slate Material Editor icon.

3. In the Slate Material Editor, go to the Material/Map Browser, and from the list double-click on the Standard material type. This will add a Standard material node to the View area (Figure 7.47). Then double-click on the material node's title bar to activate the material parameters on the right of the Slate.

Figure 7.47

**Standard material in the Material/Map Browser**

4. The most logical thing to start with is the color. The base color of an object is defined by the Diffuse parameter—although Ambient is also locked to Diffuse, which is fine.

Figure 7.48

**The Diffuse parameter color swatch**

5. Click on the color swatch to the right of the Diffuse parameter to open the Color Selector, as shown in Figure 7.48. Pick any color at this point. Once you have chosen your color, click the Close button, and you will see that the sphere icon at the top of the material node has changed to that color.

## Choosing a Surface Type

The next step is to decide what the surface of your object will be. Will it be shiny or matte? You will need a shiny surface, because real pool balls are glossy. We will have to adjust the specular highlights using the Blinn's controls.

1. Go to Specular Highlights under Blinn Basic Parameters. Set the Specular Level to 98 and the Glossiness to 85. Keep Soften at the default. The specular graph in Figure 7.49 is quite sharp.

2. That is it for the basic material. Now apply the material to the object by dragging from the node's output socket (the dot on the right of the material node, as shown in Figure 7.50) onto the object in the viewport. The sphere will change to the color

Figure 7.49

**Specular Highlights settings for the pool ball**

you chose for the Diffuse parameter, and in the sample slots the corners will become outlined with white triangles.

As a matter of fact, gray corner triangles on a sample slot in the Material Editors mean that the material is applied to an unselected object in the scene. When the corner triangles are solid white, the material is "hot" and its assigned object is currently selected, as shown in Figure 7.51. So you can see the nodes sample slot better, double-click the small slot next to the title bar to enlarge it.

The material in the editor is now the material assigned to the object. If you were to change any of the parameters of the material, it would be instantly updated on the object. Once you assign a material, there's usually no need to return to the object's default color, although you may find yourself replacing the material with another material frequently.

Figure 7.52 shows you what the pool ball should look like, most noticeably its specular highlight. However, viewing in the viewport isn't the same as a rendered image. The viewport gives the lowest level of quality, and it should not be used to make final decisions on the look of your material. Instead, it should be used as a point of reference.

Figure 7.53 shows this pool ball rendered. Rendering (covered in detail in Chapter 11) combines the materials, lights, shadows, and environments within a scene to create the final look. Notice how much more detailed the specular highlight is in the render. To check your render, click the Render icon ( ) in the Main toolbar.

Figure 7.50

**Apply materials by dragging from the material node's output socket to the object.**

Figure 7.51
**Material node**

Figure 7.52
**The pool ball in a viewport**

Figure 7.53

**The pool ball rendered**

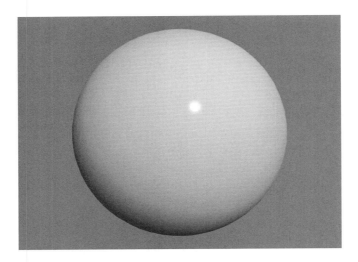

## Placing a Map on the Pool Ball

This simple material is only part of the story. Just creating a sphere and making it shiny and giving it color doesn't make a realistic ball. Pool balls have a graphic stripe or number in a circle. You still need to add the markings of a real pool ball, not just a solid color. Figure 7.54 shows some real pool balls. You can't create the needed detail using the basic parameters of the Standard material. What you need is a bitmap.

Figure 7.54

**Pool balls**

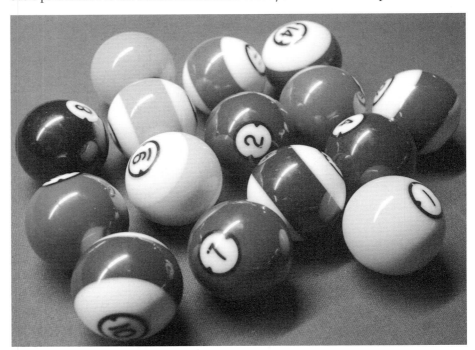

This procedure has to do with texture placement. As you gain more experience, you'll learn how to prepare your texture images for your models. A bitmap replaces the diffuse color with an image. The image you use can be hand drawn and scanned, created in a program such as Adobe Photoshop, or taken with your digital camera. The image we are going to use (Figure 7.55) was created in Photoshop. A white circle with the number 2 is in the middle and one that is cut in half is on either side.

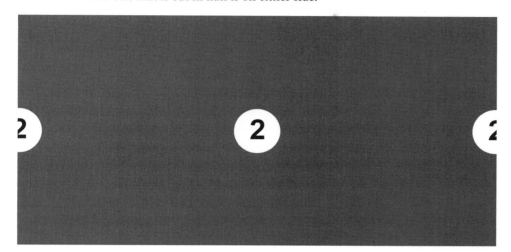

Figure 7.55

**The proposed bitmap texture for the ball**

The theory behind this image is quite simple. Pool balls have the number on opposite sides of the ball. In your texture map, you'll need to make two number 2s on the blue backdrop. The two halves of the white circle and the number 2 will simply tile together when the texture image wraps around the sphere, much like how a wrapper wraps around a piece of candy. This way you have two number 2s on the ball, easy as pie. To apply this bitmap as a texture, follow along here:

Figure 7.56

**Choose Bitmap from the Material/Map Browser.**

1. Go to the Slate and from the Material/Map Browser, click on the Maps → Standard rollout and either double-click or click and drag from Bitmap to the view area (see Figure 7.56). The Select Bitmap Image File dialog box immediately comes up.

2. Navigate to the PoolBallColorTexture.tif file in the SceneAssets\Images folder of the Pool Ball project downloaded from the web page and copied to your hard drive. See Figure 7.57.

Figure 7.57

**Choose** PoolBall-
ColorTexture.tif
**in the Select Bitmap
Image File
dialog box.**

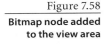

3. Now in the view area you should see a Bitmap node next to the Material node, as shown in Figure 7.58. These nodes still need to be wired together. Drag from the output socket of the Bitmap node to the input socket of the Diffuse Color slot (see Figure 7.59). When you make the connection, another node will be wired along with the bitmap node called a Controller node. A Controller node allows you to adjust or animate a map's values. See Figure 7.60.

Figure 7.58

**Bitmap node added
to the view area**

Figure 7.59

**Linking the Bitmap node to the Standard material node, Diffuse Color**

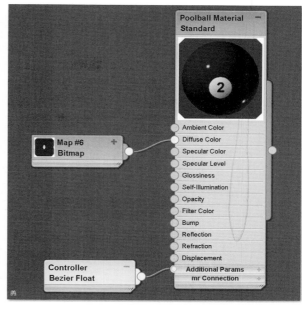

Figure 7.60

**The Controller node is added.**

4. Double-click on the Bitmap node to bring up its parameters. There are several rollouts that we will ignore for now. The most important rollouts in the Bitmap section are Bitmap Parameters and Coordinates. The Bitmap Parameters rollout deals with the actual bitmap image; the Coordinates rollout controls how the bitmap image moves relative to the surface of the object. Leave all the settings at their defaults. See Figure 7.61

> If you ever need to change a bitmap image in a texture already applied, simply go to the bitmap's parameters and under the Bitmap Parameters rollout, click on the bar with the filename to the right of the Bitmap parameter. The file browser will reopen. Choose another image file, and it will replace the current bitmap file.

5. You will be able to see the bitmap in the sample slot, but not in the viewport. To fix this, click the Show Standard Map in Viewport button (▨) on the Slate's toolbar at the top of the Slate's interface below the menus.

6. Now render the ball to check the map's appearance. With your Perspective viewport active, click the Render icon (the teapot). Figure 7.62 shows the pool ball with the mapping.

Figure 7.61

**The Slate shows the parameters for your bitmap image.**

**MAPPING COORDINATES**

When you put a 2D image onto a 3D object, think of it as being "projected" onto the surface, as if you had a white object and a slide projector were projecting a picture onto the white surface. Mapping coordinates describe how the image is projected or wrapped around the surface. Coordinates are spelled out in terms of *U*, *V*, and *W*. *U* is the horizontal dimension, *V* is the vertical dimension, and *W* is the optional depth. All primitives have mapping coordinates, including our sphere. That doesn't necessarily mean the image will wrap itself correctly, although it works fine for our Pool Ball exercise (imagine that!). Merely having the mapping coordinates only means the map will show up. To edit the mapping coordinates, you need to use the Coordinates rollout. You will learn more about mapping coordinates as well as UV unwrapping work later in this chapter.

Figure 7.62

**The ball with the mapped image**

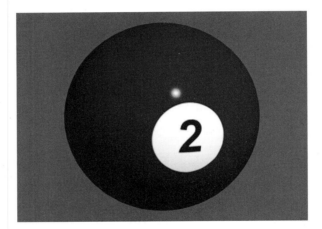

## Adding a Finishing Touch—Reflection Mapping

With the image applied, the pool ball looks pretty good at this point (Figure 7.62)—but it can be better. The small nuances are what really make a render look good. One thing this pool ball is missing is a reflection of its environment. Now, short of creating and texturing a pool table and several other pool balls, we need to make a cheat.

There are two ways to create reflections: the "faking it" method (using mapping) and the raytrace method. Both methods require us to go to the Maps rollout in the Material Editor. We are going to use the cheat and add a bitmap into the Reflection map slot. We are going to use the "faking it" method.

Raytrace is a rendering methodology that traces rays between all the lights in the scene with all the objects and the camera. It can provide true reflections of objects in the scene. Chapter 11 covers raytracing in more depth.

To fake the reflection, you'll need an image that looks like the "room" around the ball. We are going to use a photograph taken for this occasion and saved as the image file ReflectionMap.tif in the SceneAssets\Images folder of the Pool Ball project from the companion web page (Figure 7.63).

**Figure 7.63**

**The reflection map used to "cheat" the reflections on the pool ball**

This image has all the elements that you might see around a pool ball—specifically, more pool balls! To add this image as a reflection for the ball, follow these steps:

1. Go to the Slate and in the Material/Map Browser, drag a bitmap into the view area. Navigate to ReflectionMap.tif in the SceneAssets\Images folder of the Pool Ball project you downloaded to your hard drive, then click the Open button.

2. In the view area drag from the output socket of the Bitmap node to the input socket of the Reflection slot.

3. Do a quick test render with the Render icon (the teapot icon in the Main toolbar). The reflections are pretty strong (Figure 7.64).

4. You need to adjust how much reflection is on the ball. In the view area, go to the Controller Bezier Float node connected to the Reflection Amount parameter, expand the node by clicking on the plus sign next to the title. Change the Value to 0.2 as shown in Figure 7.65. Test-render the pool ball again. You should notice a much nicer level of reflection (Figure 7.66). Voilà! Save the file.

**Figure 7.64**

**The reflections are a bit heavy. If you could reduce the amount of reflection, they'd be better.**

Figure 7.65
**Change Value in the
Controller Bezier
Float to 0.2.**

Figure 7.66
**The reflections look
much better and
add realism to the
pool ball.**

# 3ds Max Gallery

*On the following pages,* you will find a combination of images from the book and images created by a few artists fairly new to 3ds Max, most of whom are students at The Art Institute of California–Los Angeles, where one of the authors teaches. We hope these images will inspire your own creativity as you become more familiar with 3D in general and 3ds Max specifically. On the Internet, you can find a wealth of information about schools and programs such as The Art Institute of California–Los Angeles, where you can continue your education in CG work.

Some of these artists have been using 3ds Max for only a short period of time, and already they've been able to use the tools and techniques they've learned to channel their artistic eye and creativity into some beautiful and interesting imagery.

**ABOVE:** The toy rocket that we modeled in Chapter 5, "Modeling in 3ds Max: Part II," is textured in Chapter 7, "Materials and Mapping." Use this photo to study how the surface of the rocket reflects its environment and how its coloring reacts to light, especially as you light and render the rocket in Chapter 10, "3ds Max Lighting," and Chapter 11, "3ds Max Rendering." **BELOW:** By the end of Chapter 7, your rocket will look like this color image. By applying materials, you set a look for the model that is further refined in the lighting and rendering stages of production.

ABOVE: As you finish with the rocket example in Chapter 11, your rocket will take on a whole new life. Lighting touches and reflections of the rocket's environment will bring your model to life. BELOW: The chess set, used throughout Chapters 10 and 11 to illustrate lighting and rendering topics, is rendered in color for your reference.

**ABOVE:** A color version of Figure 7.170 to help you visualize the UV seams needed for the exercise in Chapter 7. **BELOW:** A color version of Figure 7.171 from Chapter 7. Use this to help you lay out the UVs for the soldier.

**ABOVE:** A color version of Figure 7.178 from Chapter 7 shows in better detail the layout for UVs for the soldier model. These UVs are laid out in such a way as to fit the painting for the soldier's uniform. **BELOW:** This color version of Figure 7.182 shows the color texture map for the soldier from Chapter 7's exercise. Notice how the color map lines up with elements laid out in the UVs.

**ABOVE:** A normal map is used to add extra detail to a low polygon model. Although normal maps are not covered in this book, this map was put on the soldier to increase its detail level when rendering in Chapter 11. The colors of the map direct pixel values in the final detail to add high polygon mesh detail into a low polygon mesh version of that model. This greatly reduces the polygon count without losing much overall detail. **BELOW:** The soldier from Chapter 7 is compared here as a color version of Figure 7.188 to compare using a bump map to the same render without the bump.

**ABOVE:** The final textures for the soldier completed in Chapter 7. This is a higher quality print of Figure 7.190. **BELOW:** These purple spheres were rendered in mental ray with Final Gather and are shown here for comparison. They are color versions of Figures 11.90 (middle) and 11.91 (bottom). Notice there is more bounced light and purple color spill on the floor in the bottom image.

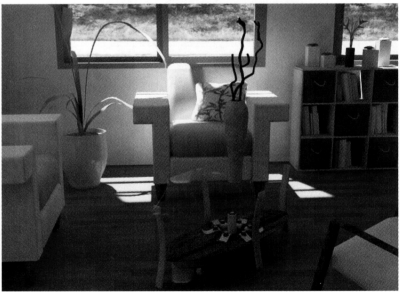

**ABOVE:** Darlene Gauci created this living room scene for her modeling class as an interior design student at The Art Institute of California—Los Angeles. Photometric lighting and mental ray give this image a natural and realistic appearance. **BELOW:** Another angle of Darlene Gauci's living room shows the striking light coming through the window.

**ABOVE:** Federico Esparza's fantasy rifle model is inspired by popular game designs and was created for his Principles of Modeling class. **BELOW:** Federico's tank is featured in Chapter 11's HDRI lighting tutorial. Inspired by a tank game asset used in THQ's popular game *Warhammer 40,000: Dawn of War*, Federico's model was created for one of his modeling classes at The Art Institute.

**ABOVE:** Anthony Gonzales created this Ford Mustang for his Principles of Modeling class at The Art Institute. **BELOW:** This vintage Nash car was modeled as coauthor Randi learned various modeling tools way back in the olden days. Randi dusted off this model recently and rendered it with Final Gather as a sample for her students to design and model their own cars in her class.

**ABOVE:** David Pounce created this AK-47 assault rifle model as an *asset model*, a model used as a prop or set piece in a game, as part of a modeling exercise. **BELOW:** The tank and soldier from Figure 11.133 in Chapter 11 are shown here rendered with an HDRI image.

**ABOVE:** Who wouldn't want to nap in a bedroom like the one modeled, textured, and lighted by Ghazaleh Pourkazemi for his Camera and Lighting Techniques class as an interior design student at The Art Institute? The lighting lends an interesting mood to the warmth of the bedroom. **BELOW:** Ghazaleh Pourkazemi created this morning view of a kitchen, flooding the open space with light to show off the large, well-designed space. Textures help sell the look of his interior design.

**ABOVE:** Ghazaleh Pourkazemi's living room uses clever texture mapping of photos for the fireplace and the outside view through the picture windows of this lake house. **BELOW:** The Daylight System in mental ray adds a very nice early morning look to the Red Rocket from Chapter 11. This is a color version of Figure 11.122 from the chapter.

**ABOVE:** Jesse Doyle, a student of USC Cinema-Television School's Division of Animation and Digital Art created this model as he taught himself 3ds Max before entering school. The organic forms in this "Alien Mech" vehicle model have an interesting and appealing look. **BELOW:** A wireframe view of Jesse Doyle's model gives you an idea of how detailed the mesh needed to be to conform to this design. The vehicle is meant to hover, as witnessed by the slipstreams emanating from the downward thrusters. These images were both rendered with the popular and powerful third-party VRay renderer from Chaos Group.

**ABOVE:** Jesse Doyle created these images of Sony's PSP to further his education in 3ds Max. His goal was to create a fairly accurate representation of the Sony PSP with a single polygonal object using polygonal modeling. Texturing was all done using 3ds Max materials and Adobe Photoshop/Illustrator. **BELOW:** Desiree Herr, a student of interior design at The Art Institute of California—Los Angeles, created this urban loft condo and filled it with golden afternoon light using mental ray rendering.

**ABOVE:** Desiree Herr shows a spartan corner of her urban loft, contrasting some warm light coming through the front door glass, all using Final Gather in mental ray. **BELOW:** Desiree Herr relies on Final Gather light bounce to fill the space in her loft condo design. She created a soft and warm light filling the space using photometric lights in the scene.

If you have lost the view of your pool ball somehow, or if you simply want to center it in the Perspective viewport (or any other viewport), press the Z shortcut to focus the viewport on all the objects in the scene. In this case, it will center the pool ball.

## Background Color

You may notice that the background in the renders in Figures 7.64 and 7.66 is gray, whereas your renders' backgrounds are (probably) black. There are many reasons why you would want to control the background color, which you can do with a simple setting change. You may want a specific color to offset your scene (for example, blue to represent the sky) or you may want a picture in your background.

To change the background of your renders, go to the Main Menu bar and choose Rendering → Environment. The Background parameter is at the top of the dialog box (Figure 7.67). Click on the color swatch and choose your color. That's it!

To add an image to the background, click on the bar marked None to add a bitmap, just as you did with the bitmaps on the pool ball. Once you do, the image will render in the background with your scene. To change the image, click that bar (which at that point should list the path and filename of the current image) to go to the Material/Map Browser, where you can select a new bitmap and image.

Figure 7.67

**The Environment and Effects dialog lets you change the background color.**

## Mapping, Just a Little Bit More

Now that you know how to add maps to a material, removing them is very simple. In the Compact Material Editor for the parent material's parameters (not the map's parameters), right-click on the map name and select Clear from the context menu, as shown in Figure 7.68.

If you don't want to clear the map entirely, but just need to turn it off for a little while, you can just uncheck the box to the left of the parameter name, as shown in Figure 7.69. Check it again to use that map again.

In the Slate, selecting a map's node and pressing Delete on your keyboard will disconnect the map from the material, but will also delete the map node itself along with its

Controller node. If you wish to temporarily disconnect a node, simply click on the connecting wire between the nodes to select it, and then press Delete. This will delete the connection, but keep the nodes intact though disconnected. You can simply rewire the connection between the nodes as needed.

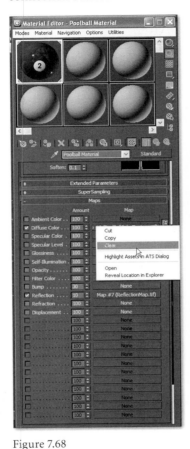

Figure 7.68

**Removing a map from a parameter**

Figure 7.69

**Unchecking the box next to a mapped parameter will temporarily remove the map from the parameter.**

## Seeing More Sample Slots

In the Compact Material Editor, if you have a scene with several materials, and you need to see more sample slots than the default in the Material Editor, simply right-click on any slot and select either 5 × 3 Sample Windows or 6 × 4 Sample Windows from the context menu. See Figure 7.70. This will help you navigate a heavy scene that has tons of materials that you need to modify. In the following figures, you can see the sample slots multiply!

Figure 7.70

**To show more sample slots in the Compact Material Editor, use the right-click menu and choose either 3 × 2, 5 × 3, or 6 × 4 rows.**

Figure 7.71

**Magnify gives you a larger view of your material.**

As you've seen, the sample slots for any given material in the Material Editor constantly update to show you any changes you've made to that material. However, if you want a larger image than the relatively small sample slot, double-click on the slot or right-click on the slot and select Magnify from the context menu. A larger window (Figure 7.71) opens (which is resized by dragging the corners of the window) with a sample of that material. By default it will update automatically as you make changes to the material.

You've already noticed that there are at most only 24 sample slots in the Compact Material Editor when you expand to 6 × 4 Sample Windows as in Figure 7.70. This does not limit to 24 the number of materials you can use. You should consider both Material Editors as a scratchpad of sorts. You can create as many materials as you'd like in a 3ds Max scene; however, only 24 can be loaded in the Material Editors at the same time.

If you click the Get Material button in the Compact Material Editor, you can list all the materials that are used in the scene. When the Material/Map Browser is open, click to expand the Scene Material rollout for the Browse From parameter, and all of the materials assigned in the scene will be listed. When an object's material is not shown in a sample slot, it does not mean it has been deleted. You can load it back into any sample slot for editing at any time.

Figure 7.72

**The Sample Slots rollout in the Slate Material Editor**

Figure 7.73

**Applying materials to a mesh's sub-object polygons is easy.**

For the Slate, in the Material/Map Browser you can see the Sample Slots rollout. All 24 slots are visible, as shown in Figure 7.72. This also applies to the Compact Material Editor.

## Assigning Materials to Sub-Objects

You've seen several times how to assign a material to an object. You can, for instance, drag from the output socket of the material node in the Slate to the object in a viewport or, if you are using the Compact Material Editor, you can drag the sample slot with the material you created onto the object in your scene. You can also select an object in the viewport, and then select a Sample Slot material and click the Assign Material to Selection button (⬛) in the both Compact and Slate Material Editors.

You may want to assign materials to sub-object polygons as well as whole objects. One approach is to use the Multi/Sub-Object material type briefly discussed earlier in the chapter.

Figure 7.74

**The Material/Map Browser has many different maps.**

There is a much easier way to assign materials to sub-objects, however. Just select the appropriate polygons on the surface (the object must be an Editable Poly or have an Edit Poly modifier applied), and assign the material as you regularly would (using the Assign Material to Selection button or dragging the material or the wire from the output of the material node to the selected polygons in the viewport). A sphere with several polygons assigned to different materials is shown in Figure 7.73.

Once you apply a material to a sub-object, a new Multi/Sub-Object material is created in the scene automatically. You can load the new Multi/Sub-Object material by using the eyedropper to click on the object in the viewport to load the material into a sample slot.

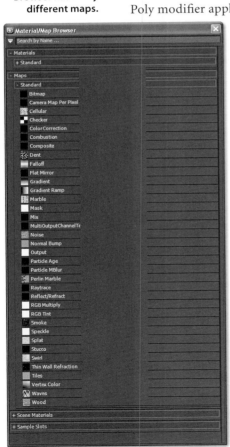

## Exploring the Various Map Types

By now you've noticed that the Material/Map Browser has different maps you can access (as shown in Figure 7.74). The most popular map types are described here.

### 2D Maps

2D maps are two-dimensional images that are typically mapped onto the surface of geometric objects or used as environment maps to create a background for the scene. The simplest 2D maps are bitmaps; other kinds of 2D maps are generated procedurally.

*Procedural maps* are generated entirely within 3ds Max and rely on a set of parameters you set for their look. Images brought in the way the pool ball's color and reflection maps were brought in are not procedural maps. They are *bitmaps*—that is, raster image files. For more on raster image files, see Chapter 1, "Basic Concepts."

Click on the Standard Maps category in the Material/Map Browser to see the available 2D maps.

## Bitmap

As you've already seen, a *bitmap* is an image file that you load into 3ds Max. It can be a photo, a scan, or any image that is readable by 3ds Max.

## Checker

A procedural map, the checker map is a checkerboard pattern that is generated in 3ds Max. Its parameters in the Slate (shown in Figure 7.75) control the look of the checkerboard.

Figure 7.75

**The checkerboard pattern**

The Tiling values under the Coordinates rollout determine the number of checkers. The higher the number, the more checkers. The two color swatches, of course, control the two colors of the checkerboard; black and white are defaults. You can either click the color swatch to change the color, or you can click the Map bars (labeled *None* until you assign a map) next to each color. The Blur parameter allows you to blur the edges of the checkers, and the Soften parameter under the Checker Parameters rollout blurs the checkers together.

## Gradient

A *gradient is* a procedural map (the parameters are shown in Figure 7.76) that grades from one color to a second color to a third color.

In the Coordinates rollout, the parameters are much the same as they are for the checker map. These coordinates are pretty much the same for all procedural maps, as they allow you to position the map as you need on the object by setting the options such as Tiling and Offset.

Figure 7.76

**The gradient map**

The colors for the gradient are set by Color #1, Color #2, and Color #3. You can also map these colors. The Color 2 Position parameter sets the *relative* location of the middle color to the upper and lower colors—i.e., 0.5 is the middle because the other colors are at 0 and 1.0.

Notice the material preview that used to be a sphere is a cylinder. You can change the object type from the right-click menu. Right-click on the material node, go to Preview Object Type, and choose Cylinder (Figure 7.77).

### Gradient Ramp

Similar to the Gradient map, but much more powerful, the Gradient Ramp is a procedural map that allows you to grade from and to any number of shades. Gradient Ramps are perfect for creating maps that fall off (for example, for opacity effects where the opacity fades away). See Figure 7.78.

Use the sliders along the ramp in the Gradient Ramp Parameters rollout to set the position of the gray value. Click in the ramp to create a new slider at that grayscale value. The black and white sliders at the very ends do not move. To delete a slider, right-click on it, and choose Delete from the context menu that appears. Notice the value and position readout above the ramp. As you can see in the view area, the more colors added to the ramp, the more controllers added to the Gradient Ramp node. It gets pretty messy! If you want only the children to the Gradient Ramp hidden, right-click on the node and from the menu choose Hide Child Tree (Figure 7.79).

Figure 7.78

**The Gradient Ramp node**

You don't necessarily need the controller showing because you can edit the color through the material's Parameters menu. When you finish designing the material, you may want to hide all the materials children, so right-click in the view area, choose Hide Children from the menu, and the material node's children will be hidden.

## 3D Maps

Similar to 2D maps, which are generated in two dimensions, 3D maps are patterns generated procedurally in all three dimensions. For example, Marble has a grain that goes through the assigned geometry in *X, Y,* and *Z.* If you cut away part of an object with Marble assigned as its texture, the grain in the cutaway portion matches the grain on the object's exterior.

When you create a 3D map, notice that the Coordinates rollout has Tiling and Offset parameters in three axes, whereas the 2D maps have only *U* and *V.*

Try using some of the 3D maps (such as Marble, Noise, and Wood) to see how they work on a simple object in your scene. They all have basically the same Coordinates rollout; however, each has its own Parameters rollout to control the color and other settings.

## Marble

A Marble map creates veins of colors that run through an object. The 3D aspect of the map allows it to spread across all three dimensions, creating a more realistic texture. Color #1 and Color #2 control the two colors of a Marble map, while the third color is a grainy blend of the two together, as shown in Figure 7.80.

Figure 7.79

**The right-click menu for the Gradient Ramp node**

Figure 7.80

**The Marble map**

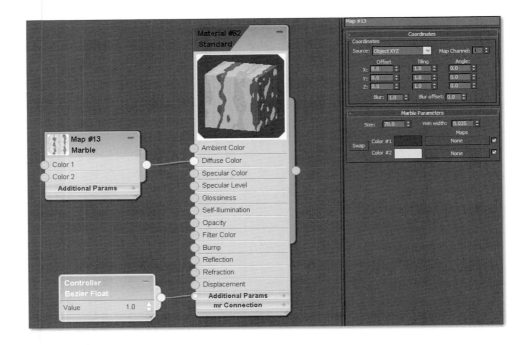

## Noise

Noise is a great way to easily add some randomness to a parameter or to add a bit of randomness to a surface's color or specular highlight, for example. See Figure 7.81.

Figure 7.81

**The Noise map**

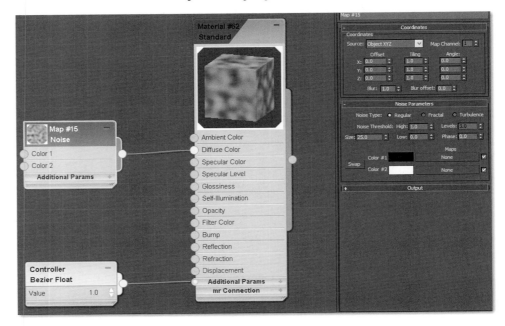

Used sparingly, noise can add great detail to highlights for any shiny object when mapped to the specular color. In this case, just make sure the colors in the noise do not contrast too much against each other, which would make the map faint.

### Wood

Wood is a quick way to add wood grain to a material. See Figure 7.82.

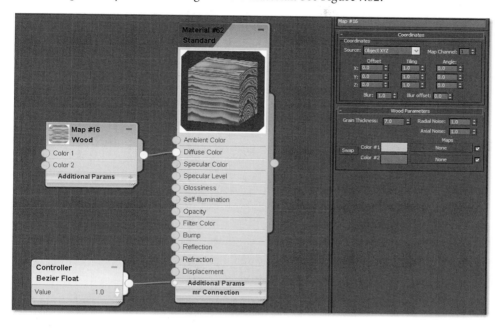

**Figure 7.82**

**The Wood effect**

Just like with the Marble map, you can set the color of the wood grain with Color #1 and Color #2. Adding Radial Noise and Axial Noise values will make the wood appear to have more burls.

### Compositor and Color Modifier Maps

In image processing, *compositing images* refers to superimposing two or more images to combine them in a variety of ways. In CG, compositors are meant specifically for compositing colors or maps together for some advanced effects. Color Modifier maps alter the color of pixels in a material for some advanced effects. Color modifiers and compositor maps will not be covered in this book.

## Using Opacity Maps

Opacity mapping allows you to cut out parts of an object by making those parts invisible. You can also create wonderful fading effects using opacity maps. With opacity mapping, you don't have to model certain details, which can be a real time saver. In this example, you will create a chain-link fence. However, you will not model a fence. You will create it entirely from mapping. To make a chain-link fence, follow these steps:

1. Open the Chain Link Opacity Map.max file in the Texture Scene Files folder from the companion web page. Open the Slate and from the Material/Map Browser double-click on the Standard material to add it to the view area. First you are going to add a bitmap to the diffuse color, so from the Maps → Standard rollout, double-click Bitmap and navigate to the Texture Scene Files folder from the web page. Choose Chain Link.tif (shown in Figure 7.83). This will add the Chain Link.tif bitmap node to the View Area. To link the node to the material, drag from the Bitmap output socket to the Diffuse Color input socket.

Figure 7.83

**Chain Link texture map**

2. To make the Bitmap parameters show up, double-click on the Bitmap node. Go to the Coordinates rollout and change both the U and V Tiling parameters to 3.0. This will scale down the image across the surface of the object, because the image repeats three times.

3. Apply the material to the Plane geometry in the scene. Click the Show Standard Map in Viewport button. Render, and you will see something similar to Figure 7.84. As you can see, the chain-link image appears on the plane, but you can't see the objects on the other side.

Figure 7.84

**The chain-link fence is rendered.**

4. Back in the Material/Map Browser, drag a bitmap to the Opacity input socket. This automatically links the nodes and brings up the Select Image Map File dialog box. Navigate to the Texture Scene Files folder downloaded from the web page and select Chain LinkOP.tif (Figure 7.85).

5. The Tiling values for the Opacity Map must be the same as for the Diffuse Map; otherwise, the transparency of the fence will not line up with the links of the fence. Double-click the opacity map node, then go to the Coordinates rollout and change both the U and V Tiling to 3.0. Render to see the results shown in Figure 7.86. Save the file.

Figure 7.85

**Chain Link opacity map**

You can see immediately how useful opacity mapping can be. 3ds Max uses the white portions of the image map to display full opacity, whereas the black areas become transparent. If you did not have an opacity file such as the one in this exercise, you could easily create one by painting a black-and-white matte of the color image that you are using for the material.

Figure 7.86

**The render when both the U and V Tiling are set to 3.0**

## Mapping the Rocket

Earlier in this chapter, you turned a boring sphere into an exciting pool ball using Diffuse Color and Reflection maps. Now let's dive into mapping the rocket we modeled in Chapter 5, "Modeling in 3ds Max: Part II," to get it ready for lighting and rendering in Chapters 10 and 11, respectively.

To give you a rounded experience and a basis for comparison, we will use the Compact Material Editor for the following exercise, in which we create materials and map the Red Rocket model. We will then use the Slate at the end of this chapter, when we map the soldier from Chapter 6, "Character Poly Modeling."

Study the full-color image of the rocket shown in Figure 7.87. (It's also shown in the color section of this book.) That will give you an idea of how the rocket is to be textured. Let's begin with the wheels.

Figure 7.87

**Let's texture the rocket!**

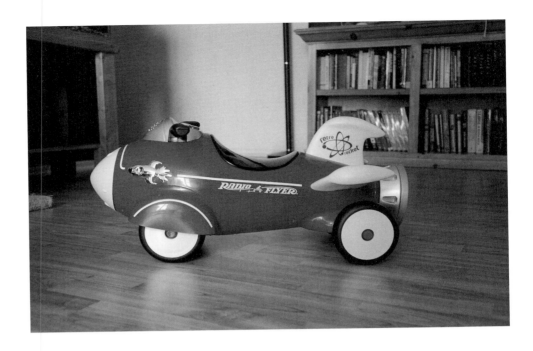

## The Wheels

The wheels of the real toy rocket are made of plastic that is fairly smooth, shiny, and reflective. The black tires are different from the wheels: they have a rough, bumpy surface (Figure 7.88). The bumpiness breaks up the shininess, similar to what happens when you throw a handful of sand into a pool of water. The surface is still shiny and reflective but is distorted by the bumpiness, giving an appearance of a slightly matte finish.

The black part of the tire has a slight bumpiness, which changes the shininess, making the surface appear more matte.

Figure 7.88

**The tire is a rough black plastic.**

Just a simple ——— shiny white plastic

A simple shiny ——— red plastic

Since the tire was created from a single primitive and then modified, we don't have separate objects to which to apply materials. One option is to break apart the object so it has distinct areas (distinct objects), but this method adds an extra complication because we have to manage more objects. To avoid this, we are going to use a texturing technique using Multi/Sub-Object (MSO) materials. This material was explained earlier in the chapter; now let's put it into practice.

## Selecting Polygons and Named Selection Sets

With a Multi/Sub-Object material, you select the polygons on the objects you want to assign a particular type of material, as opposed to selecting the entire object. The hardest part of creating an MSO material is selecting those polygons. However, there are a few things that will make selecting at the sub-object level easier.

Selecting by region (see the "Selection Tool Icons" section of Chapter 3, "The 3ds Max Interface") allows you to use the mouse to select one or more objects by defining an outline or area, instead of simply clicking them. There are five different types of regions from which to choose; the default is a rectangle region. For this task, your best bet is probably to use the Lasso region selection (which works just like the Lasso tool in Adobe Photoshop) to select the polygons around the wheel that demarcate the tire portion of the wheel.

Start by opening your final rocket model from your work in Chapter 5, or open the ROCKET_MATERIAL_WHEEL_START.max file from the Scenes folder of the Red Rocket project downloaded from the web page. This file has the rest of the rocket hidden using the Layer Manager. To unhide the other parts of the rocket, use the Layer Manager. Keep the other parts hidden for now, though.

1. Press F4 so you can see the edges on the shaded model. Press F2 so that when you select the polygons, they will be shaded and easier to see.

2. Select the wheel and go to the Polygon Modeling tab of the Graphite Modeling Tools. If the Graphite Modeling Tools don't show up, click on the Modify tab. Select Polygon to enter Polygon Selection mode (you can also press 4 for Polygon mode).

3. Click the Select Region flyout (Figure 7.89) and select the Lasso Selection Region icon from the flyout. (Feel free to try the other region selection methods, too). Using the Lasso tool, click and drag in the viewport around the polygons you want to select to define a lasso region.

> Holding down the Ctrl key lets you add polygons to your selection, and holding down the Alt key lets you remove polygons from your selection.

4. Click the Select Object tool in the Main toolbar. Then select the polygons that make up the tire portion of the wheel, as shown in Figure 7.90.

Figure 7.89

**The Select Region flyout**

Figure 7.90

**The wheel is composed of three distinct sections.**

Select these polygons
for the tire part of the wheel.

Select these for the
middle part of the wheel.

Select these for the
white part of the wheel.

Be careful to use the Select Object tool, not the Select and Move tool. You do not want to accidentally move any of the polygons while you are trying to select them.

5. Another method to try in selecting the polygons for the black (tire) part of the wheel is to use Edge mode. Arc rotate so you are viewing the back side of the wheel. Go to Edge mode, and select a single edge on the perimeter of the wheel (Figure 7.91).

6. In the Modify Selection tab. click Loop, which will select all the edges that are touching head to toe. Then click Grow four times. Hold down the Ctrl key and click the Polygon mode.

7. Once you have selected all the tire polygons on the wheel object, as shown in Figure 7.92, save the selection as a selection set.

Figure 7.91

**Select a single edge on the perimeter of the wheel.**

Single edge
selection

Figure 7.92

**Select all the tire polygons.**

Figure 7.93

**Named Selection Sets field**

Figure 7.94

**Using named selection sets**

8. With the polygons selected, enter the name **Wheel_Black** in the Named Selection Sets field and press Enter (Figure 7.93).

From here on, you can select all those polygons quickly by selecting them from the Named Selection Sets pull-down menu shown in Figure 7.94.

9. Once you have saved the selection set, select the white portion of the wheel, as shown in Figure 7.95 as well as in Figure 7.90. Save a named selection set called **Wheel_White**.

Figure 7.95

**Select the white part of the wheel.**

10. Finally, select the middle part of the wheel (the bolt) as called out in Figure 7.90 and shown in Figure 7.96, and create a named selection set called **Wheel_Bolt**.

Figure 7.96

**Select the middle part of the wheel, the bolt.**

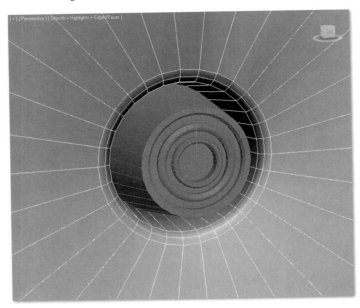

### Creating a Multi/Sub-Object Material

Now that you have made your selections for the wheel, you will create the Multi/Sub-Object material for the wheel, consisting of three distinct parts: black tire, white hubcap, and red bolt.

1. Open the Compact Material Editor and select a sample sphere. We will start with the Red material for the bolt. Name the material **Red Bolt,** as shown in Figure 7.97.

2. In the Blinn Basic Parameters rollout, select the color box next to Diffuse that controls the base color of an object; the Color Selector will open. Create a red color with the values of Red: 200, Green: 0, Blue: 0, as shown in Figure 7.98. Click Ok.

Figure 7.97

**Name the material Red Bolt.**

Figure 7.98

**Create a red color.**

3. Change the specular highlights to make the surface appear shiny. Set the Specular Level, which controls the intensity of the highlight, to 90 and set the Glossiness, which controls the size of the highlight, to 80.

4. Select another sample sphere and set its name to **Wheel White**. Change the Diffuse Color to White. Set Specular Level to 90 and Glossiness to 80, as with the Red material.

5. Select a third sample sphere in the Material Editor and name it **Wheel Black**. Change the diffuse color to black. Because the highlights on the tire will be different, set the Specular Level to 50 and Glossiness to 20.

6. Make sure you are in Polygon mode. If the wheel bolt isn't already selected, go to the Named Selections Set drop-down list and select Wheel_Bolt. This will select all the polygons you selected for the bolt part of the wheel.

7. Press F2 so that the selected polygons are no longer shaded full red and you can just see the edges around the poly colored red, instead. This makes it easier to see the applied material in the viewport.

8. Go to the Material Editor, select the Red Bolt material, and drag it to the selected polygons to assign it to those polygons.

9. Go to the Named Selection Sets list and choose Wheel_White, and then go to the Material Editor and grab the Wheel White material and drag it to the selected polygons, assigning the material.

10. In the Named Selection Sets list, choose Wheel_Black to select those polygons. Drag the Wheel Black material from the Material Editor to the selected polygons.

11. Your wheel now has three distinct materials applied to its appropriate parts. Save your work!

Although there are different ways to create a Multi/Sub-Object material, this method of creating an MSO material is perhaps the most straightforward and the easiest to implement in this scenario.

### Loading the MSO Material into the Material Editor

Congratulations! You have created a Multi/Sub-Object material, even though it may not appear that way. What you did was create three separate materials and apply them to sub-objects on the Wheel object. What 3ds Max did was work behind the scenes to create the MSO material. How mysterious! The three materials you see in the Material Editor are now just instances of the main or *parent material* called the Multi Sub-Object material. We will load this material into the ME so you can see it in the following steps.

1. Exit Polygon mode by clicking on the polygon icon in the Graphite Modeling Ribbon. Open the Compact Material Editor, and select a sample sphere that isn't being used.

2. Next to the material title is an eyedropper icon (  ). Click the eyedropper, and then click on the wheel. The MSO material should be loaded into the Compact Material Editor, as shown here.

3. The Compact Material Editor parameters for the wheel's MSO material are shown in Figure 7.99. Change the name of the MSO material to **Wheel**.

Figure 7.99

**The Multi/Sub-Object material for the wheel**

Materials originally applied to the wheel that are instanced to the Multi/Sub-Object material

Multi/Sub-Object material

Allows you to add more materials

This is the material that is there by default and can be removed using the Set Number button.

The originally created materials

The names are the same as those of the originally created materials.

### Fine-Tuning the Materials

Continue with your own scene file. Select the Perspective viewport and press F9 for a Render Last of the wheel (F9 is the shortcut key for a Render Last). Keep in mind that the rest of the rocket is hidden and accessible through the Layer Manager.

The rendered result (shown in Figure 7.100) looks a bit flat. Specular highlights help make a 3D object look real, but highlights don't show up on flat surfaces.

For example, in Figure 7.101, you can see three cylinder objects of varying flatness. The cylinder with the most rounded sides shows the highlight the most.

You can see a highlight on the black tire part of the wheel, but there's no highlight anywhere on the white hubcap, and only a little highlight on the red bolt. One solution is to add more curves to your model to try to bring out the specular highlights; another solution is to change your material somehow. This decision can be made depending on how close you will see the wheel in any of your shots. If the wheel is seen only from a distance, there is no need to further detail the model. Because we will be seeing the wheel only from a distance, we will alter the material. We can add a few things to bring out the shine in the material.

Figure 7.100

**The rendered wheel is a bit flat looking.**

Figure 7.101

**Flat objects do not show off their specular highlights particularly well.**

Usually shiny objects are also reflective, so if we add reflections to the flat hubcap surface, the render would look more convincing. As with the Pool Ball exercise earlier in the chapter, you can fake the reflections for a very convincing result, especially when you do not have a full CG environment built for the rocket that would allow true raytraced reflections (for more on raytracing, see Chapter 11).

To assign a reflection map to the wheel, follow these steps.

1. In the Compact Material Editor, select the Red Bolt material. In the Maps rollout, click None (to the right of Reflection). Choose Bitmap from the Material/Map Browser, navigate to the SceneAssets\Images folder in the Red Rocket project, and select the rocket Rocket Refmap Blur.jpg image file. If you don't see this map, make sure the Files of Type field is set to JPG.

2. Render a frame of the wheel bolt. Now the wheel's bolt will look like a perfect mirror, because the Reflection amount is being used at 100 percent.

3. In the Material Editor tools, navigate up a level () to the Maps rollout and change the Reflection Amount to 30.

4. Repeat the preceding steps for the other two wheel materials. Figure 7.102 shows the wheel rendered with the mapped reflection. You should notice a subtle difference between Figure 7.102 and Figure 7.100, which shows the wheel with no reflections. You can adjust the Reflection Amount to taste.

The mapped reflection helps give the wheel more substance, as it makes the material more convincing when rendered. A true reflection, as you will see with raytracing in

Chapter 11, will give you more accurate reflections, provided you are rendering in a created environment, which we are not. Figure 7.103 shows an example of a raytraced reflection rendered in a simple 3D room. The wheel on the left is the fake mapped reflection; the wheel on the right is the raytraced reflection showing the accurate environment.

Figure 7.102

**The wheel rendered with mapped reflections**

Figure 7.103

**The wheel on the left has a mapped reflection, and the wheel on the right has a raytraced reflection.**

### Applying a Bump Map

We are almost but not totally done with the wheel. The black part of the wheel is only halfway there. One important feature of the wheel is the bumpiness on the surface (refer to Figure 7.88 earlier in the chapter). This bumpiness changes all the specular and reflective properties on that part of the wheel. Bump mapping is very common in CG. It adds a level of detail to an object fairly easily by creating bumps and grooves in the surface and giving the object a tactile element. Bump mapping uses the intensity values (aka the brightness values) of an image or procedural map to simulate bumpiness on the surface of the model, without changing the actual topology of the model itself. You can create some surface texture with a bump map; however, you will not be able to create extreme depth in the model. For that, you may want to model the surface depth manually or use displacement mapping instead. To add a bump map to the tire, follow these steps:

1. In the Compact Material Editor, you should have the Wheel Black material selected and the Maps rollout open from the previous series of steps.

2. Click the None button next to the Bump map. In the Material/Map Browser, choose Noise.

Noise is a map of color patterns that is generated procedurally in three dimensions so you don't have to fuss with mapping coordinates. (Mapping coordinates specify the location of an image on your object, as discussed later in the chapter.)

3. When you place the Noise map in the Bump map slot, you will automatically be taken to the Parameters for the Noise map in the Compact Material Editor (Figure 7.104). Change the Size to 0.02. Click the Go to Parent icon ( ) to move up a level to the main Material parameters.

4. Go to the Maps rollout and increase the Bump Amount from 30 (the default) to 60.

5. Render; you should now see a texture on the tire (Figure 7.105) that resembles the real bumpiness of the tire in Figure 7.88.

The wheel is complete!

Now you'll need to apply the MSO material you created to the other three wheels. There's a hard way to do this, and an easy way. The hard way is to select the polygons for the tire, the hubcap, and the bolt for each wheel, and apply the MSO material. The easy way is to copy the finished wheel, place it where the other three wheels are located, and delete the original wheels. Just make sure to unhide the rest of the rocket using the Layer Manager.

Figure 7.104

**Noise Parameters rollout**

Figure 7.105

**Add a bump map to the wheel.**

## Creating Material Libraries

While a material is in the Material Editor or applied to an object, it is part of the scene and is saved with the scene, whether it is displayed in a sample slot in the Material Editor or not. However, for complicated scenes it is inconvenient to have all the materials active in the Material Editor, because you are limited to only 24 sample slots. Once you get to your 25th material, you will have to store some of the materials elsewhere, such as in a

Material Library, to make available slots for editing in the Material Editor. You can later bring those stored materials back into the Material Editor easily.

To create a Material Library, follow these steps:

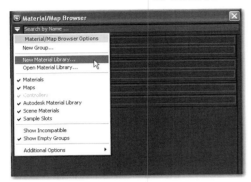

Figure 7.106

**The Material/ Map Browser options menu**

1. In the Compact or Slate Material Editor, select the Material node or sample sphere with the Wheel Multi/Sub-Object material.

2. Click on the Get Material button in the Compact Material Editor ( ).

3. In the Material/Map Browser, click on the Options button ( ), which is in the upper-left corner. This opens the menu shown in Figure 7.106

4. Choose New Material Library from menu and name the Library **Red Rocket** (Figure 7.107).

5. Now the Material/Map Browser has a rollout, Red Rocket. Drag and drop the MSO material (and any other material from your scene) from the Material Editor to the Material/Map Browser's Red Rocket rollout. This automatically loads it into the Red Rocket library.

Figure 7.107

**Name the library Red Rocket.**

6. To save the library to a location to be used at another time, right-click on the Red Rocket title bar; you will see the path it is set up in. Choose Save As (Figure 7.108).

Figure 7.108

**Save the Red Rocket library.**

7. Save the Library in the MaterialLibraries folder in the Red Rocket project. Name it **Red Rocket.mat**. (There already is a file in that folder called ROCKET.mat for your reference.)

You can also load a library from a 3ds Max scene file, instead of a Material Library file (.mat). When you click Open Material Library from the Material/Map Browser's option menu, choose Open Material Library and then choose 3ds Max (*.max) from Files of Type. Select and load the .max scene file. All materials assigned in that scene are then listed in the browser. To convert the collection of materials to a library file, click Save and save it as a MAT file (.mat).

You can load the scene file ROCKET_MATERIAL_WHEEL_FINAL.max from the Scenes folder of the Red Rocket project on the web page to skip to this point or to check your work.

# Mapping the Fins: Introduction to Mapping Coordinates

An image map is two-dimensional; it has length and width but no depth. Geometry in 3ds Max, however, extends in all three axes. How is a material that contains 2D image maps applied properly to a 3D scene object? Are the maps projected in a single direction onto the object's surfaces or do they envelop the object cylindrically or spherically? The answer depends on the type of mapping coordinates applied to the object. Mapping coordinates define how and where image maps are projected onto an object's surfaces and whether the maps are repeated across those surfaces.

Mapping coordinates can be applied to objects in several ways. The Generate Mapping Coords option is on by default. When primitive objects are created and the Generate Mapping Coords option is checked at the bottom of the Parameters rollout, the appropriate mapping coordinates are created automatically.

Loft objects, which are covered in Chapter 5, control mapping in the Mapping section of the Surface Parameters rollout. The Length Repeat value determines how many times the material's maps are repeated along the length of the Path object, and the Width Repeat value determines how many times the maps are repeated around the scene object.

> If any part of your rocket is hidden in the scene file, especially if you started with the scene files from the web page, unhide those parts in the Layer Manager.

## The Base Material

The top vertical fin on the rocket's tail is nothing special as far as materials are concerned. It is white plastic that is just a bit shiny and has a decal, as you can see in Figure 7.109. At this point, you easily can create the material itself:

1. Open the ROCKET_MATERIAL_FIN_START.max file from the Scenes folder of the Red Rocket project, and continue with the ROCKET_MATERIAL_WHEEL_FINAL.max or the file you have created.

2. Open the Compact Material Editor and select an available sample sphere. In the Blinn Basic Parameters, click the color swatch next to the Diffuse, and make it white.

3. Name the material **Fin_Decal**. Unlike the side fins, the top fin has a decal on its side, so it will have its own material. Apply the material to the Fin object by dragging and dropping the sample sphere from the Material Editor to the fin.

4. Back in the Material Editor, in the Specular Highlights group of the Basic Blinn Parameters set the Specular Level to 80 and the Glossiness to 60. When you render, the base color may look a bit gray; that is just the basic lighting in the scene. See Figure 7.110.

Figure 7.109

**The top vertical fin of the rocket**

Figure 7.109

**The top vertical fin of the rocket**

5. We need to add reflections for the fin. Go to the Maps rollout in the Material Editor, click None next to the Reflection map, and select Bitmap from the Material/Map Browser. Navigate to the SceneAssets\Images folder in the Red Rocket project and select `Rocket Refmap Blur.jpg` to assign it as the reflection map.

6. The Compact Material Editor will display the Bitmap Parameters rollout. Go up a level by clicking on the Go to Parent icon. Go to the Maps rollout and turn the Reflection Amount down to 35.

7. Render. You'll see a plain, white, shiny fin, as shown in Figure 7.111.

Figure 7.110

**Fin with basic material applied**

Figure 7.111

**Turn the Reflection amount down to 35 to achieve this render.**

## Adding the Decal

The main feature of this vertical fin is its decal. This is an image that we need to add to the material. The image is a 2D image and won't be as easy to apply as the 3D noise map we used earlier for the bump map of the tire. The decal will become a part of the Diffuse color; we will replace the color we created for Diffuse with the image itself.

1. In the Compact Material Editor, select the Fin_Decal sample sphere. Make sure you are at the top level of the material and can see the Maps rollout.

2. Click None next to the Diffuse Color map. Choose Bitmap from the Material/Map Browser, navigate to the SceneAssets\Images folder in the Red Rocket project, and choose RedRocketDecal.tif.

3. In the Material Editor toolbar, click the Show Standard Map in Viewport button (⊞). This will display the decal in the viewport. Figure 7.112 shows the mapped decal on the top fin.

Figure 7.112

**The decal isn't mapping properly to the top fin.**

Don't panic just yet. Every object in 3ds Max has a set of mapping coordinates that tell the program how to place a 2D image onto your geometry. Honestly, 3ds Max gets it wrong most of the time the first time you try to map a 2D image.

4. In the Material Editor's parameters for the decal, go to the Coordinates rollout (shown in Figure 7.113); this area is where you adjust the map. Details about the parameters in this section are discussed in the "Coordinates Rollout Explanation" sidebar.

5. The decal needs to be rotated, scaled, and positioned. In the Material Editor, under the Coordinates rollout, change Angle W to 90.

Applies the map as a texture map to a surface.
Select the type of coordinates from the Mapping list.

Uses the map as an environment map.
Select the type of coordinates from
the Mapping list.

Texture:

Figure 7113

**The Coordinates rollout for the bit-map parameters**

Changes the position of the map
over the surface of the geometry.
U moves the bitmap horizontally;
V moves it vertically.

Enviro:

Determines the number of times
the map is repeated along each axis

Turns the Tile feature
on/off per axis

Rotates the map about the *U*-, *V*-,
or *W*-axes (in degrees)

6. Set the Tiling to U: 1.6 and V: 2. With bitmap coordinates, the higher the number, the smaller the map will become, in order to allow it to repeat or tile. In this case, we do not want the bitmap to repeat; we're just using the values to shrink the size of the decal on the surface. To turn off the tiling, simply uncheck the Tile boxes.

7. Set the Offset to U: −0.11 and V: 0.05.

The size and placement of the decal are not bad, but there are still copies of the decal on all the sides of the top fin, as shown in Figure 7.114.

This happened because the model for the top fin started out as a box with six sides, so the Material Editor put a decal on each side of the geometry. This method works if the bitmap image has a random pattern and you don't mind having that image on all sides of the object. Here, the mapping coordinates inherent in the top fin geometry will not allow us to place the decal on *just* the sides of the fin.

In the next section, we will use a modifier to change the mapping coordinates on the Top Fin object.

Figure 7.114

**Copies of the decal are still on all sides of the top fin.**

### COORDINATES ROLLOUT EXPLANATION

The Coordinates rollout in the bitmap parameters for a 2D image has several options, as you can see in Figure 7.113. Here is a brief explanation of the settings:

**Applies the map as a texture map or environment** You can select the type of coordinates from the Mapping pull-down menu. As you can see in Figure 7.113, there are different coordinate choices for Textures or Environments.

**Offset UV** Changes the position of the map over the surface of the geometry. *U* moves the bitmap horizontally, and *V* moves the bitmap vertically on the surface.

**Tiling UV** Determines the number of times the map is repeated along each axis.

**Angle UVW** Rotates the map about the *U*-, *V*-, or *W*-axis in degrees.

## Using a UVW Mapping Modifier

Instead of dealing with the surface's own mapping coordinates as we have been doing, we are going to use a modifier to replace those coordinates on the geometry. The *UVW Mapping modifier* makes the decal act more like a real decal that we can control by moving a modifier gizmo around to place the coordinates as we please. (For more on UVW mapping, see the sidebar "Understanding UVW Mapping" later in this chapter.)

The UVW Mapping modifier is commonly used to apply and control mapping coordinates. You select the type of mapping projection, regardless of the shape of the object, and then set the amount of tiling in the modifier's parameters. The mapping coordinates applied through the UVW Mapping modifier override any other mapping coordinates applied to an object, and the Tiling values set for the modifier are multiplied by the Tiling value set in the assigned material. Figure 7.115 shows the parameters for the UVW Mapping modifier.

### CREATING THE UVW MAPPING MODIFIER

To use the UVW Mapping modifier to properly map the decal to the fin, follow these steps.

1. Go back to the Compact Material Editor and set the coordinates in the bitmap parameters for the decal back to their default values:

   **Offset:** U: 0.0, V: 0.0

   **Tiling:** U: 1.0, V: 1.0

   **Angle:** W: 0.0

   **UV Tile boxes:** Check Off to turn the Tiling feature off

2. Select the fin and go to the Modify panel. From the Modifier List drop-down, choose UVW Mapping.

**Figure 7.115**

**The UVW Mapping modifier's parameters**

3. In the Modifier Stack, you can see the UVW Mapping modifier stacked on top of the Editable Poly. You will also see an orange gizmo next to the top fin geometry.

When you apply the UVW Mapping modifier to your object, the gizmo always conforms to the shape of the object. Because this is a decal, we want the image to keep its original proportions.

4. Go to the UVW Mapping modifier parameters and, in the Alignment section, click the Bitmap Fit button (shown in Figure 7.116).

5. This will take you to the Select Image dialog box. Navigate to the SceneAssets\ Images folder in the Red Rocket project and select the file `RedRocktDecal.tif`. This will change the size of the UVW Mapping gizmo to the size and aspect of the image rather than the geometry.

**Figure 7.116**

**The Alignment section for the UVW Mapping modifier parameters**

### ADJUSTING THE UVW MAPPING GIZMO

Now we will adjust the UVW Mapping Gizmo in the following steps:

1. In the Modifier Stack, click the plus sign in the black box next to the UVW Mapping modifier, and select Gizmo. See Figure 7.117.

2. Now look at the top fin in the viewport, and you should see the plane-shaped Modifier gizmo. You will now be able to transform it to suit where you need the decal placed.

3. Switch to the Rotate tool, and rotate 75 degrees on the *X*-axis.

4. Switch to the Scale tool (press R), and scale down the gizmo to 40 percent. Then switch to the Move tool (W) and center the decal on the fin as shown in Figure 7.118.

5. In the viewport, the decal looks like a bright white rectangle, while the rest of the top fin is gray. That is okay. Render, and you will see something similar to Figure 7.119.

**Figure 7.117**

**Select the sub-object Gizmo mode for the UVW Mapping modifier.**

Figure 7.118

**Center the decal on the fin.**

Figure 7.119

**Render, and the decal will look much better on the fin.**

## CORRECTING THE PROJECTION

While the decal on this side of the fin looks fine, if you look on the other side of the fin, the decal is flipped. The type of UVW Mapping modifier projection we are using (planar mapping) is useful only when one side of an object needs to be mapped. In this case we need the decal to show up correctly on the other side of the fin. What do we do now?!?

1. Go to the UVW Mapping modifier parameters, and select Box under Mapping.

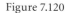

Figure 7.120

**The decal shows in places we don't want.**

2. This works, but now we have the decal in places we don't want, as shown in Figure 7.120. This is because Box mapping projects the image from six sides, using a planar map for each side, but uses the sided-surface *normal* (a vector that defines which way a face or vertex is pointing) to decide the mapping direction. So, we are going to trick the modifier and remove the depth.

3. In the parameters for the UVW Mapping modifier, change the Height parameter to 0.01, as shown in Figure 7.121.

4. The copies of the decals we don't want on the fin should disappear. On the sides where we don't want the decal, we have scaled the Box Projection gizmo down to almost nothing; the projections for those sides are actually still there but now they are very small and not noticeable on the fin. This isn't the most sophisticated way to fix the issue, but it works for our needs. In CG, whatever works is the best course of action. See Figure 7.122 for final results.

Figure 7.121

**Change the Height parameter to 0.01.**

We can't change the Height parameter of the UVW Mapping modifier gizmo to 0 because then the modifier won't work properly. A very small value such as 0.01 works very well instead.

Figure 7.122

**Fin with final materials**

### ADDING THE MATERIAL TO THE MATERIAL LIBRARY

This is a good time to add this decal material to the Material Library.

1. Select the Fin_Decal material in the Material Editor and click the Get Material button ( ).

2. In the Material/Map Browser, go to the Material/Map Browser Option button ( ). Choose Open Material Library and navigate to the MaterialLibraries folder in the Red Rocket project.

3. Choose the file Red Rocket.mat from the MaterialLibraries folder. Then drag the Fin_Decal material from the Material Editor to the Red Rocket library in the Material/Map Browser.

4. Right-click on the Red Rocket title bar and choose the path and save.

5. Render out the fin and check your work. Save your scene file.

You can load the scene file ROCKET_MATERIAL_FIN_FINAL.max in the Scenes folder of the Red Rocket project to skip to this point or to check your work.

### UNDERSTANDING UVW MAPPING

The UVW Mapping modifier consists primarily of a yellow gizmo that determines how the image maps are projected onto the surfaces of an object. The images are projected outward or inward from the gizmo and extend through the assigned objects to all surfaces. The size and orientation of the gizmos affect how the maps are projected onto the relevant objects. The properties of the different mapping types are listed here:

**Planar** Projects the image map perpendicular to the perimeter of the rectangular gizmo.

**Cylindrical** Projects the map outward from the center of a cylindrical gizmo as if the map were wrapped around the object in two axes.

**Cap** Projects the map to the end caps of the cylindrical gizmo in a planar fashion.

**Spherical** Projects the map outward from the center of a spherical gizmo as if the map were completely enveloping the object. The top and bottom of the image maps are gathered at the poles of the gizmo and may cause some distortion.

**Shrink Wrap** Similar to the Spherical method, except that the four corners of the image map are gathered at a single location.

**Box** Projects the image in six perpendicular planes from the center of the gizmo.

**Face** Applies the image map to each face of an object regardless of its size or orientation.

**XYZ to UVW** Used with procedural maps, such as Noise or Smoke, to control the maps when the object changes size.

## Mapping the Body

The rocket body is made up of three texturing areas:

**The main body**: red with a white decal

**The control panel:** a gray metallic material

**The nose:** white plastic with teardrop embossed features

The easiest way to texture is to use the Multi/Sub-Object material technique you used on the wheel. The body has a logo on it, so it will have the same issue as the fin: The logo image will appear on the opposite side of the object when you use Planar mapping. Another way of dealing with the logo-flipping issue is to apply the material to each side separately. You would apply the same material to specific selected polygons on each side of the object, but 3ds Max lets you apply two maps and two UVW Mapping modifiers instead of one. This gives you independent control over each side of the rocket body.

> This is the technique you would use if you wanted to put a different design on the other side of your model.

1. Open the ROCKET_MATERIAL_BODY_START.max.

2. Select the rocket and go to the modeling ribbon. Go to Polygon mode and select the polygons on one half of the rocket. This is accomplished most easily in the Top viewport.

The Seat and Control panel polygons are also selected now. We want to deselect them for now. To do this, go to the modeling ribbon, and under Polygon Modeling select Ignore Backfacing; see Figure 7.123.

This allows you to select only the polygons facing you. Hold down Alt while you select what you want to subtract from any selection. This can be a bit tedious, but it must be done. Once finished, your selection should resemble Figure 7.124.

### Creating the Material

We'll begin by creating a material for the red body.

1. Open the Compact Material Editor, select a sample sphere, and click on the color swatch next to Diffuse. Change the color to red (with values of R: 200, G: 0, B: 0). Name the material **Rocket Body Right**.

2. Drag and drop the new material onto the selected polygons of the rocket to assign the material to that half of the rocket.

3. Go to the Maps rollout and click on None next to Diffuse Color. Choose Bitmap from the Material/Map Browser and navigate to the SceneAssets\Images folder in the Red Rocket project and

Figure 7.123

**Select Ignore Backfacing**

Figure 7.124

**Select one half of the rocket's body, without the seat or control panel polygons.**

select the file RocketBodyRight.tif. On the toolbar, click the Show Standard Map in Viewport button (). Don't worry if the map doesn't look correct.

4. Use the Go to Parent button in the Material Editors toolbar and navigate to the top level of the material. In the Specular Highlights section of the Material Editor, change the Specular Level to 90 and Glossiness to 80.

5. Go to the Maps rollout and click None next to Reflection, and from the Material/Map Browser choose Bitmap. Navigate to the SceneAssets\Images folder in the Red Rocket project and select the file Rocket Refmap blur.jpg for the reflection. Go back to the Maps rollout and change the Amount value next to Reflections to 20.

6. Press the F9 key to do a Render Last. The decal will probably be tilting (Figure 7.125), so we see part of it toward the front and the seat of the rocket.

Figure 7.125

**The decal is tilting.**

7. Go back to the Material Editor, and in the Coordinates rollout uncheck the Tile UV boxes to turn off tiling. Don't worry if the map doesn't look quite right yet. The map on the rocket may appear in a strange layout, such as shown previously, or may even be a strange color (in some rare cases).

The model still needs mapping coordinates. We will get to them later.

### Flipping the Decal

In the following steps, we will create a copy of the one side's material and flip it for the other side.

1. Go back to the modeling ribbon, and select the polygons on the opposite side of the rocket. Remember to deselect the Seat and Control panel polygons.

2.  In the Compact Material Editor, drag and drop the Rocket Body Right material sample sphere onto an available sample sphere to make a copy of the material. Rename the material Rocket Body Left.

3.  Go to the Maps rollout for this new material and click the button next to Diffuse Color to take you to the bitmap parameters. Click the bar with the image path and, in the file selection window, select RocketBodyLeft.tif for a flipped version of the previous color map.

4.  In the Coordinates rollout, change the Map Channel parameter to 2, as shown in Figure 7.126. This lets you have many different sets of coordinates on the same object simultaneously. Don't worry that the Red Rocket graphic disappears; it will return when we add the UVW Mapping modifier for the left of the rocket.

Figure 7.126

**Change to Map Channel 2 in the Coordinates rollout of the bitmap.**

5.  Drag and drop the flipped material onto the selected polygons of the rocket (representing the other side of the rocket).

We are now adding the mapping coordinates. We have two materials for each side of the rocket. The right side of the rocket has Map Channel 1 and the left side has Map Channel 2. We are going to start by adding and editing the mapping for the right side with Map Channel 1.

6.  Go into the Modify panel and click the Editable Poly entry to leave the sub-object selection level. Then, from the Modifier List, choose the UVW Mapping modifier. We are going to keep it on the default mapping setting, which is Planar. In the Alignment parameters of the modifier change to the *X*-axis, as shown in Figure 7.127.

Figure 7.127

**Change to X in Alignment parameters of the UVW Mapping modifier.**

7.  Click the Bitmap Fit button, navigate to the SceneAssets\Images folder in the Red Rocket project, and select the file RocketBodyRight.tif. This will change the Modifier gizmo to make it the same size as the bitmap image, keeping the image's scale proportional.

8.  In the Modify panel, go to the Modifier Stack and click on the black box with the plus sign next to the UVW Mapping modifier. Click on Gizmo to allow you to transform the image (via the gizmo) without affecting the object.

9.  Move the Modifier gizmo so the white stripe in the decal is lined up approximately with the front of the rocket, as shown in Figure 7.128.

10. Exit the UVW Mapping modifier gizmo sub-object mode by clicking the modifier in the stack.

Figure 7.128

**Line up the stripe in the material just like the real rocket's stripe.**

11. Add a second UVW Mapping modifier onto the rocket, and change the Map Channel to 2 (Figure 7.129).

Figure 7.129

**Select Map Channel 2 in the UVW Mapping modifier.**

12. In the Alignment parameters of the second UVW Mapping modifier, change the axis to *X*. Click on the Bitmap Fit button, navigate to where the `RocketBodyLeft.tif` bitmap is found, and click Open.

13. Go to the Modifier Stack, click the Gizmo sub-object, and move the bitmap gizmo to line up the image with the map on the opposite side of the rocket.

If you render, you should now see the stripe decals on the side of the rocket, as shown in Figure 7.130.

Figure 7.130

**A render of the rocket shows how the decal is mapped on the body.**

## Adding a Seat

We don't have to worry about mapping the polygons of the seat for the rocket because we have a model of a seat to add.

Go to the Application menu and choose Import → Merge, navigate to the Scenes folder in the Red Rocket project, and select the file SEAT.max and click Open to merge in the seat geometry, as shown in Figure 7.131. The extra geometry adds detail to the model by giving it a nicer seat. If you had to, you could forgo the seat geometry, instead selecting the seat polygons and assigning a glossy black material to them.

The control panel and Nose materials still need to be created and added to the model.

Figure 7.131

**Adding the seat**

## The Control Panel

In this section, we will texture the control panel.

1. As you have done before, create a new material in an available sample sphere in the Material Editor and set its color to gray. If you prefer, you can just use the default gray (R150, G150, B150).

2. Set the Specular Level to 50 and the Glossiness to 20.

3. Name this new material **Control Panel**.

For the control panel, we should add just a little bit of bumpiness to the surface to give the panel a better feel.

4. Select the Control Panel material in the Material Editor. In the Maps rollout, change the Bump Amount to 20 and click None to create a map.

5. Select Noise from the Material/Map Browser to add a Noise texture to the bump map.

6. In the Noise Parameters rollout for the Noise map, change the Size to 0.02.

Finally, let's add a reflection map to the control panel, as we did with the body of the rocket.

7. In the Material Editor, click Go to Parent, then select the Maps rollout, set the Reflection Amount to 10, and click None next to Reflection to add a map.

8. Select Bitmap from the Material/Map Browser and navigate to the Red Rocket project's SceneAssets\Images folder to select Rocket Refmap blur.tif.

9. In a viewport, select the rocket, enter Polygon mode, and select the polygons that make up the control panel, as shown in highlight in Figure 7.132. Drag the Control Panel material onto the selected polygons to assign the material.

Figure 7.132

**Select the polygons of the control panel.**

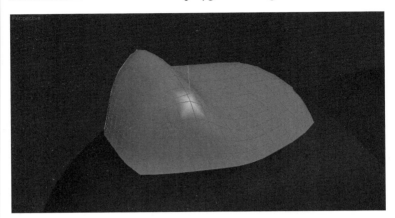

10. Click on the Editable Poly level when you are finished. If you don't, the two UVW Mapping modifiers will be applied only to the control panel polygons.

Because the buttons of the control panel are separate objects, you easily can create colorful materials for them, using more or less the same settings from the previous materials. Simply assign each button its own material for its own distinctive color. If you are using ROCKET_MATERIAL_BODY_START.max, the finished control panel buttons are hidden in their own layer. Open the Manage Layer dialog box and unhide the layer.

Voilà! All that remains now are the thruster and the nose of the rocket.

### Bring on the Nose, Bring on the Funk

The material for the nose is pretty similar to the material we just created for the control panel, except the Diffuse color should be white.

1. Copy the Control Panel material by dragging it onto an empty sample sphere in the Compact Material Editor and changing its Diffuse color to white. Feel free to adjust the Specular settings as you see fit. (A Specular level of 90 and a Glossiness value of 80 work very well.) Name the new material Nose.

   The control panel had a slight bump map on the material. Let's remove that from the Nose material.

2. Select the Nose material in the Compact Material Editor. Right-click on the map bar next to the Bump parameter, and select Clear from the context menu, as shown in Figure 7.133.

Figure 7.133

**Clear the Bump bitmap.**

The Nose material now has no bump map, but it retains the reflection map from the control panel's material, saving us a little bit of work.

3. Select the polygons of the nose, shown in a box in Figure 7.134, and drag the material from the Material Editor to the selected polygons to assign the material. When you're finished, click Editable Poly to return to object mode.

Figure 7.134

**Select the polygons of the nose.**

4. Save your work, and make sure to version up the file as not to overwrite your previous scene file. The Rocket's side decals will look wrong until you click the top UVW Mapping modifier.

## The Thruster

The final part of the rocket model to texture is the thruster. Using the experience you've already gained from texturing the rest of the rocket, this will be a breeze. If you prefer, you can load the ROCKET_MATERIAL_THRUSTER_START.max file from the Scenes folder of the Red Rocket project, or just continue with your own scene.

Figure 7.135 shows the thruster. Notice the round bulbous section in the left image. This is the middle yellow part of the thruster.

In this section, we'll experiment with a selection technique to make it easier to isolate the middle, yellow part of the thruster. Also remember to use the Layer Manager to unhide any parts of the rocket that may be hidden in your scene.

1. Select the thruster and enter Polygon mode. Select the center ring of polygons of the thruster, highlighted in Figure 7.136.

If the Thruster object is not an editable polygon in your scene, add an Edit Poly modifier to the object before continuing.

2. In the modeling ribbon, in the Modify Selection tab, click the Grow button five times to enlarge your selection to include all the polygons that make up the yellow round inside of the thruster, highlighted in Figure 7.137.

3. Open the Material Editor and select an available sample sphere. Name this material Thruster Yellow Light. If there are no available sample slots, right-click on a slot and choose 5 × 3 Sample Slots from the menu.

4. In the Blinn Basic Parameters rollout, click on the color swatch next to Diffuse and change the color to yellow (R: 255, G: 210, and B: 0).

5. In the Specular Highlights section, change Specular Level to 90 and Glossiness to 80.

6. To give the yellow material a bit of a lightness, change Self Illumination to 50 and Opacity to 90.

Figure 7.135

**The Thruster object has a yellow part, the circle in the middle, and the outside housing.**

Figure 7.136

**Select the center ring of polygons of the thruster.**

Figure 7.137

**Click the Grow button in the Modify Selection tab.**

7. Go to the Maps rollout and change the Reflection Amount to 50 and add a bitmap to Reflection. Navigate to the SceneAssets\Images folder in the Red Rocket project and select the file `Rocket Refmap blur.tif` to add a reflection map similar to the rest of the rocket.

8. Drag and drop the material to the selected polygons.

9. To save a lot of time, we can easily select the other polygons of the thruster. With the round center polygons still selected, choose Edit → Select Invert.

10. Drag and Drop the Control_Panel material onto the selected polygons. Done! Figure 7.138 shows the textured thruster.

11. Unhide all the other parts of the rocket using the Layer Manager, as needed, and render a frame of the fully textured rocket, as shown in Figure 7.139 and Figure 7.140.

All the parts of the rocket now have materials applied. Save your work, pat yourself on the back, and have a nice smoothie to celebrate. All the parts of the rocket now have materials applied.

Figure 7.138
**The textured thruster**

Figure 7.139
**The rocket!**

Figure 7.140
**The rocket from behind**

## Mapping the Soldier

In this exercise, we will apply materials and maps to the soldier model from Chapter 6. For this process, we will first UV unwrap the model so we can lay out the colors and patterns for the soldier's uniform and general look. This process essentially creates a flat map that can be used to paint the textures in a program such as Photoshop. Having properly laid out UVs will make the mapping process much easier.

We have already created the textures (i.e., the maps) we intend to use for the soldier using Adobe Photoshop.

The remainder of this chapter will show you how to prepare the model for proper UVs and how to apply the maps we have already painted. We will not be showing the actual painting process in Photoshop, as it goes beyond the purposes of this book.

### UV Unwrapping

Figure 7.141

**Add an Unwrap UVW modifier.**

Set your project to the Soldier project downloaded from the companion web page at www.sybex.com/go/intro3dsmax2011. Open the scene file SoldierTexture_v01.max from the scenes folder of the project, or use your own final model scene file from Chapter 6. Keep in mind that any design changes you made to your own soldier model may cause discrepancies in the UV unwrapping and mapping steps completed in the following sections.

In this section, we will unwrap the UVs for the soldier model by creating seams on the soldier's body that will define body shapes on a flat blank canvas that can be used later for painting the textures for those parts of the body. For example, we will begin by creating seams to define the shapes of the arms, so we know where in Photoshop to paint the sleeves of the uniform.

Begin defining UVs with the following steps:

1. Turn on Smooth + Highlights + Edged Faces view for your viewports.

2. With your model selected, go to the Modifier List drop-down panel and add an Unwrap UVW modifier to it, as shown in Figure 7.141.

3. Expand the Unwrap UVW modifier in the Modifier Stack and enter into Face mode, as shown in Figure 7.142.

4. Turn off Show Map Seam under the Parameters rollout. This turns off the green highlight on the edges, which is generated by default and is not useful in its current state.

5. Click the Point to Point Seam button toward the bottom of the Command panel under the Map Parameters rollout (Figure 7.143). This tool will let us re-route the seams to where we want them.

Figure 7.142

**Enter into
Face mode.**

Figure 7.143

**Click the Point to
Point Seam button.**

6. With Point to Point Seam enabled, click on the center of a pair of intersecting edges about where you want to define the left shoulder (Figure 7.144). A dashed line "rubber band" appears next to your cursor, letting you know that the tool is waiting for the next point to be selected.

7. Select the next intersecting edges in the loop around the shoulder. This creates a blue highlight across the edges (see Figure 7.145).

Figure 7.144

**Pick this edge intersection to begin
defining the left
shoulder.**

**NAVIGATING VIEWPORTS WHILE POINT TO POINT SEAM IS ACTIVE**

While Point to Point Seam is active, you can navigate using all the viewport navigation tools to look around the model. After you've done so, 3ds Max still remembers the last intersection you clicked and draws an accurate seam at the next click.

8. Continue around the shoulder until you have a complete loop, ending with the intersection you started with in step 6. Also, you can right-click then start or continue the picks without overlapping the picks.

9. Select the bottom-most edge intersection on the underarm and continue selecting edge intersections all the way to the middle point of the wrist, as shown in Figure 7.146. You will have to switch to Wireframe (press F3) view to pick the last point (Figure 7.147) at the end of the forearm.

10. Click the right mouse button to deactivate the Point to Point Seam tool's rubber banding, but still keep the button active, then continue cutting a new set of UVs for the right arm as you did for the left arm.

11. Right-click the mouse, and box out areas under the arms on both sides as shown in Figure 7.148. In Figure 7.148, you can see the seams block out the area under the arm and continue down to the belt line, and across the top of the beltline around the waist. If you miss-click a point, you can use the Undo button.

Figure 7.145
**Pick these edge intersections.**

Figure 7.146
**Select the intersections under the arm.**

Figure 7.147

**Switch to Wireframe view to pick the last intersection for the forearm/wrist.**

Figure 7.148

**Add these seams to define the torso areas under the arm.**

12. Using the Point to Point Seam tool, cut seams for the two gloves lengthwise down the middle from wrist to wrist. You can see this progression for the left-hand glove start in Figure 7.149. Begin at the wrist on the side of the thumb and work your way around to the opposite side of the wrist. Remember, you may need to enter Wireframe view mode (F3) to select the proper edge intersection points. Figure 7.150 shows the seam working around the hand.

13. Open the Material Editor (Slate or Compact) and apply an unused Standard material to your entire model if it doesn't already have one. Double-click on the Diffuse Color input socket of the material (Figure 7.151) to open the Material/Map Browser (Figure 7.152). Under the Maps → Standard rollout, select Checker and click OK.

14. In the Slate, double-click the Checker Map title bar to open its parameters. Change the U and V Tiling parameters for the checker map from 1 to 5 so the checker texture (Figure 7.153) gives you better visual feedback as to how your UVs are coming along as you fix them. At the top of the Slate, click on Show Standard Map in Viewport if you cannot see the map on your model in the viewports (Figure 7.154).

Figure 7.149

**Cut a new seam along the glove, starting as shown.**

Figure 7.150

**Work your way around the glove.**

Figure 7.151

**Double-click the Diffuse Color input socket.**

Figure 7.152

**Double-click to create a Checker map for the diffuse color.**

Figure 7.153

**Set the U and V Tiling to 5.**

Figure 7.154

**Click the Show Standard Map in Viewport button.**

## Pelting the Left Arm UVs

Save your work now before continuing with the next set of steps to unfold the UVs for the arms into usable patterns to paint the textures. You can pick up with the scene file SoldierTexture_v02.max from the Scenes folder of the Soldier project from the companion web page to check your work so far or to skip to this point.

1. With Face mode selected in your Unwrap UVW modifier, and Point to Point Seam unselected, click on a polygon on the left forearm of your model. Next, in the Command Panel at the bottom of the Map Parameter rollout, click on the Exp. Face Sel to Seams button. If the seams were created correctly in the previous set of steps, a selection of faces on the arm will turn red in your viewport (Figure 7.155).

2. Now we need to unfold the UVs to create the pattern to paint on in Photoshop (or another image editor). To unfold the UVs into a usable pattern, click on the Pelt button in the Map Parameters rollout, as shown in Figure 7.156.

3. When you click Pelt, 3ds Max opens the Edit UVWs dialog box as well as the Pelt Map dialog box. In the Edit UVWs dialog box, click the View menu and check off Show Grid and Show Map to simplify the UV view as shown in Figure 7.157.

Figure 7.155

**The arm's faces are selected.**

Figure 7.156

**Click on Pelt to unfold the UVs of the arm.**

Figure 7.157

**The Edit UVWs and Pelt Map dialog boxes showing the arm UVs**

4. To unfold the map, click on the Start Pelt button in the Pelt Map dialog box. This moves the UVs in the Edit UVWs dialog box in real time. This procedure keeps unfolding the UVs until you stop it, so wait a couple of seconds for the UVs to stop moving, and click on Stop Pelt. Figure 7.158 shows the results.

Figure 7.158

**Pelting the arm UVs**

5.  You're almost done with the arm, but if you check the checkerboard texture in your viewport you can see that some of the checks are bigger than others. To fix this, click the Settings box next to the Relax button in the Pelt Map dialog box, and change the drop-down option to Relax by Face Angles (Figure 7.159). Click the Set as Default button since you will be going through these steps on each part of your model.

6.  Now, click on Start Relax. Wait until the UVs stop moving and click on Stop Relax. Checking your texture in the viewport now shows the checkerboard how we want it (Figure 7.160).

7.  In the Pelt Map dialog box, click on the Commit button at the bottom, or your changes won't take. Also, you want to exit out of the Edit UVWs dialog.

Figure 7.159

**Set the drop-down menu to Relax by Face Angles.**

Figure 7.160

**The arm UVs are pelted and relaxed the way we need them.**

### Pelting the Right Arm UVs

Repeat Steps 1–7 for the right arm. You can see in Figure 7.161 that the right arm is now laid out—pelted and relaxed.

Figure 7.161

**The right arm is pelted and relaxed.**

**Figure 7.161**

**The right arm is pelted and relaxed.**

### Unwrapping and Using Pelt for the Head

Save your work now before continuing with the next set of steps to unfold the UVs for the head. You can pick up with the scene file SoldierTexture_v03.max from the Scenes folder of the Soldier project downloaded from the companion web page to check your work so far or to skip to this point.

For this section, since it is a bit hard to see where to seam, we went into the Material Editor to the Standard Checker material we created. In the Maps rollout, we unchecked Diffuse Color to turn off the checker pattern.

The head poses a problem: Each part (helmet, goggles, mask) is a separate object modeled in Chapter 6 that was attached together into one Editable Polygon. That means when we look closely at the geometry, there is some object penetration. This makes it very hard to clearly see some of the areas we need to seam. We will use a sub-object visibility technique to control what we are viewing in the following steps.

Figure 7.162

**Go into Element mode to select the helmet.**

1. Select the Soldier, and in the Modify panel's Modifier Stack, go to Editable Poly, and select Element, as shown in Figure 7.162. Element mode allows you to select separate objects that are attached together into a single object.

When you do this you will get the warning shown in Figure 7.163. Select Yes. Every time you move between the Unwrap UVW modifier and the Editable Poly modifier, you will see this warning; if that gets annoying, check the Do Not Show This Message Again option. The warning tells you that any changes you make to that level of the model will ripple throughout the rest of the stack and may mess up other parts of your work. Since we are simply using the Element mode to hide parts of the head of the model to make seaming easier to see, we need not worry that anything will change.

2.  Select the helmet, then in the modeling ribbon go to the Visibility tab and click Hide Unselected, as shown in Figure 7.164. That this will hide all unselected elements in the model, leaving the helmet as the only visible object. Yay!

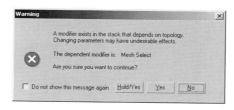

**Figure 7.163**

**Topology dependency warning**

3.  Exit Element mode by clicking Editable Poly in the Modifier Stack. Now go back up to the Unwrap UVW modifier and click on Face. Go back down to the Map Parameters rollout and click the Point to Point Seam button. Following the line in Figure 7.165, create a new seam on the helmet.

4.  When the seam is has been created, go back down to the Editable Poly → Element mode in the Modifier Stack, and in the Visibility tab click the Unhide All button. Then select the goggles, go to the Visibility tab, and click Hide Unselected button. Repeat step 3 on the Goggles using Figure 7.166 as your guide for the seams.

**Figure 7.164**

**Hide Unselected hides all the elements except the helmet.**

**Figure 7.165**

**Create a new seam on the helmet.**

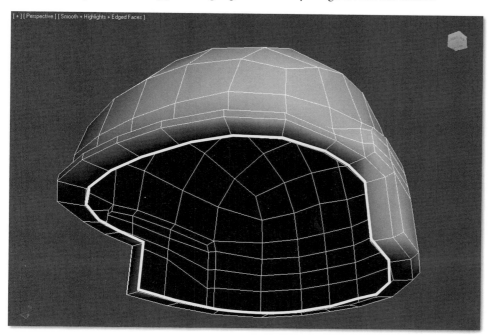

Figure 7.166

**Goggle guide for
the seams**

5. Repeat the process individually for the mask, the head, and the helmet straps, using Hide Unselected to isolate each of the three elements as you work on them. Then follow the same process as before to create seams as shown in Figure 7.167 for the face mask, Figure 7.168 for the head, and Figure 7.169 for the helmet strap.

6. Open the Material Editor, and in the soldier's checker material go to the Maps rollout and check the box next to Diffuse Color to turn on the checkers again. We will need the checkers when we pelt the model.

Figure 7.167

**Seams for soldier face mask**

Figure 7.168

**Seams for the soldier head**

Figure 7.169

**Seams for the soldier helmet strap**

Figure 7.170

Follow these out-
lines to create the
rest of the model's
seams. This image is
also in the color sec-
tion of this book.

## Seaming the Rest of the Body

Use the Point to Point Seam tool to block out the rest of the model's parts and then pelt map them as you did for the arms. Refer to Figures 7.170 and 7.171 for the placement of seams on the model's body. These figures are also shown in the color section of this book.

## Unfolding the Rest of the Body

Save your work before continuing with the next set of steps. You can pick up with the scene file SoldierTexture_v04.max from the Scenes folder of the Soldier project down-loaded from the companion web page to check your work so far or to skip to this point.

1. In the Modify Panel, click the Face button. Then click a single polygon on the hel-met. Then select the Exp. Face Sel to Seams. This will select all the polygons associ-ated with the seams you created for the helmet.

Figure 7.171

**Follow these outlines to create the rest of the model's seams for your model. This image is also in the book's color section.**

2. Click the Pelt button. This will open the Edit UVWs dialog box and the Pelt Map dialog box. First click Start Pelt. You will see the UVs moving around; when they stop moving, click the Stop Pelt button.

3. Now click on the Settings button next to the Start Relax button. Make sure the drop-down menu is set to Relax by Face Angles and click the Save as Default button. Then exit out of the Relax Tool dialog box.

4. Click the Start Relax button again, and when the UVs stop moving, click Stop Relax. For the remaining objects you don't have to go into the settings box: Just hit Start Relax.

5. Select the Commit button. The checkers pattern on the helmet should look organized and even.

Now that you are finished with the helmet, make your way down the body using Pelt and Relax to lay out the UVs on the remaining parts of the body, checking each one off as you go.

Save your work now before continuing with the next set of steps. You can pick up with the scene file SoldierTexture_v05.max from the Scenes folder of the Soldier project to check your work so far or to skip to this point.

As you can see in Figure 7.172, when the UVs are finished, the checker pattern for each separate part of the soldier is a different size.

1. In the Modify panel, click the Face button if it isn't already selected. Then click away from the Soldier model and drag a selection box around the whole model to select all the polygons as shown in Figure 7.172.

Figure 7.172

**Soldier model with all the polygons selected**

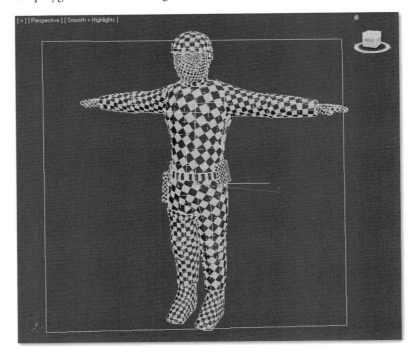

2. Under the Parameters rollout in the Unwrap UVW modifier click the Edit button. What you will see is a mess; these are all the unwrapped UVs piled on top of each other.

3. In the Edit UVWs menu, go into Tools → Relax. Click Start Relax. Be patient and wait for the movement to slow down or stop before pressing Stop Relax. Then exit out of the Relax Tool dialog box. This will relax all of your UVs together uniformly, ensuring that they all have the same UV real estate. This is important so that all the elements carry the same relative texture space as each other, as shown in Figure 7.173.

4. Keep the Edit UVWs dialog open. Deselect the UVs by clicking away from the model. You should see what is shown in Figure 7.174.

Figure 7.173

**Soldier model with all UVs relaxed uniformly**

Figure 7.174

**The Edit UVWs dialog box with the soldier UVs in a pile**

Because you are still in Face mode in the Unwrap UVW modifier, if you click anywhere on the pile of UVs you will select a face. What we want to do now is to select an individual e element's full set of UVs so that we can lay them out separately, giving them some space on the flat blank canvas that can be used later for painting the textures for those parts of the body. The easiest way is to select a face, then go down to the toolbar at the bottom of the Edit UVWs dialog box and check Select Element, as shown in Figure 7.175.

This will allow you to select all the UVs associated with an element (such as the helmet only). When you select something in the Edit UVWs dialog box it will show up

Figure 7.175

**Check Select Element.**

selected on the model in the viewports, as shown in Figure 7.176. This will help you know what parts you are moving around in the Edit UVWs dialog. Also in the Edit UVWs dialog box you can use all the navigation tools you use in the viewports to pan and zoom. In the following steps, you will start placing the UVs for each element within the thick blue bordered box in the Edit UVWs dialog box to lay out the entire soldier's UVs for textures.

1. In the Edit UVWs dialog box, drag a selection box around all the UVs. Using the Scale tool in the Edit UVW dialog box, scale the UVs about -25%. Now you should be able to see the blue border box in the Edit UVWs dialog box, as shown in Figure 7.177.

Figure 7.176

**Select an element in the Edit UVWs dialog box, and it will show as selected on the model.**

Figure 7.177

**Scale down the UVs until they fit in the blue box.**

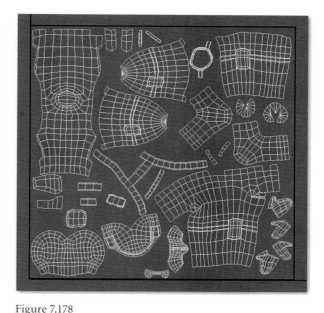

Figure 7.178

**UVs correctly placed within the UV space. This image is also included in this book's color section.**

2. Click on the Select Element option, then start moving and rotating the elements to separate each element's UV layout from the others by selecting the UV points and moving them within the blue box to eventually match the layout in Figure 7.178. Figure 7.178 is also shown in the color section of the book for clarity. The goal is to fit the UVs into this box without going outside of it, and without overlapping any of the UVs. Anything outside this box will end up tiling (or have no texture at all), and any overlapping UVs will share parts of the texture from another element. Either way, that's not good.

3. If you find that there simply isn't enough room to fit all of the UVs in, select all the UVs again, and scale them down together uniformly as you did in Step 1, and continue placement. Figure 7.178 shows the UVs laid out and correctly placed within the usable UV space.

4. In the Edit UVWs dialog, select Tools → Render UV Template to open the Render UVs dialog box shown in Figure 7.179. In that dialog, click the Render UV Template button to create an image of your UVs, as shown in the Render Map dialog box in Figure 7.180.

5. Save the UV layout image by clicking the Save Image icon in the Render Map dialog box (Figure 7.181). Once saved, this image can be opened in your favorite image editor and you can use the pieces as guides to paint the soldier's textures.

Figure 7.179

**Render UVs dialog box**

Figure 7.180

**The UV rendered image**

Figure 7.180

The UV rendered image

Figure 7.181

**Save the UV image.**

With the UV layout image saved, you can go into Photoshop (or image editing software of your choice) and create a texture to place on your model. The UV image was taken into Photoshop and with a combination of painting and cutting/pasting of photos, the final map for the soldier was created (Figure 7.182). Figure 7.182 is also in the color insert of this book.

The texture map, as you can see, places painted parts of the soldier's body according to the UV layout we just created. For example, you can clearly see the soldier's vest painted in the upper-left corner of the texture image file, with the back of the vest in the upper part, the neck hole in the middle, and the front of the vest below.

The more you unwrap UVs for models, the easier it becomes to anticipate how to paint the textures. Unwrapping a human character model like this soldier, even a simple model like this, is not an easy affair, but is the cornerstone to successfully creating good looking assets for games or animations.

Figure 7.182
**The final map for
the soldier.**

In the following sections, we will show you how to apply the maps to the material for the soldier, as well as explore bump and normal maps to give the soldier added detail.

## Applying the Color Map

Save your work now before continuing with the next set of steps. You can pick up with the scene file SoldierTexture_v06.max from the Scenes folder of the Soldier project to check your work so far or to skip to this point.

Now it is time to use the map we put so much effort into.

1.  Open the Slate. You should see the checker material we created for the soldier to help with the UVs. Drag a Standard material from the Material/Map Browser to the view area. Name it **Soldier**.

2. Double-click on the Diffuse Color input socket of the material to open the Material/ Map Browser. Under the Maps → Standard rollout, select Bitmap. When the Select Bitmap Image File dialog box appears, navigate to the /SceneAssets/images folder for the Soldier project, and select the Soldier_Color_V04.tif file.

3. Apply the material to the soldier and click on Show Standard Map in Viewport; the result is shown in Figure 7.183. BAM! Now wasn't all that hard UV work worth it?

Figure 7.183

**The soldier with the material applied.**

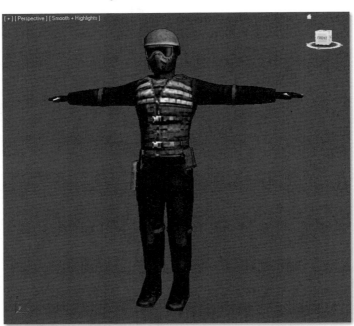

## Applying the Bump Maps

Bump mapping makes an object appear to have a bumpy or irregular surface by simulating surface delineation. When you render an object with a bump-mapped material, lighter (whiter) areas of the map appear to be raised on the object's surface, and darker (blacker) areas appear to be lower on the object's surface, as shown in Figure 7.184.

Normal mapping is a technique used for faking the lighting of bumps and dents. It is used to add details without using more polygons in the modeling process. A Normal map is usually used to fake high-resolution geometry detail while it's actually mapped onto a low-resolution mesh for efficiency's sake. The pixels of a normal map each store a vector (or simply, a direction) that describes a high resolution surface's slope at that very point on the surface. This vector is called a *normal*. The RGB channels of a normal map control the direction of each pixel's normal, enabling you to fake a high degree of surface resolution when applied to a low polygon mesh. A normal map for the soldier is shown in Figure 7.185 and in the color section of the book.

Figure 7.184
**Bump map created in Photoshop by desaturating the original color map to create light and dark areas that conform to the original color texture**

Figure 7.185
**Normal map created in Photoshop and based on the original color map. This image is also included in the book's color section.**

You can use one or both of these mapping techniques to create additional surface detail. It all depends on how much detail you want to appear. Bump maps are simpler to create, since you can usually take the color map and just desaturate it to make a grayscale image file. Normal maps are not as simple but yield better results when the object is rendered. We have both a normal map and bump map for you to use. We will continue with the Soldier material we created in the previous exercise as we add these new maps in the following steps.

1. Click on the Bump input socket of the material to open the Material/Map Browser. Under the Maps → Standard rollout, select Normal Bump.

2. Click on the title bar of the Normal Bump node to bring up the Parameters rollout shown in Figure 7.186. Click on the None button next to Normal. This will once again bring up the Material/Map Browser. Under the Maps → Standard rollout, select Bitmap. When the Select Bitmap Image File dialog box appears, navigate to the /SceneAssets /images folder of the Soldier project, and select the Soldier_Normal_V01.tif file.

Figure 7.186

**The Normal Bump node's Parameters rollout**

3. Back to the Normal Map Parameters: now click None next to Additional Bump. This will once again bring up the Material/Map Browser. Under the Maps → Standard rollout, select Bitmap. When the Select Bitmap Image File dialog box appears, navigate to the /SceneAssets/images folder from the Soldier project downloaded from the companion web page, and select the Soldier_BS_V01.tif file.

4. Go back to the Maps rollout in the main material parameters and set the Bump Amount to 100.

The Normal map is applied and finished. See Figure 7.187 for the material tree from the Slate. See Figure 7.188 for images that compare the soldier rendered with and without the Normal map. Figure 7.188's images are also shown in the book's color section. You may notice that the normal and bump maps have created a lot more detail in the soldier's body, particularly in his vest. You should notice the difference even better in your own renders.

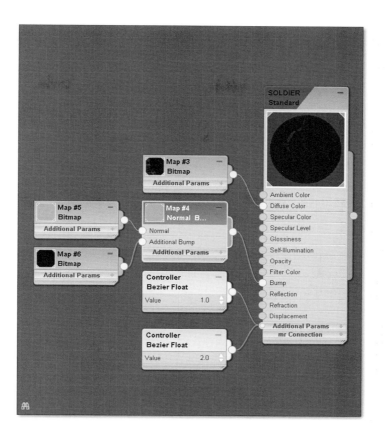

Figure 7.187
**The Slate Material Editor node tree with a Diffuse Color map and a Bump map**

Figure 7.188
**The left image is a render of the soldier without the Normal and Bump maps. The right image is rendered with the Bump/ Normal maps.**

## Applying the Specular Maps

Highlights in objects are actually a reflection of a light source, and specularity is a way to fake those reflections by placing highlights on the receiving surface that would otherwise be reflecting the light in reality. Specular maps are maps you use to define a surface's shininess and highlight color, without the complex calculations of actual reflections in the render. The higher a pixel's value (from black to white, or 0 to 1 respectively), the shinier the surface will appear at that location. Therefore, dry matte surfaces such as unpolished stone or fabric would have a very dark specular map, while polished surfaces like shiny metal or glossy plastic would have lighter specular maps.

We will be adding a specular map to the soldier to further the amount of detail we can get from the render. We are going to reuse the image that we used for the Bump map to give the soldier a bit of bling on his vest and buckles.

In the Slate, drag from the output socket of the Additional Bump bitmap to the Specular Level input socket of the Soldier material already in your scene, as shown in Figure 7.189.

The final render of the soldier is shown in Figure 7.190 as well as in the color section of the book. You can notice the improvement to the look of the soldier's vest with the added Specular Color map.

Now your soldier character is ready to use in renders, or even as a game asset. There are many online resources on how to export assets such as the soldier to your favorite game engine. We will use the soldier for rigging and animation with Character Studio in Chapter 9, "Character Studio and IK Animation," as well as use him for rendering exercises in Chapter 11.

Figure 7.189

**Dragging from the Bump map to the Specular slot.**

Figure 7.190

**Final render of
the soldier**

## Summary

Creating materials for your objects is usually the next step after modeling them. Creating materials can give you a sense of accomplishment because it is essentially the last step in making the object look as you envisioned—aside from lighting and rendering, of course.

There are several ways to create materials, from simple colors to complex mappings on distinct parameters. Finding the right combination of maps, shader types, and material types can make a world of difference in the look of your scenes. It's important to remember that like everything else in CG, applying materials takes time, and gaining wisdom with your materials and maps will come with practice.

In this chapter, you learned the basics of materials, what kinds of materials are in 3ds Max, and how to create and edit them in the Material Editor. Then you learned how choosing the appropriate type of shader will make your surface look right, and how to apply your knowledge to mapping a pool ball, reflections and all. Next you learned a few more tricks with the Material Editor and found out about the different kinds of maps available in 3ds Max. With that knowledge, you mapped the entire rocket you modeled in Chapter 5, and readied it for its next step, lighting in Chapter 10. Then you picked up the soldier model from Chapter 6 and learned how to lay out its UVs for painted textures, which you assigned at the end of the chapter using color as well as bump, normal, and specular maps.

If you'd like some additional practice, go back and adjust all the materials on the rocket with different types of materials, colors, and settings to see how they affect the render of the rocket. So far we've done all this with a minimal lighting setup. As you will see in Chapter 10, lighting plays a vital role in how you texture your model. Soon you'll find yourself tweaking settings for the specular highlights, reflections, color, and so on as you change your lighting environment to create the best render.

# CHAPTER 8

# Introduction to Animation

*The best way to learn* how to animate is to jump right in and start animating. You will begin this chapter by picking up the Mobile exercise from Chapter 2, "Your First 3ds Max Project," and adding animation to the shapes of the mobile. You'll take a good look at 3ds Max's animation tools so you can start editing animation and developing your timing skills.

Topics in this chapter include the following:

- **The mobile redux: setting up hierarchies**
- **Using dummy objects**
- **The bouncing ball**
- **Using the Track View–Curve Editor**
- **Track View**
- **Anticipation and momentum in knife throwing**

# The Mobile Redux: Setting Up Hierarchies

Do you remember way back when you were reading Chapter 2? In the exercise in that chapter, you had a chance to set up the mobile so you could become more familiar with the 3ds Max UI. Now we'll revisit the mobile and set it up to animate, and you'll learn how to create hierarchies as we go.

The first section of this chapter will take you through setting up these mobile objects for animation in hierarchies so that when one bar rotates, the shapes and any bars beneath it also rotate.

In the following section, we will tackle hierarchies and setting up the mobile objects to animate properly.

## Parent and Child Objects

Before we continue with the next step in the Mobile exercise, let's take a look at hierarchies in action. Here is a quick introduction to how hierarchies work.

In the following steps, we will create a hierarchy of a few boxes to see how the relationship works when parents move, taking their children with them, and how children can move independently under their parents.

Figure 8.1

**Create and line up three boxes.**

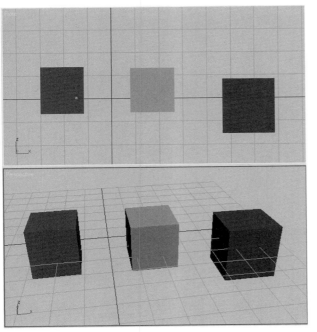

1.  Start a new scene. In the Create panel under Standard Primitives, click Box to create a new box. Click and drag in the Front viewport and draw out a box. When you are happy with the size of the rectangle, release the mouse button and then drag the mouse further to pull out the third dimension of the box to give it depth. Click again when you are happy with the 3D box, and 3ds Max will create it. Your cursor will still be active in the Create Box tool. Click and drag to create two more boxes of approximately the same size to the right of the first box, as shown in Figure 8.1.

2.  You need to set up a hierarchy so that the box on the right is a child of the box in the middle, which in turn is a child of the box on the left, like a row of ducks. In the Main toolbar across the top of the UI, click the Select and Link tool ( ). The Select and Link tool works upward, meaning you select the bottom of the hierarchy and work your way up, as you'll see next.

3. In either the Front or Perspective viewport, click the box on the right and then drag the mouse over to the box in the middle. A dashed line will appear and the cursor will change to the "Select and Link" icon while you do this, as shown in Figure 8.2. When you release the mouse button, the parent box will flash a white outline. This indicates that the link worked. The box on the right is now a child of the box in the middle.

Figure 8.2

**Notice the cursor cues.**

4. Click the Move tool ( ⊕ ) and select the middle box. Move it around in the viewport. The box on the right (the child) will now follow, as shown in Figure 8.3. Click the child box on the right, and move it. Notice the child can move independently of its parent (the box in the middle).

5. Click the Select and Link tool ( ⊗ ) again. This time click on the box in the middle and drag it to the box on the left. Select and move the box on the left, and all the boxes will follow.

Now let's set a few keyframes on these boxes to get our juices flowing.

Figure 8.3

**The box follows as you drag it.**

## Setting Keyframes

The Time Slider is at the bottom of the screen, as shown in Figure 8.4. The Time Slider is used to change your position in time, counted in *frames*. As you read in the previous chapter, frames are the common increment for denoting time in an animation. You'll read more about the Time Slider in the next chapter.

Figure 8.4

**The Time Slider allows you to change your position in time and scrub your animation.**

You can click and drag the horizontal bar to change the frame in your animation on the fly. This is called *scrubbing* animation. The bar displays the current frame/end frame. By default, your 3ds Max UI may show a start frame of 0 and an end frame of 30. Let's set the Time Slider to start at 0 and end at 100. To the right of the Time Slider, click the Time Configuration button, as shown in Figure 8.5.

In the Time Configuration dialog box, set the End Time value to 100 as shown in Figure 8.6, and then click OK. Your Time Slider will change to show a range of 0 to 100 frames. Click and drag the slider to the left so your current frame is 0. Now, in the lower-right corner of the UI, click the Auto Key button, as shown in Figure 8.7. Both the Auto Key button and the Time Slider will turn red. This means that any movement in the objects in your scene will be recorded as animation. How exciting!

Figure 8.5

**Click the Time Configuration button.**

Figure 8.6

**Set the End Time to 100.**

Figure 8.7

**Auto Key button**

Figure 8.8

**Move the boxes at frame 20.**

Move the Time Slider to the right to frame 20. Select the box on the left (the top parent) and move it across the Front viewport to the left along the *X*-axis. Next, click and move the middle box down on the *Y*-axis in the viewport, as shown in Figure 8.8.

Now scrub the timeline between 0 and 20, and you will see your animation. Even though you did not set any keyframes on the box to the right, it will follow along with both the left box and the middle box, doing a combination of their moves. The middle box goes with its parent (the left box) and its own animation, sliding down the viewport on the *Y*-axis. This is a simple hierarchy showing you how the relationships between objects build animation. You will use the same theory to build the animation for the Mobile exercise.

Before you continue on to the next exercise, make sure to turn off Auto Key.

## Hierarchies for the Mobile

Set your 3ds Max project folder by choosing Application menu → Manage → Set Project Folder and selecting the Mobile project that you downloaded from this book's companion web page (www.sybex.com/go/intro3dsmax2011) to your hard drive.

Let's start with a simple hierarchy scheme much like the preceding Boxes exercise. Start with the Mobile_v01.max scene file in the Mobile\Scenes folder in the Mobile project downloaded from this book's companion web page.

You will create the hierarchies for the animation of the mobile using the following steps:

1. Remember, the Select and Link tool works from the children up the hierarchy to the top parent. You will link the shapes to their respective bars up the mobile. Click the Select and Link tool (🔗) and then select the triangle. Drag the cursor to its bar, as shown in Figure 8.9. The triangle is now linked to the bar above it.

2. With the Select and Link tool still active, click and drag from the donut to the bar above it, as shown in Figure 8.10.

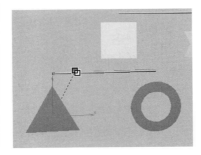

Figure 8.9

**Drag from the triangle to link it to the bar.**

Figure 8.10

**Link the donut to the bar.**

3. With the Select and Link tool, click and drag from the bottom bar that holds the triangle and donut to the square shape above it, as shown in Figure 8.11. The bar is hanging from that square as if this were a real mobile, so you would link it as such. If you want to check your work, select and move the square. The objects beneath it will move with the square. Just make sure to press Ctrl+Z to undo any moves you made to check the linking.

4. Now you just need to use the same steps to link the rest of the mobile:

   a. Click and drag with the Select and Link tool from the square to the bar above it.

   b. Link from the star to its bar.

   c. Link from the bar above the star and square to the top bar, as shown in Figure 8.12.

Figure 8.11
**Link the bar to the square.**

Figure 8.12
**Link one bar to another.**

   d. Link from the hexagon to its bar.

   e. Link from the circle to its bar.

   f. Link from the bar above the circle and hexagon to the top bar, as shown in Figure 8.13.

Figure 8.13
**Link the circle's bar to the top one.**

You can refer to Figure 8.14 for a diagram of the linking order. It doesn't matter in what order you link the pieces, as long as you link from the bottom pieces up the chain.

Figure 8.14

The linking order determines the hier-archy of the mobile.

## Pivot Points

Now you've linked all the pieces of the mobile and created your first animation hierarchy. It's time to rotate parts of the mobile and test your handiwork. This will be the last step before you animate the mobile. To test the mobile, select the bottom bar and rotate it on the *Z*-axis in either direction. Figure 8.15 shows the rotation of the bottom bar. Notice that the Rotate gizmo is at one end of the bar and not in the middle. You should also notice that the bar (along with the triangle and donut) is rotating around the end of the bar, although it should rotate in the middle, where the string would be hanging it from the square right above it.

Your results might be slightly different from what is shown here. Your bar might not rotate around the same end or it might rotate somewhere else along the cylinder. This is

Figure 8.15

The bottom bar is rotating around its own end instead of its middle.

perfectly normal. The important thing is where the *pivot point* of the object is—and that pivot should ultimately be in the middle of the bar.

Simply put, the pivot point of an object in 3ds Max is the point about which it rotates. It is also the point on the object that defines the point in coordinate space where the object resides. So a coordinate of (2, 6, 0) for the position of a cube, for example, technically describes the pivot point of that cube to be at the location (2, 6, 0).

Because the pivot point of the bottom bar is not in the middle of the bar, you will have to move the pivot point to the middle. To do so, follow these steps:

1. Use Ctrl+Z to undo any rotations you have already put on the bottom bar. Click the Move tool (  ) or press the hot key W for the Move tool, and select the bottom bar if it is not currently selected. In the Command panel, switch to the Hierarchy panel, as shown in Figure 8.16, by pressing the Hierarchy Panel tab ( ).

2. At the top of the Hierarchy panel, make sure the Pivot button is active and then click the Affect Pivot Only button to activate it (the button will change color). This will tell 3ds Max to move only the pivot point of the currently selected object and not to move the entire object. Your gizmo will change, as shown in Figure 8.17.

3. Click the *X*-axis Move handle (the small red arrow inside the larger outline of an arrow) and move the pivot point along the length of the bar to the middle of the bar, as shown in Figure 8.18.

**Figure 8.17**

Again, the gizmo cues you to what action is being taken: You're moving only the pivot point.

**Figure 8.18**

Move the pivot to the middle of the bar.

**Figure 8.16**

**The Hierarchy panel**

4. In the Hierarchy panel, click the Affect Pivot Only button again to turn it off. Your cursor will return to the normal Move tool gizmo. Select the Rotate tool from the Main toolbar ( ) and rotate the bottom bar again. The bar will now rotate around its middle as it should, with the triangle and donut in tow, as shown in Figure 8.19.

5. To make sure the pivot points are all in the middle of the respective bars, check the other bars in the mobile. If necessary, use the previous steps to relocate the pivots to their proper places.

You can check your work against the Mobile_v03.max scene file in the Mobile\Scenes folder from the companion web page. Once the pivot points are all placed properly on the mobile's bars, you are ready to animate. Grab a cold drink; you deserve it!

**Figure 8.19**

**The bottom bar now rotates properly.**

# Ready, Set, Animate!

In this animation, we will rotate *only the bars* of the mobile. Don't worry about rotating or animating the shapes for now. We will revisit this exercise later in this chapter.

You can use your own file, or you can download the Mobile_v03.max scene file in the Mobile\Scenes folder on the web page. In this file, the mobile is already linked properly for this animation and all the pivots are placed at the middle of each bar. To animate the mobile, follow these steps:

1. Scrub the Time Slider to 0. If it is not already on, turn on the Auto Keyframe feature by clicking the Auto Key button (Auto Key). Both the Auto Key button and the Time Slider will turn red.

2. Move the Time Slider to frame 50. Click the Rotate tool (or press the hot key E for the Rotate tool), and select and rotate the bottom bar (which will also rotate the triangle and donut beneath it). You can rotate the bar in either direction on the Z-axis, as shown in Figure 8.20. Give it a few full rotations all the way around. Don't be shy.

3. You can scrub the animation to check it out. The bottom bar and its shapes should be spinning. Make sure you go back to frame 50 in the Time Slider. With the Rotate tool still active, select the second bar from the bottom (the bar with the square and the star), and rotate it in either direction on the Z-axis. Figure 8.21 shows how the bottom bar follows along.

Figure 8.20 _____
**Rotate the bottom bar with some gusto!**

Figure 8.21 _____
**Rotate the second bar, and the bottom bar follows.**

4. While still at frame 50, select the third bar from the bottom (the bar with the circle and the hexagon) and rotate it in either direction on the $Z$-axis. The circle and hexagon rotate with the bar, as shown in Figure 8.22.

5. With the Rotate tool, select the top bar and rotate it in either direction on the $Z$-axis. The entire mobile will rotate along with it, because the top bar is the top parent of this hierarchy (Figure 8.23).

Figure 8.22

**The shapes rotate properly.**

Scrub your animation, and you'll see that the mobile is in full swing! The bars rotate and carry with them the shapes and bars beneath them, according to the previously set hierarchy. If your shapes or child bars are not rotating with their parent bars, check your hierarchies or redo that portion of the exercise. We will pick up animating the rest of the mobile in the next section.

You can use your own file, or you can download the Mobile_v04.max scene file in the Mobile\Scenes folder on the web page.

Understanding the underlying technique used here is important, so doing the exercise more than once is not a bad idea. These things can be frustrating, so take it easy and when you get confused or stuck, back up and try again. For now, take a break, save your work and get ready for the next section.

Figure 8.23

**The whole mobile rotates along with the top bar.**

## Animating the Rest of the Mobile

Let's pick up where you left off and finish the animation using the hierarchies that were just set up.

You can begin this exercise by using your own Mobile file, or you can download Mobile_v05.max from the Mobile\Scenes folder in the Mobile project on the companion web page. This scene file is the same as the file you ended up with in the previous section (Mobile_v04.max), except this version takes the animation of the bars to frame 100 instead of frame 50, giving you a little more room to play.

## Animating the Shapes

With the Mobile_v05.max scene open (or your own file), scrub through the animation to become familiar with the scene. The intent here is to create a hierarchy in the mobile and animate the bars. Now you will add rotation to the shapes hanging from the bars. Figure 8.24 shows the mobile in mid-animation.

Figure 8.24

**The mobile!**

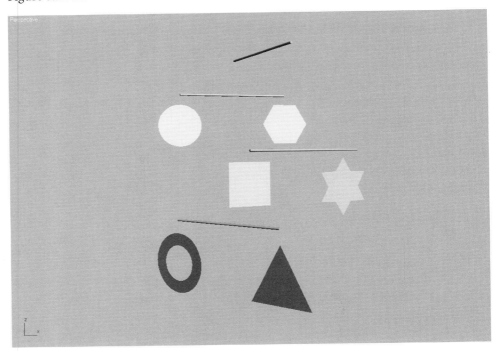

To add animation to the shapes under the bars, follow these steps:

1. Go to frame 0 of the animation, and click the Auto Key button ( Auto Key ) at the bottom of the UI to turn it on if it's off.

2. Select the triangle hanging from the bottom bar, and go to frame 50. Rotate the triangle on the Z-axis in either direction at least a full turn of 360 degrees, as shown in Figure 8.25. Don't scrub your animation yet.

3. Still at frame 50, select the square on the bar above, and rotate that shape on the Z-axis several hundred degrees in either direction. Figure 8.26 shows the rotation of the square. The bottom bar goes along with the square's rotation because this is how they were linked earlier in this chapter. Don't scrub your animation yet.

4. Still at frame 50, select the star and rotate it several hundred degrees on the Z-axis in either direction (Figure 8.27).

Figure 8.25

**Rotate the triangle 360 degrees or more on the Z-axis.**

Now scrub your animation and check the results. In theory, all the bars should rotate and so should the shapes hanging on the bars. When you scrub, however, the mobile will seem to have lost its mind. The shapes will rotate completely off-axis, as if you have set rotation keyframes on the *X*- and *Y*-axes as well as the intended *Z*-axis. The same will occur with the lower bar. It will go off its axis and rotate in an unpredictable manner. This behavior is explained in the next section, with easy solutions to fix the issue.

Figure 8.26

**The square is rotated, and its child bar goes along for the ride.**

## Making a Mistake

Have we gone mad? Why would we purposely show you an incorrect work-flow? Because learning from missteps is as important to learning CG as learning the correct steps is. Being able to troubleshoot is essential to becoming good in CG, and the more trouble you get yourself into, the better you will become at digging your way out.

This example of strangely rotating hierarchies is an isolated issue that is called *gimbal lock* in many CG circles. Different CG packages have different ways of interpreting exactly how an object rotates when it is rotating along more than one axis. Imagine three cars all staring each other down at a three-way intersection—with the traffic light out. Who goes first in this situation is important to the flow of traffic at the intersection. When a 3D package calculates rotations, it needs to know which axis to rotate first before tending to the rotation of the other axes. In 3ds Max, the *animation controller* is the traffic light directing the animation. With gimbal lock, you have an incorrect interpretation of the rotations, so the resulting animation seems off-axis.

Figure 8.27

**Rotate the star on the *Z*-axis.**

In this exercise, the multiple rotations inherited by the child shapes and bars from their parents caused havoc with their own rotations, so the axes became confused and everything looks just plain wrong. The easiest way to fix this issue is to reassign the animation controllers in charge of the rotations for those objects to one that will not lock up.

### Animation Controllers

By default, 3ds Max assigns an Euler XYZ controller to the rotations of objects. This is the best controller to use in the majority of circumstances. In this example, however, it doesn't quite work. To assign a different controller, follow along here:

1. Turn off Auto Key. Select the square; you will start with that object. Switch to the Motion panel (click the Motion tab—![icon]—in the Command panel, as you see in Figure 8.28). Open the Assign Controller rollout. You'll see that the Rotation controller for the square is set to Euler XYZ.

2. Select Rotation: Euler XYZ from the list in the Motion panel, as shown in Figure 8.28. Click the Assign Controller button (![icon], found right under the Assign Controller

Figure 8.28

**The Assign Control-
ler rollout in the
Motion panel.**

rollout heading) to open the Assign Rotation Controller dialog box (Figure 8.29).
Choose TCB Rotation from the list then click OK. If you do not first select the controller from the Controller list, the Assign Controller button will be grayed out and
unusable.

3. The square and the bar linked beneath it should snap
back into axis. Scrub the animation, and you'll see that
the square and the bar beneath it are behaving as you
would expect: They are rotating on the Z-axis only, as
they should. Figure 8.30 shows the resulting animation. Notice that the star and triangle are still rotating
off-axis.

4. Select the triangle and repeat steps 2 and 3 to assign a
TCB Rotation controller to the triangle. Do the same
for the star. Figure 8.31 shows the proper rotations of
the shapes and the bars—but looks are deceiving. We're
not done yet!

Figure 8.29

**Choosing TCB Rotation limits
your options and the rotation.**

If Euler XYZ caused such a ruckus, why isn't TCB
Rotation the default for rotating objects? For one thing,
the editing options you have with an Euler XYZ controller
are head and shoulders above what you get with TCB Rotation. With Euler XYZ,
3ds Max splits the *XYZ* rotation animation into three separate tracks to give individual
control over each axis. This is ideal.

Figure 8.30

**You've fixed the rotation of the square and its
children.**

Figure 8.31

**The mobile seems to rotate properly, but does
it really?**

In addition, the TCB Rotation has taken the several hundred degrees of rotation you have animated, and cut it down to keep values under 180 degrees of rotation at most. The square, triangle, and star don't seem to be rotating the several hundred degrees you intended.

**Figure 8.32**

Edit your controller in the Key Info rollout.

> It is not a good idea to change the default animation controllers based solely on your experience with this exercise. On the other hand, if you run into a gimbal lock situation in the future, you'll have a good idea what caused it, and you'll be able to troubleshoot it quickly.

### Editing the TCB Rotation Keyframes

To fix the problem of the objects not rotating the several hundred degrees you want, you will have to manually edit the controller to allow a greater degree of rotation:

1. Select the square and open the Key Info rollout (Figure 8.32). Go to frame 0.

2. The Key Info rollout shows you the properties of the animation on the selected object on a key-by-key basis. If everything is grayed out, use the arrows at the top of the rollout to move through the keyframes. Go to the first keyframe at frame 0 (shown as Time: 0 in the rollout). The Angle displays the orientation of the square at the beginning of the animation: 120. Use the arrows at the top of the rollout again to move to keyframe 2 (Time: 50).

3. The Angle parameter should change to a value of 117.643 (your value may differ, as long as the rotation looks correct). The *X* parameter value reads –1.0. The *X*, *Y*, and *Z* parameters represent the direction in the respective axes. The value –1 means the square is rotating backward. Don't get confused because this value is now in *X* and not *Z*. Remember, you gave up the individual controls for *X*, *Y*, and *Z* when you changed from the Euler XYZ controller. While at this second keyframe (at frame 50), check Rotation Windup at the bottom of the rollout, and enter the value **500** for Angle. You must first turn on Rotation Windup to enter **500** for the Angle (Figure 8.33).

**Figure 8.33**

Adding more rotation to the square in the Key Info rollout

4. Scrub your animation, and the square will rotate more, as you first intended. Repeat steps 2 and 3 for the triangle and star to fix their rotations with the TCB Rotation controller. At this point, you can save the 3ds Max file for use in the next section.

Any parameter that is animated has a controller. A controller essentially deals with all the animation functions in the scene for 3ds Max, such as storing keyframe values. Interpolating in-betweens is handled by the controllers. By default, the Position XYZ controller is assigned to an animation on an object's position and an Euler XYZ is assigned to its rotation. These controllers are the most useful as they split the *X*, *Y*, and *Z* into separate tracks to give individual control over each axis. You will have the opportunity to work with and edit individual tracks later in this chapter.

# Using Dummy Objects

The preferred way to circumvent this particular issue of rotation confusion is by using helper objects in 3ds Max called *dummy objects.* Changing the controller for an object is not always the best solution—particularly if the range of movement will be changed. You saw this problem when you changed to TCB Rotation before you had to fix it in Key Info to add more rotation. Using dummy objects, you can insert a helper in the hierarchy that will negate the gimbal lock issue and make it very clear to 3ds Max how the rotations should proceed. As a matter of fact, it's common for animators to make copious use of dummies as controllers for their animation *rigs.* A rig is essentially any setup in the scene that helps you animate objects in the scene.

Dummies (called *null nodes* in other CG applications, such as Maya) are very useful nonrendering objects that can be used in several ways. In this case, they serve as placeholders and are used directly in the hierarchy to straighten out the rotation confusion. They serve as parents to the mobile shapes that may come down with rotation confusion or gimbal lock.

### The Way to Really Set Up the Mobile: Placing Dummies in the Hierarchy

You can begin this exercise either by using your own Mobile file before the steps in the last section or by opening Mobile_v06.max from the Scenes folder in the Mobile project you downloaded from the companion web page to your hard drive.

To create dummy objects for the animation hierarchy, follow these steps:

1. Go to the Create Panel. Click on the Helpers button ( ▣ ), and click on Dummy (Figure 8.34).

2. Go to Frame 0. There are no Parameter rollouts or settings for the dummy. Move your cursor to the Front viewport, center it over the circle, and then click and drag to create a dummy like the one in the top of Figure 8.34. Create a dummy that is slightly larger than the circle.

### Linking the Dummies

If you scrub the animation, you will notice that the circle moves along with the rotation of its parent bar, as it did before. This is because the dummy is not part of the hierarchy yet. You are going to change the structure of the hierarchy in order to

Figure 8.34

**Click Dummy (left). This creates a dummy object to fit over the circle (right).**

break the relationship of the circle with its parent object and restructure it to add the dummy between the bar and the circle. This is done by relinking the new order.

3. Make sure the Time Slider is at frame 0. Go to the Main toolbar and click on the Select and Link tool (🔗). Use the Select and Link tool to select the circle, and then click and drag it to its dummy object. Make sure you don't let go until the cursor changes to the icon to make the proper link, as shown in Figure 8.35.

> To jump to the beginning of an animation, just press the Home key on your keyboard; this is a shortcut to jump to the start. Likewise, pressing the End key will take you to the end of an animation.

4. You're not done yet. If you scrub the animation, the circle will no longer move with its parent bar. You have to link the dummy to the bar. Select the dummy, and click and drag to the parent cylinder (Figure 8.36). This completes the new hierarchy. Now the circle is the child of the dummy, and the dummy is the child of the parent bar above it. Play the animation, and you will see the dummy moving along with the mobile, with the circle in tow.

5. Fantastic! Now it is time to animate the circle itself. Move to the end of your time-line (frame 100; press the End key), and click the Auto Key button at the bottom of the interface (you can also press the N key to toggle Auto Key on and off). Select the circle, and rotate a few hundred degrees on the *Z*-axis in either direction. Do not rotate the dummy, just the circle. Figure 8.37 shows how the circle rotates within the dummy, which then follows the bar's rotation.

6. Repeat steps 1 and 2 to create dummies for the other objects in the mobile. Relink the objects to their dummies, as you did in steps 3 and 4. Animate the shapes them-selves to your heart's content as in step 5. If you see funky rotation on the dummies and objects, either you have made an error in the linking order, or you have ani-mated the dummies rotating and not the shapes themselves.

Play the animation. As you can see, the funky rotation is gone and now you have a perfectly normal rotation without having to change the animation con-trollers. The bar's rotation moves the dummy below it, and the dummy pulls the circle. Because the bar is not directly pulling the circle, the circle is free to rotate without rotation confusion.

Once you feel confident with how this exercise works, you should have a pretty solid idea of how hierarchies work in animation. Feel free to go through this entire exercise another time before moving on.

**Figure 8.35**

**Drag to link from the circle to the dummy object.**

**Figure 8.36**

**Link the circle's dummy to the bar.**

**Figure 8.37**

**Success! The circle is now rotating properly.**

**Editing Dummies—Using the Align Tool**

Each dummy gets its orientation from the viewport in which you create it. When you place one of the mobile's dummies, you don't need to have it aligned perfectly with the shape for which the dummy is being used. However, it is a good idea to match things up as best as you can to keep track of which dummy goes with which shape.

Let's say you created a dummy and it is nowhere near its object. The Align tool can move the dummy so it is centered on the object. To see how the Align tool works, follow along with these steps:

1. Turn off Auto Key and go to Frame 0. Create a dummy of any size anywhere in the mobile scene (Figure 8.38).

2. Make sure the dummy is selected. Go to the Main toolbar and select the Align tool (). Move your cursor to the hexagon to which you want to align the dummy, and click the hexagon. The Align Selection dialog box will open (Figure 8.39).

Figure 8.38
**Create a dummy.**

Figure 8.39
**The Align Selection dialog box.**

Figure 8.40
**Aligned to center**

3. The Align Selection dialog box gives you the choice of aligning an object along any axis, orienting the object (this feature is for rotations), and aligning for the object's scale. Keep the checks on in the *X*, *Y*, and *Z* Position boxes, but change the Current and Target Object to Center and then press OK. The dummy will match up with the hexagon shape as shown in Figure 8.40.

Although it may seem like more work, using dummies is a great workflow for animation. It keeps the scene's animation neater and better defined. As you gain more experience, you will begin to learn when you should use dummies in your hierarchy to make the animation workflow smooth.

# The Bouncing Ball

A classic exercise for all animators is to create a bouncing ball. As a matter of fact, you will find bouncing ball tutorials almost everywhere you look. Although you will see it as a straightforward exercise, there is so much you can do with a bouncing ball to show character that the possibilities are almost limitless. Animating a bouncing ball is a good exercise in physics as well as cartoon movement. You'll first create a rubber ball, and then you'll add cartoonish movement to accentuate some principles of the animation techniques discussed in Chapter 1, "Basic Concepts." Aspiring animators will be able to use this exercise for years and always find something new to learn about bouncing a ball.

In preparation, download the Bouncing Ball project from the companion web page to your hard drive. Set your current project by choosing Application menu → Manage → Set Project Folder and selecting the Bouncing Ball project that you downloaded.

## Animating the Ball

Your first step is to keyframe the positions of the ball. As introduced in Chapter 1, *keyframing* is the process—borrowed from traditional animation—of setting positions and values at particular frames of the animation. The computer interpolates between these keyframes to fill in the other frames to complete a smooth animation.

Open the `Animation_Ball_00.max` scene file from the BouncingBall\Scenes folder you downloaded.

You'll start with the *gross animation*, or the overall movements. This is also widely known as *blocking*. First, move the ball up and down to begin its choreography.

Follow these steps to animate the ball:

1. The first thing you need to do in this scene is to move the pivot point for the ball from the center of the ball to the bottom of the ball. Select the ball, then go to the Hierarchy panel ( ). Choose Pivot, and under the Adjust Pivot rollout, click the Adjust Pivot Only button. Zoom in on the ball in the Front viewport and move the pivot so that it is at the bottom of the ball. Then click on the Affect Pivot Only button again to deactivate— but you already knew that.

2. Turn on the Auto Key button (keyboard shortcut N) and move the Time Slider to frame 10. With the ball selected, move it along the Z-axis down to the ground plane. That will be 0 units on Z when you release the mouse button in the Transform Type-In at the bottom of the interface. You can also just enter the value and press Enter (Figure 8.41).

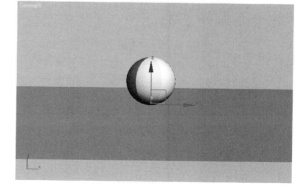

Figure 8.41

**At frame 10, move the ball to meet the ground plane.**

This has created two keyframes, one at frame 0 for the original position the ball was in, and one at frame 10 for the new position to which you just moved the ball.

### Copying Keyframes

Now you want to move the ball up to the same position in the air as it was at frame 0. Instead of trying to estimate where that was, you can just copy the keyframe at frame 0 to frame 20.

You can see the keyframes you created in the timeline. They are red boxes in the timeline. Red keys represent Position keyframes, green keys represent Rotation, and blue keys represent Scale. When a keyframe in the timeline is selected, it turns white. In Figure 8.42, the keyframe at frame 0 is selected and is white.

1. Select the keyframe at frame 0; it should turn white when it is selected. Hold down the Shift key on the keyboard (this is a shortcut for the Clone tool), and click and drag the selected keyframe to move it to frame 20. This will create a keyframe with the same animation parameters as the keyframe at frame 0.

Figure 8.42

**The selected key in the timeline is white.**

2. Click and drag on the Time Slider to scrub through the keyframes. Turn off Auto Key.

## Using the Track View–Curve Editor

Right now the ball is going down and then back up. To continue the animation for the length of the timeline, you could continue to copy and paste keyframes—but that would be very time-consuming, and you still need to do your other homework and clean your room. A better way is to loop or *cycle* through the keyframes you already have. An *animation cycle* is a segment of animation that is repeatable in a loop. The end state of the animation matches up to the beginning state, so there is no hiccup at the loop point.

In 3ds Max, cycling animation is known as *Parameter Curve Out-of-Range Types*. This is a fancy way to create loops and cycles with your animations and specify how your object will behave outside the range of the keys you have created. This will bring us to the Track View, which is an animator's best friend. You can go through the Track View's UI in the "Track View" section later in this chapter at any time, or you can hang tight and see how you work with Curve Editor first using the Bouncing Ball exercise. You will learn the underlying concepts of the Curve Editor as well as its basic UI throughout this exercise. Feel free to reference the "Track View" section as you continue.

The Track View is a function of two animation editors, the Curve Editor and the Dope Sheet. The Curve Editor allows you to work with animation depicted as curves on a graph that sets the value of a parameter against time. The Dope Sheet displays keyframes over time on a horizontal graph, without any curves. This graphical display simplifies the process of adjusting animation timing because you can see all the keys at once in a spreadsheet-like format. The Dope Sheet is similar to the traditional animation exposure sheets or X Sheets.

Navigation inside the Track View–Curve Editor is pretty much the same as navigating in a viewport; the same keyboard/mouse combinations work for panning and zooming.

You will use the Track View–Curve Editor (or just Curve Editor for short) to loop your animation in the following steps:

1. With the ball selected, in the menu bar choose Graph Editors → Track View - Curve Editor. In Figure 8.43, the Curve Editor displays the animation curves of the ball so far.

Figure 8.43

**The Curve Editor shows the animation curves of the ball.**

2. A toolbar runs across the top of the Curve Editor under the menu bar. In that toolbar, click the Parameter Curve Out-of-Range Types button ([⊠]), shown in context in Figure 8.44.

Figure 8.44

**Parameter Curve Out-of-Range Types button**

3. This will open the Param Curve Out-of-Range Types dialog box (Figure 8.45). Select Loop from this dialog box by clicking its thumbnail. The two little boxes beneath it will highlight. Click OK. To read up on the other Parameter Curve Out-of-Range Types available, see the "Parameter Curve Out-of-Range Types" sidebar later in this chapter.

Figure 8.45

**Choosing to loop your animation**

4. Once you set the curve to Loop, the Curve Editor displays your animation as shown in Figure 8.46. The out-of-range animation is shown as a dashed line. Scrub your animation in a viewport and see how the ball bounces up and down throughout the timeline range.

Figure 8.46

**The Curve Editor now shows the animation looped curve.**

## Reading Animation Curves

As you can see, the Track View–Curve Editor (from here on called just the Curve Editor) gives you control over the animation in a graph setting. Curves allow you to visualize the interpolation of the motion. Understanding what animation curves do in the Curve Editor is critical to getting your animation to look right. Once you are used to reading animation curves, you can judge an object's direction, speed, acceleration, and timing at a mere glance.

The Curve Editor's graph is a representation of an object's parameter, such as position (values shown vertically) over time (time shown horizontally). Every place on the curve represents where the object is; a keyframe does not need to be on the curve. So, the shape of the curve makes a big difference in the motion of the object.

Here is a quick primer on how to read a curve in the Curve Editor.

In Figure 8.47, an object's Z Position parameter is being animated. At the beginning, the curve quickly begins to move positively (that is, to the right) on the Z-axis. The object shoots up and comes to an *ease-out*, where it decelerates to a stop, reaching its top height. The ease-out stop is signified by the curving beginning to flatten out at around frame 70.

Figure 8.47

**The object quickly accelerates to an ease-out stop.**

## PARAMETER CURVE OUT-OF-RANGE TYPES

There are several ways to interpret the curves of an animation when they are out of range, meaning when they extend before your first keyframe and beyond your last keyframe. The Parameter Curve Out-of-Range Types dialog box is opened through the Curve Editor with this toolbar button ( ). The types are the following:

**Constant**  Used when you do not want any animation out of range. This curve type will hold the value of the end and/or beginning key of the range for all frames. Constant is the default out-of-range type.

**Cycle**  Used when you need the animation to loop or cycle by repeating the same animation that is within the range. If the first keyframe does not line up with the last keyframe of the curve range, there will be an abrupt "jump" from the last key to the first with every cycle. If the start and end values do not need to match, and that hiccup in the cycle is desired, use Cycle.

**Loop**  Used when you need the animation to loop or cycle smoothly despite any differences in the start and end keyframe values. Loop repeats the same animation in the curve range, but it also interpolates between the last and first keyframes in the range to create a smooth loop in the cycle. Loop's ability to create a smooth loop can go only so far before it acts like a Cycle (e.g., when the key values at the start and end are too disparate).

*continued*

## PARAMETER CURVE OUT-OF-RANGE TYPES *(continued)*

**Ping Pong**  Used when you want your animation to oscillate back and forth. Ping Pong repeats the same animation in the range, but it plays it front to back and then back to front, and so forth, to alternate the playback, as shown here.

**Linear**  Used when you need your animation to continue at the same speed as its beginning or end. The animation curve is projected out from the range in a straight line, picking up the trajectory from the shape of the start or end of the curve, as shown here.

**Relative Repeat**  Used when you need your animation to repeat as in a cycle and to continue building on itself as it cycles. Each repetition is offset by the value at the end of the range, as shown here.

You can select any one of these types for either the before or after by clicking one of the smaller boxes below the thumbnails. You can set both the before and after out-of-range type by clicking the thumbnail of the type itself.

In Figure 8.48, the object slowly accelerates in an *ease-in* in the positive *Z* direction until it hits frame 75, where it suddenly stops.

Figure 8.48

**The object eases in to acceleration and suddenly stops at its fastest velocity.**

In Figure 8.49, the object eases in and travels to an ease-out where it decelerates, starting at around frame 69, to where it slowly stops, at frame 75.

Figure 8.49

**Ease-in and ease-out**

Finally, in Figure 8.50, the object jumps from its Z Position in frame 24 to its new position in frame 25.

Figure 8.50

**Step interpolation makes the object "jump" suddenly from one value to the next.**

Figure 8.51 shows the Track View–Curve Editor, with its major aspects called out for your information. See the "Track View" section later in this chapter for a more thorough explanation of the UI and toolset for the Track View.

Figure 8.51

**The Curve Editor**

Refining the Animation

Now that you've played back the gross animation of the bounce, how does it look? Not like a ball bouncing, really, but the framework is getting there. Notice how the speed of the ball is consistent. If this were a real ball, it would be dealing with gravity; the ball would speed up as it gets closer to the ground and there would be "hang time" when the ball is in the air on its way up as gravity takes over to pull it back down.

This means you have to edit the movement that happens between the keyframes. This is done by adjusting *how* the keyframes shape the curve itself, using tangents. When you select a keyframe, a handle will appear in the UI, as shown in Figure 8.52 and close up in Figure 8.53.

Figure 8.52

**The ball's animation curve**

This handle adjusts the tangency of the keyframe to change the curvature of the animation curve, which in turn changes the animation. There are different types of tangents, depending on how you want to edit the motion. By default the Smooth tangent is applied to all new keyframes. This is not what you want for the ball, although it is a perfect default tangent type to have.

Figure 8.53

**The keyframe's handle**

### Editing Animation Curves

Let's edit some tangencies to better suit your animation. The intent is to speed up the curve as it hits the floor and slow it down as it crests its apex. Instead of opening the Curve Editor through the menu bar, this time you are going to use the shortcut. At the bottom-left corner of the interface, click the Open Mini Curve Editor button shown in Figure 8.54. You may have to close the large Curve Editor dialog first.

This Mini Curve Editor is almost exactly the same as the one you launch through the Main Menu bar. A few tools are not included in the Mini Curve Editor toolbar, but you can find them in the menu bar of the Mini Curve Editor. Figure 8.55 shows the Mini Curve Editor open in the 3ds Max UI.

Figure 8.54

**The Open Mini Curve Editor button**

Figure 8.55

**The Mini Curve Editor**

To edit the curves, follow these steps:

1. Scroll down the List Controller window on the left of the Mini Curve Editor by dragging the Pan tool (the hand cursor) to find the Ball object's position. Click on the Z Position track. This will bring only those curves to the Key Editing window that you want to edit, as you saw in Figure 8.55.

2. The Z Position curve is blue, as is almost everything relating to the *Z*-axis. The little gray boxes on the curves are keyframes, as you saw in Figure 8.51. Select the keyframe at frame 10. You may need to scrub the Time Slider out of the way if you are on frame 10. The key will turn white when selected. Remember, if you need to zoom or pan in the Curve Editor's Key Editing window, you can use the same shortcuts you would use to navigate in the viewports. You will change this key's tangency to make the ball fall faster as it hits and bounces off the ground.

3. In the Mini Curve Editor toolbar, change the tangent type for the selected keyframe from the Auto default to Fast by selecting the Set Tangents to Fast icon (). When you do this, you will see the animation curve change shape as shown in Figure 8.56.

Figure 8.56

**The effect of the new tangent type**

4. Select the Camera viewport and play the animation. You can easily correlate how the animation works with the curve's shape as you see the Time Slider travel through the Mini Curve Editor as the animation plays.

## Finessing the Animation

Although the animation has improved, the ball has a distinct lack of weight. It still seems too simple and without any character. In situations such as this, an animator can go wild and try several different things as he or she sees fit. This is where creativity helps hone your animation skills, whether you are new to animation or have been doing it for 50 years.

Animation shows change over time. Good animation conveys the *intent*, the motivation for that change between the frames.

### Squash and Stretch

The concept of *squash and stretch* has been an animation staple for as long as there has been animation. It is a way to convey the weight of an object by deforming it to react (usually in an exaggerated way) to gravity, impact, and motion.

You can give the ball a lot of flare by adding squash and stretch to give your object some personality. Follow along with these steps:

Figure 8.57

**Dragging the Time Slider**

1. The Auto Key Animation button should still be active. If it isn't, press the N key to activate it. In the Mini Curve Editor, drag the yellow double-line Time Slider (called the Track Bar Time Slider) to frame 10. (See Figure 8.57.) Click and hold the Scale tool to access the flyout. Choose the Select and Squash tool ( ). Center the Scale cursor over the Z-axis of the Scale Transform gizmo in the Camera viewport. Click and drag down to squash down about 20 percent. This will scale down on the Z-axis and scale up on the X- and Y-axes to compensate (Figure 8.58).

2. Move to frame 0. Click and drag up to stretch the ball up about 20 percent (so that the ball's scale in Z is about 120), as shown in Figure 8.59. Adjust your viewport as necessary so you don't move the ball out of frame. When you scrub through the animation, you will see that at frame 0 the ball stretched and then the ball squashes and stays squashed for the rest of the time. You'll fix that in the next step.

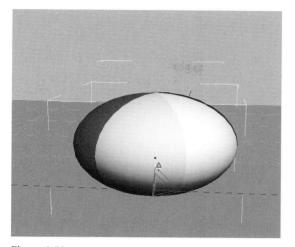

Figure 8.58

**Use the Squash tool to squash down the ball on impact.**

Figure 8.59

**Stretch the ball when it is at its apex.**

You need to copy the Scale key from frame 0 to frame 20 first, and then apply a loop for the Parameter Out-of-Range Type. Because the Mini Curve Editor is open, it obstructs the timeline; therefore, you should copy the keys in the Mini Curve Editor. You can just as easily do it in the regular Curve Editor in the same way:

Figure 8.60

**Select the Move Keys Horizontal tool.**

3. In the Mini Curve Editor, scroll in the Controller window until you find the Scale track for the ball. Highlight it to see the keyframes and animation curve. Click and hold the Move Keys tool in the Mini Curve Editor toolbar (⬚) to roll out and access the Move Keys Horizontal tool (Figure 8.60).

4. Click and drag a selection marquee around the two keyframes at frame 0 in the Scale track to select them. Hold the Shift key, and then click and drag the keyframes at frame 0 to frame 20 (Figure 8.61).

Figure 8.61

**Use the Move Keys Horizontal tool to drag the selected scale keyframes.**

5. In the Mini Curve Editor's menu bar, select Controller → Out-of-Range Types. Choose Loop, and then click OK. Play the animation. The curves are shown in Figure 8.62.

Figure 8.62

**The final curves**

### Setting the Timing

Well, you squashed and stretched the ball, but it still doesn't look right. That is because the ball should not begin to squash too long before it hits the ground. It needs to return to 100 percent scale and stay there for a few frames. Immediately before the ball hits the ground, it can squash into the ground plane to heighten the sense of impact. The following steps are easier to perform in the regular Curve Editor rather than in the Mini Curve Editor. Close the Mini Curve Editor by clicking the Close button shown in Figure 8.63.

Figure 8.63

**Close the Mini Curve Editor.**

Open the Curve Editor to fix the timing, and follow these steps as if they were law:

1. Move the Time Slider to frame 8; Auto Key should still be active. In the Curve Editor, in the Controller window select the ball's Scale track so that only the scale curves appear in the Editing window. In the Curve Editor's toolbar, select the Add Keys button ( ). Your cursor will change to an arrow with a white circle at its lower right. Click on one of the Scale curves to add a keyframe on all the Scale curves at frame 8. Because scales *X* and *Y* are identical, you will see only two curves instead of three.

2. Because they are selected, the keys will be white. In the Key Status tools, you will find two text type-in boxes. The box on the left is the frame number, and the box on the right is the selected key's (or keys') value. Because more than one key with a different value is selected, there is no number in that type-in box. Enter **100** (for 100 percent scale) in the right type-in box, and 3ds Max will enter a value of 100 for the scale in *X*, *Y*, and *Z* for the ball at frame 8, as shown in Figure 8.64.

3. Move the Time Slider to frame 12, and do the same thing in the Curve Editor. These settings are bracketing the squash so that the squash happens only a few frames before and a few frames after the ball hits the ground, as shown in Figure 8.65. Press the N key to deactivate Auto Key. Save your work.

Figure 8.64

**Enter a scale of 100.**

Figure 8.65
**Much less squash!**

Once you play back the animation, the ball will begin to look a lot more like a nice cartoonish one, with a little character. Experiment with changing some of the scale amounts to have the ball squish a little more or less, or stretch it more or less to see how that affects the animation. See if it adds a different personality to the ball. If you can master a bouncing ball and evoke all sorts of emotion with your audience, you will be a great animator indeed.

## Moving the Ball Forward

Make sure you set your current project to the Bouncing Ball project. Then you can load the `Animation_Ball_01.max` scene file from the Bouncing Ball project folder on your hard drive (or from the companion web page ) to catch up to this point or to check your work.

Now that you have worked out the bounce, it's time to add movement to the ball so that it moves across the screen as it bounces. Layering animation in this fashion, where you settle on one movement before moving on to another, is common. That's not to say you won't need to go back and forth and make adjustments through the whole process, but it's generally nicer to work out one layer of the animation before adding another. The following steps will show you how:

1. Move the Time Slider to frame 0. Select the ball with the Select and Move tool, and move the ball in the Camera viewport to the left so it is still within the camera's view. That's about –30 units on the X-axis (Figure 8.66).

2. Move the Time Slider to frame 100. Press the N key to activate Auto Key again. Move the ball to the right to about 30 units along the X-axis.

3. Don't play the animation yet; it isn't going to look right. Go to the Curve Editor, scroll down in the Controller window, and select the X Position track for the ball (Figure 8.67).

When you created the keyframes for the up and down movement of the ball (which was the Z-axis), 3ds Max automatically created keyframes for the X and Y Position tracks, both with essentially no value. To fix it, keep following these steps:

4. Select the keyframes on the X Position track at frame 10 and frame 20, and delete them by pressing the Delete key on your keyboard.

Figure 8.66

**At frame 0, move the ball to the left side of the viewport.**

Figure 8.67

**The X position of the ball does not look right.**

5. Select the Parameter Curves Out-of-Range Types button (), and select Constant. This will remove the loop from the X Position track but won't affect the Z Position track for the ball's bounce (Figure 8.68). Press the N key to deactivate Auto Key. Play the animation. You can use the / (slash) button as a shortcut to play the animation.

Figure 8.68

**The X Position curve for the ball's movement**

6. There is still a little problem. Watch the horizontal movement. The ball is slow at the beginning, speeds up in the middle, and then slows again at the end. It eases in and eases out, as you can see in the curve in Figure 8.68. This is caused by the default tangent, which automatically adds a slowdown as the object goes in and out of the keyframe. In the Curve Editor, select both keys for the X Position Curve and click on the Linear Tangent ( ![icon] ) to create a straight line of movement so there is no speed change in the ball's movement left to right.

Figure 8.69 shows the proper curve.

Figure 8.69

**The X Position curve for the ball's movement now has no ease-in or ease-out.**

## Adding a Roll

You need to add some rotation, but there are several problems with this. One, you moved the pivot point to the bottom of the ball in the very first step of the exercise. You did that so the squashing would work correctly—that is, it would be at the point of contact with the ground. If you were to rotate the ball with the pivot at the bottom, it would look like Figure 8.70.

Figure 8.70

**The ball will not rotate properly because the pivot is at the bottom.**

### Using the XForm Modifier

You need a pivot point at the center of the ball, but you can't just move the existing pivot from the bottom to the middle—it would throw off all the squash and stretch animation. Unfortunately, an object can have only one pivot point. To solve the issue, you are going to use a modifier called *XForm*. This modifier has many uses. You're going to use it to add another pivot to the ball in the following steps:

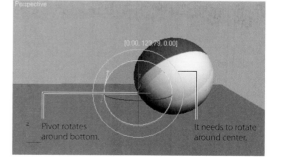

1. Double-check that Auto Key is deactivated. The button is red when it is active.

Select the ball. From the menu bar, select Modifiers → Parametric Deformers → XForm. You may also select it from the Modifier List from the Modify panel. XForm will be added to the ball in the Modifier Stack, and an orange bounding box will appear over the ball in the viewport. XForm has no parameters, but it does have sub-objects, as you can see in Figure 8.71.

Figure 8.71

**The XForm modifier in the Modifier Stack**

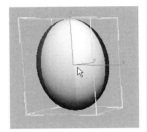

**Figure 8.72**

**Moving the XForm's center**

**Figure 8.73**

**The sphere's pivot point is still at the bottom.**

2. Expand the Modifier Stack by clicking the black box with the plus sign next to XForm. Then click Center. In the next step you will use the Align tool to center the XForm's center point on the ball.

3. Click the Align tool, and then click on the ball. In the dialog box, make sure the check boxes for X, Y, and Z Position are checked, which means those axes are active. Now click Center under Target Object, and then press OK. The XForm's center will move, as shown in Figure 8.72.

Now to be clear, this isn't a *pivot point*. This is the *center point* on the XForm modifier. If you go to the Modifier Stack and click on the sphere, the pivot point will still be at the bottom, as shown in Figure 8.73.

The XForm modifier allows the ball to rotate without its squashing and stretching getting in the way of the rotation. By separating the rotation animation for the ball's roll into the modifier, the animation on the sphere object is preserved.

### Animating the XForm Modifier

To add the ball's roll to the XForm modifier, follow along with these steps:

1. Turn on Auto Key and choose the Select and Rotate tool.

2. In the Modifier Stack, click on Gizmo for the sub-object of XForm. This is a very important step because it tells the modifier to use the XForm's center instead of using the pivot point of the ball.

3. Move the Time Slider to frame 100 and rotate the ball 360 degrees on the *Y*-axis (you can use Angle Snap Toggle to make it easier to rotate exactly 360 degrees). Click on the XForm modifier to deactivate the sub-object mode. Play the animation.

> **THE BALL DOESN'T ROTATE 360 DEGREES!**
>
> If you rotate the ball in step 3 360 degrees but the ball does not animate, 3ds Max could potentially be interpreting 360 degrees to be 0 degrees in the Curve Editor, thereby creating a flat curve. If this is the case, you can try rotating the ball 359 degrees instead to force the animation to work. You could also manually change the value in the Curve Editor for the keyframe at frame 100 to be a value of 360.

The ball should be a rubbery cartoon ball at this point in the animation. Just for practice, let's say you need to go back and edit the keyframes because you rotated in the wrong direction and the ball's rotation is going backward. Fixing this issue requires you to go back into the Curve Editor as follows:

Open the Curve Editor (mini or regular). Scroll down in the Controller window until you see the Ball tracks. Below the Ball's Transform track is a new track called Modified Object. Expand the track by clicking on the plus sign in the circle next to the name. Go to the Gizmo track and select the Y Rotation track (Figure 8.74).

You will see the Function curve in the Edit Keys window. You want the keyframe at frame 0 to have the value 0 and the keyframe at frame 100 to be 360 degrees. Select both keyframes and change the tangents to Linear, as shown in Figure 8.75.

Close the Curve Editor and play the animation. Play the `bounce ball.avi` QuickTime movie file located in the RenderOutput folder of the Bouncing Ball project to see a render of the animation. You can also load the `Animation_Ball_02.max` scene file from the BouncingBall project folder to check your work.

Figure 8.74

**The XForm's gizmo selected in the Controller window**

Figure 8.75

**Setting the rotation of the ball**

## Bouncing Ball Summary

Working with the bouncing ball gave you quite a bit of experience with the 3ds Max's animation toolset. There are several ways to animate a bouncing ball in 3ds Max. It is definitely a good idea to try this exercise a few times at first, and then to come back to it later—after you have learned other 3ds Max techniques.

If you are interested in seeing the differences in workflow between 3ds Max and Maya, you can see how to animate the bouncing ball with a similar ball exercise in *Introducing Maya 2011* (Sybex, 2010).

## Track View

As you have already seen, the Track View–Curve Editor is a powerful tool for creating and editing your animation scenes. In this section, the user interface for the Track View is laid out and explained as a brief reference for you. Figure 8.76 shows the Track View–Curve Editor.

Figure 8.76
**The Track View–
Curve Editor**

The Curve Editor can be a bit daunting at first. Now that you've had some experience with it in this chapter, it should seem pretty straightforward. The left side of the window (called the Controller window) displays the objects in the scene in an outline format. These objects have subheadings called *tracks* under them. Each track will define animation on one axis of movement or rotation or scale, or one parameter that is keyframed. When you click on a track, its animation information will display in the graph area on the right. In the Curve Editor, you can access the curves and keyframes to edit the animation. In the Dope Sheet version of the Track View, you can access keys in a different manner, as discussed in the next chapter.

You can switch between the Curve Editor and the Dope Sheet by selecting the desired window in the Modes menu in the Track View menu bar. Most of the tools discussed here are also accessible through the menu bar and the toolbars. The toolbars are divided into function sets.

## Key Tools Toolbar

The following table lists the tools used in editing keys in the Curve Editor window. You used a few of these tools in the Bouncing Ball animation.

| ICON | NAME | FUNCTION |
|---|---|---|
| | Filters | Filters the display in the Curve Editor to make viewing complicated scenes easier. |
| | Move Keys | Lets you select a keyframe and move it freely in the graph. |
| | Move Keys Horizontal | Lets you select a keyframe and move it horizontally to change its timing only. |
| | Move Keys Vertical | Lets you select a keyframe and move it vertically to change its value only. |
| | Slide Keys | Lets you select keyframes and move the group, and slide the adjacent keys away as you move the group. |
| | Scale Keys | Lets you select keys and scale them to expand or compress the amount of time between them. |
| | Scale Values | Lets you select keys and increase or decrease the values of the keys proportionally without moving them in time. |
| | Add Keys | Add keys to an existing animation by clicking a curve. |
| | Draw Curves | Draw new curves or revise existing curves by drawing directly on the animation curve graph. |
| | Reduce Keys | Reduce keys when you have more keys than necessary on a curve. |

## Key Tangency Toolbar

As you saw with the bouncing ball, changing the tangency on a few keys can dramatically alter the look of your animation. By default, new keys are set to Auto tangents, which generally keep the curve smooth. 3ds Max sets an appropriate tangency automatically; however, you can easily change the tangency by manually moving the handles on the keyframes. Once you select an Auto tangent's handle, 3ds Max will automatically shift the handle to a custom handle, allowing you to move it. The following table lists the icons for the tangency tools.

| ICON | NAME | FUNCTION |
|---|---|---|
| | Set Tangents to Auto | This flyout icon boasts three tools for controlling Auto tangents. In the flyout, the top icon sets both handles to Auto, the middle icon sets the In tangent, and the bottom icon sets the Out tangent to Auto. |
| | Set Tangents to Custom | Custom tangents allow you to move the handles to form your own curvature. If you hold the Shift key as you drag a tangent handle, it will break continuity with the other handle, allowing you to have a different In tangency than Out tangency. |
| | Set Tangents to Fast | Sets the tangent to accelerate into or out of a keyframe quickly, or both. |
| | Set Tangents to Slow | Sets the tangent to go slowly into or out of the keyframe, or both. |

*continued*

*continued*

| ICON | NAME | FUNCTION |
|---|---|---|
| | Set Tangents to Step | Sets the tangent to "jump" from one value to the next in a single frame. The animation will be frozen until the next keyframe, when it will jerk to that position or value. |
| | Set Tangents to Linear | Sets the tangency to a straight linear progression into or out of the keyframe, or both. |
| | Set Tangents to Smooth | Attempts to keep the curve smooth across all values to achieve a more realistic motion in many cases. |

## Curve Toolbar

The Curve tools act on the animation curves themselves, allowing you to easily make changes to an animated track. You will run into some of these tools as you become more experienced with Max. Don't worry about memorizing all these functions.

| ICON | NAME | FUNCTION |
|---|---|---|
| | Lock Selection | Locks the current selection so you don't accidentally select something else. |
| | Snap Frames | Snaps keys to frames when you move them. When off, you can move keys to sub-frames (i.e., in-between frames). |
| | Parameter Curve Out-of-Range Types | Allows you to set the behavior of your animation before and beyond the keyframed range. |
| | Show Keyable Icons | Toggles an icon to tell you whether a track is keyable or not. Red is keyable; black is not. |
| | Show All Tangents | Toggles the display of tangent handles on all curves in the graph. |
| | Show Tangents | Toggles the display of tangent handles on individual curves. |
| | Lock Tangents | Locks a selection of tangent handles so you can adjust them all at once. When off, however, you have access to only one tangent handle at a time. |

## Biped Toolbar

These Curve Editor Biped tools make the process of using the Curve Editor for biped animation streamlined. Biped tools will be covered in the next chapter. The following table lists the icons and their names for your reference. The functions are obvious based on the tool names. The Biped toolbar is visible only if you have a biped in your scene.

| ICON | NAME |
|---|---|
| | Show Biped Position Curves |
| | Show Biped Rotation Curves |
| | Show Biped X Curves |
| | Show Biped Y Curves |
| | Show Biped Z Curves |

## Navigation Toolbar

These tools are for Track View navigation. Tools such as Pan, Zoom, and Zoom Region work the same as in the Viewport Navigation tools. Some of the tools are designed specifically for the Track View. A few often-used icons are listed in the following table:

| ICON | NAME | FUNCTION |
|---|---|---|
| | Pan | Use this tool to drag the key window. You can also use the middle mouse button. |
| | Zoom Horizontal Extents flyout | Adjusts the display so that the entire active time segment is shown. |
| | Zoom Value Extents flyout | Adjusts the display so that the full heights of the curves are visible. |
| | Zoom | Zooms both time and value proportionally together. |
| | Zoom Region | Lets you drag a region to scale the display to fit. |

# Anticipation and Momentum in Knife Throwing

This exercise will give you more experience animating in 3ds Max. In it, you'll animate a knife being thrown at a target. You will edit more in the Curve Editor (yeah!) and be introduced to the concepts of anticipation, momentum, and secondary movement.

In preparation, download the Knife project from this book's companion web page to your hard drive. Set your 3ds Max project folder by choosing Application menu → Manage → Set Project Folder and selecting the Knife project that you downloaded.

## Blocking Out the Animation

To begin this exercise, open the Animation_Knife_00.max file in the Knife project and follow along here:

1. Move the Time Slider to frame 30 and activate the Auto Key button.

2. Move the knife to the target object, as shown in Figure 8.77.

3. Move the Time Slider to frame 15, where the knife is halfway between its start and the target, and move the knife slightly up on the *Z*-axis so that the knife moves with a slight arc (Figure 8.78).

Figure 8.77

**Move the knife to the target at frame 30.**

Figure 8.78

**Move the knife up
slightly at frame 15.**

4. For now, change the frame range in the Time Slider so you're working between frame 0 and frame 30. Click the Time Configuration button () at the bottom of the UI next to the navigation controls. Figure 8.79 shows the Time Configuration dialog box. In the Animation section, change the End Time to 30 from 100 and click OK. The Time Slider will reflect this change immediately.

5. Play your animation, and you should see the knife move with a slight ease-in and ease-out toward the target, with a slight arc up in the middle. You want the position of the knife to start at frame 10, so open the Curve Editor and scroll down in the Controller window until you see the X, Y, Z Position tracks for the knife. Hold the Ctrl key and select all three tracks to display their curves (Figure 8.80).

6. Drag a selection marquee around the three keys at frame 0. In the Keys toolbar, select and hold the Move Keys tool ( ) to access the flyout icons, and select the Move Keys Horizontal tool in the flyout ( ). Use this tool to move the keys to frame 10 (Figure 8.81).

7. This will compact the curve, as shown previously, so you will need to move the keys at frame 15 (Figure 8.81) to the new middle, frame 20 (Figure 8.82).

Figure 8.79

**Change the frame range in the
Time Configuration dialog box.**

That's it for the gross animation (or blocking) of the shot. Did you have fun?

Figure 8.80

**The initial Curve Editor for the knife**

Figure 8.81

**Keys from frame 0 moved to frame 10. Select the keys at frame 15 for the next step.**

Figure 8.82

**Move the keys to the new middle.**

## Trajectories

When it comes to animation, it is very helpful to be able to see the path your object is taking over time. These paths are known as *trajectories* in 3ds Max 2011. The easiest way to see the trajectories is to select the knife object, go to the Motion panel, and click Trajectories, as shown in Figure 8.83. Your viewports will display a red curve to show you the path of the knife's motion as it arcs toward the target, as shown in Figure 8.84.

The large hollow square points on the trajectory curve represent the keyframes set on the

Figure 8.83

**Turning on Trajectories for the knife**

Figure 8.84

**The curve shows the trajectory for the knife's motion.**

knife so far. Let's adjust the height of the arc using the trajectory curve. Turn on the Sub-Object button at the top of the Motion panel (Figure 8.85).

Figure 8.85

**Choose the Sub-Object level.**

Keys is your only sub-object choice in the pull-down menu to the right of the button. Select the middle keyframe and move it up or down to suit your tastes, as shown in Figure 8.86. Once you settle on a nice arc for the path of the knife, turn off the Trajectories mode by clicking the Parameters button in the Motion panel.

As you can imagine, the Trajectories options can be useful in many situations. It not only gives you a view of your object's path, but it also allows you to edit that path easily and in a visual context, which can be very important.

Figure 8.86

**Raise the arc of the knife by altering its trajectory.**

## Adding Rotation

The next step is to add a bit of rotation to the knife. As an animator, you need to research and gather as much information about your subject matter as you can. Throwing knives is usually a bad idea, but you can throw something else—ideally something that is shaped and weighted like a knife—at a target (the inanimate kind) to see how to animate your knife. Almost invariably, you'll find that the object will have to rotate once or twice before it hits its target. To add rotation to your CG knife, follow these steps:

1. Move to frame 30, and press the E key for the Select and Rotate tool. Auto Key should still be active. In the Perspective viewport, Rotate on the *Y*-axis 443 degrees, as shown in Figure 8.87.

2. Scroll down to find the X, Y, and Z Rotation tracks, and select them. Select the keys at frame 0 then use the Move Keys Horizontal tool to shift the keyframes to frame 10. Press N to deactivate the Auto Key. Figure 8.88 shows the Curve Editor graph for the knife.

3. Play the animation, and you will see that the knife's position and rotation eases in and eases out. A real knife would not ease its rotations or movement. Its speed would be roughly consistent throughout the animation.

Figure 8.87
**Rotate on Y.**

Figure 8.88
**Move the first Rotation keyframes to frame 10.**

4.  Go back to the Curve Editor, change Move Keys Horizontal back to Move Keys. Then select the X Position track, select all the keyframes, and switch the tangent to Linear. Now select the Z Position track; you'll need to finesse this one a bit more than the X Position track. You are going to use the handles on the tangents that appear when you select a key. These handles can be adjusted; just center your cursor over the end and click and drag using the Move tool. Figure 8.89 illustrates how you want the Z Position animation curve to look. This will give the trajectory a nice arc and a good rate of travel.

Figure 8.89
**Adjust the curve for the knife's arc through the air.**

5.  Now it is time to edit the Rotation keys. In the Curve Editor scroll to find the X, Y, and Z Rotation tracks. The first thing you can do is add a bit of drama to the knife to make the action more exciting. To this end, you can say that the rotation on the knife is too slow. Select the X Rotation track and select its key at frame 30. In the Key Stats, change the value to −52. The higher the value, the faster the knife will rotate. This will add one full revolution to the animation and some more excitement to the action.

6.  Adjust the tangent handles to resemble the curve shown in Figure 8.90. The knife will speed up just a little bit as it leaves the first rotation keyframe. The speed will be even as it goes into the last keyframe.

Figure 8.90

**Match your curve to this one.**

With just a little bit of fast rotation as the knife leaves frame 10, you give the animation more spice. A little change in the curve can make a big difference in an animation—every little bit counts. The knife should now have a slightly weightier look than before, when it rotated with an ease-in and ease-out.

## Adding Anticipation

Instead of making the knife just fly through the air toward the target, you should animate it to move back first to create *anticipation*, as if an invisible hand holding the knife pulled back just before throwing it to get more strength in the throw. This anticipation, although it's a small detail, can add a level of nuance to the animation that enhances the total effect. Follow these steps:

1.  Move the Time Slider to frame 0. Go to the Curve Editor, scroll the Controller window, and select the X Rotation track for the knife. In the Curve Editor toolbar, click the Add Keys button ( ), bring your cursor to frame 0 of the curve, and click to create a keyframe. This creates a key at frame 0 with the same parameters as the next key, as shown in Figure 8.91.

2.  Select the Move Keys tool and select the key at frame 10. In the Key Stats type-in, change the value of that key to 240. If you play back the animation, it will look weird. The knife will cock back really fast and spin a bit. This is due to the big hump between frames 0 and 10.

Figure 8.91

**Adding a key to the beginning to create anticipation for the knife throw**

3. Keep the tangent at frame 0 set to the default, but change the tangent on the key at frame 10 to Linear. Play back the animation. You'll have a slight bit of anticipation, but the spice will be lost and the knife will look less active and too mechanical.

4. To regain the weight you had in the knife, press Ctrl+Z to undo your change to the tangency on frame 10 and set it back to what you had (just like Figure 8.91). You may have to undo more than once. Now, select the Move Keys Vertical tool and select the In tangent for keyframe 0. This is the tangent handle on the left of the key, as shown in Figure 8.92.

Figure 8.92

**The In tangent is the one on the left.**

It's very common to try something in the course of your work, and rely on Undo to get back to the starting point. You can sometimes expect to use Undo several times when you find yourself at a dead end.

5. Press Shift and drag the tangent handle down to create a curve that is similar to the one shown in Figure 8.93. By pressing Shift as you dragged the tangent handle, you broke the continuity between the In and Out handles, so that only the In handle was affected. Play back the animation. It should look much better now.

Remember, the smallest tweaks in the Curve Editor can have a huge positive or negative impact on your animation.

Figure 8.93

**To create a believable anticipation for the knife throw, set your curve to resemble this one.**

## Follow-Through

The knife needs more weight. A great way to show that in animation is by adding follow-through. The follow-through for the knife would be having the knife sink into the target a little bit and push back the target as it transfers momentum to the target. For more on momentum, see the "Momentum" sidebar later in this chapter.

### Knife Follow-Through

To add follow-through to your animation, follow these steps:

Figure 8.94
**Time Configuration button**

1. You want to sink the knife into the target after it hits. Select the Time Configuration button (shown in Figure 8.94), and change the End Time to 45 to add 10 frames to your frame range. Click OK. This will not affect the animation; it will merely append 10 frames to the current frame range.

2. Select the knife and go to frame 30, where it hits the target. In the Curve Editor, select the X Position track of the knife. Add a keyframe with the Add Keys tool at frame 35.

3. Note the value of the key in the type-in boxes at the bottom of the Curve Editor (*not* the type-in boxes at the bottom of the main UI). In this case, the value in this scene is about −231. You will want to set the value for this key at frame 35 to about −224 to sink it farther into the target. If your values are different, adjust accordingly so you don't add too much movement. Also make sure the movement flows *into* the target and not back out of the target as if the knife were bouncing out.

4. Keep the tangent for this new key set to Auto. With these relative values, scrub the animation between frames 30 and 35. You should see the knife's slight move into the target. The end of your curve should look like the curve in Figure 8.95.

5. You still need to add a little bit of follow-through to the rotation of the knife to make it sink into the target better. In the Curve Editor, select the X Rotation track to display its curve. Add a key to the curve at frame 35. The value of the key at frame 30 should already be about −652. Set the value of the keyframe at frame 35 to be about −655 (Figure 8.96). Keep the tangent set at Auto.

Figure 8.95
**Your animation should end like this.**

Figure 8.96
**Set −655 at frame 35.**

Be careful about how much the knife sinks into the target. Although it is important to show the weight of the knife, it is also important to show the weight of the target; you do not want the target to look too soft. Make sure your key values at frame 35 for the X Position and X Rotation are not too much.

## Transferring Momentum to the Target

To make the momentum work even better for the knife animation, you will have to push back the target as the knife hits it. The trouble is, if you animate the target moving back, the knife will float in the air. You have to animate the knife *with* the target. However, animating them separately in the hopes they will match up will frustrate you and will more than likely look bad.

If you think that hierarchy has to be involved here, you are absolutely right. Basically, the knife will have to be linked to the target so that when the target is animated, the knife will follow precisely, because it is stuck in the target.

This won't mess up the animation of the knife. Because the knife will be the child in the hierarchy and can have its own animation separate from the target, you can link it after you are finished with the knife animation. Just follow these steps:

1. Go to frame 30, where the knife impacts. Choose the Select and Link tool. Select the knife and drag it to the target as shown in Figure 8.97. Nothing should change until you animate the target object.

Figure 8.97

**Link the knife to the target, and then rotate the target back slightly.**

2. Move the Time Slider to frame 34 and press the N key to activate the Auto Key tool. With the Select and Rotate tool, select the target object and rotate it back about 5 degrees, as shown in the second image in Figure 8.97. The pivot of the target has already been placed properly, at the bottom back edge.

3. Go to the Curve Editor, scroll to find the Y Rotation track for the target object, select the keyframe at frame 0, and move it to frame 30. Then hold the Shift key, and click and drag the keyframe (which will make a copy of it) to frame 37. Your curve should resemble the curve in Figure 8.98.

Figure 8.98

**The target will rock back and forth on impact.**

4. Change the tangent for the key at frame 30 to Fast and leave the other key tangents alone.

5. Add a little wobble to the target to make the animation even more interesting. This can be done very easily in the Curve Editor. Use Add Keys to add keys at frames 40 and 44. Using the Move Keys Vertical tool, give the key at frame 40 a value of about 1.7. Your curve should resemble the one in Figure 8.99.

6. Finally, add a little slide to the target. Using the Select and Move tool, move the Time Slider to frame 37, and move the target just a bit along the *X*-axis. Go to the Curve Editor, scroll to the X position of the target object, select the keyframe at frame 0, and move it to frame 30 so the move starts when the knife hits the target. Change the tangent for frame 30 to Fast and leave the other tangent at Auto.

Figure 8.99

**The target anima-tion curve**

Done! Play back your animation. Experiment and change some of the final timings of the target's reaction to the impact, as well as some of the values, to see how small changes can make big differences in the way the weights of the knife and target look to the viewer.

**MOMENTUM**

Understanding what momentum is and how it works is pretty important for an animator. When an object is in motion, it has momentum. The amount of momentum is calculated by multiplying the mass of the object by its velocity. The heavier something is, or the faster it is moving, the more momentum it has and the bigger the bruise it will leave if it hits you.

That's why a tiny bullet can cause such a great impact on a can of stew, for example. Its sheer speed greatly increases its momentum. Likewise, a slow-moving dump truck can bash in your car, relying on its sheer mass for its tremendous momentum.

Basically, when one moving object meets another object that is moving or not, momentum is transferred between them. That means when something hits an object, that target is somehow moved if there is sufficient momentum transferred to it.

It follows that the more mass an object has, the more momentum will transfer to the target. Also, the more velocity an object has, the more momentum will be transferred to the target on collision. You will be able to show the mass of an object in animation by showing how much momentum it transfers when it impacts another object. This could be as simple a as knife hitting a target and moving it back, as you animated in the exercise in this chapter, or as complicated as a heavyset man walking down the street. In the latter case, because the pavement can't give way underneath the man, the momentum that is transferred is reflected back to the man and absorbed by his body. That makes his body bend and flex and his big belly jiggle up and down with each step.

Impact is a perfect opportunity for an animator to show his subject's mass in motion, and it is always intrinsic in good animation.

You can see a sample render of the scene in the `knife_animation.mov` QuickTime file in the RenderOutput folder of the Knife project on the companion web page (or copied onto your hard drive). You can also download the `Animation_Knife_01.max` scene file from the Scenes folder of the Knife project to check your work.

*Introducing Maya 2011* (Wiley, 2010) includes an ax-throwing exercise that teaches the same kinds of animation concepts as the knife-throwing exercise in this chapter. Check it out if you are curious about how 3ds Max and Maya animate similar scenes.

# Summary

In this, the first of two chapters on animation, you learned the basics of creating and editing animation. You learned about hierarchies and how to link objects together to create a hierarchy useful for our mobile animation as well as how pivot points are used. You also learned how to create animation using the Auto Key function.

You learned how to fix hierarchy problems in animation and how to use dummy objects to help you animate properly. You bounced a ball to learn timing issues and how to edit animation curves through the Curve Editor. You then learned the ins and outs of the Track View–Curve Editor before moving on to a thrown knife to learn about trajectories and the concepts behind using secondary movement to help give your animation weight.

Animation can be a lot of fun, but it is also tedious and sometimes aggravating. A lot of time, patience, and practice are required to become good at animation. It all boils down to how the animation makes you think. Is there enough weight to the subjects in the animation? Do the movements make sense? How does nuance enhance the animation? These are all questions you will begin to discover for yourself. This chapter merely introduced you to how to make things move in 3ds Max. It gave you some basic animation techniques to help you develop your eye for motion. Don't stop here. Go back into the chapter and redo some of the exercises. Try different variations on the same themes. Keep working.

# CHAPTER 9

# Character Studio and IK Animation

*At one time or another,* almost everyone in the 3D community wants to animate a character. This chapter examines the 3ds Max 2011 toolsets used in the process of character animation. In this chapter, you will learn about two of the three components that make up Character Studio, a full-featured package incorporated into 3ds Max that is mostly for animating bipedal characters, including humans, aliens, robots, and anything else that walks on two feet, though you can have characters with more than two feet in certain situations.

Although Character Studio (CS) creates an instant structure for a character, you will also work with Inverse Kinematics (IK), which creates hierarchical structures for animating individually linked objects.

*Character animation* is a broad and complex field that nearly everyone wants to experiment with at some point. This chapter introduces you to the basics of using Character Studio and Bones. Further investigation into these tools is a must if you want your animation to be full of life and character.

Topics in this chapter include the following:

- **Character animation**
- **Character Studio workflow**
- **Creating a biped**
- **Animating a biped**
- **Associating a biped with the soldier model**
- **Using Inverse Kinematics**

# Character Animation

The character animation CG specialty is easily one of the toughest specialties to master. It takes an exceptional eye and a special insight to become an amazing animator. To use one word, good character animation comes down to *nuance*. Because we as people move ourselves and are surrounded by other people who move, we are innately critical when a character is not well animated. That is because the detail and nuance in movement is so inherent, so ingrained in our experience, that we never really think twice when we see someone move. We just intrinsically *know* how they move the way they do. However, we do notice when that nuance is missing in an animation of a person. As observers, we may not know exactly what is missing, but we instinctively know that something is wrong and it looks funny.

When you animate a character, you have to have a keen eye for detail and an understanding of how proportions move on a person's body. Setting up a CG character to walk *exactly* like a human being is amazingly complicated. You must account for muscles, bone structures, and a host of other details that most 3D software does not begin to address.

However, good animation for a character is actually not very difficult right out of the box. Character systems such as Character Studio (CS) make it a breeze to set up characters and have them moving in a walk cycle very quickly. Don't limit your character animation studies to Character Studio, though. While learning and mastering how CS works and how to animate with it, you mustn't lose sight of the fact that you are trying to learn *how to animate* as opposed to learning how to run a piece of software. Never let mastery of a software program be your primary mission. You will quickly limit yourself that way.

In other words, once you gain a solid grasp of how CS and other character tools work, use them to learn how to really animate. Character Studio is just a means to an end. You're here to learn to animate, not to learn how to run CS. Now that we have that out of the way, we can concentrate on getting you comfortable with CS. Have fun!

# Character Studio Workflow

Character Studio is a system built into 3ds Max to help automate the creation and animation of a character, who may or may not be exactly a *biped* (two-footed creature). Character Studio comprises three basic components: the Biped system, the Physique and Skin modifiers, and the Crowd system. Biped and Physique are used to pose and animate a single character, and the Crowd system is used to assign similar movements and behaviors to multiple objects in your 3ds Max scene. This chapter covers the Biped and Physique features, but Crowd is beyond the scope of this book.

The first step in the Character Studio workflow is to build or acquire a suitable character model. The model should be *bipedal*, meaning it stands on two feet. In the future, however, you needn't limit yourself to strictly humanoid models; CS is perfectly useful for animating anything from a human to a dinosaur to a bumblebee, as long as the model's configuration allows it. The second step in the process is to *skin* (bind) the character model to the skeleton so the animation drives the model properly.

Models should typically be in the reference position known as the "da Vinci pose," where the feet are shoulder width apart and the arms are extended to the sides with the palms down, as shown in Figure 9.1. This allows the animator to observe all of the model's features, unobstructed by the model itself, in at least two viewports. This layout of a model is a standard in the CG industry because it facilitates skinning the model to its skeleton.

Again, the term *bipedal* refers to any character with two feet. In 3ds Max, a *biped* is a predefined, initially humanoid, structure. It is important to understand that you animate the biped that is associated with your model, and not the model itself. Once the model is bound to the skeleton, the biped structure *drives* the model. You would use the Physique modifier in CS to create that relationship between the skeleton and the model.

Using the Physique modifier ensures that your model follows the biped's animation. You will work with attaching a model to a biped using Physique later in this chapter. You can also use another 3ds Max methodology, the Skin modifier, to attach the model to the biped skeleton. The differences between the two methodologies are explained next.

## Physique versus Skin

Currently, 3ds Max has two modifiers that essentially do the same thing. Physique and Skin can both be used to transfer the movement of a skeletal system such as a biped to a mesh, making the character move with the skeleton rig. Of the two, Physique is the older modifier. In 3ds Max's first releases, Character Studio, which included Physique in its package, was developed by Unreal Pictures as the first major plug-in for 3ds Max and was sold as a separate program.

Over time, however, users demanded that a program similar to Physique be included as part of the base 3ds Max package. Autodesk, responsive to the needs of its users, developed the Skin modifier to satisfy the customers' need. However, when CS was bundled free of charge

Figure 9.1

**A bipedal character in the reference position**

with 3ds Max, Physique was included, and so the base 3ds Max package included two modifiers to do the same character-skinning task.

Over time, Skin has had numerous improvements that add to its capabilities, while Physique has more or less remained the same. Because both can accomplish the same work, you can choose which one you want to learn. It comes down to personal taste; some users swear by Physique, others swear at it—and the same goes for Skin. Physique is covered in this chapter and will be your introduction to how to attach a model to a biped skeleton. Once you feel you understand the methodology, try your hand at using Skin the next time.

## General Workflow

Figure 9.2

**The default biped**

The default biped, shown in Figure 9.2, consists of legs, feet, toes, arms, hands, fingers, pelvis, spine, neck, and head. After your model is ready, you will create a biped and, using its parameters and the Scale transform, fit the biped closely to the model. The better the biped to model relationship, the easier the animation will be.

> ### BONES AND SKIN
>
> The Bones system and Skin modifier have capabilities similar to those found in Character Studio. Bones is a series of linked, hierarchical components that are used, in conjunction with the Skin modifier, to control the displacement of a model similar to the Biped and Physique method. Many animators prefer Bones. They appreciate the finer control they are able to achieve over the character's motion and motion restrictions. With finer control comes more work; Bones requires a more tedious setup process to create a skeleton than Biped.

Once the biped is fit snugly to the model, you select all of the components of the model, not the biped skeleton, and apply the Physique or Skin modifier in a process often referred to as *skinning*. It may take a while to properly test and refine the relationship between the model and the biped to get it to an acceptable level.

The final step is animating your character. You can accomplish this by adding to the biped any combination of default walk, run, and jump cycles included with CS, then applying any freeform animation to the character, and finally refining the animation keyframes in the Dope Sheet. Don't expect the default walk, run, and jump cycles to create realistic motion, though. They are just a starting point and must be tweaked to achieve acceptable movements. Character animation is about nuance and subtlety, and those artistic touches take a significant amount of time and effort to master.

> In a student or prospective employee's work, we can immediately spot default or "canned" animations that are straight out of the program's library of motions. Default cycles are a great place to get your start. Don't let yourself stop with canned motions, though. You will have to imbue your own sensibility into a character to really make it as a good animator.

The best way to start is to jump in and examine the tools available. In the next section, you will work with a biped and adjust the parameters and components to modify it.

# Creating a Biped

As stated previously, you should create your model first and then create and modify your biped to fit the model. In this section, however, you are going to examine the procedure for creating and modifying a biped first so you can gain an understanding of its capabilities. Later in this chapter, we will revisit the methods for adjusting your biped specifically to match a model.

## Placing a Biped in a Scene

Let's create a Biped system for your scene so you can get a feel for how CS works. Unlike many of the objects that you've created so far, Biped is located under the Systems category of the Create tab in the Command panel, as shown in Figure 9.3.

Figure 9.3
**Click the Systems button.**

Follow these steps to create and adjust a biped:

1. From the Command panel, select Create → Systems → Biped.

2. Click and drag in the Perspective viewport to create the biped shown in Figure 9.4.

   The first click sets the insertion point. Dragging defines the height of the biped system and defines all of the components. All of the biped's components are sized relative to the biped's Height parameter.

With this action, you created 30 visible and 5 hidden objects arranged in a linked hierarchy, not just a single object. All of the elements on the left side of the biped's body are blue, and all of the elements on the right side are green. This coloring scheme is carried throughout 3ds Max.

Figure 9.4
**Create a basic biped.**

3. Go to Tools → New Scene Explorer, which opens up a *modeless* dialog box (one that floats so you can still edit your scene while it is open). Figure 9.5 shows the Scene Explorer that opens when you invoke the New Scene Explorer command; it is for viewing hierarchies, among other things. After you expand each entry, all of the objects are indented from the edge of the dialog box, indicating that they are subordinate to, or children of, the objects above them in the list.

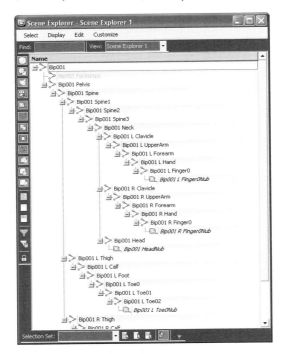

4. Close the Scene Explorer.

5. While the biped is still selected, go to the Command panel and expand the Create Biped rollout if necessary. This rollout is where changes to the biped's structure are made. You can increase the number of fingers and toes and the number of links in each to match your model. You can add a tail or ponytail by increasing the number of links for these parameters. You can even discard the arms altogether.

Adding neck links will make your biped taller, but adding spine links won't—it will only subdivide the torso area for more control in the midsection.

6. Change the parameters as you like. The biped in Figure 9.6 includes additional fingers and toes, as well as a tail and a ponytail.

The root object of the hierarchy is named Bip001, for the first biped that you create in a scene, and all the associated objects will have a Bip001 prefix. Changing the name of the object in the Name and Color rollout changes only the name of the root object and does not cascade throughout the hierarchy. Changing the name in the Root Name section of the Create Biped rollout, however, affects all of the objects in the biped.

**Figure 9.6**

**A biped with modified parameters**

## Modifying a Biped

Bipeds are very generic in appearance. You will rarely, if ever, use the default biped in an actual animation beyond learning CS. Luckily, bipeds have a complete set of tools available for modifying their structure and their behavior to match a model. You will have to select an appropriate editing mode to access the appropriate tools to adjust your biped. This section covers the tools used to adjust the size of a biped's individual elements.

If you haven't already, create a biped in your scene as discussed earlier. To begin modifying the biped, follow along here:

1. Clear your selection set by clicking the Select Object button () in the Main toolbar and then clicking on any blank area of a viewport. Nothing in your scene should be selected.

2. Click any part of your biped to select it. Bipeds react differently than other objects. Selecting any single component of the biped opens the entire Biped object for editing.

**Figure 9.7**

**Biped parameters are on the Motion tab of the Command panel.**

3. Click the Motion tab of the Command panel (Figure 9.7). The purpose of a biped is to create an animation, so all of the biped's parameters, including those that control animation as well as appearance, are consolidated under the Motion tab of the Command panel, and not under the Modify tab as you may initially think.

4. In the Biped rollout, click the Figure Mode button (  ) to display the rollouts that pertain to the biped's configuration, not its animation or footstep control. The Figure Mode button turns dark to indicate the current mode that the system is using.

5. Expand the Structure rollout to access the same parameters that were used when you first created the biped to adjust its basic configuration. Make any additional modifications that you choose.

In the Body Type drop-down menu at the top of the Structure rollout, you can change the overall appearance of the biped from the default Skeleton to Male, Female, or Classic. The body type has little to do with the biped's capabilities and is more a matter of preference.

6. Select the biped's left upper arm. In the Main toolbar, click the Select and Rotate button.

7. In the Main toolbar, set the reference coordinate system for the current Rotate tool to Local, as shown in Figure 9.8. Most transforms that are applied to a biped are applied in the Local coordinate system so they are relative to the object rather than the world or the current viewport.

8. Place your cursor over the green *Y*-axis ring of the Rotate Transform gizmo and drag upward to rotate the upper arm upward, as shown in Figure 9.9. Notice that the arm rotates at the shoulder as it's supposed to. The pivot point is already placed correctly.

   All of the pivot points for the biped elements are already placed at the top of the objects. For example, the upper arm pivots at the shoulder, the lower arm pivots at the elbow, and the hand pivots at the wrist. This is one of Character Studio's great time savers.

9. Click the Scale transform in the Main toolbar and change the reference coordinate system to Local.

10. Click and drag the *X*-, *Y*-, and *Z*-axis handles of the Scale Transform gizmo individually, as shown in Figure 9.10. The *Y* and *Z* handles make the upper arm large or small, causing your biped to bulk up or thin out. Dragging the *X* handle changes the length of the upper arm. For the best reference, you should observe the changes in all of the viewports while you're adjusting the scale.

11. Select and adjust the left lower arm, hand, and fingers to suit yourself. Don't worry about the right side yet; we will discuss that shortly.

Figure 9.9

**Rotating a biped component**

Figure 9.10

**Use all the viewports to monitor the size and shape.**

12. Select each of the spine links and scale them to give your biped a nice, tapered torso. Dragging the *X* handle upward will scale the links vertically and push the elements above them upward, increasing the height of the biped. Scaling the top spine link in the positive *Z* direction will push the clavicles and all other arm components outward, as shown in Figure 9.11. The clavicles are linked to the middle of the top spine link and can be protruded by that link. If necessary, scale the clavicle to extend beyond the top spine link.

Figure 9.11

**Scaling the top spine link pushes the arms outward.**

13. Select and scale the pelvis to spread the hips out further.

14. Similar to what you did in steps 11 and 12, use the Scale transform to adjust the scale of the biped's left upper and lower leg and foot to your liking (Figure 9.12).

Figure 9.12

**Scale the legs and foot to the appropriate size.**

As you can see, creating a biped is fairly simple. You simply click and drag to place the system, and drag to set the biped's height and proportionate size. You then adjust the parameters of the structure in the Motion panel. Finally, you position and adjust the size of each of the biped's components using the transforms to fit the needs of your intended character model.

## Copying and Pasting Postures

Most characters are basically symmetrical, with some variations in their surface appearance to make them look less perfect and a bit more natural. Character Studio allows you to set the structure and form—called the *posture*—for elements on one side of a biped's body and then paste those features to the elements on the other side. For instance, when the length, width, and pose of the left arm, hand, and fingers are tweaked to your satisfaction, you can paste the same dimensions and orientations to the relative components on the right side. You don't need to model the opposite side independently.

To follow along with these steps, you can continue with the previous exercise or open CSBiped1.max from the Chapter 9 files on this book's companion web page at www.sybex.com/go/intro3dsmax2011.

1. Select the biped and access Figure mode if necessary.

2. Double-click the left upper arm. Double-clicking an object selects that object as well as all the objects below it in the hierarchy. In this case, you are also selecting the lower arm, hand, and all finger joints when you double-click the upper arm (Figure 9.13).

Figure 9.13

**Select the entire arm and hand by double-clicking the upper arm.**

Figure 9.14

**Create the collection.**

3. Open the Copy/Paste rollout.

4. Postures must be saved as collections prior to being pasted. Click the Create Collection button (as shown in Figure 9.14) and then rename the collection from the default Col01 to **Left Arm**.

5. Click the Copy Posture button just below the Posture button to copy the selected posture to the Clipboard. A preview of the copied posture will appear in the Copied Postures area of the Command panel, as shown in Figure 9.15.

6. Click the Paste Posture Opposite button ( ). The size, scale, and orientation of the selected objects will be applied to the reciprocal objects on the opposite side of the biped, as shown in Figure 9.16.

Figure 9.15

**Copy the posture.**

Figure 9.16

**Pasting a posture to the other side of a biped**

> Copied postures are not limited to being pasted within a single biped; they can also be pasted to other bipeds. Simply copy the posture, select any part of another biped, and then click the Paste Posture button ( 🖺 ).

7. Repeat steps 2 through 6 to copy the posture of the left leg to the right leg.

As you've seen in this section, modifying a biped's appearance and posture is pretty easy! You select any of the biped's components, use the Rotate and Scale transform tools, and change the components' size and orientation as needed for your character. Later in this chapter, you will explore the procedures for fitting a biped to a specific model to ensure a smooth animation setup.

Now is a good time to save your scene before you proceed to the next section.

## Animating a Biped

Bipeds can be animated in several ways, including footstep-driven animation and free-form animation. Just as it sounds, with *footstep-driven animation* you add visible Footstep objects to your scene and direct the biped to step onto those footsteps at particular points in time to suit your animation intent. Footsteps can be added individually or as a set of walk, run, or jump steps; they can be moved or rotated to achieve the desired result and direction. When using footstep-driven animation, the legs and feet of the biped are not the only things animated; the hips, arms, tails, and all other components are animated too. A short animation sequence can generate hundreds, or even thousands, of animation keys.

Footstep-driven animation is often a good starting point, but it is rarely the complete solution to your animation needs. For example, there is no method for turning a biped's head or raising its arms using footsteps.

Even when footsteps are used to create the initial movement of a biped, freeform animation must be used to augment and tweak the character's motion. *Freeform animation* is when you animate the components of the biped manually, as you would animate any other object, such as a bouncing ball. To refresh yourself, you can refer back to Chapter 8, "Introduction to Animation," which includes using the Auto Key method and the Track View—Curve Editor mode.

Animation keys that are added to the selected Biped objects appear in the track bar, just like other objects, where they can be moved, modified, or deleted to adjust the animation. Some character animators forgo footstep-driven animation altogether and use freeform animation exclusively. They enjoy the finer control freeform animation gives them when they create keys only where they choose and not throughout the automated footsteps. In this section, you will explore both the footstep-driven and freeform methods for animating a biped.

## Moving the Biped into Place

As a system, bipeds can't be moved by using the Move transform in the Main toolbar. To position a biped correctly, you must first select and move the root object using the Body Vertical and Body Horizontal buttons. We will go over this in the following steps.

Continue with the previous exercise or open CSBiped2.max from the Biped Scene Files folder on the companion web page. If you open the web page file, select the biped and enter Figure mode.

1. In the previous exercise, if you scaled either of the leg elements along the *X*-axis, the feet of the biped moved off the construction plane—also known as the Home Grid—as shown in Figure 9.17. The Home Grid is where the new footsteps will be placed, so you will want the biped's feet to be at that elevation.

2. Turn on the grid, if necessary, using the G shortcut key. Maximize the Front viewport and zoom so that you can see the dark, horizontal line indicating the construction plane, the feet, and the pelvis. The pelvis isn't really important at this point, but the root object located inside of it is.

Figure 9.17

**Keep track of the position as you scale.**

3. In the Track Selection rollout, click the Body Vertical button (see Figure 9.18). This selects the diamond-shaped Bip001 object, which is the root object of the hierarchy, and activates the Move Transform gizmo.

4. Use the Move Transform gizmo to move the biped until the feet rest on the Home Grid, as shown in Figure 9.19.

5. Switch back to a four-viewport display.

Figure 9.18

**The Body Vertical button**

## Adding Footsteps

Adding footsteps is as simple as adding a specified number of steps with a particular gait, or clicking the mouse button to place footsteps individually. We'll try both methods in this chapter. First, let's begin by placing a series of footsteps. Here's how:

1. With the biped selected, click the Footstep Mode button in the Biped rollout (    ). The rollouts change to display the tools for adding

Figure 9.19

**Moving the biped to the Home Grid**

Figure 9.20

**Create footsteps with a walk gait.**

Figure 9.21

**Creating multiple footsteps**

and controlling a biped's motion. The Footstep mode and Figure mode are exclusive; you cannot be in both modes at the same time.

2. In the Footstep Creation rollout, make sure that the walk gait is selected and then click the Create Multiple Footsteps button, as shown in Figure 9.20, to open the Create Multiple Footsteps dialog box.

3. In the dialog box that appears, you will assign Footstep properties for the number of steps you want, the width and length of each step, and which foot to step with first. Set the number of footsteps to 8 and leave the other parameters at their default values, as shown in Figure 9.21. Click the OK button.

4. Zoom out in the Perspective viewport to see the footsteps you just created (Figure 9.22). Look at the Time Slider, and note that the scene now ends at frame 123; that's 23 more frames than the 100 frames the scene had at the beginning of this chapter. 3ds Max recognized that it would take the biped 123 frames, or just over 4 seconds, to move through the eight steps that it was given.

Figure 9.22

**Zoom out to review the footsteps.**

5. Click the Play Animation button () in the Playback Controls area. What happens? Nothing. The biped must be told explicitly to create animation keys for the steps that you have just added to the scene. Drag the Time Slider back to frame 0.

6. In the Footstep Operations rollout in the Command panel, click the Create Keys for Inactive Footsteps button shown in Figure 9.23. The biped will drop its arms and prepare to walk through the footsteps that are now associated with it.

**Figure 9.23**

**The Create Keys for Inactive Footsteps button**

7. Click the Play Animation button again. This time the biped walks through the footsteps with its arms swinging and its tail swaying back and forth.

## Controlling the View

Now the problem is that if you zoom in on the biped and play the animation, it walks off the screen so you cannot see the end of the walk cycle. What good is that? Motion cycles can be very linear and difficult to track, so Character Studio contains the In Place mode to follow a biped's animation. While in the In Place mode, the biped will appear to stay in place while the scene moves around it in relation. The In Place mode cannot be used in a Camera viewport, however.

1. Go to frame 0 then zoom in on the biped in the Perspective viewport.

2. At the bottom of the Biped rollout, click the Modes and Display text with the plus sign to the left of it, as shown in Figure 9.24. This is actually a small rollout located inside of another rollout that expands to show additional display-related tools.

3. In the Modes and Display rollout, click the In Place Mode button (see Figure 9.25).

4. Click the Play Animation button again. This time the biped will appear to be walking in place while the footsteps move underneath it, as shown in Figure 9.26. Stop the animation playback when you're ready.

**Figure 9.24**

**Expand the Modes and Display rollout.**

**Figure 9.25**

**Click the In Place Mode button.**

**Figure 9.26**

**The biped does not change position in the viewport when it is in the In Place mode.**

Using the In Place mode helps you work out the way a character moves without having to navigate throughout 3D space with your viewport; so you won't need to hunt down your biped. It is important to closely watch the cycle movement and try to finesse parts to suit the character, to make it the best animation you can.

The In Place mode is great for tweaking your animation cycle because the viewport moves with the character in 3D space and you can concentrate on how its body is moving.

**WALK, RUN, OR JUMP?**

What is the difference between a walk, run, or jump gait in 3ds Max? The difference is not speed or length of stride; it's the number of feet that the biped places on the ground at any given moment. In a walk gait, the biped has either one foot or both feet on the ground at all times. During a run sequence, the biped has either one foot on the ground or, in midstride, zero feet on the ground. When the biped is executing a jump sequence, it has either both feet on the ground or zero feet on the ground while it is airborne. You can use any of these gaits or mix and match them to begin your character's motion.

### Adding a Run-and-Jump Sequence

Creating a footstep cycle does not limit you to these footsteps. Any extra footstep sequences can be added to a biped. These new footsteps are appended to any existing footsteps. This, in turn, extends the length of the animation, if necessary, to accommodate the additional footsteps. In the next exercise, you will add footsteps to the existing animation cycle.

Continue with the previous exercise or open CSBiped3.max from the Biped Scene Files folder on the companion web page, select any biped component, and access Footstep mode from the Motion panel.

1. Click the Run button (![]) in the Footstep Creation rollout. This will apply a run gait to any footsteps you will add to your current footsteps in the Create Multiple Footsteps dialog box.

2. Click the Create Multiple Footsteps button to open the Create Multiple Footsteps dialog box.

3. Change the number of footsteps to 10 and click the OK button.

4. In the Footstep Operations rollout, click the Create Keys for Inactive Footsteps button to associate the new footsteps with the biped.

5. Click the Play Animation button. The biped walks through the first 8 steps and then runs through the next 10. As you can see, the run sequence meets the definition of a run, but it is far from realistic. In the next activity, you'll learn how to add to or modify a biped's motion with freeform animation to make a better cycle.

6. Click the Jump button in the Footstep Creation rollout, and then click the Create Multiple Footsteps button.

7. In the Create Multiple Footsteps dialog box, set the number of footsteps to 4 and click the OK button. Because a jump is defined as a sequence with either two feet or zero feet on the ground at a time, four jump steps will equal two actual jumps.

8. Click the Create Keys for Inactive Footsteps button to associate the new jump footsteps with the biped.

9. Press the Play Animation button. The biped will walk, run, and then end the sequence with two jumps.

The Actual Stride Height parameter in the Create Multiple Footsteps dialog box determines the height difference from one footstep to the next. For example, to animate your biped walking up a flight of stairs, you would set Actual Stride Height to the same value as the riser height of each stair, so each footstep would correspond to a stair-step.

## Adding Freeform Animation

Good animation rarely, if ever, comes from a first try. When you set your keys initially, you will need to edit them to suit good timing and form, as well as to fix any issues that may come up. Character animation is relational: When one part of the body is in one movement, another part of the body is in an accompanying or supportive or even opposite form of movement. When you are walking and your right leg swings forward in a step, your right arm swings back and your left arm swings out to compensate. With character work, you have to remain cognizant of the entire body of the character and how it moves.

As with everything that is automated, the walk, run, and jump cycles that CS creates definitely need some work before they will be acceptable as good animation; they definitely lack the human touch, which is the hallmark of good animation. For example, based on a standard CS cycle, the biped's head never turns, the torso is very stiff, and the arms swing similarly regardless of the gait type selected. When animating using CS, you will need to add the little nuances of movement that make animation interesting and personable. You will need to add animation to the biped to gain personality. Luckily, you can easily add or modify the biped's existing animation keys with freeform animation using the Auto Key button and the Dope Sheet. The following exercises contain examples of freeform animation.

### Moving the Head

Any character's head will move along while the character walks. The following steps will guide you through the process of creating head movement for your biped. Continue with the current project scene or open the CSBiped4.max file from the Biped Scene Files folder on the companion web page.

1. Select one of the biped's components and, if necessary, exit the Footstep mode by clicking the Footstep Mode button.

2. Drag the Time Slider to frame 50, approximately the point when the biped lifts its left foot off of footstep number 2.

Footsteps are numbered, starting with the number 0 and initially alternating from the left to the right side. They are also color-coded, corresponding to the biped, with blue footsteps on the left and green footsteps on the right.

3. Select the biped's head and note the animation keys that appear in the track bar, as shown in Figure 9.27.

Figure 9.27

**Selecting a component of the biped reveals all of that object's animation keys in the track bar.**

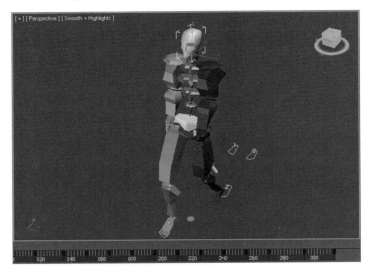

Figure 9.28

**Delete the keys on either side of frame 50.**

4. In the track bar, select the two keys on either side of the current frame, right-click either one, and then delete them (see Figure 9.28).

5. Click the Auto Key button ( Auto Key ) to turn it on.

6. Click the Rotate Transform button and rotate the head, as shown in Figure 9.29, to the left and up, as if the character sees somebody in a second floor window off-screen. A new key will be created at frame 50, recording the time and value of the head's rotation.

7. Scrub the Time Slider back and forth. Watch the head rotate from a neutral position to the orientation that you created and then rotate back to the neutral position.

8. Select all the keys between frame 50 and frame 100 (but not keys at frames 50 and 100). Delete them. This will make room for the new key that you are about to create. If animation keys are too close together, the animation could appear jerky.

Figure 9.29

**Rotate the head to the left and up.**

9. Select the key at frame 50, hold the Shift key down, and drag a copy of the key to frame 90, as shown in Figure 9.30. Use the readout at the bottom of the 3ds Max window to drag the key with precision. Copying the key will cause your biped to hold that neck pose for 40 frames, or about one and one-third seconds. Scrub the Time Slider to review the animation.

Figure 9.30

**Drag to copy the key.**

10. Select the biped's left upper arm.

11. In the track bar, select and delete all keys between frames 50 and 100. The animation keys for the arms define their swing motion. If you scrub the Time Slider or play the animation, the biped will hold its arm unnaturally stiffly for 60 frames because you deleted the animation keys between two points where it holds its hand forward. That's OK; we're just making room for some new keys.

12. Move the Time Slider to frame 60. This is the location for the first new animation key.

**Moving the Arms**

Now it's time to animate the arms, which are essential components in any walk cycle. To do so, follow these steps:

1. Rotate the upper arm upward, so that it points to the same location at which the head is looking.

2. Continue adjusting the biped's left arm, hand, and fingers until they appear to be pointing at something, as shown in Figure 9.31. You may need to turn off In Place mode to zoom in to the arm and hand.

Figure 9.31

**Rotate the biped's arm, hand, and fingers to assume a pointing posture.**

3. Double-click on the left upper arm to select it and all of the components below it in the hierarchy.

4. In the track bar, select the key at frame 60, hold the Shift key down, and drag it to frame 85 to create a copy of that key.

5. Drag the Time Slider and watch the Perspective viewport. The biped will walk for a bit, notice something off-screen, point at it, and drop its arm while looking forward again before breaking into a run and then a jump.

6. Click the Auto Key button to turn it off.

### Completing the Motion Sequence

The CSBiped5.max file in the Biped Scene Files folder on the companion web page contains the completed scene to this point.

For additional practice, add keys to the animation of the biped's arms when it jogs through the run cycle. For example, when the left foot is fully extended and the heel plants on the ground, the right arm should be bent at the elbow and swung forward and slightly in front of the biped's body. As the right foot swings forward during the next step, the right arm should swing backward and assume a nearly straight posture. Bend each of the spine links and swing both arms backward to prepare the biped for each of the jumps. Use the Body Vertical button in the Track Selection rollout to lower the pelvis into a pre-launch position, as shown in Figure 9.32, before the biped launches into its upward motion. Remember to make sure the Auto Key button is turned on to record all the changes that you make as animation keys.

Figure 9.32

**Use the Body Vertical button to position the biped for a jump.**

### Modifying Animation in the Dope Sheet

What if you need to change the animation that is generated with CS? To that end, you will need to edit the keyframes of the biped once you are happy with the base animation cycle. For this, you need to use the Track View–Dope Sheet. The Track View–Curve Editor, as you have already seen, is used to edit the function curves between animation keys; however, the Track View–Dope Sheet interface is cleaner and is used to edit the specific value and position of the keys. It is not a different set of keyframes or animation; it's just a different way of editing them. Furthermore, access to editing the footstep keys is available only in the Dope Sheet. In this exercise, you will add individual footsteps and modify the footstep timing in the Dope Sheet to make the biped dance and jump.

> Control of footstep animation is not available in the Track View–Curve Editor. You can, however, convert footstep animation to freeform animation using the Convert button (  ) in the Biped rollout. All existing animation will be retained, but the footstep-driven feature will be replaced by simple function curves that can be edited in the Curve Editor.

### Adding Footsteps Manually

With the following steps, you will manually add footsteps to your biped character:

Create a new scene with a biped or open CSBiped6.max from the Biped Scene Files folder on the companion web page. This is a biped with no footsteps applied.

1. Enter the Footstep mode.

2. In the Footstep Creation rollout, click the Walk button and then the Create Footsteps (at Current Frame) button, as shown in Figure 9.33.

3. In the Top viewport, click in several locations around the biped to place alternating left and right footsteps to your liking.

4. Change the gait to a jump, and then click the Create Footsteps (Append) button (see Figure 9.34) to create additional footsteps. Create about 12 footsteps in all.

5. When you are done, use the Move and Rotate transforms to adjust the footstep locations and orientations as desired. Your Top viewport should look similar to Figure 9.35.

6. In the Footstep Operations rollout, click the Create Keys for Inactive Footsteps button and then play the animation.

7. Character Studio doesn't have a collision detection feature, so it is very possible that limbs will pass through one another, which is quite uncomfortable in real life. If this happens, the footsteps must be modified to eliminate these conditions. If necessary, move any footsteps that cause collisions or other unwanted conditions during the playback.

**Figure 9.33**

**The Create Footsteps (at Current Frame) button**

**Figure 9.34**

**The Create Footsteps (Append) button**

**Figure 9.35**

**Manually place the footsteps in the Top viewport.**

## Using the Dope Sheet

In Chapter 8, you experimented with the Track View–Curve Editor and learned how to adjust the values of animation keyframes while observing the values between keyframes displayed as a function curve. When the Track View is in Dope Sheet mode, frames are displayed as individual blocks of time that may or may not contain keys. Although you cannot see the flow from key to key that the Curve Editor displays with its curves, the Dope Sheet mode has its advantages. For one, the Dope Sheet has the ability to add Visibility tracks to control the display of an object, as well as Note tracks for adding text information regarding the keys. Notes are helpful when you are working with other animators, or even when you want to remind yourself of something later on regarding that animation.

Using the Track View–Dope Sheet, you can adjust the point in time when a foot plants on or lifts off the ground, how long the foot is on the ground, and how long the foot is airborne. Rather than appearing as single-frame blocks in the Dope Sheet, like other keys do, footstep keys appear as multiframe rectangles that identify each foot's impact time with the footstep. Let's try the Dope Sheet on for size here:

1. Exit the Footstep mode.

2. In the Main toolbar, choose Graph Editors → Track View - Dope Sheet. The Dope Sheet will open.

3. In the Navigation pane on the left, scroll down until you find the Bip001 entry. Expand the Bip001 and Bip001 Footsteps entries. The footstep keys appear as rectangles in the Key pane. As expected, the left keys are colored blue and the right keys are colored green. If necessary, click the Zoom Region button ( ) in the lower-right corner of the Dope Sheet window and drag a zoom window around the footstep keys, as shown in Figure 9.36. The region will expand to fit the key pane.

Figure 9.36

**Zoom to the Footstep keys.**

4. Select a few Footstep keys in the panel on the right.

The white dot on the left side of a selected key identifies the frame when the heel of the biped's foot first impacts the footstep. Similarly, the white dot on the right side of a selected key identifies when the biped's foot lifts off a footstep (Figure 9.37). A blue key overlapping a green key indicates that both feet are on the ground. A vertical gray area with no footstep indicates that the biped is airborne and neither foot is on the ground.

Figure 9.37

**The dots indicate when contact begins and ends. You can drag a dot to change the duration of contact.**

5. Select the first key (numbered 0), place the cursor over the right edge of the key (as shown in the second image in Figure 9.37), then drag the dot to the right to extend the length of time that the biped's foot is on the ground.

> You can't move the end of one footstep key beyond the beginning of another one, and you must maintain a one-frame gap between same-side footsteps. You can't move a key to a point in time beyond the active time segment, nor can you modify keys for footsteps that have been created but not yet associated to the biped. In addition, footsteps must be at least two frames long.

6. The double vertical line in the Dope Sheet's Key pane is another Time Slider that allows you to scrub through the animation. Drag the Dope Sheet's Time Slider to a point in time when the biped is airborne, as shown in Figure 9.38.

Figure 9.38

**Drag the Time Slider until the biped is airborne.**

A biped's airborne time is calculated using the standard physics values for acceleration due to gravity: 32 ft/s$^2$ or 9.8 m/s$^2$. The biped does not simply hover at a user-defined altitude by moving it on the $Z$-axis and setting a key, as you would do with most other 3ds Max objects. Therefore, increasing the airborne time by increasing the gap between footsteps will boost the height to which the biped rises, acting against the gravitational force pushing it downward.

7. Select the last four jump keys and drag them to the right to create a gap approximately 30 frames wide, as shown in Figure 9.39. This will cause the biped to be airborne for about one second.

Figure 9.39

**Create a key gap to get your biped airborne.**

It is possible to move a footstep beyond the limits of the active time segment in the Dope Sheet. For example, in a 100-frame animation, you can move the last footstep to start at frame 105 and end at frame 123. When you play the animation, it will begin to loop at frame 100, and you will never see the animation created by the last keys. Use the Alt+R key combination to extend the active time segment to include all existing keys.

8. Click Alt+R to lengthen the active time segment, then move the Time Slider to the frame when both feet are planted before the jump starts. Turn on the Auto Key button.

9. Deselect any keys by clicking a blank area in the Key pane.

10. To prepare the biped to leap, select the Bip001 object and move it downward, causing the biped to bend its knees more. Rotate the spine links, neck, and head to bend the torso forward and tuck the chin. Rotate both arms backward into a pre-jump posture, as shown in Figure 9.40. Be sure to choose Local as the reference coordinate system for the Rotate transform.

11. Move the Time Slider forward until the biped is at the apex of the jump. Rotate the biped's components into positions you like, such as the split shown in Figure 9.41. Delete any animation keys that may interfere with your desired motion, and turn off Auto Key.

The CSBiped7.max file in the Biped Scene Files folder on the companion web page contains the completed exercise so you can check your work.

As you saw in this section, there are several ways to animate a biped, including the footstep-driven method, the freeform method, and a combination of techniques. You can also modify the animation in the track bar, with the Auto Key button, and with Track View–Dope Sheet. The next section addresses the methods for associating your biped with a 3D model, also known as skinning.

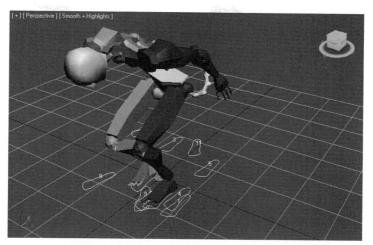

Figure 9.40

**Prepare your biped to jump.**

Figure 9.41

**Position your biped in mid-jump.**

## Associating a Biped with the Soldier Model

The purpose of a biped is to be the portal through which you add animation to your model, rather than animating the model itself using direct vertex manipulation or deforming modifiers. Any motion assigned to a biped is passed through it to the nearest vertices of the associated model, essentially driving the surfaces of the model. For this reason, it is important that the biped fit as closely as possible to the model.

## Creating and Modifying the Biped

In the following steps, you'll create and adjust a biped to fit to a character model. Set your project to the Soldier project available for download from the companion web page at www.sybex.com/go/intro3dsmax2011. You can then open the CSSoldier.max file from the Scenes folder of the Soldier project. It contains a completed soldier model in the reference position. Be sure to set the project folder to the root folder for the CSSoldier project.

1. With the soldier model file open, select the character, right-click in a viewport, and choose Freeze Selection. This will prevent you from inadvertently selecting the soldier instead of the biped.

2. Create a biped with a height about the same as the soldier's. This will size most of the biped's parts similar to those of the soldier, as shown in Figure 9.42.

Figure 9.42

**Create a biped about the same height as the soldier model.**

3. With the biped still selected, click the Motion tab of the Command panel and enter Figure mode. Changes to the biped's features or pose must be made in Figure mode to be retained by the system.

4. Use the Body Vertical and Body Horizontal buttons in the Track Selection rollout and the Move Transform gizmo to position the biped's pelvis in the same location as the model's pelvis, as shown in Figure 9.43. With the pelvis located properly, scaling the legs or spine to match the model's proportions will be much easier. Check to make sure the location is correct in all of the viewports.

    As you did earlier in this chapter, you will modify one side of the biped to fit the model and then paste that posture to the other side.

5. In the Front viewport, select the pelvis and scale its width so that the biped's legs fit inside the soldier's legs. Scale the pelvis in the Right viewport so that it roughly encompasses the soldier's lower region. See Figure 9.44. Make sure the coordinate system for the Scale transform is set to Local.

Figure 9.43

**Match the positions of the biped pelvis and the model pelvis.**

Figure 9.44

**Scale the pelvis to fit.**

### VIEWING FROZEN OBJECTS

If your background color is similar to the default shade of gray that Max uses to depict frozen objects, the model may seem to disappear against the background. There are several solutions to this situation:

- You can go to Object Properties, turn off Show Frozen as Gray, turn on See-through, and set all viewports to Smooth + Highlights mode.

- You can change the shaded color in the Customize User Interface dialog box (Customize → Customize User Interface → Colors).

- You can change the viewport background color in the Customize User Interface dialog box (Customize → Customize User Interface → Colors).

6. Select the biped's left upper leg, and then scale it along the X-axis until the knee aligns with the soldier's knee. Scale it on the Y- and Z-axes until it is similar in size to the soldier's thigh, as shown in Figure 9.45.

7. Select the biped's left calf. In the Right viewport, rotate the calf to match the model and then scale it on the X-axis until the biped's ankle matches the soldier's ankle. You may need to select the left foot and use the Move transform, in the Front viewport, to orient the calf to the model. Scale the calf to match the proportions of the soldier's calf.

Modifying a biped to match a model can be a time-consuming task that requires continual tweaking and modification. Moving the foot as described in the previous step may require that the upper leg's proportions be readdressed. Don't expect to perform this task quickly without making any revisions to components on which you have previously worked. The better the biped matches the model now, the easier the animation will be later.

8.  Continue working down the leg by scaling the biped's foot to match the soldier's. Be sure to check the orientation of the foot in the Top viewport. In the Structure rollout, use the Ankle Attach parameter to move the biped's ankle slightly backward, as shown in Figure 9.46.

Figure 9.45
**Scale the length, width, and depth of the biped's upper leg to match the soldier's thigh.**

Figure 9.46
**Increasing the Ankle Attach parameter to move the ankle**

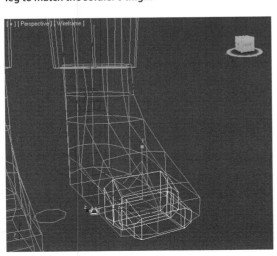

9.  In the Structure rollout, change the number of toes to 1 and toe links to 2. Because the soldier is wearing boots, a single, wide toe will suffice.

10. Scale and move the biped's toe to match the model's boot. Be sure to scale the toe links on the *Z*-axis, as shown in Figure 9.47.

Figure 9.47
**Match the model's boot and the biped's toe.**

11. Double-click the left upper leg to select it and all of the objects below it in the hierarchy. Create a collection and then copy/paste the posture of the left leg to the right as you did in the "Copying and Pasting Postures" section in this chapter. The model is not perfectly symmetrical; make any necessary changes to the right side of the biped.

## Adjusting the Torso and Arms

Similar to the method used to adjust the legs, you will use the Scale and Rotate transforms to fit the biped to the model. The locations of the arms rely on the scale of the spine links. You can continue with your file from the previous exercise or open CSSoldier2.max from the Scenes folder of the Soldier project available on the companion web page. Just make sure your project is set to the Soldier project.

1. In your scene (or the one from the web page), select the biped, and then access Figure mode, if you need to.

2. Select each of the spine links in turn, and then rotate and scale them to fit the soldier's torso. Only the lowest spine link can be moved, and this will move all of the links above it as well. Each spine link should be scaled down slightly on the X-axis to lower the biped's clavicles to match the model's, as shown in Figure 9.48.

3. Move, rotate, and scale the left clavicle as required to place the biped's shoulder socket in the proper location.

4. Scale and rotate the left upper arm and left forearm using the same techniques you used to adjust the biped's legs.

5. Scale and rotate the left hand as required to fit the model.

Once the fingers have been adjusted, you cannot go back and change the number of fingers or finger links. If you do, all modifications to the fingers will be lost.

6. The hands need only two fingers (the second finger is actually the thumb) and two links each. Adjust the biped's fingers to match the model's fingers, as shown in Figure 9.49. This can be one of the most tedious tasks in character animation, depending on the complexity and orientation of the model's fingers. Take your time and get it right. (Would you rather do it right or do it over?)

7. When you are done, paste the posture to the right side of the biped and make any required changes.

**Figure 9.48**

Match the biped's clavicles to the model.

**Figure 9.49**

Match the biped's fingers to the model's.

### Adjusting the Neck and Head

The neck and head will seem easy to adjust when compared to the hands. You need to make sure the neck links fill the soldier's neck area, and scale the head to fit. Follow along here:

1. In the Structure rollout, increase the number of neck links to 2.

2. Move, scale, and rotate the neck links to match the proportions of the model's neck, as shown in Figure 9.50.

3. Move and scale the head to the approximate size of the soldier's head, as shown in Figure 9.51.

That's it. The biped has been created and adjusted to fit the 3D model, and half the battle is over. Next you will tie the biped to the model and make adjustments to the skinning process. Now would be a good time to save your work and take a break.

Figure 9.50

**Adjust the neck links to match the model's neck.**

Figure 9.51

**Matching the head**

## Applying the Physique Modifier

The Physique modifier is the tool used to skin the 3D model to the biped so that all of the biped's animation is passed through to the model. It's important to remember that the modifier is applied to the model and not to the biped. Continue with the previous exercise or open CSSoldier3.max from the Scenes folder of the Soldier project on the companion web page to follow these steps:

1. Right-click in any viewport and select Unfreeze All from the Quad menu to unfreeze the soldier model.

2. Select all of the biped's components by double-clicking the Bip001 object.

> If you have trouble double-clicking the Bip001 in a dense model, try selecting Bip001 using the Select from Scene dialog box and then pressing Ctrl+Page Down to select everything below it in the hierarchy.

3. In the Named Selection Sets field in the main toolbar, enter the name **SoldierBiped** to save the biped as a named selection set (see Figure 9.52). This makes it easier to select all the components for the biped in one fell swoop by selecting its name from the drop-down list on the Main toolbar.

> By creating named selection sets, you can quickly access all of the desired components by selecting the named selection set from the drop-down list on the main toolbar. For reference, see Chapter 3, "The 3ds Max Interface," for the icons and functions of the named selection sets.

4. Select the Soldier model and click the Modify tab of the Command panel.

5. Expand the Modifier List and select the Physique modifier, as shown in Figure 9.53.

6. In the Physique rollout, click the Attach to Node button ( 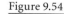 ). The button will turn dark and wait for you to identify the root object in the hierarchy that controls the mesh.

**Figure 9.52**
**Create the name selection set.**

7. Press the H key to open the Pick Object dialog box. This method will be easier than trying to click on the object directly in a cluttered scene. Select the Bip001 Pelvis object and click the Pick button, as shown in Figure 9.54.

8. In the Physique Initialization dialog box, accept the defaults and click the Initialize button. The cursor will briefly turn into a coffee cup to indicate that the initialization is in progress. It will return to normal when the process is complete.

## Testing the Model

The most time-consuming part of the process is complete. You have created a biped, adjusted all of its component parts to fit your model, and applied the Physique modifier to link the model to the biped. The next step is to test the model by adding animation.

1. Select any element of the biped and click the Motion tab of the Command panel.

2. Enter Footstep mode.

3. Add a footstep sequence as you did in the "Animating a Biped" section of this chapter. Don't forget to create keys for the inactive footsteps. Exit Footstep mode when you are done.

4. Activate In Place mode, and then zoom and pan the Perspective viewport to get a good view of the action.

**Figure 9.53**
**Select the Physique modifier.**

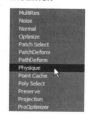

**Figure 9.54**
**Use the Pick Object dialog box to select the root object in a cluttered scene.**

Figure 9.55

**The rendered soldier during a walk cycle**

5. Exit Footstep mode, then select the SoldierBiped named selection set from the drop-down list on the Main toolbar.

6. Right-click in any viewport and choose Hide Selection from the Quad menu to hide the biped and obtain an unobstructed view of the model.

7. Click the Play Animation button. Your soldier will walk through the scene. It should be similar to the rendered soldier shown in Figure 9.55.

As you can see, you still need to do a little work to successfully rig this character. Certain parts of the model seem to drag other nearby parts of the model along with them. This is particularly visible in the feet and arms. This is fixed in the next section.

### Tweaking Physique

Each element in the biped has an area of influence, called an *envelope*, that determines which parts of the model it affects. The biped's left foot, for instance, should control the movement of only the model's left foot and the lower part of the ankle. In our case, the envelopes extend to affect some of the vertices on the opposite side. To fix the envelopes, follow this procedure:

1. Right-click in the viewport and choose Unhide by Name from the quad menu. In the Unhide dialog box, click Display → Expand All. Select all of the Biped objects, then click the Unhide button to unhide the biped.

2. Scrub the Time Slider until the left foot rests on the ground after its first step. In the Right viewport, zoom into the feet and legs then render the viewport. Figure 9.56 shows the condition where the left foot drags along some of the vertices from the right foot.

3. Select the mesh, then, in the Modify panel, click the Hide Attached Nodes option at the bottom of the Physique Level of Detail rollout. This will turn on the sides of the biped temporarily and display the links as thin orange lines.

Figure 9.56

**There is a problem with the feet.**

4. In the Modifier Stack, expand the Physique modifier and select the Envelope sub-object, as shown in Figure 9.57.

5. Select the orange links for the left foot and toes. The inner and outer envelopes appear as shown in Figure 9.58. Also, notice that the model's vertices that are affected by the links are displayed in the viewport as small crosses.

Figure 9.57

**Select the Envelope sub-object level.**

6. In the Envelope Parameters section of the Blending Envelopes rollout, click the Inner button, then reduce the Radial Scale value (see Figure 9.59) until the envelope just encompasses the boot in the Front viewport. Clicking the Inner button causes changes to affect only the inner bound of the envelope.

7. Repeat the procedure with the Outer button selected and watch the vertices from the opposite foot become unselected as the envelope shrinks.

8. Switch to the Right viewport and use the Strength parameter and the Scale transform, alternately with the Inner and Outer buttons selected, to adjust the size and shape of the envelopes. The goal is to have the foot links affect only the boot and ankle.

9. Repeat this procedure with the remaining links in the model. You can use the Parent Overlap and Child Overlap options to determine how much one link affects the vertices controlled by the links before or after it in the hierarchy. You may also want to add some freeform animation to make the character livelier.

Inner envelope — — Outer envelope

**Figure 9.58**

**Select the Envelope sub-object level**

The completed Character Studio Soldier exercise can be found in the CSSoldier Complete.max file in the Scenes folder of the Soldier project on the companion web page.

As we mentioned at the beginning of the chapter, Character Studio is a very complete character animation package, and we've barely scratched the surface here. There are tools for saving biped configurations and sequences of animation. You can mix animation sequences from different files to create an entirely new motion. When the model does not skin as well as you need, you can use envelopes to refine the skinning process further, define vertices to be excluded from a specific Biped object's influence, or include bulge conditions to define the model's behavior depending on the angle between subsequent biped elements. The list goes on, but the good news is that the CS tutorials and help system that ship with 3ds Max are very thorough, and you should find the information in those places to expand your Character Studio skills once you have a solid footing with the basics of CS. It's important to realize that animation requires nuance, and the best animation with the simplest rig and setup will beat a mediocre animation created with a more wonderful, complicated, ingenious setup.

**Figure 9.59**

**Reduce the radial scale**

## Using Inverse Kinematics

When a hierarchy is set up through linking, the result is a kinematic chain. As you saw in Chapter 8, transforms are passed from a parent object to all of the child objects down the chain. Imagine your arm is a system of linked 3ds Max objects; when you pivot your forearm (the parent) at the elbow, your hand (the child) and your fingers (the descendants) are also transformed to maintain the relationship between the objects. This is known as Forward Kinematics (FK) and is the default method of passing transforms in a hierarchy.

When Inverse Kinematics (IK) is used, the child object is transformed while the parent and ancestor objects maintain their relationships throughout the chain. Using the same arm example, lifting your arm by grabbing and pulling up on a finger would raise the hand, which would raise the forearm, causing a curl at the elbow. With IK, the end of the chain, the child, is positioned in your animation and the rest of the chain upstream rotates and pivots to fit the new layout of the chain to achieve a possible pose. IK setups require the use of an IK solver to determine how the parent objects react to the child transforms and joint constraints to prevent unnecessary twists in the motion.

In the following exercise, we will play some more with toys of war by linking a machine gun mounted on a tank model. Here, the goal is to arrange the IK setup so that the gun pivots vertically at the joints only and then pivots at the turret.

### Linking the Objects

The machine gun unit consists of the gun itself, two two-component pivot assemblies, two shafts, and the turret. The gun is at the top of the hierarchy, and the turret is at the bottom.

1. Open the IKGun1.max file from the Biped Scene Files folder on the companion web page.

2. Begin by linking the Gun object to the PivotTop object, the cylindrical object near the gun. The PivotTop object will flash briefly to signify that is has been linked. If you are having difficulty selecting the proper object directly, press the H key to open the Select Parent dialog box.

3. Continue creating the hierarchy by also linking the PivotTopRing to PivotTop, Pivot-Top to Shaft1, and then Shaft1 to PivotBottom.

Figure 9.60

**The Select from Scene dialog box showing the hierarchy**

4. Complete the setup by linking PivotBottomRing to PivotBottom, PivotBottom to Shaft2, and Shaft2 to Turret. If you open the Select from Scene dialog box and make sure Display Subtree is checked, you hierarchy will look like Figure 9.60.

### Creating Joint Constraints

The gun assembly should be able to rotate in only certain ways. The gun itself should pivot only perpendicular to the PivotTop object, for example. This is accomplished by constraining the Rotate transform for the PivotTop object, the parent of the gun, to a single axis. The transforms can further be restricted by limiting the range of motion an object can rotate within an acceptable axis. This method is used to prevent the gun barrel from rotating to the point where it disappears within the tank body to which it may be attached. Both of these tasks are accomplished under the Hierarchy tab of the Command panel, as you will see in the following steps:

1. In the Command panel, click the Hierarchy tab ( 🔲 ).

2. Click the IK button and then, in the Inverse Kinematics rollout, click the Interactive IK button, as shown in Figure 9.61. The IK button will turn light gray to signify which family of rollouts is displayed. The Interactive IK button will turn dark to indicate that this feature is active and any transforms applied to objects in the hierarchy are applied in IK mode.

3. In the Perspective viewport, select and move the Gun object along the *X*-axis. The gun's orientation changes and all of the hierarchy elements, including the turret, change to maintain the connection, but they all rotate oddly. This is because the orientation at the joints is not constrained to a single axis or limit of degrees.

4. Undo any transforms that were applied.

5. Select the PivotTop object. In the Rotational Joints rollout, uncheck the X Axis and Z Axis Active check boxes.

6. Check the Limited check box in the Y Axis section. Decrease the From parameter to approximately −65 by dragging the spinners. The Pivot and its children will rotate in the viewport and then snap back to their original orientations when the mouse is released. Drag the To spinner to approximately −40, as shown in Figure 9.62. Limiting the orientation restricts how far the object can rotate in a particular axis, and dragging the spinners instead of typing in the values gives visual feedback regarding the axis about which the object is rotating.

7. Select Shaft1 and uncheck the Active option for the *X*-, *Y*-, and *Z*-axes in the Rotational Joints rollout. Repeat the process for the Shaft2 and Gun objects. None of these objects needs to rotate on their own; they just need to follow their parent objects.

8. Select the PivotBottom object. Check the Active and Limited options in the *Y*-axis area. Set the From value to −4 and the To value to 30. Uncheck the X Axis and Z Axis Active options.

9. Select the Turret object. Only the Z Axis option should be checked so the turret can rotate only laterally, and not flip over. Do not check the Limited option; the turret should be able to rotate freely.

10. In the Object Parameters rollout, check the Terminator option to identify the turret as the top object in the IK structure (see Figure 9.63).

11. Select the Gun object and then click the Link Info button at the top of the Hierarchy panel. In the Rotate section of the Locks rollout, check the X option, as shown in Figure 9.64. The gun should now not rotate on any axis except the local *X*-axis.

**Figure 9.61**

**The Interactive IK button**

**Figure 9.62**

**Drag the To: spinner to −40.**

**Figure 9.63**

**Check the Terminator option.**

Figure 9.64

**Lock the X Rotate axis.**

12. Select the Turret object and check the X, Y, and Z options in the Move section (see Figure 9.65) to lock any movement for the turret. The turret should be fixed in place. In a complete 3ds Max scene, the turret would be linked to a larger structure to define its transforms.

13. Click the IK button at the top of the Hierarchy panel, and then click the Interactive IK button again to turn it on if necessary. Test your IK chain by moving the gun. As it moves, the other objects in the chain will reorient to maintain the proper relationships with their parent objects.

14. Turn off the Interactive IK button when you are done.

## Applying the IK Solver

Figure 9.65

**Lock all the Move axes for the Turret.**

An IK solver calculates the controls required to position and orient the members of an IK chain when one or more members is moved or rotated. The IK solver defines the top of the chain and identifies the goal, or the base of the chain. The IK solver precludes the need to activate the Interactive IK mode in the Hierarchy panel whenever IK is required.

The two appropriate IK solvers for this situation are the HI (History Independent) solver and the HD (History Dependent) solver. The HI solver is better suited for long animation sequences and character animation, and the HD solver is better suited for machine animation. Because this animation is for a machine, in this case a tank, the HD solver will be used here.

Continue with the previous exercise or open the IKGun2.max file from the Biped Scene Files folder on the companion web page.

1. Undo any transforms that were applied in your own scene during the previous exercise.

2. Choose Edit → Hold from the Main menu. Some IK operations, including applying an IK solver, are not always undoable through the Undo command. If the result of the IK solve is not correct, choose Edit → Fetch to restore your scene to the point just before you executed the Edit → Hold.

Figure 9.66

**A line stretches from the gun's pivot to the cursor.**

3. Select the Gun and choose Animation → IK Solvers → HD Solver. A rubber band line will stretch from the gun's pivot point to the cursor, as you can see in Figure 9.66.

4. Place the cursor over the Shaft2 object and click to define it as the end of the IK chain. The IK chain should now be bound to the object that has been designated as the Terminator.

When the cursor is moved over the other viewports while an IK solver is being assigned, the view will update to show the rubber banding line projecting from the object to the cursor in that particular viewport. The viewport does not have to be the active viewport for this viewport change to occur.

5. The End Effector acts as the pivot point of the Terminator object and can be used to straighten out the chain without actually moving the child object. On the Motion panel, in the IK Controller Parameters rollout, click the Link button in the End Effectors area and then click on the turret. Turret appears in the End Effector field.

6. Select the gun and use the Move transform to test your IK setup. Moving the gun forward, backward, up, or down will now cause the two pivots to rotate within their limits.

The HD solver's IK components are not listed in the Select Objects dialog box, because they act on behalf of the objects to which they are assigned. To modify any of its properties, select the object and open the Motion panel of the Command panel. The IK Controller Properties rollout contains the options for modifying the IK chain.

## Summary

This chapter introduced you to two powerful tools for reducing the time and effort required to animate objects and characters. Character Studio is a fantastic tool that speeds up the process of character animation. Using the Biped system, you can quickly create and adjust the substructure that controls a 3D model. Once the Physique modifier associates or skins the model to the biped, character animation can be added using footstep-driven or freeform animation.

IK is used throughout mechanical design and character animation, and it is another 3ds Max tool that you may find invaluable once its workflow becomes second nature to you. The exercises in this chapter examined the basics of an IK setup and the basic use of an IK solver for a mechanical animation of a gun. The IK setups can include several IK chains controlling the transforms for different components of the same model. Easily selected controls can be placed in the scene for simple selection and manipulation of a complex model's components. IK can also be used for organic character animation, because 3ds Max has different types of IK for character work as well (such as the HI IK or Limb Solver IK). This chapter covered only one type of IK (using the HD solver) for a simple use of IK. Most practical applications will use the HI system; however, for the purposes of this book, familiarizing you with the simpler HD solver primes you for further study in 3ds Max IK systems.

# CHAPTER 10

# 3ds Max Lighting

*Light is everything.* By light we see, and by light we show. Light reveals the world around us and defines shape, color, and texture. Computer graphics hang on every word light has to whisper. Without faithful lighting, any good computer graphic will fall to its knees and fail. Lighting is the most important aspect of CG, and it just simply cannot be mastered at a snap of the fingers. The trick to correctly lighting a CG scene is understanding how light works and seeing the visual nuances it has to offer.

In this chapter, you will study the various tools used to light in 3ds Max. This chapter will serve as a primer to this most important aspect of CG. It will start you on the path by showing you the tools available and giving you opportunities to begin using them.

Topics in this chapter include the following:

- **Basic lighting concepts**
- **Three-point lighting**
- **3ds Max lights**
- **Common light parameters**
- **Ambient light**
- **Lighting the Red Rocket**
- **Atmospheres and effects**
- **Light Lister**

# Basic Lighting Concepts

On a conceptual level, the lighting in 3ds Max mimics the real-world direct-lighting techniques used in photography and filmmaking. Lights of various types are placed around a scene to illuminate the subjects, as they would be for a still life or a portrait. Your scene and what's in it dictate, to some degree at least, which lights you put where. A number of considerations must be kept in mind when settling on a methodology and light types for Computer Graphics (CG), but the overall concept of lighting is strikingly similar between a real-world set lighting and CG.

At the basic level, you want your lights to illuminate the scene. Without lights, your cameras have nothing to capture. Although it seems rather easy to throw your lights in, turn them all on, and render the scene, that couldn't be further from the truth.

Lighting is the backbone of CG. Although it is technically easy to insert and configure lights, it is *how* you light that will make or break your scene. That skill really comes only with a good deal of experience and experimentation, and it requires a good eye and some patience.

In this chapter, you will learn the basic procedures for lighting a scene in 3ds Max. No single chapter could explain everything about lighting, and no beginner or intermediate CG student should expect to quickly master the art of lighting CG. In short, lighting touches every single aspect of the CG pipeline. A strong lighter understands modeling form and is able to make adjustments to enable efficient lighting. Lighters understand motion and how to light for it. They understand textures and materials, and they frequently are tasked with creating or adjusting materials to work perfectly with their lights. Strong lighters are also rendering experts. When it's time to render, they must know what is and is not doable in a scene. They must diagnose problems and overcome obstacles to make sure every frame is rendered faithfully and with artistic merit.

## Develop Your Eye

As corny as it sounds, to be an artist, you must learn to see. This is especially true for CG lighting. There are so many nuances to the real-world lighting around us that we take them for granted. We intuitively understand what we see and how it's lit, and we infer a tremendous amount of visual information without much consideration. With CG lighting, you must re-create these nuances for your scene. That amounts to the work of lighting.

The most valuable thing you can do to improve your lighting technique is to relearn how you see your environment. Simply put, you must refuse to take for granted what you see. If you question why things look the way they do, you'll find that the answers almost always come around to lighting.

Take note of the distinction between light and dark in the room you're in now. Notice the difference in the brightness of highlights and how they dissipate into diffused light and then into shadow.

When you start understanding how real light affects objects, you'll be much better equipped to generate your own light. After all, the key to good lighting starts with the desire to simply create an interesting image.

## Your Scene and Its Needs

Your scene needs a careful balance of light and dark. Too much light will flatten your image and lose details in form. This is the first mistake many beginners make; they tend to over-light to make sure everything is lit. Figure 10.1 is a rendering of a chessboard that has too many bright lights. The lighting only flattens the image and removes any sense of depth and color.

On the other hand, under-lighting a scene will make it muddy and gray and pretty lifeless. Your details will end up covered in darkness, and everything will flatten out as well. Figure 10.2 shows you the same chessboard that is under-lit. You hardly notice the details in the mesh.

Your first job as a lighter is to find the balance between over-lighting and under-lighting. It sounds simple, and it is—although it requires lighting a shot several times and test rendering it to check the outcome. Like a photographer, you want your image to have the full range of exposure. You want the richest blacks and the brightest whites in your frame to give it a deep sense of detail. Figure 10.3 shows you a fairly well-balanced lighting for the same chessboard. The light and shadow complement each other, and the lighting works to show off the features of the objects in the scene.

Figure 10.1
**An over-lit chessboard**

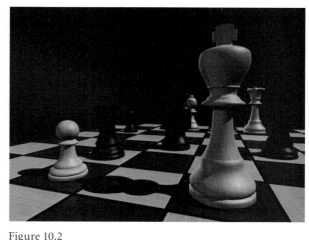

Figure 10.2
**An under-lit chessboard**

## Three-Point Lighting

Three-point lighting is a traditional approach to lighting a television shot. After all these years, the concepts still carry over to CG lighting. In this setup, three distinct roles are used to light the subject of a shot. More than one light can be used for each of the three roles, but the scene should in effect seem to have only one primary or *key* light, a softer light to fill the scene, and a back light to make the subject pop out from the background.

Figure 10.4

**A three-point lighting schematic**

This does not mean there are only three lights in the scene. Three-point lighting suggests that there are three primary angles of light for your shot, dependent on where the camera is located.

Three-point lighting ensures that your scene's main subject is well lit and has highlights and a sense of lighting direction using shadow and tone. Figure 10.4 shows you a plan view of the three-point lighting layout. The subject is in the middle of the image.

### Key Light

A *key light* is placed in front of the subject for the primary light. The key is placed off to one side to give a sense of direction to the light, because one side will be brighter than the other. Shadows will fall from this light to heighten the sense of direction and increase the depth of the shot.

Although it is possible for several lights to fulfill the role of key light in a scene—for example, three overhead ceiling lights—one light should dominate, creating a definitive direction. Figure 10.5 shows the subject being lit by a single key light.

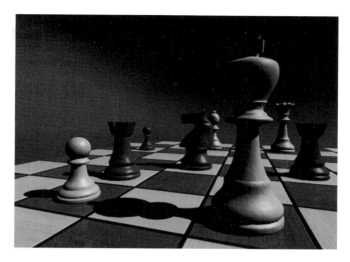

Figure 10.5

**Key light only**

Here, the key light produces a moody still life. It may be composed of more than one 3ds Max light, although the intent would be that all the lights that comprise the key should come from roughly the same angle.

## Fill Light

A more diffused light than the key light, the *fill light* seems directionless and evenly spread across the subject's dark side. This fills the rest of the subject with light and decreases the dark area caused by the key light.

The fill light shouldn't necessarily cast any shadows onto the subject or the background. In fact, the fill light is actually used to help bring up the darkness and soften the shadows created by the key light. Figure 10.6 shows the same still life with an added fill light in the scene. The fill light clearly softens the shadows and illuminates the dark areas that the key light misses by design.

Figure 10.6

**A fill light is now included.**

In most cases, you'll need to place the fill light in front of the subject. The fill, however, is aimed so that it shines from the reverse side of the key light. This angle intentionally targets the dark side of the subject. Even though the still life in Figure 10.6 is still a fairly moody composition, much more is visible than with only the key light in Figure 10.5.

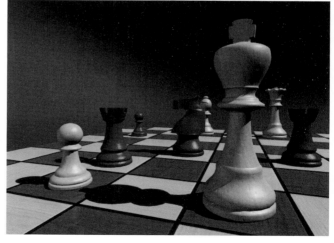

## Back Light

The *back light*, also called a rim light, is placed behind the subject to create a bit of a halo, which helps make the subject pop out in the shot. As a result, the subject has more presence against its background. Figure 10.7 shows how helpful a back light can be.

Figure 10.7

**A back light makes the subject pop right out.**

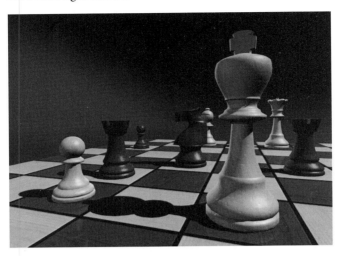

The back light brings the chess pieces out from the background and adds some highlights to the edges, making the composition more focused.

Don't confuse the back light with the background light, which lights the environment behind the subject.

## Three-Point Lighting in Action

The focus of a three-point lighting system is the primary subject of the shot. This means the lighting is based on the position and angle of the subject to the camera. When a camera is moved for a different shot, even within a scene of the same subject, a new lighting setup is more than likely required. This makes three-point lighting shot-specific and not scene-specific. Of course, once you have a shot set up with the lighting you like, changing it slightly to suit a new camera angle is much easier than starting from scratch.

When the lighting is completed for the subject of a shot, the background will probably need to be lit as well. For the background, you would typically use a directed primary light source that matches the direction of the key light. This becomes your background's main light. Then you would use a softer fill light to light the rest of the background scene and to soften the primary shadows.

## Practical Lighting

*Practical lighting* is a theatrical term describing any lights in a scene that are cast from lighting objects within the scene. For example, a shaded lamp on a nightstand in the background of a scene set in a bedroom would need practical lighting when the light is turned on. The practical lighting shouldn't interfere with the main lighting of the scene, although if the scene's lighting is explicitly coming from such a source, you will have to set up your key light to match the direction and general mood of the practical light in the shot.

Not every light-emitting object in your CG scene automatically calls for its own light in 3ds Max. Rendering tricks such as glow (see Chapter 11, "3ds Max Rendering") often are used to simulate the effect of an active scene light. This way, you don't need to actually use a 3ds Max light. Of course, if you need the practical light to illuminate something in the scene, you need to create a light for it.

# 3ds Max Lights

3ds Max has two types of light objects: Photometric and Standard. *Photometric lights* are lights that possess very specific features to enable a more accurate definition of lighting, as you would see in the real world. Photometric lights have physically based intensity values that closely mimic the behavior of real light. We will touch on these lights as we cover mental ray rendering in the next chapter. *Standard lights* are still extremely powerful and capable of realism, but they are more straightforward to use than Photometric lights and less taxing on the system at render time.

> A chessboard scene is included on the companion web page. To practice the lighting techniques as you read through this chapter, set your project to the Lighting Scene Files project downloaded from the web page and load the Chess_Board_Start.max file in the Scenes folder.

## Default Lights

What happens if you have no lights at all in your 3ds Max scene? In this case, the scene is automatically lit by *default lighting*. When you add light objects, the default lighting is replaced entirely by the new lights. There is very little you can do with the default lighting; it is there for your convenience so you easily can view an object in Shaded mode and test render without creating a light first.

### One or Two Default Lights

When you use default lighting, there is only one light. However, you can customize the configuration so that you can have two lights for default lighting.

To change to two default lights, in the main menu bar choose Views → Viewport Configuration, which opens the Viewport Configuration dialog box. From there, choose the Lighting and Shadows tab. In this dialog box, you can choose whether you want Scene Lights, which illuminates the viewport using light objects, or Default Lights, which is one

Figure 10.8

**You can choose one or two lights for your default lighting.**

light or two lights. If there are no lights in the scene, it defaults to one light. Figure 10.8 shows the Viewport Configuration dialog box's Lighting and Shadows tab.

In a single default light, you have a single key light. This light is linked to the viewport, and it moves with the point of view. Setting up the default lighting to have two lights adds a single fill light that is placed opposite the key light. The key is always placed in front of the object being viewed, on its upper-left side. The default fill light, if added, is created behind and to the lower right of the object. The link between the default light and the viewport is broken when you have two default lights. In Figure 10.9, there is a sphere on the left with a single default light. In the middle is the same sphere with two default lights. In the image on the right, the two default lights are no longer connected to the viewport.

In Figure 10.10 and Figure 10.11, you can see how the second default fill light works for the chessboard. Figure 10.10 has the single default light, and Figure 10.11 has two default lights. You can see the addition of a second set of highlights on the chess pieces in Figure 10.11 due to the added fill light.

Figure 10.9

**The default light and the viewpoint**

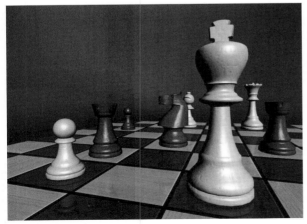

Figure 10.10

**A single default light provides a key light.**

Figure 10.11

**Two default lights provide a key light and a fill light.**

### Converting Default Lights

Remember that the default lights have no parameters and cannot be edited. You can, however, convert the default lighting into light objects that can be edited. To do this, the 2 Lights Default Lights option must be selected in the Viewport Configuration dialog box's Lighting and Shadows tab.

To add the default lighting to your scene, choose Create → Lights → Standard Lights → Add Default Lights to Scene, as in Figure 10.12. If you have 1 Light default lighting, this menu option will be grayed out and the dialog box shown in Figure 10.13 will open, giving you the option to add either one or both default lights to the scene.

3ds Max will bring the default lights in as Omni lights (which you will learn about soon). Once you add the default lights, you can edit them like any other light. However, it's always best to just begin lighting the scene with your own lights created from scratch.

Figure 10.13

**The Add Default Lights to Scene dialog box**

### Using Default Lights

Once you add a light, any default lighting that has not been added to the scene will be removed. Likewise, if you remove all the lights in a scene, 3ds Max will re-create the default lighting. Figure 10.12 shows how to add two default lights as Omni lights (the diamond shapes) in the sphere's scene.

Use default lighting as a temporary solution. It gives you an easy way to have a constant light that travels with the viewport's point of view—provided it's the single default light. This helps you see the detail in your modeling, animation, and texturing without having to worry about creating and placing lights, especially lights that would follow the viewport.

## Standard Lights

The lights in 3ds Max try to mimic the way real lights work. For example, a light bulb that emits light all around itself would be an Omni light in 3ds Max. A desk lamp that shines light in a specific direction in a cone shape would be a spotlight. Each of the different Standard lights casts light differently. We will look at the most commonly used lights.

3ds Max has a total of eight light types in its Standard Light collection. The following lights are in the collection:

Target Spotlight

Free Spotlight

Target Direct Light

Free Direct Light

Omni Light

Skylight

mr Area Omni Light

mr Area Spotlight

The last two on this list have the prefix "mr" to signify that they are mental ray–specific lights. An advanced renderer, mental ray is commonly used in production today. It offers many sophisticated and frequently complex methods of lighting that enhance the realism of a rendered scene. It is fairly complex and will be covered in the next chapter.

After you read this chapter, you should be familiar enough with lighting to get started and try new things without using any advanced lighting and rendering methodologies.

Figure 10.14

**A Target spotlight**

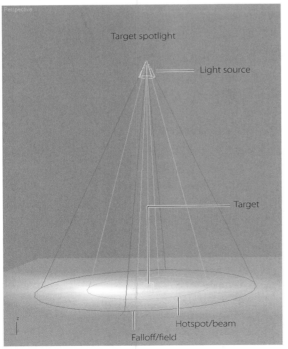

### Target Spotlight

A *Target spotlight,* as shown in Figure 10.14, is one of the most commonly used lights because it is extremely versatile. A spotlight casts light in a focused beam, similar to a flashlight. This type of lighting allows you to light specific areas of a scene without casting any unwanted light on areas that may not need that light. You can control the size of the *hotspot.* This is the size of the cast beam.

The light is created with two nodes, the light itself (*light source*) and the Target node, at which the light points at all times. This way you are able to animate the light following the subject of the scene easily, as a spotlight would follow a singer on stage. Select the target and move it as you would any other object in 3ds Max. The Target spot will rotate to follow the target. Similarly, you can animate the light source, and it will orient itself accordingly to aim at the stationary target. (You may also animate both if you prefer.)

## CREATING A TARGET SPOT

Create a Target spot by going to the Create panel and clicking the Lights button (  ) to access the light creation tools shown in Figure 10.15.

Figure 10.15

**Light creation tools**

In any scene, click the Target Spot button, and in the Top viewport, click and drag to create a Target spotlight, as shown in Figure 10.16.

Figure 10.16

**Target Spotlight created in the Top viewport**

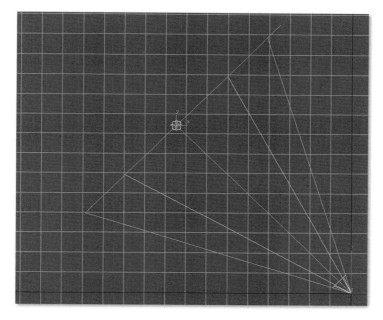

## FALLOFF/FIELD

Select the light source of the Target spot. Go to the Modify panel (  ), and open the Spotlight Parameters rollout shown in Figure 10.17.

Figure 10.17

**Spotlight Parameters rollout**

The falloff, which pertains to Standard lights in 3ds Max, is represented in the viewport by the area between the inner lighter-yellow cone and the outer darkeryellow cone. The light diminishes to 0 by the outer region.

The *falloff* is the area in which the intensity of the beam falls off, or dissipates, creating a soft area around the hotspot circle (where the light is the brightest), as shown in Figure 10.18.

Figure 10.18

**The falloff of a hotspot**

**SPOTLIGHT SHAPE**

You can also change the shape of a spotlight from circular to rectangular by selecting either Circle or Rectangle in the Spotlight Parameters rollout. In addition, using the aspect value, you can set the height-to-width ratio for the hotspot for a Rectangle spotlight. Figure 10.19 shows a rectangular spot with an aspect of 4.0.

When rendered, the rectangular spot looks like the image in Figure 10.20.

Figure 10.19

**A spotlight can also be rectangular.**

Figure 10.20

**The rendered image**

## SELECTING THE LIGHT

You can move (and animate) the entire light, including the target, by selecting the light object in the viewport by the line that connects the light source and the target in the middle of its display, as shown on the left in Figure 10.21. To access the parameters of the light, you have to select the light, as shown on the right. The target does not list any parameters for the light.

Figure 10.21

**Selecting the light**

## INTERACTIVE CONE SETTINGS

3ds Max has the ability to control the Hotspot/Beam and the Falloff/Field parameters in the viewport. Follow these steps to interactively change a spotlight's hotspot and falloff.

1. Select the spotlight's source.

2. Click the Select and Manipulate tool in the Main toolbar ( ).

3. Click and drag the green circles at the end of the spotlight cone to set the hotspot and falloff ranges, as shown in Figure 10.22.

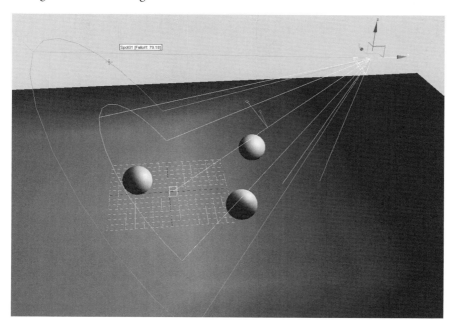

Figure 10.22

**Setting the hotspot and falloff ranges**

### Target Direct Light

A *Target Direct light* has Target and Light nodes to help you control the direction and animation of the light. It also has a hotspot and beam, as well as a falloff, much like the Target spot. However, where the Target spot emits light rays from a single point (the light source) outward in a cone shape, the Target Direct light casts parallel rays of light within its beam area. This helps simulate the lighting effect of the sun, because its light rays (for all practical purposes on Earth) are parallel. Figure 10.23 shows a Target Direct light in a viewport.

Because the directional rays are parallel, the Target Direct lights have a beam in a straight cylindrical or rectangular box shape instead of a cone.

You can create a Target Direct light much the same way as a Target spot.

1. Select Target Direct from the Create panel and click in an Orthographic window to set the light and define the target direction and length of the light by dragging.

2. Select the light for the Target Direct light and open the Modify panel.

In the Directional Parameters rollout, you'll find the same parameters for the Target Direct light that you had for the Target spot. The procedure to select the light is the same as for the Target spot, as well. You can select the middle of the light for the whole object, or you can select either the target or light. You have to select the light to bring up the parameters for the light object.

Figure 10.23

**A Target Direct light**

Although the spotlight and the directional light don't seem to be very different, the way they light is strikingly different, as you can see in Figure 10.24.

Figure 10.24

**A Target spot (left) and a Target Direct spot (right)**

The spotlight rays cast an entirely different hotspot and shadow than the directional light, despite having the same values for those parameters.

> It's preferable to create lights in one of the Orthographic viewports because it gives you a better idea of size and direction than a Perspective or Camera viewport.

## Free Spotlight

A *Free spotlight* is virtually identical to a Target spot, except that this light has no target object. You can move and rotate the free spot however you want, relying on rotation instead of a target to aim it in any direction. A Free spotlight is shown in Figure 10.25.

Figure 10.25

**A Free spotlight does not have a target.**

Figure 10.26

**Spotlight General Parameters rollout.**

To create a Free spotlight, choose Free Spot in the Create panel, click in a viewport, and drag to set its initial direction and length. The one other difference between a Free spotlight and a Target spotlight is that whereas the length of the Target spotlight is controlled by its target, a Free spot has a parameter in the General Parameters rollout of the Modify panel, as shown in Figure 10.26. You set the length by adjusting this unmarked value next to the Targeted check box. You will study the General Parameters rollout later in this chapter.

Adjusting the length of a spotlight will not matter when the light is rendered; however, seeing a longer light in the viewports can help you line up the light with objects in the scene. Likewise, you can shorten the length of the light to clear some wireframe clutter from your viewports.

Spotlights (including Target spots) are great for key lighting because they are very easy to control and give a fantastic sense of direction.

### Free Direct Light

The *Free Direct light* is identical to the Target Direct light, but it doesn't have the Target node. Its parameters are the same as the Free spot's, and it is selected and moved in the same way. Figure 10.27 shows a Free Direct light.

Directional lights (including Target directs) are great lights to use as key lights. You can also use them for fill lights, although the hotspot size must be large to avoid seeing the edges of the hotspot.

Figure 10.27

**A Free Direct light**

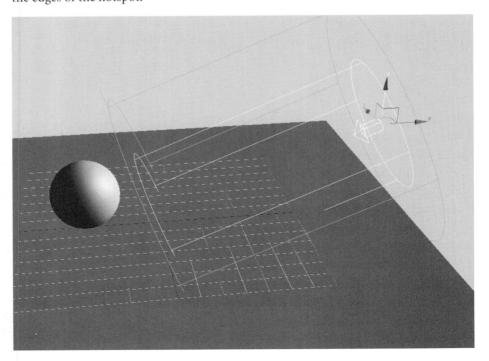

Directional lights are also used frequently to simulate sunlight, although their beams must be quite wide to avoid any chance of seeing the hotspot or falloff area.

## Omni Light

The *Omni light* in 3ds Max is a point light that emanates light from a single point in all directions around it. Figure 10.28 shows an Omni light.

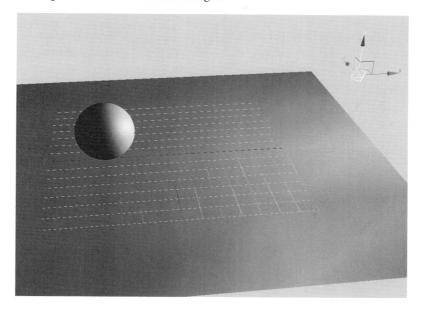

Figure 10.28

**An Omni light is a single-point source light.**

Figure 10.29

**Omni light General Parameters**

Unlike the spot and directional lights, the Omni light does not have a special rollout, and its General Parameters rollout is much simpler, as shown in Figure 10.29.

An Omni light is shown rendered in Figure 10.30. Notice how the ground plane is brighter directly below where the light sits.

Figure 10.30

**An Omni light lights the sphere and floor.**

Omni lights are not as good for simulating sunlight as directional lights are. The Omni light's rays spread from a single point source, so by the time they reach their subjects, the light direction and shadows will be too disparate across the scene. In Figure 10.31, the Omni light in the image on the left creates different shadow and lighting directions for all the objects in the scene, and the directional light in the image on the right creates a uniform direction for the light and shadow, as would the sun here on Earth.

Figure 10.31

**Omni light (left)
and directional
light (right)**

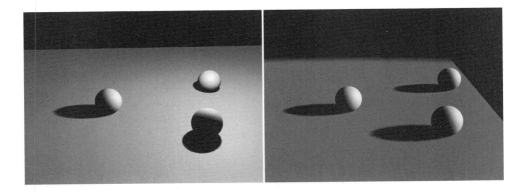

Try to avoid casting shadows with Omni lights, because they will use a lot more memory than a spotlight when casting shadows.

Omni lights are good for fill lights as well as for simulating certain practical light sources that have a brighter center and fall off evenly around that bright spot on all three axes. You could even use Omni lights for all three points in your three-point lighting system, as shown in Figure 10.32 on the chessboard scene. This lighting gives the scene a nice soft feel with crisp shadows.

Figure 10.32

**Using Omni lights
for all three points
in a three-point
lighting system**

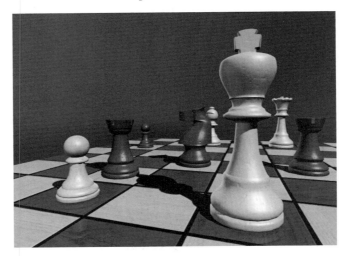

## Skylight

*Skylight* is a special 3ds Max light used with an advanced rendering method to quickly generate a scene rendered in a soft outdoor light. We will not be covering this advanced lighting and rendering methodology; however, here is a quick introduction to the light itself.

Figure 10.33 shows a Skylight high above the scene with the three spheres. It is created by selecting the Skylight button in the Create panel and clicking to place it in a viewport.

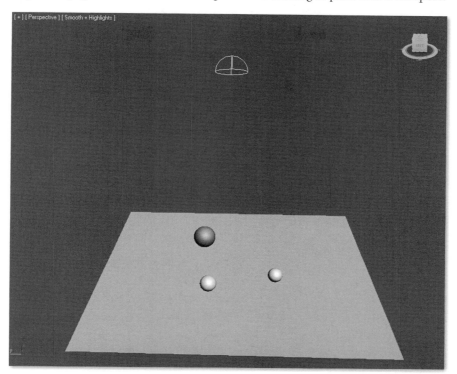

Figure 10.33

**A Skylight placed over the spheres and ground plane**

The Skylight Parameters rollout is shown in Figure 10.34.

The Skylight is used to create a soft, global lighting to simulate light from the sky. This look is often seen with renders using Global Illumination or Radiosity. In these lighting/rendering solutions, the Skylight creates a sky dome that sits around the objects in the scene. Light is emitted from the entire surface area of the dome to cast an even light throughout the scene, much as the sky lights an outdoor area.

The rendering of a Skylight scene, as shown in Figure 10.35, is flat and bright. There is no definition because shadows are not enabled.

Turning on shadows gives you a beautiful render, as shown in Figure 10.36, with soft shadows and contact shadows that really make the spheres look as if they are sitting outside in afternoon light.

The render time for this frame, however, is significantly longer than that for any of the other renders so far in this chapter. Calculating soft light such as this is quite intensive unless a lighting plug-in such as Light Tracer is enabled in the render setup.

Figure 10.34

**The Skylight Parameters rollout**

Figure 10.35
**The Skylight flattens the spheres and blows them out.**

Figure 10.36
**Turning on shadows for the Skylight dramatically increases render times, but it gives a nice effect with soft shadows, mimicking a Radiosity effect.**

## Common Light Parameters

Most of the parameters for the Standard lights are the same for all the lights and will be described in this section. You may want to create a spot or directional light so you can follow along with the information about light parameters given here.

### General Parameters Rollout

Figure 10.37
**The General Parameters rollout is the same for all the Standard lights.**

The General Parameters rollout for all the Standard lights (except for Skylight) is shown in Figure 10.37. In the Light Type section, you can change the type of light that is currently selected. Simply choose the type (Spot, Directional, Omni) from the drop-down menu. 3ds Max will replace the light with the new light type; it won't change its position or orientation. This can be immensely helpful when you are deciding which light will work best for a scene. Otherwise, you would have to delete and re-create lights to find the solution that best suits your scene.

You can turn a Free Spot or Free Directional to a target of the same kind by checking the Targeted check box. Of course, the On toggle controls whether the light is on or off in the scene.

In the Shadows section of the General Parameters rollout for these lights, you will find the controls for the shadow-casting properties of the selected light. Use the drop-down menu to select the type of shadows to cast. The two most frequently used shadow types, Shadow Map and Ray Traced Shadows, are discussed later in the chapter.

The Use Global Settings toggle can be very useful. When it is turned on, all of the lights in your scene will be set to use the same Shadow parameters of the light you have selected and for which you have enabled Use Global Settings. This is useful in the event you need the same type of shadows cast from all the lights in the scene. It can save you the hassle of specifying the settings for all the lights. It does, however, limit you to the same shadow settings for all the lights. While you are learning, you should leave Use Global Settings off and set each light manually as needed. Again, shadows are covered a little later in this chapter.

## Intensity/Color/Attenuation Rollout

The Intensity/Color/Attenuation rollout, shown in Figure 10.38, is used to adjust your light's brightness and color settings.

### Light Intensity

The Multiplier parameter works like a dimmer switch for a light. The higher the value is, the brighter the light will be. The Multiplier can go into negative values. A negative amount will subtract light from your scene, allowing you to create dark areas within lit areas or to remove excess light from a surface that has unwanted spill light.

### Light Color

The color swatch next to the Multiplier field is used to add color to your light. Simply click on the color swatch to open the Color Selector. The darker the color is, the darker the light will be.

### Light Decay

Under the Decay section, you can set the way your light fades across distance. This is not the same as falloff with spots and directional lights, though. Falloff occurs on the sides of a hotspot, whereas *decay* happens along the path of the light as it travels away from the light. Figure 10.39 shows a light with no decay type set. Figure 10.40 shows the same light with its decay type set to Inverse. Figure 10.41 shows the same light with the decay type set to Inverse Square. Notice the decay rate increases with each successive figure.

If no decay is set for a light, its intensity remains at full strength from the light to infinity. An Inverse decay diminishes the intensity of the illumination over distance traveled according to some brainy formula. An Inverse Square decay more closely resembles the decay of real-world light, and it is a stronger rate of decay than Inverse decay. Use this decay rate to drop off the effect of a light quickly before it reaches too far into the scene; however, you may need a stronger Multiplier value to increase your light's intensity to compensate for the much faster decay.

Figure 10.38

**The Intensity/Color/ Attenuation rollout**

Figure 10.39

**A light with no decay evenly illuminates all the numbers.**

Figure 10.40

**A light with Inverse decay illuminates the back numbers less.**

Figure 10.41

**A light with Inverse Square decay illuminates the first two numbers and begins to lose the remaining three.**

In Figure 10.42, you can quickly see and set the start of a decay in spot and directional lights by changing the Start value in the Decay section of the rollout.

Figure 10.42

**Seeing the start of a light's decay helps you understand how it will illuminate your scene.**

In Figure 10.43 you can see a decay start that is closer to the light, and its effect on the render in the top-left corner. The start of the decay is moved closer to the spheres in Figure 10.44.

Figure 10.43
**A decay start**

Figure 10.44
**A decay start closer
to the spheres**

## Light Attenuation

Light attenuation is another way to diminish the intensity of a light over distance. With attenuation, however, you have more implicit control on the start and end of the fade, and you can specify an area where the light fades in and then fades out. To do this, set the Attenuation distances to the desired effect.

### NEAR ATTENUATION GROUP

The following values set the distances where the light fades into existence:

**Use** Toggles on/off the use of near attenuation for the light.

**Show** Displays the near attenuation range settings in viewports. For spotlights, attenuation ranges appear as lens-shaped sections of the cone. For directional lights, the ranges appear as circular sections of the cone. For Omni, the ranges appear as spheres. By default, Near Start is dark blue and Near End is light blue.

**Start** The distance at which the light starts to fade in.

**End** The distance at which the light reaches its full intensity.

Figure 10.45 shows a render of near attenuation at work. The first numbers are darker than the back numbers. Figure 10.46 shows a spotlight and the Attenuation display in the viewport.

Figure 10.45

**Near attenuation fades in the light.**

Figure 10.46

**The spotlight displays the attenuation distances.**

### FAR ATTENUATION GROUP

The following values set the distances where the illumination fades out of existence:

**Use** Toggles on/off the use of far attenuation for the illumination.

**Show** Displays the near attenuation range settings in viewports. For spotlights, attenuation ranges appear as lens-shaped sections of the cone. For directional lights, the ranges appear as circular sections of the cone. For Omni, the ranges appear as spheres. By default, Near Start is dark blue and Near End is light blue.

**Start** The distance at which the illumination starts to fade away.

**End** The distance at which the illumination has faded to nothing.

Figure 10.47 shows a render of the far attenuation on the same set of numbers, using the same light as before. Now the lights fade into darkness the farther back they are in the scene, which is similar to decay. Figure 10.48 shows the Far Attenuation display for the spotlight. Figure 10.49 shows the Attenuation display for an Omni light in a viewport.

**Figure 10.47**

**Far attenuation fades out the light.**

**Figure 10.48**

**The spotlight displays the attenuation distances.**

**Figure 10.49**

**The Attenuation display for an Omni light**

You can always use both near and far attenuation to set a sliver of light in your scene, as shown in Figure 10.50. As you can see, attenuation is a more precise way than decay to set a diminishing light intensity.

Figure 10.50

**Using both near and far attenuation gives you a slice of light where you need it.**

Both decay and attenuation are important to use when the light needs to be realistic. Light decays in real life; your renders will assume a higher fidelity when the lights in them decay. The effect may be subtle, but it can make a large difference.

## Advanced Effects Rollout

Figure 10.51

**Advanced Effects rollout**

The Advanced Effects rollout (shown in Figure 10.51) enables you to control how a light affects the surfaces it illuminates. You can increase or decrease the contrast and softness of a light's effect on a surface. You can also dictate which component of the light is rendered on the surface.

### Contrast and Soften

By adjusting the Contrast and Soften Diffuse Edge values, you can alter the way the light hits your surface. The image in Figure 10.52 was rendered with default Contrast and Soften Diffuse Edge values. The image in Figure 10.53 was rendered with a Contrast value of 25 and a Soften Diffuse Edge value of 50. It has deeper contrast, but with slightly softer values leading from the diffuse color.

**Contrast**  Changes the contrast level between the diffuse and ambient areas of the surface when lit.

**Soften Diffuse Edge**  Controls the softness of the edges between the diffuse and ambient areas of the lit surface.

Figure 10.52

**Using default Contrast and Soften Diffuse Edge values**

Figure 10.53

**Using a Contrast setting of 25 and a Soften Diffuse Edge setting of 50**

## Light Components

Light in a CG program is differentiated into an *ambient*, a *diffuse*, and a *specular* component. The ambient component of light is the general ambient light in a scene. There is no direction to ambient light, and the light itself is cast evenly across the extent of the scene. The diffuse component of light is the way it illuminates an object by spreading across its surface. The specular component of light is how the light creates highlights on a surface, especially when that surface is glossy. (You may want to review the discussion of these components in Chapter 7, "Materials and Mapping.")

In the Affect Surfaces section of the Advanced Effects rollout, you can toggle on the Diffuse, Specular, and Ambient Only check boxes to render only those components of the light on the surfaces they illuminate. This is a good way to separate your renders into lighting components that you can later control in compositing, although it leads to a longer workflow.

Figure 10.54 is rendered with the diffuse component of the lights in the scene. Figure 10.55 shows only the specular highlights rendered. Figure 10.56 shows only the ambient light rendered on the objects.

Figure 10.54

**Only the diffuse component of the lights is rendered.**

Figure 10.55
**Only the specular component of the lights is rendered.**

Figure 10.56
**Only the ambient light in the scene is rendered.**

## Ambient Light

Ambient light in 3ds Max is not a light per se; it is a global setting in the render environment. Ambient light, in short, is an even light with no direction or source. It is a way to globally brighten the entire scene to add an even light to all objects. Using too much ambient light will wash out your objects and give you flat renders.

Figure 10.57

**The Environment and Effects dialog box**

To set an ambient light level in your scene, in the main menu select Rendering → Environment to open the Environment and Effects dialog box shown in Figure 10.57.

To set an ambient light, click on the Ambient color swatch under the Global Lighting section and pick an appropriate color. The brighter the color, the brighter the ambient light will be throughout the scene.

> You can also create an ambient light in your scene by creating an Omni light and toggling on the Ambient Only check box under the light's Advanced Effects rollout.

## Lighting the Red Rocket

Now that we have an overview of how lights work in 3ds Max, let's put them to good use and light the Red Rocket textured model from Chapter 7. Because lighting goes hand in hand with rendering, we will create the basic lighting setup based on the three-point system discussed earlier in this chapter. We'll work more with the lighting and settings when we get to Chapter 11, "3ds Max Rendering."

Occasionally, setting a project and opening a scene file fails to open all the appropriate image files used in the scene. In these cases, you will have to reconnect the image files needed by navigating to their folders (usually in the project's SceneAssets/Images folder) and picking the files manually. 3ds Max will give you the error message and give you a chance to replace the files when you first open the scene.

Set your current project to the Red Rocket project you've copied to your hard drive from this book's companion web page. Open ROCKET_LIGHT_START.max from the Scenes folder of the Red Rocket project.

This scene is very simple (Figure 10.58). It is the final rocket from Chapter 7. (If you prefer, you can use your own rocket file.)

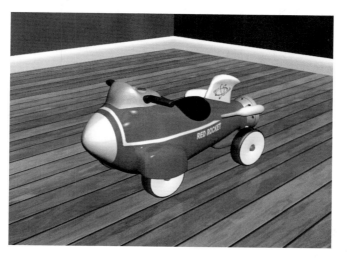

Figure 10.58

**The rocket set into a simple room**

The rocket, with all its many parts, has been frozen in the scene on the companion web page at www.sybex.com/go/intro3dsmax2011 so you can work freely without worrying about selecting objects other than the lights. The rocket and the room it is in can be unfrozen by going to the Layer Manager and clicking the Unfreeze icon next to the Rocket layer (as shown in Figure 10.59).

To begin lighting the rocket, follow along here:

1. Go to the Create panel and select the Lights icon ( ) to bring up the selection of lights you can create.

2. Click the Target Spot button to create a Target spot. Go to the Top viewport, and click and drag from the right side of the viewport toward the middle, as shown in Figure 10.60. The click will create the light; the drag places the target.

Figure 10.59

**Use the Layer Manager to unfreeze parts of the scene.**

To unfreeze objects, click on the snowflake icon.

Figure 10.60

**Click and drag from the right side toward the middle.**

When you create your first light, the Camera viewport will turn dark momentarily. This is because when you create a light, the default lights are removed from the scene.

3. Move to the Front viewport, select the light, and move it up as shown in Figure 10.61. If your front view is not visible, simply select one of the viewports and press F for the Front viewport.

Figure 10.61

**Move the light.**

4. Name the light **Key Light**. This light will have shadows and give the scene its main source of light and direction.

5. Go to the Modify panel, check the On box under Shadows, and set Shadow Type to Shadow Map. This is the default shadow type. Later in the chapter, we will expand on all the shadow types and their uses in 3ds Max.

6. Go to the Intensity/Color/Attenuation rollout in the Modify panel, and set the Multiplier setting to 0.8. As you learned earlier in the chapter, the Multiplier setting acts like a dimmer switch and controls the light's brightness.

7. In the Spotlight Parameters rollout, change the Hotspot/Beam parameter to 18 and the Falloff/Field value to 38. Both these parameters affect the width of the cone of light. The closer the two values are, the sharper the edge of the light will be; the farther they are from each other, the softer the light will be.

Try a render (press F9 for a Render Last), and you will see the rocket as shown in Figure 10.62.

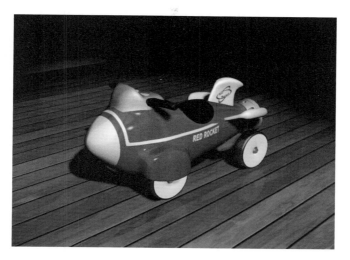

Figure 10.62

**Rendering the rocket with the first light in place**

Not bad, but look at how dark the shadow is. Once we add a fill light, the shadows will be better. For the fill we'll use an Omni light. You may also notice that the rocket looks a bit like it is floating above the ground. Let's address that issue first, in the following steps:

1. Select the key light (the Target spot), and in the Shadow Map Params rollout (Figure 10.63), change the Bias parameter to 0.1. Bias moves the shadow toward or away from the object. The shadow is too far away from the rocket, and that is why in Figure 10.62 it appears to be floating.

Figure 10.63

**The Shadow Map Params rollout**

2. In that same rollout, change the Size parameter to 1500. Size specifies the amount of resolution in the shadow; the more the pixels the more crisp the edge of the shadow will appear.

3. Go back to the Create panel to create another light. Click to create an Omni light. In the Top viewport, click in the bottom-left corner of the room to place the Omni as shown in Figure 10.64.

4. In the Front viewport, move the light up about half the height of the backdrop.

5. The Omni is just a fill light in this scene, so we don't want any shadows from it. Furthermore, we will turn off specular highlights on the rocket from this light to make sure the render looks as if there is only one light in the room. By default, shadows are

always off, but we must turn off specular highlights manually. With the Omni light selected, go to the Modify panel and, under the Advanced Effects rollout, uncheck Specular as shown in Figure 10.65.

Figure 10.64

**Place an Omni light in the scene.**

Figure 10.65

**Advanced Effects rollout**

6. Go to the Intensity/Color/Attenuation rollout for the Omni light, and change the Multiplier to 0.3.

7. Render again (press F9), and you'll see the render looks better but the rocket's shadow is still dark (Figure 10.66).

Figure 10.66

**The rocket with a key and fill light**

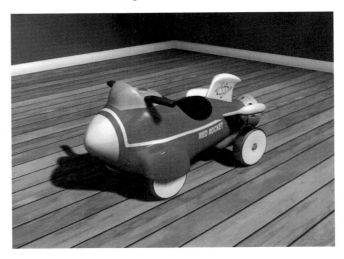

8. To fix the darkness of the shadow in Figure 10.66, we could add more lights to the scene, but then the scene would get too bright. The solution is to adjust the density of the shadow (you will see more on shadows in the next section). Select the key light, go to the Modify panel, and in the Shadow Parameters rollout, change the Object Shadows Dens parameter to 0.8 (Figure 10.67).

9. Press F9 for another Render Last (or press the teapot icon in the Main toolbar), and you will see that the rocket's shadow looks much better (Figure 10.68).

This exercise used what is arguably the most popular shadow-casting method. There are other ways to cast different types of shadows, each with its own advantages and distinct look. In the following section, we will explore different shadowing techniques.

When creating shadows, don't be too quick to smother your scene with light, or too eager to show off your careful modeling work and textures. Leaving objects in shadow and darkness is as important as revealing them in light. You can say a lot visually by not showing parts of a whole, and leaving some interpretation to the audience.

Using shadows intelligently is very important in lighting your scenes. Without the shadows in the rocket scene, the rendered image would look weird. The rocket would float in the scene and have no contact with its environment. You would also lose a great deal of the sense of direction without shadows.

A careful balance of light and dark is important for a composition. The realism of a scene is greatly increased with the simple addition of well-placed shadows. Don't be afraid of the dark. Use it liberally, but in balance.

You can create the following types of shadows in 3ds Max:

- Advanced Ray Traced
- mental ray Shadow Map
- Area Shadows
- Shadow Map
- Raytraced Shadows

Each type of shadow has its benefits and its drawbacks. The two most common types used are Shadow Maps (which you've already seen) and Raytraced shadows.

Controls in the Shadow Parameters rollout and the shadow type–specific rollouts are available when you select the shadow type.

Figure 10.67

**The Shadow Parameters rollout**

Figure 10.68

**The rocket is lit!**

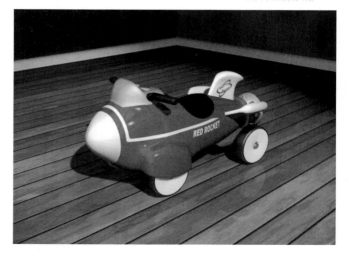

## Shadow Parameters Rollout

The settings in the Shadow Parameters rollout govern the common parameters for all shadow types discussed here. In this rollout, you can adjust the color of your shadow as well as its density (i.e., how dark it appears). See Figure 10.69. You should always check your light's Multiplier values to make sure your fill light does not wash out your shadows before you adjust the shadow parameters themselves. For instance, the fill light generally has a lower intensity than the key light.

Click on the color swatch to pick a color for your shadows. More often than not, you will have your shadow colors at black or close to black. You can also control the density of the shadows by adjusting the Density value. As you can see in Figure 10.69, adjusting the density changes how much of the shadow is rendered. A Density of 0 will turn off your shadows, in essence.

Figure 10.69

**Shadow density**

Interestingly enough, you can also apply a map to your shadow by checking the Map box and clicking on the button currently labeled None. From there, you can choose a map. In Figure 10.70, a checker map was mapped to the shadow on a fruit arrangement. Notice how the checker pattern shows up just in the shadows between and on the fruit.

Figure 10.70

**You can map a texture to the shadow, as shown on this fruit still-life render.**

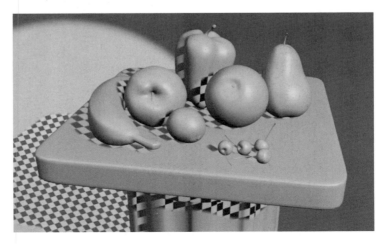

## Selecting a Shadow Type

For the most part, you will be more than happy with the results from a Shadow Map shadow in your scenes. However, to get shadows to respond to transparencies, you will need to use Raytraced shadows. Additionally, if you need to soften your shadows the farther they are cast from the object, you will need to use Area shadows. These shadow types are discussed next.

### Shadow Maps

The Shadow Map is a generated bitmap file during a pre-rendering pass of the scene. This map is used to place the shadows in the final render. It is often the fastest way to cast a shadow. However, Shadow Map shadows do not show the color cast through transparent or translucent objects. Once you select Shadow Map in the General Parameters rollout for a light, the Shadow Map Params rollout appears. It was shown earlier in Figure 10.63.

Because this shadow type relies on maps, it is important to be able to control the resolution of the generated maps. When you are close to a shadow, in order to avoid jagged edges around it the resolution needs to be higher for the cast shadow than it would if it were farther from the camera.

The following parameters are useful for creating Shadow Maps:

**Bias** The shadow is moved, according to the value set, closer to or farther away from the object casting the shadow. Figure 10.71 shows how the bias moves the shadow away the higher the value is set.

Figure 10.71

**The bias offsets the shadow from the casting object.**

Bias = 6.0

Bias = 1.0 (normal)

**Size** Detailed shadows will need detailed Shadow Maps. Increase the Size value, and 3ds Max will increase the number of subdivisions for the map, which in turn increases the detail of the shadow cast. Figure 10.72 compares using a low Shadow Map Size setting to using one four times larger. Notice how the shadows on the left (Size = 1024) are somewhat mushy and less noticeable, and the shadows on the right (Size = 4096) are crisp and clean. You don't want to set your Shadow Map size to be too high, though. It will increase render time for little to no effect. A size around 2048 is good for most cases. Scenes like this chessboard that have a large scale to them will require higher Size values, such as the 4096 used. The rule of thumb is to use the lowest Size value that will get you the best result for your scene.

> In some scenes, you may discover that no Shadow Map Size setting will give you good results (for instance, in large outdoor scenes). In these cases, you will have to revert to a different shadow method, such as Raytraced shadows.

**Sample Range** This creates and controls the softness of the edge of shadow-mapped shadows. The higher the value is, the softer the edges of the shadow will be. Figure 10.73 shows you how soft edges (on the left) can make the lighting seem weaker or farther away from the subject than crisp shadows (on the right).

Figure 10.72

**The Shadow Map Size setting affects the shadow detail.**

Figure 10.73

**Soft-edge shadows versus crisp-edged shadows**

### Raytraced Shadows

*Raytracing* involves tracing a ray of light from every light source in all directions and tracing the reflection to the camera lens. You can create more accurate shadows with raytracing than with other methods. However, the render takes significantly longer to calculate. Raytraced shadows are always hard edged, yet they are realistic for transparent and translucent objects. Figure 10.74 shows a pair of chess pieces rendered with a plane casting a shadow over them. The plane has a checker mapped to its opacity, so it has alternating transparent and opaque squares defining the checkerboard. On the left side of the image in Figure 10.74, the light is casting Shadow Map shadows, while on the right the light is casting Raytraced shadows.

Figure 10.74

**Ray Traced shadows react to transparencies, and Shadow Maps do not.**

Use Raytraced shadows when you need highly accurate shadows or when Shadow Map resolutions are just not high enough to get you the crisp edges you need. You can also use Raytraced shadows to cast shadows from wireframe rendered objects.

The Ray Traced Shadow Params rollout (see Figure 10.75) controls the shadow. The Ray Bias parameter is the same as the Shadow Map Bias parameter in that it controls how far from the casting object the shadow is cast.

Figure 10.75

**Ray Traced Shadow Params rollout**

## Creating Soft Shadows Due to Distance

The only way you will be able to create a natural shadow that softens the farther it gets from the casting object is to use Area shadows. These types of shadows are natural. If you notice a telephone pole's shadow, the farther the shadow is from the pole, the softer the shadow becomes. Adding such a shadow to a render can greatly increase the realism of the scene.

To enable a soft shadow such as this, select Area Shadows as your shadow type. At default parameters, the Area shadow will work for you to generate nicely soft shadows. Figure 10.76 shows a regular Raytraced shadow. Figure 10.77 shows an Area shadow at the default settings.

Figure 10.76

**A Raytraced shadow is too hard-edged.**

Figure 10.77

**An Area shadow begins to soften at the ends.**

Go to the Area Shadows rollout shown in Figure 10.78. To adjust the softness of the shadows, you will not want to increase the Sample Spread value, because that parameter, just like the Sample Range of the Shadow Map shadow, softens the entire shadow. A true shadow is crisp where it meets the casting object and softens as it casts away.

To further soften the ends of the shadows, in the Area Light Dimensions section of the rollout, set the Length to 80 and the Width to 60. This will increase the softness of the shadow in a realistic way while keeping the contact shadow crisp. However, the render, shown in Figure 10.79, does not look very good. The soft ends are very grainy.

You will need to increase the quality of the shadow, so set Shadow Integrity to 6 and Shadow Quality to 10. The render will take longer, but you will get a beautiful shadow, as shown in Figure 10.80.

Figure 10.78

**The Area Shadows rollout**

Figure 10.79

**The render with Length set to 80 and Width set to 60**

Figure 10.80

**Increase the shadow quality to obtain a very realistic shadow.**

## Atmospheres and Effects

Creating atmospheric effects with lights, such as fog or volume lights, is accomplished through the Atmospheres & Effects rollout in the Modify panel for the selected light, as shown in Figure 10.81.

Using this rollout, you can assign and manage atmospheric effects and other rendering effects that are associated with lights. In the following exercises, you will learn how to create a volumetric light (similar to a flashlight shining through fog). You will also learn how to exclude objects from a light so that the light does not illuminate them. This is an important trick to know.

Figure 10.81

**Atmospheres & Effects rollout**

### Creating a Volumetric Light

Let's create a fog light now.

1. Open the ROCKET_AMOSPHERE_START.max scene file in the Lighting Scenes folder on the companion web page. Go to Create panel → Lights and click on the Target Direct light. Move your pointer to the Top viewport, and click and drag from the top of the viewport down toward the rocket.

   As shown in Figure 10.82, the light begins outside the room the rocket is in. This scene is already equipped with two Omni lights to act as fill lights in the room.

2. Move to the Front viewport and move the light up along the *Y*-axis, and then move the target so it is centered to point the light directly on the rocket, as shown in

Figure 10.83. Make sure the light is shining into the room from outside through the window.

3. Activate the Camera viewport and do a Render Last (F9); you will see that the scene is being lit from the direction of the light (Figure 10.84).

This first render probably looks very odd. The rocket and floor have reflections on them, so they show up even if there is no light in the scene at all. That is the way reflections work.

Figure 10.82

**The light begins outside the room the rocket is in.**

Figure 10.83

**Move the light up and move the target.**

Figure 10.84

**A test render of the rocket**

### Adding Shadows

Now you need some shadows in the scene.

1. In the General Parameters rollout for the light, go to the Shadows section and check the box to enable shadows. Select Shadow Map from the drop-down menu. This will turn on Shadow Map shadows for this light.

2. Go to the Shadow Map Params rollout and set the size to 2048; this will add some sharpness to the shadow's edge and make it more like a daylight shadow. Also change the Bias setting to 0.1, which will move the shadow so it is under the rocket. If you do a Render Last, you won't see any shadows (as shown in Figure 10.85).

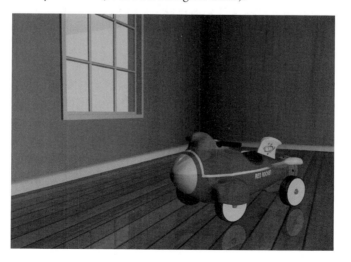

Figure 10.85

**You won't see any shadows if you do a Render Last.**

This is because the window is blocking the light. The window glass object has a material that has its Opacity turned down to 0. However, Shadow Map shadows don't recognize transparency in materials. To solve this problem, you need to exclude the window-glass object from the light.

### Excluding an Object from a Light

1. The Exclude button is in the General Parameters rollout for the light, just below Shadows. Click the Exclude button to bring up the Exclude/Include window shown in Figure 10.86.

Figure 10.86

The Exclude/Include window allows you to exclude certain objects from being lit by the light in the scene.

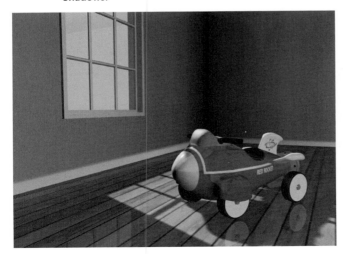

Figure 10.87

Shadows!

2. Click on the Glass object and press the right arrows in the middle of the window (Figure 10.86) to add the Glass object to the other side, excluding the object from receiving light and casting light. Click OK.

3. Render your scene to take a look. Now you can see shadows. We didn't exclude the whole window with its frame because the inside frame is a nice detail to cast shadows. Figure 10.87 shows the render with the shadows.

## Adding a Volumetric Effect

The whole point of this exercise is to add volume to the light. This will give this scene some much needed atmosphere.

Figure 10.88

**The Add Atmo-sphere or Effect settings**

1. Go to the Atmospheres & Effects rollout for the light. Select Add from the rollout to open the Add Atmosphere or Effect window, which is shown in Figure 10.88.

2. In the window, select Volume Light and click OK to add the effect to the light. Volume Light will be added to the rollout, as shown in Figure 10.89.

3. Render the scene. You should see a render similar to Figure 10.90.

To adjust the volume light, select the Volume Light entry in the rollout and click the Setup button. This will bring up the Environment and Effects dialog box. Scroll down to the Volume Light Parameters section to access the settings for the volume light, shown in Figure 10.91. Experiment with different settings to see how the volume light renders.

You can use `Rocket_Atmosphere_Final.max` in the Scenes folder of the Lighting scene Files project from the companion web page to see the results of this work, and to adjust as you wish.

Figure 10.89

**Add Volume Light to the rollout area.**

Figure 10.90

**Volume light!**

Figure 10.91

**The Environment and Effects window displays the Volume Light parameters.**

## Volume Light Parameters

The default parameters for a volume light will give you some nice volume in the light for most scenes, right off the bat. If you want to adjust the volume settings, you can edit the following parameters:

**Exponential** The density of the volume light will increase exponentially with distance. By default (Exponential is off), density will increase linearly with distance. You will want to enable Exponential only when you need to render transparent objects in volume fog.

**Density** This value sets the fog's density. The denser the fog is, the more light will reflect off the fog inside the volume. The most realistic fogs can be rendered with about 2 to 6 percent Density value.

Most of the parameters are for troubleshooting volume problems in your scene if it is not rendering very well. Sometimes you just don't know what that problem is and you have to experiment with switches and buttons. The Noise settings are another cool feature to add some randomness to your volume:

**Noise On** This toggles the noise on and off. Render times will increase slightly with Noise enabled for the volume.

**Amount** This is the amount of noise that is applied to the fog. A value of 0 creates no noise. If the Amount is set to 1, the fog renders with pure noise.

**Size, Uniformity, Phase** These settings determine the look of the noise and let you set a noise type (Regular, Fractal, or Turbulence).

Adding atmosphere to a scene can heighten the sense of realism and mood. Creating a little bit of a volume for some lights can go a long way to improving the look of your renders. However, adding volume to lights can also slow your renders, so use them with care. Also be aware that adding too much volume to a scene may look peculiar; use volumetric light sparingly and with good reason. Reserve it for when it is called for in the scene and will add ambience to the image.

# Light Lister

If several lights are in your scene and you need to adjust all of them, selecting each light and making one adjustment at a time can become tedious. This is where 3ds Max's Light Lister comes in handy. Accessed through the Main Menu bar by choosing Tools → Light Lister, this floating palette gives you control over all of your scene lights, as shown in Figure 10.92.

This is the perfect tool to edit your lights once you have them set up initially. You can choose to view/edit all the lights in your scene or just the ones that are selected. Using this easy dialog box gives you instant access to almost all the important light parameters in one place. When you adjust the values for any parameter in the Light Lister window, the changes are reflected in the appropriate place in the Modify panel for that changed light.

Figure 10.92

**The Light Lister window**

# Summary

Lighting is the aspect of CG that is arguably the most difficult to master (some users think it's even harder than character animation), and it is the most easily criticized. People in the CG industry can tell very quickly when lighting is done poorly.

In this chapter, you began by reviewing some key concepts in CG lighting, including three-point lighting. Then you learned the different types of lights that 3ds Max has to offer, from default lights to Target spots, and how to use them. You dove into the common light parameters to gauge how best to control the lights in your scene before you moved on to creating various types of shadows. You ran through a set of short exercises in which you created a volumetric light for a fog effect and finished with a tour of the Light Lister window.

Several books are devoted to CG lighting. It is a craft that takes getting used to. This chapter introduced you to the concepts and tools you need to begin, and the next chapter will take this knowledge further into rendering. Now it's your turn to take the models you have created (and the ones you will create in the future), texture them, and light scenes with them to develop an eye for the ins and outs of lighting.

There really is no quick way to learn how to light. It would be quite a disservice to pretend that a chapter, or even an entire book, will give you everything you need to know. Take the information and references in this chapter and apply them on your own. Working on your own may not sound like fun, and it may not seem as easy as being guided step by step, but it is the best education you will get.

# CHAPTER 11

# 3ds Max Rendering

*Rendering is the last step* in creating your CG work, but it is the first step to consider when you start to build a scene. During rendering, the computer calculates the scene's surface properties, lighting, shadows, and object movement, and then it saves a sequence of images. To get to the point where the computer takes over, you'll need to set up your camera and render settings so that you'll get exactly what you need from your scene.

This chapter will show you how to render your scene using 3ds Max's scanline renderer and how to create reflections and refractions using raytracing. In addition, this chapter will introduce you to the popular mental ray renderer and HDRI lighting workflow.

Topics in this chapter include the following:

- **Rendering setup**
- **Motion blur**
- **Previewing with ActiveShade**
- **Cameras**
- **Safe Frame**
- **Render elements**
- **Rendering effects**
- **Raytraced reflections and refractions**
- **Bringing it all together: Rendering the rocket**
- **mental ray Renderer**
- **Final Gather with mental ray**

# Rendering Setup

In a manner of speaking, everything you do in CG can be considered setup for rendering. More specifically, your render settings and what final decisions you make about your 3ds Max scene ultimately determine how your work will look. In many ways, you should be thinking about rendering all along—especially if you are creating 3D assets for a game, where the 3D scenes are rendered in real time by the game engine. If you create models and textures with the final image in mind and gear the lighting toward elegantly showing off the scene, the final touches will be relatively easy to set up.

To set the proper settings, begin with the Render Setup dialog box.

Figure 11.1

**The Common tab in the Render Setup dialog box**

## Render Setup Dialog Box

The Render Setup dialog box is where you define your render output for 3ds Max. You can open this dialog box by clicking the Render Setup icon (□) in the Main toolbar, by selecting Rendering → Render Setup, or by pressing F10. You've already seen how to render (□) a frame in your scene to check your work. The settings in the Render Setup dialog box are used even when the Render button is invoked; so it's important to understand how this dialog box works. Figure 11.1 shows the Common tab in the Render Setup dialog box.

### Common Tab

The Render Setup dialog box is divided into five tabs; each tab has settings grouped by function. The Common tab stores the settings for the overall needs of the render—for example, image size, frame range to render, and type of renderer to use.

In the Common Parameters rollout, you will find the most necessary render settings. They are described in the following sections.

#### TIME OUTPUT

In this section, you can set the frame range of your render output by selecting one of the following options (as shown in Figure 11.2):

**Single** This option renders the current frame only. The frame range is set to Single by default.

**Active Time Segment** This option renders the frame range in the timeline.

**Range** This option renders the frame range specified in the text boxes.

Figure 11.2

**Time Output sets the frame range of your render.**

**Frames** This option renders the frames typed in the text box. You can enter frame numbers separated by commas or specified as ranges, such as 3–13, to render only the specified frames.

**Every Nth Frame**  This option is enabled when you are rendering more than one frame. It allows you to render every *n*th frame, where *n* is a whole number, so you can specify how many frames to skip.

Typically, you will be rendering single frames as you model, texture, and light the scene. The closer you are to final rendering, especially for scenes with moving cameras or lights, the more likely you will need to render a sequence of images to check the animation of the scene and how the lighting works. This is where the Every Nth Frame function comes in very handy. Using it, you can render every fifth frame, for example, to quickly see a render test range of your scene without having to render the entire frame range.

You should always test render at least a few frames of an animation before you render the entire frame range, because the smallest omission or error can cost you hours of rendering and effectively bottleneck production flow and get several people annoyed at you. This practice is a good habit to start. Whenever you want to launch a render of the entire scene, render at least one frame to check the output. If you have animated lights or cameras, use the Every Nth Frame option to test a few frames.

**Area to Render**  This is where to go if you want to render only part of your frame. This is especially useful when you are testing the look of a single part of your frame, or even a single object, without having to wait for the rest of the frame to process. Here you can choose View, Selected, Region, Crop, or Blowup. For example, when set to Region, a re-sizeable box appears in your viewport as well as the Rendered Frame Window where you can select the region of the frame you wish to render.

### OUTPUT SIZE

The image size of your render, which is set in the Output Size section (as shown in Figure 11.3), will depend on your output format—that is, how you want to show your render. Chapter 1, "Basic Concepts," explains the popular resolutions used in production.

**Figure 11.3**

**Output Size sets your output format size.**

**Resolution**  By default, the dialog box is set to render images at a resolution of 640 × 480 pixels, defined by the Width and Height parameters, respectively. This resolution has an image aspect of 1.333, meaning the ratio of the frame's width to its height.

**Image Aspect Ratio**  Changing the Image Aspect value will adjust the size of your image along the Height parameter to correspond with the existing Width parameter to accommodate the newly requested aspect ratio. Different displays have different aspect ratios. For example, regular television is 1.33:1 (simply called 1.33) and a high-definition (HD) television is a widescreen with a ratio of 1.78:1 (simply called 1.78). The resolution of your output will define the screen ratio.

**Pixel Aspect Ratio**  Pixel Aspect affects the image because it actually changes the shape of the pixel from a square to a rectangle. This reflects how TV screens (standard definition, not HD) display images. When output is displayed on a TV screen, the image will be squeezed slightly horizontally. Therefore, renders are created a bit wider so that when they are displayed on a TV screen, they will appear normal. This is especially visible when you render a round object, as shown in Figure 11.4. On the left, the sphere is rendered with a pixel aspect of 1.0 (i.e., a 1:1 ratio). On the right, the sphere is rendered with a pixel aspect of 0.9 (i.e., a 0.9:1 ratio). However, when the sphere on the right is displayed on a standard TV, it will appear round and not stretched in this manner.

Figure 11.4

**Rendering a round object for display on a TV screen**

You hardly ever have to worry about pixel aspect ratios. They are mentioned only for those who may be outputting directly to DV tape or DVD. Luckily, in the Output Size section of the Render Setup dialog box there is a drop-down menu for choosing presets from different film and video resolutions. Custom is the default, and it allows you to set your own resolution. You can also select one of the preset resolution buttons. For DVD or TV output, you should select the NTSC D-1 (video) preset. For output to a DV tape, you should select the NTSC DV (video) preset. They both have a pixel aspect ratio of 0.9 to account for the TV "squeeze." Of course, if you (or your client) are in Europe or in another place where the PAL standard is used, you will need to select the PAL equivalents of the aforementioned presets, because TV resolutions and frame rates differ internationally. For more on aspect ratios and frame rates, see Chapter 1.

The higher the resolution, the longer the scene will take to render. Doubling the resolution might quadruple the render time. To save time when you're working with large frame sequences, you can render tests at half the resolution of the final output and render every fifth frame or so.

The image quality of a render also affects how long a render will take. In addition to turning down the resolution for a test, you can use a lower-quality render and/or turn off certain effects, such as Atmospherics (volume lights, for example, that simulate light cutting through fog). Quality settings are explained in the following section.

Figure 11.5

**Options section gives you global toggles.**

### OPTIONS

The Options section (shown in Figure 11.5) lets you access several global toggles. Three boxes are checked by default. You can toggle the rendering of specific elements in your scene. For example, if you are using Atmospherics (volume light) or Effects (lens flare) and don't want them to render, you can uncheck the appropriate box(es). This is a shortcut to turn off the effect or atmosphere.

## RENDER OUTPUT

What good does it do to render a scene if you don't save the files? When you are done setting up the dialog box for your image output, you need to tell 3ds Max where to render the images and what file format to use. Use the Render Output section as shown in Figure 11.6 to indicate that the file should be saved.

The image format can be selected to be a single image file or sequence of image files that form a sequence, or it can be a movie file such as a QuickTime. In fact, 3ds Max supports many image file formats. The most common movie format is arguably QuickTime. A sequence of frames is typically rendered to Targa or TIFF files.

**Figure 11.6**

**The Render Output section is used to indicate the location and format of the image files.**

### Choosing a Filename

To specify a location and file type to render to, click the Files button to open the Render Output File dialog box shown in Figure 11.7. Select the folder to which you want to render, and set the filename. You can set the file type using the Save As Type pull-down menu.

Proper file naming is very important when you render a scene, particularly when you are rendering a sequence of images and have hundreds of frames. Saved images are usually identified by a filename, a frame number, and an extension in the form `filename_####.ext`—for example, `stilllife_0234.tif`. This format is used in production facilities and accepted by most compositing programs, such as Combustion or After Effects.

**Figure 11.7**

**The Render Output File dialog box defines how the render saves to disk.**

| Name ▲ | Size | Type |
|---|---|---|
| testrange_v010000.tif | 1,013 KB | TIF Image |
| testrange_v010002.tif | 1,013 KB | TIF Image |
| testrange_v010004.tif | 1,013 KB | TIF Image |
| testrange_v010006.tif | 1,013 KB | TIF Image |
| testrange_v010008.tif | 1,013 KB | TIF Image |
| testrange_v010010.tif | 1,013 KB | TIF Image |
| testrange_v010012.tif | 1,013 KB | TIF Image |
| testrange_v010014.tif | 1,013 KB | TIF Image |
| testrange_v010016.tif | 1,013 KB | TIF Image |
| testrange_v010018.tif | 1,013 KB | TIF Image |
| testrange_v010020.tif | 1,013 KB | TIF Image |
| testrange_v010022.tif | 1,013 KB | TIF Image |
| testrange_v010024.tif | 1,013 KB | TIF Image |
| testrange_v010026.tif | 1,013 KB | TIF Image |
| testrange_v010028.tif | 1,013 KB | TIF Image |
| testrange_v010030.tif | 1,013 KB | TIF Image |
| testrange_v010032.tif | 1,013 KB | TIF Image |
| testrange_v010034.tif | 1,013 KB | TIF Image |
| testrange_v010036.tif | 1,013 KB | TIF Image |
| testrange_v010038.tif | 1,013 KB | TIF Image |
| testrange_v010040.tif | 1,013 KB | TIF Image |
| testrange_v010042.tif | 1,013 KB | TIF Image |
| testrange_v010044.tif | 1,013 KB | TIF Image |
| testrange_v010046.tif | 1,013 KB | TIF Image |
| testrange_v010048.tif | 1,013 KB | TIF Image |
| testrange_v010050.tif | 1,013 KB | TIF Image |
| testrange_v010052.tif | 1,013 KB | TIF Image |
| testrange_v010054.tif | 1,013 KB | TIF Image |
| testrange_v010056.tif | 1,013 KB | TIF Image |
| testrange_v010058.tif | 1,013 KB | TIF Image |
| testrange_v010060.tif | 1,013 KB | TIF Image |
| testrange_v010062.tif | 1,013 KB | TIF Image |
| testrange_v010064.tif | 1,013 KB | TIF Image |

Figure 11.8

**Image filenames without a separator between the filename and frame number are confusing to look at and might play out of sequence.**

When you enter the filename for an image sequence, you can include an underscore (the _ character) *after* the filename and before the frame number to help differentiate the two. This is especially useful if you use version numbers in your scene names. If you don't use an underscore (or similar character) between the filename and frame number, your rendered image files can be confusing, as shown in the file list in Figure 11.8.

It's a good idea to name your rendered images according to the scene's filename. This way you can always know from which scene file a rendered image was produced, without rooting through several files and/or guessing.

The extension portion of the image filename is a three-letter abbreviation that corresponds to the type of file you are rendering. By specifying a file format in the Save As Type drop-down menu, you automatically set the extension for the file in its filename. This way you ensure that you can identify the file type.

## Image File Type

You can save your images in a wide range of formats when you render with 3ds Max. The format you choose depends on your own preference and your output needs. For example, JPEG (Joint Photographic Experts Group) files may be great for the small file sizes preferred on the Internet, but their color compression and lack of alpha channel (a feature discussed below) make them undesirable for professional film or television production work beyond test renders and *dailies*—meetings at which the day's (or week's) work on a production is looked at and discussed.

Furthermore, for two reasons it's best to render a sequence of images rather than a movie file. First, you want your renders to be their best quality with little to no image compression. Second, if a movie render fails, you must re-render the entire sequence. With an image sequence, however, you can pick up where the last frame left off. The best file formats to render to are Targa and TIFF (Tagged Image File Format), though the decision can come down to personal preference. For example, OpenEXR is an incredibly robust file format to work with in compositing and is preferred by many professional artists.

These file formats enjoy universal support, have little to no image quality loss due to compression, and support an alpha channel. Almost all image-editing and compositing packages can read Targa- and TIFF-formatted files, so either is a safe choice most of the time. For more on image formats, see Chapter 1.

While we're on the subject of image files, let's look at what makes them up. Computer images are composed of red, green, and blue channels. Each channel specifies the amount of that primary additive color in the image. (See Chapter 1 for more on how computers define color.) In addition, some file formats can also save a fourth channel, called the *alpha channel*. This channel defines the transparency level of the image. Just as the red channel defines how much red is in an area of the image, the alpha channel defines how transparent the image is when layered or composited on another image. If the alpha channel is black, the image is perfectly see-through. If the alpha channel is

Figure 11.9
**Alpha channel**

white, the image is opaque. The alpha channel is also known as the *matte*. An object that has a transparency in its material, such as the wine bottle shown rendered in Figure 11.9, will render with a gray alpha channel.

The alpha channel is displayed in the Rendered Frame Window (Figure 11.10). You have seen this window display your test renders several times throughout this book.

Figure 11.10
**Rendered Frame Window**

To view an image's alpha channel in the Rendered Frame Window, click the Display Alpha Channel icon. To reset the view to RGB (full-color view), click the Display Alpha Channel icon again. You can also see how much red, green, or blue is present in the frame by clicking any one of the red, green, and blue disc icons that are the Enable RGB Channel icons, as shown in Figure 11.10.

To save an image you like in the Rendered Frame Window, click the Save Image button. The Clone Rendered Frame Window button is quite useful in that it creates a copy of this window for you so you can compare a newer render to an older render without needing to save the images.

To copy a rendered image into another program, click the Copy Image icon, which will copy the image onto the Windows Clipboard. This image will then be available when you open other programs. You can paste it quickly into another application in fewer steps than before by using this feature.

## Render Processing

When you click the Render button in the Render Setup dialog box, the Rendering dialog box pops up (Figure 11.11). This dialog box shows the parameters being used, and it displays a progress bar indicating the render's progress. You can pause or cancel the render by clicking the appropriate button. Rendering can consume most, if not all, of your system's resources. (It may also consume more than your system's resources, which usually results in a crash!) Pausing a render will not let you access your scene in 3ds Max, but it will stop the process on your system momentarily so that you can tend to another PC task.

Figure 11.11

The Rendering dialog box shows you everything you want to know about your current render.

## Assign Renderer

The Assign Renderer rollout (Figure 11.12) displays which renderers are assigned to your scene. Four types of renderers are available in 3ds Max by default (without any additional plug-ins installed) as shown in Figure 11.13:

**Default Scanline Renderer**  The Scanline Renderer renders the scene as a series of horizontal lines.

**mental ray Renderer**  This is a general-purpose renderer that can generate physically correct simulations of lighting and material effects.

**VUE File Renderer**  The VUE File Renderer creates VUE (.vue) files, typically for natural environments.

**Quicksilver Hardware Renderer**  Quicksilver is a renderer new to 3ds Max 2011 that engages the CPU and the graphics card's processor (GPU) to quickly render your scene. This is useful for test renders and for quickly approximating how gaming engines may look.

Figure 11.12
**Assign Renderer rollout**

VUE and Quicksilver are not covered in this book because they are advanced renderers; however, mental ray rendering is covered later in this chapter.

## Rendering the Bouncing Ball

Figure 11.13
**Choose Renderer dialog box**

Seeing is believing, but doing is understanding. In this exercise, you will render the Bouncing Ball animation from Chapter 8, "Introduction to Animation," to get the feel for rendering an animation in 3ds Max. Just follow these steps:

1. Set your Project folder to the Bouncing Ball project that you downloaded to your hard drive from the companion web page at www.sybex.com/go/intro3dsmax2011. Open the `Animation_Ball_02.max` file in the Scenes folder. Let's render a movie to see the animation.

2. Open the Render Setup dialog box. In the Time Output section, select Active Time Segment: 0 to 100.

3. In the Output Size section, select the 320 × 240 preset button and leave Image/Pixel Aspect as is.

4. Leave the Options group at the default, and skip down to the Render Output section. Click the Files button to open a Render Output File dialog box. Navigate to where you want to save the output file, preferably into the RenderOutput folder in your Bouncing Ball project. Name the file **Bounce Ball**, and click the drop-down menu next to Save as Type to choose MOV QuickTime File (*.mov) for your render file type. Normally, we would render to a sequence of images rather than a movie file like this; however, for short renders a QuickTime file works out fine.

By default, 3ds Max will render your file(s) to the RenderOutput folder in the current project directory.

Apple's QuickTime movie file format gives you a multitude of options for compression and quality. The quality settings for the QuickTime file are not the same as the render quality settings.

5. After you select MOV QuickTime File and click the Save button, the Compression Settings dialog box, shown in Figure 11.14, opens. Set the parameters for the QuickTime file as indicated:

- Compression Type: Photo–JPEG
- Frames per second: 30
- Compressor Depth: Color
- Quality: High

Click OK.

Figure 11.14

**QuickTime compression settings affect the quality of the rendered QuickTime video file.**

If you are concerned about the file size of your renders, you can slide the Quality bar to a lower quality setting for the compressor. The Photo-JPEG compressor makes fairly good images with small file sizes. However, you'll want to deliver your renders at the highest quality you can muster. To improve quality, use a different compressor type. For example, Animation is lossless and makes big files, but those big files look much better.

6. Skip down to the bottom of the Render Setup dialog box, and verify that Production is selected. Select the viewport you want to render in the View drop-down menu. You need to render Camera01.

7. Click Render. The Rendered Frame Window will show you how the frames look as they render as the renderer goes through the sequence of frames, and the Rendering dialog box will appear.

After the render is complete, navigate to your render location (by default it is set to the RenderOutput folder for the Bouncing Ball project). Double-click the QuickTime file to see your movie, and enjoy a latte.

## Renderer Tab Basics

The Renderer tab, found in the Render Setup dialog box, has options that determine the look and quality of the render. The options that are displayed in this tab depend on which renderer you assigned to render your scene. We will cover the Default Scanline Renderer in the following sections and mental ray a bit later in the chapter. This rollout sets the parameters for the Default Scanline Renderer.

### Options

Most of the features in Options (Figure 11.15) are used to make rendering a scene more efficient. If you want to do a quick render of an animation, for example, turn off Mapping and Shadows. You will still see the movement, but the processing will go faster.

Figure 11.15

**The Options section of the Renderer tab in the Render Setup dialog box**

### Antialiasing

*Aliasing* is the staircase effect you see in an image just at the edge of a line or area of color, particularly when that edge is at an angle, as shown in Figure 11.16.

*Antialiasing* can smooth this stepped effect on diagonal or curved lines. It blurs and mixes the color values of pixels adjacent to the jagged line or curve, as shown in Figure 11.17. Turning off this feature will speed up your renders, but the quality loss will be noticeable.

Turning off Antialiasing disables the Force Wireframe setting. Geometry renders according to the material assigned to it even if Force Wireframe is turned on. Turning off Antialiasing also disables Render Elements. If you need to render elements, be sure to leave Antialiasing on (Figure 11.18).

Figure 11.16

**Aliasing is the stepped effect on diagonal and curved lines. Notice the top ridges of the fruit and its stem.**

Figure 11.17

**Antialiasing helps smooth jagged diagonal and curved lines.**

Figure 11.18

**The Antialiasing group of parameters**

### Filters

Filters are the last step in antialiasing. You can use them to access different methods of calculating the antialiasing at the subpixel level in order to sharpen or soften your final output. You don't need to worry about which filter to use until you have much more rendering experience under your belt. The Area filter, which is the default filter, will work great (Figure 11.19).

**Figure 11.19**

**Filter drop-down menu**

If you are curious about the different filter types, select a filter. A short description of it will appear in the box below the Filter Maps check box.

# Motion Blur

With *motion blur,* a renderer can simulate how the eye or a camera sees an object in motion. When an object moves relatively fast, your eye (or a camera) perceives a blur on the object. Using motion blur for an animation can greatly enhance the fidelity of your render, although it adds more processing time. Use motion blur sparingly in most scenes. It takes a careful eye to choose the right blur amount for an object.

The Renderer tab in the Render Setup dialog box has two sections used for setting the type of motion blur you need.

### Object Motion Blur

The Object Motion Blur section (shown in Figure 11.20) lets you access the motion blur settings.

**Figure 11.20**

**Object Motion Blur section**

The Object Motion Blur settings are as follows:

**Duration (Frames)** The higher the Duration number, the more blur you get. You can see the difference in the motion blur for the ball in Figure 11.21.

**Samples** This setting determines how many duration subdivision copies are sampled. The higher the Samples number, the better the motion blur quality.

**Duration Subdivisions** This setting determines how many copies of each object are rendered within the duration. The higher the Subdivisions number, the smoother the motion blur will look.

**Figure 11.21**

**Different durations give different motion blur lengths.**

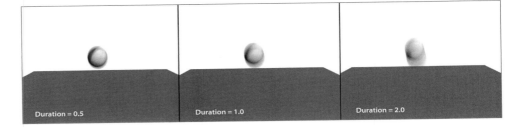

Setting the Duration very high and the Samples and Duration Subdivisions low will give you a ghosting effect that will kill the look of the motion blur. You will need to find the right balance to achieve a believable blur. Remember that less is more. Just a touch of motion blur may be all a scene needs.

## Image Motion Blur

As you'll notice in the Render Setup dialog box, Object Motion Blur is turned on by default. However, you still need to enable motion blur on a per-object basis; this means you have to toggle motion blur on for any object that you want to render with blur.

To turn on motion blur, select the object and right-click on it in a viewport. From the Quad menu, choose Object Properties. Select the type of motion blur (shown in Figure 11.22) you want, and then adjust the parameters in the Renderer tab.

The difference between Object and Image motion blur types can be seen in Figure 11.23. The bouncing ball on the left is rendered with Object motion blur, and the one on the right is rendered with Image motion blur. Both are rendered with the same Duration. The Image motion blur renders smoother, although it may not be as accurate because it is a smearing effect created *after* the object is rendered into the image. The Object blur renders the blur during the scanline rendering process itself.

For now, you only need to be concerned with the Duration parameter for an Image motion blur. This setting, as with the Object motion blur, sets the amount (and therefore the length) of the blur. Remember not to go overboard with motion blur. A little goes a long way.

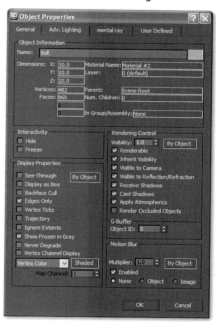

**Figure 11.22**

**Choose the type of motion blur for an object through its Object Properties dialog box.**

**Figure 11.23**

**Different motion blur types give you different results. The one on the left is Object motion blur, and the one on the right is Image motion blur.**

# Previewing with ActiveShade

ActiveShade is a fantastic 3ds Max feature that lets you interactively preview a render as you make changes in the scene. This is particularly helpful for texturing and lighting because the floating ActiveShade dialog box updates whenever you make a light or material change in the scene.

ActiveShade doesn't render Atmospheric effects.

Figure 11.24

**ActiveShade rendering toggle**

To enable ActiveShade, open the Render Setup dialog box (  ). At the bottom of the dialog box, click to toggle on the ActiveShade rendering, as shown in Figure 11.24. Pick your viewport, and either click the ActiveShade button in the Render Setup dialog box or click the Render button in the Main toolbar. The icon in the Main toolbar changes (  ) as you switch from Production rendering to ActiveShade rendering.

You can have only one ActiveShade dialog box open at a time. If you try to open another dialog box, an alert will ask whether you want to close the other dialog box.

You can also turn a viewport into an ActiveShade dialog box. Select the viewport where you want to enable ActiveShade, click on the middle Point-of-View viewport label, and from the menu choose ActiveShade, as shown in Figure 11.25.

That viewport will then become an ActiveShade viewport and will update a render every time you make changes to the scene. This helps keep the clutter of open dialog boxes to a minimum. You should switch off ActiveShade and enable Production before continuing with the rest of the chapter.

# Cameras

Cameras in 3ds Max, as shown in the Perspective viewport in Figure 11.26, capture and output all the fun in your scene. In theory, the cameras in 3ds Max work as much like real cameras as possible. Hence, the more you know about photography, the easier these concepts are to understand.

Figure 11.25

**Select ActiveShade from the context menu.**

The *camera* creates a perspective through which you can see and render your scene. You can have as many cameras in the scene as you want. However, it's a good idea to position the camera you're planning to render with where you want it for your final framing.

You can use the Perspective viewport to move around your scene as you work, leaving the render camera alone.

Figure 11.26

**A camera as seen in the Perspective viewport**

## Creating a Camera

There are two types of cameras in 3ds Max: Target and Free. A *Target camera*, much like a Target spotlight, has a Target node that allows it to look at a spot defined by where the target is placed (or animated). A Target camera is easier to aim than a Free camera because once you position the target object at the center of interest, the camera will always aim there.

On the other hand, *Free cameras* have only one node, so they must be rotated to aim at the subject, much like a Free spotlight. If your scene requires the camera to follow an action, you will be better off with a Target camera.

You can create a camera by clicking on the Cameras icon (  ) in the Create panel and selecting either of the two camera types, as shown in Figure 11.27.

Figure 11.27

**Cameras in the Create panel**

To create a Target camera, click in a viewport to lay down the Camera node, and then drag to pull out and place the Target node. To create a Free camera, click in a viewport to place it.

## Using Cameras

A camera's main feature is the *lens,* which sets the *focal length* in millimeters and also sets the *field of view* (FOV), which determines how wide an area the camera sees, in degrees. By default, a 3ds Max camera lens is 43.456mm long with an FOV of 45 degrees. This

Figure 11.28

**Stock lenses make it easy to pick the right lens for a scene.**

default lens will most likely meet all your camera needs, but in case you need to change the lens, you can use the Lens or FOV parameters to create a new lens using the spinner or by entering a value. To change a lens, you can also pick from the stock lenses available for a camera in its Modify panel parameters, as shown in Figure 11.28.

The 3ds Max Lens and FOV parameters are tied together. One drives the other because the focal length of a real lens sets the field of view.

The most interactive way to adjust a camera is to use the viewport navigation tools. You can then place the camera while you see its field of view in that viewport. The Camera viewport must be selected for the viewport camera tools to be available to you in the lower-right corner of the UI. You can move the camera or change the lens or FOV. Chapter 3, "The 3ds Max Interface," has a complete list of the tools in the "Viewport Navigation Controls" subsection. You can also change a camera by selecting the camera object and moving and rotating it just as you would any other object.

### Talk Is Cheap!

The best way to explain how to use a camera is to create one, as in the following steps:

1.  Set your project to the Rendering Scene Files project you have downloaded to your hard drive from this book's companion web page. Open the Camera Create.max scene file in the Rendering Scene Files folder downloaded from the web page. This is the chessboard from the lighting chapter, but without a camera. Creating a camera is the same as creating a light. It's easier to create a camera in the Top viewport, so you can easily orient it in reference to your scene objects. Figure 11.29 shows the intended position of a camera for this scene.

2.  In the Create panel, click the Cameras icon (🎥). Select the Target camera and go to the Top viewport. Click from the bottom of the viewport and drag to the chessboard. The first click creates the Camera object. The mouse drag and release sets the location of the target, just like creating a target light. You may need to zoom out your view to accommodate placing the camera.

3.  The camera was created along the ground plane. You need to move the entire camera up using the Front viewport. The easiest way to do this is to select the camera and target using the line that connects the camera and target. That will select both the target and camera so you can move them as a unit. Use the Move tool to relocate the camera higher in the scene to place it at the level of the chess pieces.

Figure 11.29

**The camera
would go here.**

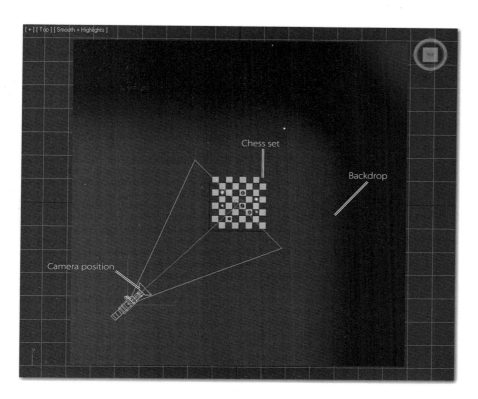

4. To see the Camera viewport, select a viewport and press the C key. This changes the viewport to whatever camera is currently selected. If there are multiple cameras in your scene and none are selected, when you press C you will get a dialog box that gives a list of the cameras from which you can choose.

5. Now Render the scene (press F9 or click the teapot icon) through the camera you just created and positioned. Find a good framing for the chessboard and set your camera.

When the camera is set up, take some time to move it around and see the changes in the viewport. Moving a camera from side to side is known as a *truck*. Moving a camera in and out is called a *dolly*. Rotating a camera is called a *roll*. Also change the Lens and FOV settings to see the results.

Zooming a lens (changing the Lens parameter) is not the same as a dolly in or dolly out. The field of view changes when you zoom, and it stays constant when you dolly. They will yield different framings.

## Animating a Camera

Now that the camera is in the scene, let's add some animation to the camera. Camera animation is done in the same way as animating any object. You can animate the camera or the target or both. You can also animate camera parameters such as Lens or FOV.

1. In the scene you just worked in, select the camera.
2. Move the Time Slider to frame 30.
3. Press the N key to activate Auto Key, or click its icon.
4. Use the Move tool to move the camera farther away from the still life. The idea is to create a dolly out of the still life.
5. Scrub through the animation and make any edit you desire.

If you are comfortable using the Perspective viewport, you can convert it to a Camera view by pressing Ctrl+C. Cool trick!

## Clipping Planes

You can limit what your camera sees in a scene. For example, in a huge scene, you can exclude or *clip* the geometry that is beyond a certain distance by using *clipping planes*. This helps minimize the amount of geometry that needs to be calculated. Each camera has a clipping plane for distance (Far Range) and foreground (Near Range), as shown in Figure 11.30 and Figure 11.31, respectively. The near clipping plane will clip geometry within the distance designated from the camera lens.

You can also use clipping planes to create a cutaway look for a model. Set your near clipping plane to a specific distance into the object, and the object will render as if it were sliced, giving you a perfect cutaway look.

Figure 11.30
**A far clipping plane cuts off the distant extents of a scene.**

Figure 11.31
**A near clipping plane cuts off the extents directly in front of a camera.**

Likewise, if you find that a model or scene you have imported looks odd or is cut off, check to make sure your clipping planes are adjusted to fit the extent of the scene, especially with imported models.

To enable clipping planes, click the Clip Manually check box and set the distances needed, as shown in Figure 11.32.

Once you turn on manual clipping planes, the camera will display the near and far extents in the viewports with a red plane marker, as shown in grayscale in Figure 11.33.

**Figure 11.32**

**Check the Clip Manually check box and set the distances.**

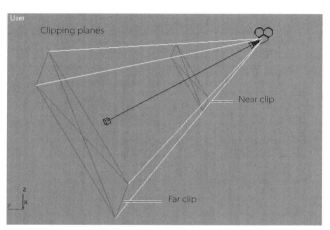

**Figure 11.33**

**When Clip Manually is enabled, a camera will display its manual clipping planes in a viewport.**

## Safe Frame

Because every TV is different, what you see on one screen may look somewhat different on a different screen. To help make sure the action of your scene is contained within a safe area on all TV screens, you can enable the Safe Frame view in any viewport. This will, as shown in Figure 11.34, show you a set of three boundaries in your viewport.

The Live area is the extent of what will be rendered. The Action Safe area is the boundary where you should be assured that the action in the scene will display on most if not all TV screens. Most TVs will display somewhere between the Action Safe and the Live areas. Finally, the Title Safe boundary is where you can feel comfortable rendering text in your frame. Because some TVs distort the image slightly at the edges, any text that

**Figure 11.34**

**Safe Frame gives you a suggested boundary for the action of your framing.**

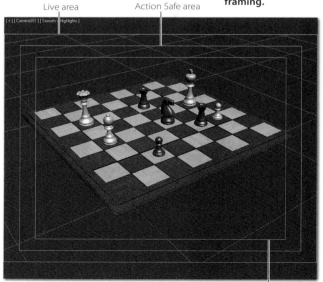

falls outside the Title Safe area may not be readable. Although they are based on TV technology from years ago, these conventions hold true in professional production to this day. The Safe Frame areas are still good guidelines to use when framing your shot.

To view the Safe Frame areas in the chosen viewport, click on the viewport's name in the upper left hand corner of the viewport to access the context menu, and then choose Safe Frame from the list.

## Render Elements

The Render Elements tab is another tab in the Rendering Scene dialog box, and is shown in Figure 11.35. You might not need this feature as a beginner, but you will be surprised at the control you get when you render your scene into separate passes to composite later. As a beginner, you should concentrate on becoming familiar with rendering and lighting. As the months pass and you feel more comfortable rendering, you should discover that most CG is layered.

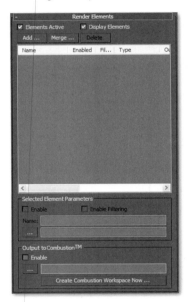

Figure 11.35

**The Render Elements tab in the Render Setup dialog box**

This means that separate passes are rendered and then layered or composited together with finer control in a program such as Photoshop for still images, and Composite, After Effects, or Nuke for image sequences. The ability to layer is another reason why rendering to image files is preferred over rendering to movie files.

However, you will need to understand compositing to be able to control and layer the elements back together.

Shadows and reflections are the main elements that you might consider rendering separately, especially when you are first learning. When these elements are separate, you gain a greater degree of control in compositing because you can affect the shadows or reflections any way you want (soften, color, transparency, etc.) as you composite them back on top of the image. For example, if you render a scene of a tree casting a shadow across a lawn, you will have to render the entire scene again if you decide to lighten the shadow color. If you have the shadow as a separate pass, you can very easily and interactively change the darkness of the shadow as you composite it in Shake, for instance.

The following list describes common elements to render:

**Alpha** Renders a black-and-white matte to be used in compositing. This is especially helpful when you need different mattes for different objects in your scene. In Figure 11.36, the chessboard is shown rendered in Alpha only.

Figure 11.36
**The Alpha element**

**Reflection**  Renders only the reflections so you can composite them separately onto the color render to have control over the amount of reflection in the final composited image, for example. Figure 11.37 shows the chess pieces' reflections in the chessboard rendered as an element.

**Refraction**  Renders only refracting elements in transparent or translucent objects, so they may be layered in the composite at a later time.

**Self-Illumination**  Renders the incandescence of an object's material separately, so its intensity may be controlled in composite.

**Shadow**  Renders only the shadows cast in the scene into the alpha channel of the image. Figure 11.38 shows the chess pieces' Shadow element. Keep in mind that you will have to render to an image format that has an alpha channel, such as TIFF.

Figure 11.37
**The Reflection element**

Figure 11.38
**The Shadow element as shown in the alpha channel of the image**

Figure 11.39

**The Specular element**

Figure 11.40

**The Z-Depth element**

**Specular**  Renders only the highlights on an object's glossy material. Figure 11.39 shows the specular highlights on the chess pieces. Look at how the nicks and scratches on the pieces are so noticeable in this element.

**Z-Depth**  Renders a grayscale image that responds to the depth of a scene. The closer an object or a part of an object is, the whiter it renders. The farther from the camera an object or its parts are, the darker the render. This pass is then used in a compositing program, such as Combustion, to create a sense of haze or blur to add a depth of field to the image. Figure 11.40 shows a Z-Depth pass generated for the chessboard scene.

Now, let's try rendering something. Follow along with these steps.

1. Select the Render Elements tab in the Render Setup dialog box, click the Add button, and select the element you want to render.

2. Once you select a render element, it will be added to the element list. Then you'll need to go down to the Selected Element parameters to input where you will save the bitmap elements when you click the "…" button (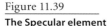), as shown in Figure 11.41. The dialog box will name the element automatically. However, when you go into the Render Element Output File dialog box to save it, you should name it again.

3. If you want each element to be rendered in its own Rendered Frame Window, check the Display Elements box. If it is unchecked, the program will render the elements to a file and the Rendered Frame Window will not show you the progress of each element.

4. Click the Render button to begin a render. 3ds Max will render the entire scene, and then output the elements as needed.

Figure 11.41

**In the Render Element Output File dialog, enter where you want to save the bitmap elements.**

# Rendering Effects

Rendering Effects offers a variety of special effects such as lens effects, film grain, and blur to add to your render. Rendering Effects allows you to create effects without having to render to see the results. They are rendered after your scene is rendered, and they are added to the rendered image automatically.

## Lens Effect: Glow

You will add a glow effect to a light bulb hanging over the chessboard in a scene.

> For this scene, we've chosen to glow the Light Bulb object. You can also glow a light; this property can be set only through Object Properties.

You will glow the Light Bulb object in the following steps:

1. Set your project to the Rendering Scene Files project you downloaded from the web page. Load the Chess_Glow.max scene file from the Rendering Scene Files project's Scenes folder.

2. Select the light bulb, and then right-click. From the Quad menu, select Object Properties, as shown in Figure 11.42.

3. In the Object Properties dialog box, go to the G-Buffer section and assign 2 as the Object ID

Figure 11.42

**Select Object Properties from the Quad menu.**

number for the glow effect, as shown in Figure 11.43. This tells 3ds Max which object gets the glow. The number you assign doesn't matter unless you want different glows on different objects. In that case, each glow object would receive its own Object ID number.

Another way you can assign glow is through the object's material. Go to the Material Editor, and in the toolbar click and hold on the Material ID Channel button. In the Slate Material Editor, you simply right-click on the material node and select Material ID Channel to access the different ID numbers to assign. The benefit of using the material for the glow is that you can glow any object that has the material applied.

4. In the menu bar, choose Rendering → Effects to open the Environment and Effects dialog box. Click the Add button. Then pick Lens Effects from the Add Effect dialog box. Figure 11.44 shows that the Lens Effects has been added.

5. Scroll down to Lens Effects Parameters, select Glow, and press the arrow button (or double-click Glow itself) to add Glow to the box on the right, as shown in Figure 11.45.

Figure 11.43

**Set a unique number for the Object ID.**

Figure 11.44

**Adding Lens Effects to the Environment and Effects dialog box**

Figure 11.45

**Adding Glow in the Lens Effects Parameters**

6.  While still in the Environment and Effects dialog box, scroll down to the Glow Element rollout. This is where you create the settings for the glow effect. There are two tabs:

    **Parameters** This tab is where you set the size and color of the glow, as shown in Figure 11.46.

    **Options** This tab is where you can assign the glow to the object desired. Under Image Sources, you have to choose how the glow will be applied to the object, through the material or object properties.

7.  Click the Options tab. Because you are creating the light bulb's glow through the Light Bulb object's Object ID, click to enable Object ID and set the Object ID parameter to 2, as shown in Figure 11.47. Leave the other parameters at their default values.

8.  Click over to the Parameters tab to set the glow's size. Setting the size for the glow can be a bit tricky because the size of the glow depends on the size of your object. Set the Size value to 5. Leave Intensity set at the default; once you render the effect, you can adjust the Intensity setting.

9.  To add color to the glow, you can use two methods: You can set the Use Source Color parameter to set the glow color to a percentage of the object's material color. You also can use the Radial Color parameters to set the colors for the inside of the glow (on the left in the Radial Color parameter) and the outside of the glow (on the right in the Radial Color parameter). In this case, set Use Source Color to 65 because the light bulb has a yellow material applied. If you have Interactive Preview enabled (see the note in this section), you can see how the glow looks. Otherwise, run a render to check the look.

10. The default intensity looks okay, but it could be brighter. Change the Intensity to 165. Render. Okay, it looks good. See Figure 11.48.

Figure 11.46

**Set the size and color of the glow.**

Figure 11.47

**Set the Object ID parameter to 2.**

Figure 11.48

**Glow!**

### Using Preview

Using the preview in the Environment and Effects dialog box as shown in Figure 11.49 (in the Effects tab), provides a much easier way to view the effects than rendering a frame does. You can select whether you want to preview all of the effects (All) in the scene or just the one you are working on (Current). Toggling Interactive updates the preview when you change the Effects parameters by opening a Render dialog box and updating it as you

Figure 11.49

**The effects preview**

make changes. Enabling Interactive may cause your computer to slow down, so leave it unchecked and use the Update Effect button when you want to see an update.

# Raytraced Reflections and Refractions

In this section, you will learn how to create realistic reflections and refractions in your renders. As you saw in Chapter 7, "Materials and Mapping," you can apply an image map to an object's material's Reflection parameter to add a fake reflection to the object. To get a true reflection of the other objects in the scene, you will need to use raytracing methodology. There are essentially two ways to create raytraced reflections in a scene: by using a Raytrace map or by using a Raytrace material.

The Raytrace material is a more detailed solution; however, it can take twice as much time as using a Raytrace map, because the Raytrace material requires more calculation.

As you learned in Chapter 4, "Modeling in 3ds Max: Part I," determining the level of detail you need for a reflective surface is important. There is no reason to use the Raytrace material for a reflection unless your camera is right up on the object. In many cases, the Raytrace map looks great and saves tons of rendering time. Keep in mind though, the amount of control you will have with a Raytrace map is significantly less than with the Raytrace material.

First you will try using the Raytrace material.

## Raytrace Material

In the following steps, you will learn how to use the Raytrace material to create reflections in a scene with a fruit still life arrangement.

### Creating the Raytrace Material

1. Set your project to the Rendering Scene Files project you downloaded from the web page. Open the Still_Life_raytrace.max file found in the Scenes folder of the Rendering Scene Files project on the web page. Change the Camera view to Camera01 in one of the viewports if it isn't already.

2. Open the Compact Material Editor and select a sample slot. Click the Get Material button (  ) and select the Raytrace material from the Material/Map Browser, as shown in Figure 11.50.

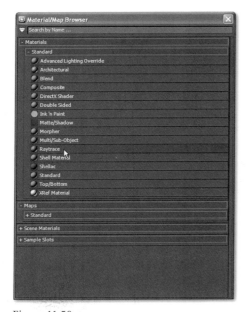

Figure 11.50
**Select the Raytrace material.**

Figure 11.51
**The Raytrace Basic Parameters rollout**

3. The parameters to create reflections are available through the Raytrace Basic Parameters rollout, as shown in Figure 11.51. Leave most of these parameters at their default values, but change the Reflect color swatch to white from black. This will set the reflection of the material all the way to the maximum reflectivity.

4. Change the Diffuse color swatch to black to turn the column that the fruit is sitting on black. This will make the column appear as a reflective black glass material in the render.

5. Apply the Raytrace material to the column in the scene. Render the Camera viewport. Figure 11.52 shows the result.

Figure 11.52
**The Raytrace material renders reflections.**

### Tweaking the Render

The render will show the Raytrace material on the column reflecting like a flat mirror. It looks very convincing, but you may notice the jagged edges or artifacts around the reflected objects. What you're seeing is aliasing in the reflections. The antialiasing filters set by default may not be enough. Clone this rendered image by pressing the Clone Rendered Frame Window icon (), which is found in the Rendered Frame Window toolbar, to make a copy of this rendered image in another window.

When the defaults aren't enough, it is time for the heavy artillery: *SuperSampling.*

Figure 11.53

**The SuperSampling rollout**

SuperSampling is an extra pass of antialiasing. By default, 3ds Max applies a single SuperSample pass over all the materials in the scene. However, if a specific material needs more antialiasing, you can apply a separate SuperSample method to that material.

In the current still life scene, select the material slot for the column's Raytrace material. Go to the SuperSampling rollout and uncheck Use Global Settings. Check Enable Local Supersampler. In the pull-down menu, choose Adaptive Halton, as shown in Figure 11.53.

The Adaptive Halton method performs well in this case. However, always try the regular patterns first; they tend to render faster. Render the scene, and you will notice a marked improvement in the quality of the reflections (Figure 11.54).

Figure 11.54

**Reflections with the Raytrace material with Local Super-Sampling enabled**

## Raytrace Mapping

You can apply raytracing only to a specific map; you can't apply it to the entire material. Because raytracing typically takes longer to render, this can save time. In this case, you will assign a Raytrace map to the Reflection map channel of a material to get true reflections in the scene, at a faster render time than using the material as you just did. Follow these steps:

1. In the scene you just worked in, open the Material Editor and select an unassigned sample slot. Keep the material set to Standard.

2. In the Map*s* rollout, click the mapping bar labeled None next to Reflection. Choose the Raytrace map in the Material/Map Browser, as shown in Figure 11.55.

   Leave the Raytrace map parameters at the default, as shown in Figure 11.56.

3. In the Material Editor's tool bar, click the Go to Parent button (⬢) .

Figure 11.55

**Choose the Raytrace map.**

Figure 11.56

**The Raytrace map parameters**

4. In the Blinn Basic Parameters rollout, change the diffuse color to black to match the black column from the previous render.

5. In the Specular Highlights section, change the Specular Level to 98 and Glossiness to 90, as shown in Figure 11.57.

6. Apply the material to the column object in the scene and Render the Camera viewport.

7. You will notice the same aliasing in the reflections as in the previous example. Set the SuperSampling as you did with the prior example, and render again.

Figure 11.57

**The Specular Highlights parameters**

Take a look at both the images created with reflections using the Raytrace material, and those created using the Standard material with the Raytrace map applied to Reflection. They look almost the same. This is good to know because it takes about half the time to render the Raytrace map. However, you will notice slightly better detail in the reflections created with the Raytrace material. You and the requirements of your scene will determine which reflection method works best in a particular situation. However, it's good always to start with the Raytrace map to see if it creates enough detail without too much bother.

## Refractions Using the Raytrace Material

Creating raytraced refractions in glass can be accomplished using the same two work-flows as raytraced for reflections. The same conditions apply here. The Raytrace material renders more nicely, but it takes longer than using a Raytrace map for the Refraction map in a material.

Keep in mind that render times are much slower with refractions, especially if you add SuperSampling to the mix—so don't freak out. Now you will create refractions using the Raytrace material:

1. In the same scene, change the Camera01 viewport to Camera02. This gives you a bet-ter view of the wine glass through which we will refract, as shown in Figure 11.58.

2. In the Compact Material Editor, select an unassigned sample slot and click the Get Material button. This material will be for the wine glass.

3. Choose the Raytrace material from the Material/Map Browser.

4. Go to the Raytrace Basic Parameters rollout, and change the color swatch for Trans-parency from black to white. (Black is opaque and white is fully transparent.)

5. Uncheck the box next to Reflect and change that spinner to 20. This sets a slight reflection for the material.

Figure 11.58

**Changing Camera01
to Camera02**

6. Take a look at the Index of Refr parameter. This value sets the *Index of Refraction* (IOR) value that determines how much the material should refract its background. For more on IOR, see the "Refractions" sidebar in this chapter. The value is already set to 1.55. Leave it at that value.

7. Go to the Extended Parameters rollout (Figure 11.59). The Reflections section of the parameters is at the bottom. Select Additive and change Gain to 0.7. This gives a bit of reflection brightness for the clear wine glass.

8. Go to the SuperSampling rollout and uncheck Use Global Setting. Check Enable Local SuperSampler and keep it set to Max 2.5 Star.

9. In the Specular Highlights group, change the Specular Level to 98 and Glossiness to 90, as shown in Figure 11.60.

10. Apply the material to the wine glass. The glass will turn transparent in the viewport. Render. Figure 11.61 shows the result.

**Figure 11.59**

**The Extended Parameters rollout for the Raytrace material**

**Figure 11.60**

**The Specular Highlights group parameters**

You will notice a very nice wine glass render, with the bell pepper refracting through it slightly. Change the Index of Refr parameter on the material to 8.0, and you will see a much greater refraction, as shown in Figure 11.62. That may work better for a nice heavy bottle, but it is too much for the glass. An Index of Refr parameter between 1.5 and 2.5 works pretty well for the wine glass, particularly at the bottom of the glass where it rounds down to meet the stem.

**Figure 11.61**

**The wine glass refraction is rendered with the Raytrace material.**

**Figure 11.62**

**A much more pronounced refraction is rendered with an IOR of 8.0.**

## Refractions Using Raytrace Mapping

Just as you did with the reflections, you will now use a Raytrace map on the Refraction parameter for the wine glass material. In the following steps, you will create another refraction render for the wine glass:

1. While still in the same scene, open the Compact Material Editor and select an unassigned sample slot. You are going to keep the material set to Standard.

2. Go to the Maps rollout and click the bar labeled None, which is next to Refraction. Choose the Raytrace map from the Material/Map Browser. The material in the sample slot will turn transparent.

3. Click the Go to Parent button to return to the material's parameters.

4. Go to the Maps rollout and click the bar labeled None next to Reflection. Choose the Raytrace map from the Material/Map Browser. Be warned that this setting will take a long time to render the image. If you have a slower computer or perhaps are in a rush, uncheck the Reflection Map box in the material's parameters to turn off the reflection entirely.

5. Click the Go to Parent button to return to the material's parameters.

6. Go to the Maps rollout and change the Reflection amount to 6. This will reduce the amount of reflection.

7. Go to the Blinn Basic Parameters rollout and change the Opacity value to 0.

8. Go to the SuperSampling rollout and uncheck Use Global Settings. Check Enable Local SuperSampler and keep it as Max 2.5 Star.

9. In the Specular Highlights group, change Specular Level to 98 and Glossiness to 90.

10. Apply the material to the Wine Glass object in the scene and render (Figure 11.63). Save the scene if you wish to keep it.

Figure 11.63

**Use Raytrace map on the Refraction parameter to create a refraction in the wine glass.**

You can control the IOR through the material's parameters in the Extended Parameters rollout, in the Advanced Transparency section, shown in Figure 11.64. Set the IOR to different numbers to see how the render compares to the Raytrace material renders.

The render will take quite some time to finish. The raytracing reflections and refractions slow down the render quite a bit. You can leave out the reflections if you'd like, but that will reduce the believability of the wine glass. You can also map a reflection as you did with the pool ball in Chapter 7; however, having true reflections will make the wine glass look much more realistic. When you raytrace both the reflection and the refraction, using the Raytrace material seems to be the better way to go.

Figure 11.64

**The Advanced Transparency section in the Extended Parameters rollout**

### REFRACTIONS

Refraction is the bending of light that creates a distortion of an image seen through a transparent or translucent object, such as glass. How light passes through from one medium, such as air, and into another medium, such as glass, determines how much light is bent and therefore how much refraction is seen. This phenomenon is simulated in a material using the Index of Refraction parameter (IOR). When there is no refraction, the IOR is set to 1; that is, there is no difference in the medium into and out of which the light is traveling. With an IOR higher than 1, the background distorts inside the object, such as when viewing a table through a crystal ball. With an IOR lower than 1, the refraction occurs at the edge of the transparent object, such as an air bubble in water.

The typical IOR value for glass is about 1.5. Because IOR relates to an object's density, you may need to adjust the IOR to get the best possible result for different types of glass, for instance. The denser the object, the higher the IOR needs to be set. Of course, refractions require that an object be semitransparent so that you can see through it to the object(s) behind it that are being refracted.

## Bringing It All Together: Rendering the Rocket

Now that you have some experience with the rendering workflow in 3ds Max, let's take a quick look at rendering a short 45-frame sequence of the rocket. You will essentially take the rocket scene laid out in the previous chapter (with the atmospheric fog light through the window we set up). You'll need to tweak a few of the scene settings, such as setting the rocket's and environment's materials to have raytraced reflections for maximum impact. You'll also animate a camera move so you can render out a sequence you can pin to your refrigerator door. Let's go!

## Creating the Camera Move

We'll begin by animating the camera.

1. Set your project to the Red Rocket project from the web page. Start by opening ROCKET_RAYTRACE_START.max.

   This file is the same one we used at the end of Chapter 10, "3ds Max Lighting," but all the Reflection maps have been taken out because we will be raytracing almost everything (Figure 11.65).

Figure 11.65

**The rocket in its room, ready to go**

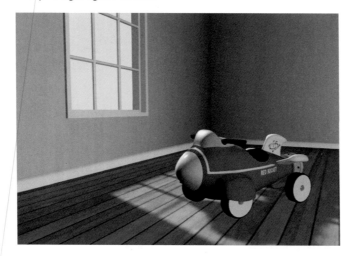

2. To begin animating, click the Auto Key button while at frame 0 (⬛Auto Key) to activate it. Go to the timeline at the bottom of the interface and move the Time Slider to 45. Now when changes are made, key frames will be created for any selected objects.

3. Select the Camera viewport because we are going to create a simple camera animation. As you saw in Chapter 3, when the Camera viewport is selected, the viewport navigation tools change, as shown in Figure 11.66. These Navigation tools make animating the camera easier.

Figure 11.66

**Camera viewport navigation tools**

4. Select the Dolly Camera tool (⬛) to move the camera closer to the rocket. Click and drag the Dolly Camera tool in the Camera viewport until you see only the front of the rocket, as shown in Figure 11.67.

5. Select the Truck Camera tool (⬛)—this icon may be hidden in the flyout under a pair of footstep icons), which allows you to pan the camera. Click and drag up and to the left in the Camera viewport to center the rocket in the viewport to match the framing you see in Figure 11.68.

6. Back to the Camera Navigation tools, select the Orbit Camera tool (⬛). Center the tool in the middle of the viewport, and click and drag to the left until you get a better view of the side of the rocket, as shown in Figure 11.69.

Figure 11.67
Dolly the camera closer to the rocket.

Figure 11.68
Truck the camera to match this framing.

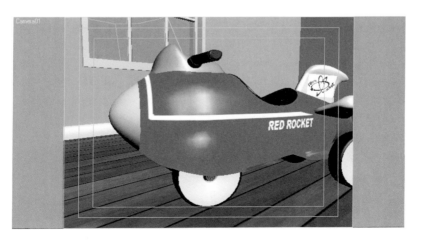

Figure 11.69
Orbit to the side of the rocket.

Figure 11.70

**The final framing for your rocket at frame 45**

Figure 11.71

**Use the animation controls to play the animation.**

7. Use the Truck Camera tool again to move the camera more to the left and to center the rocket in the viewport. Figure 11.70 should be the final position of the rocket in the camera view. Your camera move will end at this position at frame 45 of the animation.

8. Go to the animation controls shown in Figure 11.71, and play the animation you created. Make any adjustments you would like to personalize the camera move. Turn off the Auto Key button and save your file. Remember to version up your file so you don't overwrite your current work.

## Adding Raytraced Reflections

In Chapter 7, we used reflection bitmaps to fake the reflections on the rocket by using a bitmap to create the illusion of reflection. This technique usually looks very good, but there are circumstances where you need the reflections to look more accurate within the scene. This is when you use Raytrace map instead of a bitmap image. The Raytrace map calculates reflections as they work in the real world, reflecting the object's environment. Of course, in order for raytraced reflections to work, your object needs to be in an environment, much like the rocket's simple room. There has to be something around the object to reflect. To demonstrate this, we are going to add Raytrace to the rocket and the room.

### The Rocket

To add raytraced reflections to the rocket, begin here:

1. Open the Compact Material Editor, and you will see all the materials that were created earlier for the rocket.

2. In the Compact Material Editor, select the first sample sphere at the top left; this is the texture for the left side of the rocket body.

This is the only side of the rocket that will be visible in our renders, so that is the only side we will change.

3. Go to the Maps rollout, and you will see that the bitmap reflection from Chapter 7 has already been removed. If you are continuing with your own scene file, simply remove the current bitmap before continuing. To do so, just drag None from another map slot onto the Reflection channel.

4. Change the Amount value for Reflection to 20, and click None to add a map. In the Material/Map Browser, choose Raytrace.

5. Render a frame, and you should see some reflections of the room. If you want the rocket to have a higher amount of reflection, you only have to go back to the Maps rollout and make the Reflection value higher than 20.

6. Go through the materials in the Material Editor for the rocket's remaining parts to add Raytrace to their reflections as well. For those materials in the ROCKET_RAYTRACE_START .max scene, you will notice that the reflection bitmaps have already been removed from the following parts of the body to make them ready for the Raytrace map:

   - Both sides of the rocket's body (although you only see one side of the body in these renders, you may opt to put Raytrace on both.)
   - The nose
   - The fins
   - The hubcaps (white part of the wheels)
   - The tires (black part of the wheels)
   - The seat

7. Go through the Material Editor and add Raytrace to those materials. If you are continuing with your own scene, replace the reflection bitmap on the list of materials with the Raytrace map.

We aren't adding Raytrace to everything on the rocket, because Raytrace reflections take a lot more time to render. Don't bother adding them to parts of the scene that won't make a difference. Figure 11.72 shows a render of the rocket with the Raytrace map applied to the aforementioned materials.

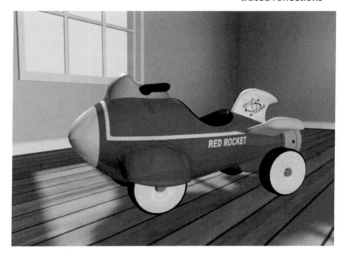

Figure 11.72

**The rocket with ray-traced reflections**

## The Room

In the room, the floors and the glass on the window should also have raytraced reflections, since reflections would look very good raytraced on these objects, especially with the camera move. Let's start with the hardwood floor.

The floors have one issue with which we have to deal. The grooves between the wood panels should not have reflections; only the panels should reflect. We need to apply a mask to the reflections to block the Raytrace from the grooves in the floor. The floor already has a bump map to mark out the grooves, so that is what we will use as the mask as well.

> If the textures we are talking about do not display in the viewports, simply select the material in the Material Editor and click on the Show Standard Map in Viewport icon in the Material Editor. If the bitmap files' paths are not connected when you open the scene file, 3ds Max will open an error dialog box, allowing you to browse for the missing image(s). This can occur when sharing projects and scenes between computers, as is a common occurrence. In this case, simply navigate to that project's SceneAssets/Images folder to find the disconnected bitmap image(s).

1. Go to the Compact Material Editor and select the sample Sphere material for the floor (the material is called FLOORS).

2. Go to the Maps rollout (Figure 11.73), change the Reflection Amount to 50, and click on None to add a map. Instead of selecting Raytrace, select Mask.

Figure 11.73

**Mask map parameters for the floor's reflections.**

3. Click on the None button next to Map, and select Bitmap from the Material/Map Browser. Navigate to the SceneAssets\Images folder of the Red Rocket project and choose WoodFloorREF.tif.

4. When the bitmap is applied, you will be in the Bitmap Parameters rollout. Go to the Coordinates rollout and change from Environ to Texture. Whenever you apply a bitmap to reflections by default, 3ds Max changes the bitmap to Environ because it is trying to behave like a real reflection. We need the mask bitmap to behave like a normal bitmap and look to the UVW Map modifier applied to the floor for its coordinates (Figure 11.74).

Figure 11.74

**Change the bitmap back to Texture instead of Environ.**

5. Now click the Go to Parent button in the Material Editor toolbar to get back to the Mask Parameters rollout. Select the None bar next to Mask and then click Raytrace from the Material/Map Browser.

6. Render the frame, and you'll notice the reflections are pretty high. But you can also see how the grooves have no reflection, so the mask works! For a better reflection, turn the Reflection Amount setting in the Maps rollout down to 10 for the floor. Click the Go to Parent button then open the Maps rollout. Figure 11.75 shows a render of the rocket.

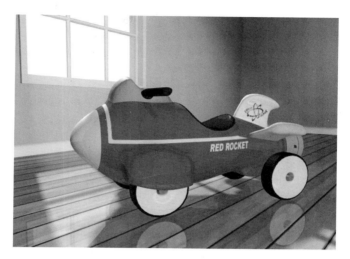

**Figure 11.75**

The reflections on the floor look great!

## Turning On the Environment Effects

Any Raytrace maps added to your scene can make the render time very long. If you are just trying to check an animation, it is wise to deactivate Raytrace while you do your test renders. To do so, open the Render Setup dialog box (press F10 or click on its icon in the Main toolbar) and click on the Raytracer tab, then go to the Global Raytracer Engine Options group, as shown in Figure 11.76. Just remember to turn it back on when your test renders are finished.

**Figure 11.76**

The Raytracer Global Parameters rollout

To round out the scene, we need atmosphere: Volume light was already added to the key light in the previous chapter, so we just need to turn it on. The Render Setup dialog box has a Deactivate button for atmospherics, so you can easily turn them on and off as you test render. To re-enable atmospherics in the render, go to the Common tab of the Render Setup dialog box and, under the Options section, check the Atmospherics box as shown in Figure 11.77.

Render the frame (Figure 11.78).

**Figure 11.77**

Re-check Atmospherics in the Render Setup dialog box → Common tab → Options section.

Figure 11.78

**The rocket is rendered with the volume light shining through the window.**

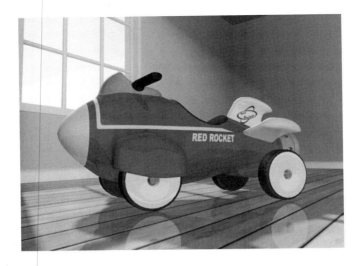

## Outputting the Render

This scene has an animated camera, so doing a simple render just won't do. We need to render out the entire 45 frames of the camera move. As you saw with the Bouncing Ball render earlier in the chapter, rendering out a sequence of images is done through the Common tab of the Render Setup dialog box.

In the Time Output section, click to select Active Time Segment: 0 to 45, as shown in Figure 11.79. The scene file you started with from the Red Rocket project will have its time segment set properly to 1 to 45. If you are working from your own scene file, however, you can either set the Active Time Segment in your scene to 1 to 45, or you can set the Range in the Render Setup dialog box manually to render from frame 1 to frame 45.

Figure 11.79

**Output Size sets the resolution of the render.**

The resolution of the render is set in Output Size. The default resolution is 640 × 480.

On a good computer, this render takes about 1 minute 20 seconds per frame with environments turned on; that means the whole 45-frame sequence will take just over one hour to render. If you want to render faster and you don't mind the render being smaller, you can render out at a smaller resolution. Half the default size is 320 × 240 and will cost you one-fourth of the higher resolution's time (15 to 20 minutes or so) to render.

Figure 11.80

**The Output Size section has preset buttons to choose the resolution, or you can input the size in the Width and Height type ins.**

To change to the lower resolution, in the Output Size section, click on the preset button 320 × 240, as shown in Figure 11.80. Now it should take just about 20 seconds per frame to render.

Go to the Render Output section of the Render Setup dialog box and click Files to open the Render Output File dialog box shown in Figure 11.81. Typically, animations are rendered out in a sequence of images, but for simplicity's sake, we will render out to a QuickTime movie as we did with the bouncing ball earlier in this chapter.

In the Render Output File dialog box (Figure 11.81), select where you want to store the rendered file, and pick a name for the QuickTime movie (`Rocket_Raytrace.mov`, for example). Then, in the Save as Type drop-down menu, choose MOV QuickTime File (.mov) and click Save. The Compression Settings dialog box will appear, as shown in Figure 11.82. Again, it is generally preferable to render to a sequence of images rather than a movie file; however, in this case a QuickTime movie file will be best.

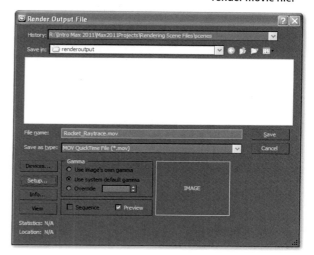

**Figure 11.81**

**Name your output render movie file.**

In the Compression Settings dialog box, select Photo–JPEG for the compression type, set Frames per Second to 30, and set Quality to Best, just as you did with the Bouncing Ball exercise. You can set the Quality slider to a lower value for a smaller QuickTime file. But remember, this Quality setting applies only to the compression of the QuickTime file and not to the render itself. Click OK to return to the Render Output File dialog box, and click Save to return to the Render Setup dialog box.

Save your scene file, and you are ready to render! Just click Render in the Render Setup dialog box, and go outside to play catch with your kids or hassle your spouse or sibling into a needless argument for a little while. In about 20 minutes (or one hour if you chose to render at 640 × 480), run back inside and play the QuickTime file saved in the location you chose earlier. Then take a huge magnet and stick your monitor to your fridge door. Voilà! You are now ready to enter the world of rendering with mental ray.

**Figure 11.82**

**The Compression Settings dialog box**

# mental ray Renderer

mental ray is a popular general purpose renderer that has fantastic capabilities. One of mental ray's strengths is its ability to generate physically accurate lighting simulations based on *indirect lighting* principles. Indirect lighting is when light bounces from one object in a scene onto another object and casts light on it. In addition, incandescence or self-illumination from one object can light other objects in the scene. A direct light such as from an Omni light is not necessarily required.

mental ray's reflections and refractions take on very real qualities when set up and lighted well. To enable mental ray, you must first select mental ray as the production renderer through the Render Setup dialog box.

## Enabling the mental ray Renderer

You first need to enable mental ray to take advantage of its rendering features. To do so, in the menu choose Rendering → Render Setup to open the Render Setup dialog box. On the Common tab, scroll down to the Assign Renderer rollout, then click the ellipses (⬚)

Figure 11.83

The Assign Renderer rollout

button for the Production entry shown in Figure 11.83. This will open the Choose Renderer dialog box (Figure 11.84).

In the Choose Renderer dialog box, highlight mental ray Renderer and then click OK. Once the mental ray renderer is assigned, you can make mental ray the default renderer by clicking the Save as Defaults button on the Assign Renderer rollout should you wish to continue using mental ray as your default renderer. Now, the Render Setup dialog box appears with the mental ray controls in tabs.

Figure 11.84

Choose mental ray Renderer from the Choose Renderer dialog box.

## mental ray Sampling Quality

Once mental ray Renderer is enabled, click the Renderer tab in the Render Setup dialog box, shown in Figure 11.85. We will explore rendering with mental ray in a later section. The following is a brief explanation of the render settings most useful for you in your work.

Under the Sampling Quality rollout are the settings to control the overall image quality of your renders. The Minimum and Maximum Samples per Pixel values govern the amount of antialiasing of your render. You should be careful not to set the samples too high to avoid needlessly long render times. Sampling is the number of times mental ray will read and compare the color values of adjacent pixels to smooth the resulting render to avoid jagged lines.

These Minimum and Maximum Samples per Pixel values set the number of times mental ray will sample a pixel to determine how best to antialias the result. The higher the number, the finer the detail and the smoother the appearance of your rendered lines will be. These settings are exponential, so a large increase will yield a much greater quality but a much longer render time. What determines the exact sample level within the minimum and maximum range set by these attributes is dependent on the Spatial Contrast values for Red, Green, Blue, and Alpha.

Spatial Contrast values determine when mental ray turns up the number of samples in a particular region of the frame. If the contrast level from one pixel to its neighbor is below the threshold value, mental ray will turn up the number of samples for that pixel to render a higher-quality result for that specific area of the frame. Therefore, the lower the values set for the Spatial Contrast, the higher the sample rate will be (within the Minimum and Maximum levels set).

Rather than setting high sample rates with just the Minimum and Maximum Samples per Pixel, lower the Spatial Contrast values equally for RGBA to force mental ray to use values closer to the Maximum Samples per Pixel value only where it needs to do so.

For example, the image shown in Figure 11.86 was rendered in mental ray with a Minimum Samples per Pixel value of 1/16 and a Maximum Samples per Pixel value of 1 using a Spatial Contrast setting of 0.1 for all four RGBA values. You can see the jagged lines on the wagon's white decal and edges quite clearly. When the Minimum Samples per Pixel value is changed to 4, the Maximum Samples per Pixel value is changed to 16, and the Spatial Contrast value is changed to 0.04 for RGBA, the render becomes much cleaner, with an acceptable increase in render times (Figure 11.87).

You can get essentially the same quality of render as shown in Figure 11.87 by setting Minimum Samples per Pixel to 16 and Maximum Samples per Pixel to 256 with a Spatial Contrast of 0.07 for RGBA, but with a much longer render time. Achieving quality without very long render times relies first on the Spatial Contrast values (lower is better), and then on the Samples per Pixel (higher is better).

Figure 11.85

**The Renderer tab shows mental ray's common settings.**

Figure 11.86

**A jagged render**

Figure 11.87

**A clean render**

## mental ray Motion Blur

Enabling motion blur in mental ray is quite simple. The Camera Effects rollout, shown in Figure 11.88, is in the Renderer tab of the Render Setup dialog box.

To enable motion blur, simply check the Enable check box in the Motion Blur group. The Shutter Duration value governs how much blur is rendered (the higher the value, the more blur is rendered), and the Motion Segments and Time Samples values set the quality of the blur (higher values give better quality blur, with higher render times).

For practice, try re-rendering the Bouncing Ball exercise from earlier in this chapter with mental ray and motion blur to compare the results from the original scanline rendering.

Figure 11.88
**The Camera Effects rollout**

# Final Gather with mental ray

A popular feature in mental ray is indirect illumination—the simulation of bounced light (explained in the next section). In the tabs at the top of the Render Setup dialog box, click the Indirect Illumination tab. There are three rollouts:

- Final Gather
- Caustic and Global Illumination (GI)
- Reuse (FG and GI Disk Caching)

## Final Gather

Final Gather is a method of mental ray rendering for estimating Global Illumination, or GI. In short, GI is a way of calculating indirect lighting. This effect allows for more accurate and physically real lighting simulations, where light can bounce in the scene and cast secondary diffused light on objects. This way, objects do not need to be in the direct path of a light (such as a spotlight) to be lighted in the scene. In short, mental ray accomplishes this by casting points throughout a scene. These light points are allowed to bounce from object to object, contributing light as they go, effectively simulating how real light photons work in the physical world.

This type of rendering can introduce artifacts or noise in the render. Finding the right settings to balance a clean render and acceptable render times is an art form all its own and is rather difficult to master. Only time and experience with Final Gather rendering will lead to mastery.

You will see how to use Final Gather later in the chapter. Figure 11.89 shows the Final Gather rollout. Some of Final Gather's options, including how to deal with quality and noise, are explained here.

## Basic Group

These are the most important parameters in the Basic section of the Final Gather rollout; they set the accuracy and precision of the light bounces, therefore controlling noise:

- FG Precision Presets slider—Sets the accuracy level of the Final Gather simulation by adjusting settings for the renderer such as Point Density, Rays per Point, and Interpolation. These settings alter how mental ray calculates the bounced light. The presets are Draft, Low, Medium, High, Very High, and Custom. (For Custom you enter your own values.) Use this slider first in setting how good your render's lighting looks. Set it low for tests and increase the precision for final renders. In Figure 11.90, three spheres are rendered with a Draft setting for Final Gather, while Figure 11.91 is set to High. Notice Figure 11.91 is a cleaner render, and also shows more of the background and the spheres than does the Draft quality in Figure 11.90. However, going too high on the Precision slider may incur substantial render times. This slider will adjust the settings for several of the values covered in the following list.

**Figure 11.90**

A Draft setting produces a test render of the spheres. This image is also included in the color section of this book

**Figure 11.91**

A High setting produces a much nicer render of the spheres. This image is also included in the color section of this book

- Multiplier/color swatch—This controls the intensity and the color of the indirect light being bounced. A value of 1.0 is the most physically accurate setting and is the default. Reducing this setting will lower the influence of the bounced light in your scene.

- Initial FG Point Density—This multiplier is one of the settings adjusted by the FG Precision Presets slider. Increasing this value will increase the quantity and density of FG "points" that are cast into the scene. For FG to work, the renderer casts these points into the scene. These points of light bounce within the scene and cast light on the objects they encounter. The higher the density of these points, the more accurate the bounced light appears. However, the higher the point density, the longer the render times. You may manually adjust this setting beyond the precision presets set by the slider.

- Rays per FG Point—This value is controlled by the Precision slider, but may also be manually set. The higher the number of rays used to compute the indirect illumination in a scene, the less noise and the more accuracy you gain, but at the cost of longer render times.

- Interpolate Over Num. FG Points—Interpolation is controlled by the FG Precision Presets slider as well as manual input. This value is useful for getting rid of noise in your renders for smoother results. Increasing the interpolation will increase render times, but not as much as increasing the Point Density or Rays values.

- Diffuse Bounces—The number of bounces governs how many times a point of light can bounce and affect objects in a scene before stopping calculation. If you set the bounces higher, the light simulation will be more accurate, but the render times will be costly. A Diffuse Bounces setting of 1 or 2 is adequate for many applications. Figure 11.92 shows the same render of the spheres as Figure 11.90, but with a Diffuse Bounces value of 5. This render is brighter and also shows color spill from the purple spheres onto the gray floor, though the grayscale image in this book will not demonstrate that adequately. You will find these two images compared in the color section of this book.

Figure 11.92

**More diffuse bounces mean more bounced light.**

- Weight—This value governs how much influence the diffuse bounces have over the lighting solution in the scene. A value of 0 uses no contribution from bounced diffuse light in the scene. A value of 1 uses the full contribution of bounced diffused light, and is the default. This will control the amount of color spilled from one surface to an adjacent surface, such as the purple spill from the spheres in Figure 11.92 and in the color section.

## Advanced Group

The Advanced group of settings gives you access to advanced ways of controlling the quality of your Final Gather renders. Some are described below in brief. You should experiment with different settings as you gain more experience with Final Gathering to see what settings work best for your scenes.

- Noise Filtering (Speckle Reduction)—The options are None, Standard, High, Very High, and Extremely High, and the default is Standard. This value essentially averages the brightness of the light rays in the scene to give you smoother Final Gather results. The higher the filtering, the dimmer your Final Gathering simulation result will be, and the longer your render times. However, the noise in your lighting will diminish.

- Draft Mode (No Precalculations)—This setting allows you turn off a good number of calculations that mental ray completes prior to rendering the scene. This will result in a faster render for preview and draft purposes.

- Max. Reflections—This value controls how many times a light ray can be reflected in the scene. A value of 0 turns off reflections entirely. The higher this value, the more times you can see a reflection. For example, a value of 2 allows you to see a reflection of a reflection.

- Max. Refractions—Similar to Max. Reflections, this value sets the number of times a light ray can be refracted through a surface. A value of 0 turns off all refraction.

## The mental ray Rendered Frame Window

When you render a frame in 3ds Max, the Rendered Frame Window opens, displaying the image you just rendered. When you render with mental ray, an additional control panel is displayed under the Rendered Frame Window, as shown in Figure 11.93.

This control panel gives you access to many of the most useful settings in the Render Settings dialog box so you can adjust render settings easily and quickly.

**Figure 11.93**

**The Rendered Frame Window now shows several mental ray controls.**

## Caustics and Global Illumination (GI) Rollout

Within the Caustics and Global Illumination (GI) rollout, you will find controls for various advanced mental ray lighting techniques. Caustics is a visual effect seen when light is reflected off a shiny or reflective surface and onto an adjacent surface in interesting light patterns. Caustics may occur also through a refractive surface, such as a glass of water, so that it indirectly lights an adjacent surface with focused light patterns.

The Global Illumination controls let you control the usage of photons by mental ray for generating Global Illumination. GI is another method of simulating bounced light that offers more options than Final Gather in the way the light is bounced. GI may also be used with Final Gather for a more physically real effect, but at the cost of high render times.

Because this book is an introductory book, we will not be covering caustics or GI.

## mental ray Materials

For the most part, mental ray treats regular 3ds Max maps and materials the same way the Default Scanline Renderer does. However, a set of mental ray specific materials exists

Figure 11.94

**Main material parameters for the Arch & Design material.**

to take further advantage of mental ray's power. In this book, we will examine the Arch & Design material used in mental ray.

The mental ray Arch & Design material works great for most hard surfaces, such as metal, wood, glass, and ceramic. It is especially useful for surfaces that are glossy and reflective, such as metal and ceramic.

To showcase these materials, we will re-texture a few parts of the red rocket from Chapter 7. Figure 11.94 shows the main material parameters for the Arch & Design materials. We will look at the features that we need for the rocket next.

1. Set your project to the mental ray project that you downloaded from the web page. Open the ROCKET_MENTAL RAY_START.max file found in the Scenes folder of the Mental Ray Scene Files project on the companion web page. This file has mental ray already assigned as the renderer. The scene has the room, the rocket's body, and the thruster already textured. There are no lights in the scene but because Final Gather is enabled, it utilizes the default lights to generate a lighted scene, as shown rendered in Figure 11.95.

2. Open the Slate Material Editor; at the top of the view area you will see the two tabs for the room and rocket. Right-click in the blank area next to the tabs, as shown in Figure 11.96, and create a new view area. Name it **More Rocket**.

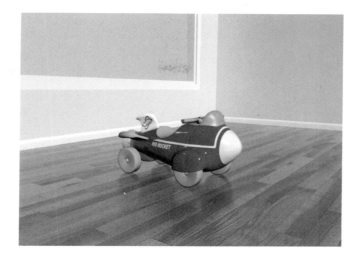

Figure 11.95

**The rocket file rendered**

3. Drag an Arch & Design material to the new View area from the mental ray material section of the Material/Map Browser.

Figure 11.96

**Create a new view area.**

4. Double-click on the thumbnail picture of the sample sphere to enlarge in the view area. This will also display the Arch & Design material in the Material Parameter Editor.

5. Name the material **Rocket Seat** and in the main material parameters → Diffuse group, click on the color swatch. Change the color to R: 0.0, G: 0.0, B: 0.0 for a pure black color.

6. Leave the Reflection values at their default. This will give the seat a slight reflection.

By default, Arch & Design materials have reflection enabled. The area below the Diffuse group in the parameter section of the Slate is the Reflection group of parameters. Reflections for this material are calculated using the Reflectivity and Glossiness values. The higher the Reflectivity value is, the clearer the reflections are. The Glossiness value controls the blurriness of the reflections from sharp (a value of 1) to completely blurred (a value of 0). When you blur your reflections, the blurrier they are, the noisier they will be in the render. You can use the Glossy Samples value to increase the quality of the blurred reflections once you set Glossiness to anything less than 1.

7. Drag a wire from the material's output socket to the seat of the rocket in the viewport (Figure 11.97).

Render the Camera viewport to see the new material on the seat. Now we will move on to the fins. There are three fins: two with a white shiny material and one with the decal already applied from Chapter 7. The rocket body and fin are already textured in this scene. To get acquainted with the Arch & Design material, we will texture just a few parts of the rocket.

Figure 11.97

**Seat material being applied to the object in the scene**

8. Drag another Arch & Design material into the new view area and name it **Fin**.

9. In the Diffuse group of parameters, click on the color swatch and change the color to white, as shown in Figure 11.98, using these values: R: 1.0, G: 1.0, B: 1.0.

10. Drag a wire from the material output socket to the objects fin04 and fin05 in the viewports. Those are the two white fins on the sides of the rocket.

Figure 11.98

**Click the Color swatch and make it white.**

The wheels will be done in the same way as in Chapter 7: by using the Multi/Sub-Object material and dragging the individually created materials to the selected polygons. The difference now is we will use the Arch & Design material instead. The wheel is divided into three materials: shiny red for the bolt, shiny white for the face, and bumpy black for the tire.

If you remember, when we first textured the wheels, we saved sub-object selections in Chapter 7. That will be useful here, too.

1. Select one of the wheels, and go into Polygon mode. Go up to the Main toolbar and click on the Named Selection Sets drop-down menu and choose Wheel_Bolt. This selects the polygons of the bolt (Figure 11.99).

Figure 11.99

**The Named Selection Sets drop-down menu**

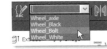

2. In the Slate Material Editor we'll next create a shiny red material. Drag an Arch & Design material to the view area. Change the Diffuse color to R: 0.8, G: 0.0, B: 0.0 and drag it onto the selected polygons of the bolt.

3. Click on the Named Selection Sets drop-down menu and choose Wheel_White. The white parts of the wheel will be selected. In the Slate, instead of creating a new material, we'll use the Fin material you've already created. Drag a wire from the existing white fin material's output socket to the selected polygons.

4. Repeat step 3, but select Wheel_Black from the Named Selection Sets drop-down. In the Slate, go to the tabs at the top of the view area and click the Rocket tab. This tab has a few materials already set up for you. Choose the Arch & Design material node called Handle_ Bar and drag it onto the selected polygons of the wheel.

5. Repeat the same process (steps 1–4) on the remaining three wheels.

6. Render the camera01 viewport. If it isn't loaded into a viewport, just select a viewport and hit the C key; this will bring up the Select Camera list. Choose Camera02. The render is shown in Figure 11.100.

Figure 11.100

**The rocket textured**

## 3ds Max Photometric Lights in mental ray Renderings

Now that you have had a basic look at the mental ray materials, let's add some lights to the scene. The idea is to set up a light that makes it appear as though the sunlight is coming through the window, lighting the rocket and the room. In Chapter 10 we looked at lighting using Standard lights, but for this section we will use more advanced lighting tools like Photometric lights and the Daylight system.

Many of the parameters for Photometric lights are the same as or very similar to the Standard lights we looked at in Chapter 10. Here, we will show you the parameters that are specific to Photometric lights. Photometric lights simulate real lighting by using physically based energy values and color temperatures.

1. Either continue with the file you are working with or open the ROCKET_MENTAL RAY_ LIGHT.max file found in the Scenes folder of the Mental Ray Scene Files project from the companion web page.

2. In the Main Menu bar, choose Create → Lights → Photometric Lights → Target Light to create a Photometric Target Light.

3.  When you click for the Photometric Target Light, you will get a pop-up recommending that you use the mr (mental ray) Photographic Exposure Control, as shown in Figure 11.101. Choose Yes.

4.  In the Top viewport, drag to create the light from below the rocket and up (Figure 11.102).

Figure 11.101

**mr Photographic Exposure Control warning**

Figure 11.102

**Create the light starting in the Top viewport.**

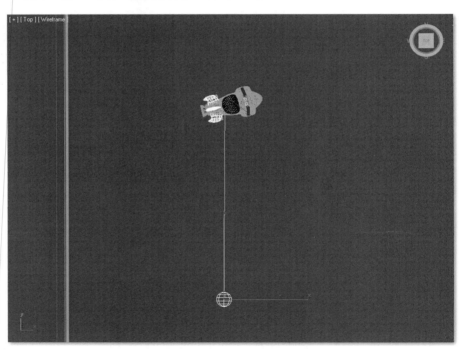

5.  Switch to the Right viewport and move the light up as shown in Figure 11.103.

6.  With the light still selected, go to the Modify panel. The first rollout under the Modifier Stack is Templates. This rollout gives you access to several light type presets to save you time in creating a light. Feel free to play around with the different presets and render the rocket frame a few times to see the differences before continuing with the exercise and the next step.

Figure 11.103

**Move the light up in the Right viewport.**

7. In the Select a Template drop-down menu, select Recessed 75W Lamp (Web). The "web" is special to Photometric lights and requires some explanation. A photometric light with a "web" distribution essentially defines the light's behavior and the light it casts. Lighting manufacturers provide web files that model the kinds of lights they make, so using these distribution patterns as templates gives you a lot of options in simulating real world lights, like this 75-watt recessed lamp. Figure 11.104 shows the distribution pattern for this light as seen in the Command panel.

Figure 11.104

**Distribution (Photometric Web) rollout**

8. We need to take care of some basic stuff now, so with the light still selected, go to the General Parameters rollout and check the Targeted box. We originally created a targeted light but when we used the template it took away the target. Having a target on a light makes it easier to edit the light's position. Checking this box turns the target back on for the light.

9. Check the Shadows On box to turn it on. In the drop-down menu, choose Ray Traced Shadows.

Figure 11.105

**Exposure Control and mr Photographic Exposure Control rollout in the Environment and Effects dialog**

10. In the Main Menu bar, choose Rendering → Environment. Under the Exposure Control rollout, click the Render Preview button (Figure 11.105). You may notice the preview will show as either very bright or very dark at first. If so, the preview function will work perfectly once you render a frame for the first time.

11. Under the mr Photographic Exposure Control rollout, select Exposure Value (EV), if it isn't already selected. Set some different values for the EV and see what happens in the Render Preview dialog box. The higher the EV number, the darker the scene will be. Set the EV value to 7 or so and render (see Figure 11.106). You can continue to work with the EV value to experiment with the luminance level. Don't go too bright in the exposure controls, it might make the scene too washed out. Be sure to set the EV back to 7 and close the Environment and Effects dialog box.

### EXPOSURE CONTROLS

Exposure controls adjust output levels and the range of colors of a rendering. These controls are similar to real-world film exposure settings on a physical camera. The mr Photographic Exposure Control rollout gives you the ability to change your rendered output easily without the need for long re-renders.

Figure 11.106

**The rocket so far**

## Photometric Light Parameters

Now let's look in the Command panel at the Photometric light's Intensity/Color/Attenuation rollout for our 75W light (Figure 11.107).

Figure 11.107

**Photometric light's Intensity/Color/Attenuation rollout in the Command panel**

The Color group of parameters controls the color temperature of the light, which you can set either with a color or in Kelvin degree value just like with real-world photographic lights. In the drop-down menu, there are different color/temp settings. The default is D65 Illuminant (Reference White).

The Intensity group of parameters controls the strength or brightness of the lights measured in lm, cd, or lx at:

- lm (lumen)—This value is the overall output power of the light. A 100-watt general purpose light bulb measures about 1750 lm.

- cd (candela)—This value shows the maximum luminous intensity of the light. A 100-watt general purpose light bulb measures about 139 cd.

- lx at (lux)—This value shows the amount of luminance created by the light shining on a surface at a certain distance.

The Dimming group of parameters is another place to control the intensity of the light. When the Resulting Intensity box is checked, the value specifies a multiplier that dims the existing intensity of the light and takes over control of the intensity. Picking up from the last step in the previous exercise, let's start to experiment with these values in the following steps:

1. With the 75W light still selected, go to the Command panel and, in the Color group under the Intensity/Color/Attenuation rollout, click the button next to Kelvin and change the value to 4000. This will give the light a bit more warmth by adding in more yellow/red.

2. In the Dimming group, uncheck the box next to the 100% spinner under Resulting Intensity to enable the Intensity parameter.

3. In the Intensity group, select cd and set the cd amount to 2500. This will brighten things up a bit.

4. Render (see Figure 11.108).

Figure 11.108

**The rocket render with color and intensity changes**

The scene still looks a bit dark and the shadows are very dark; they look like black holes. We will use Final Gather to brighten up the overall render. So far we have just used Final Gather's default settings. The one thing we need is for the rays that are generated by the light to bounce. The more bounces the light makes, the more luminance in the room. But more bounces slow down the render. It is good to balance bounces with exposure control and the intensity of the light for the best and most efficient result.

5. In the Rendered Frame Window, when you are already rendering with mental ray, the mini Final Gather panel is available for quick changes. Most of these controls also have a home in the Render Setup dialog box, and changing the value in one dialog box updates the corresponding value in the other dialog box. In the mini panel below the Rendered Frame Window (Figure 11.109), change FG Bounces to 7. Render and compare the resulting render shown in Figure 11.110 to Figure 11.108.

Figure 11.109

**This mini panel gives you access to Final Gather controls to adjust your render easily.**

Figure 11.110

**The final rocket**

## 3ds Max Daylight System in mental ray Renderings

The Sunlight and Daylight systems simulate sunlight by following the geographically correct angle and movement of the sun over the earth. You can choose location, date, time, and compass orientation to set the orientation of the sun and its lighting conditions. You can also animate the date and time to achieve very cool time lapse looks and shadow studies. In essence, this type of light works really well with mental ray and Final Gather. We will use it in the most basic way, using all of its defaults.

1.  Open the ROCKET_MENTAL RAY_FINAL.max file found in the Scenes folder of the Mental Ray Scene Files project on the companion web page. This is the file we ended with after applying the Arch & Design textures earlier in the chapter.

Figure 11.111

**Daylight system**

2.  In the Main Menu bar, choose Create → Lights → Daylight System, as shown in Figure 11.111.

    A Daylight System Creation warning will come up, asking you if you want to change the exposure controls to suit the Daylight system. Say Yes to this. See Figure 11.112.

3.  In a Top viewport, click and drag at the center of the scene. This will create a compass that is attached to the Daylight system. Make it about the size shown Figure 11.113.

Figure 11.112

**Daylight System Creation warning**

Figure 11.113

**Create the Daylight-system compass at about the size shown here.**

4. When you release the mouse button, move the mouse so the light is placed outside the walls of the room, as shown in Figure 11.114. The Daylight system is supposed to simulate the sun and sky, so it needs to be outside the room.

5. With the light still selected, go to the Modify panel and in the Daylight Parameters rollout, change the drop-down menus under both the Sunlight and Skylight parameters to mr Sun and mr Sky, respectively (Figure 11.115). When you change the Skylight, a mental ray warning will appear asking if you want to place an mr Physical Sky environment map in your scene. Click Yes (Figure 11.116).

6. Also in Daylight Parameters, under Position select Manual as shown in Figure 11.117. This will allow you to use the Move tool to move the light to where you want it. The default position represents noon. The lower the light is to the horizon in your scene, the more it will simulate darker skies at sunset. We will leave the light in the default position.

7. Select the Camera viewport and render. As you can see, it is too dark. We are trying to simulate a sunny day, and beyond the direct light coming through the window, it's pretty dark.

Figure 11.114

**Light should be outside the room.**

Figure 11.115

**Change Daylight system light to mr Sun and mr Sky.**

Figure 11.116

**Add the mr Physical Sky environment map into the scene.**

Figure 11.117

**Change the light position to Manual.**

A good tool to use in this situation is mr Sky Portal. It gives you an efficient way of using a scene's existing sky lighting within interior scenes that do not require costly Final Gather or GI resulting in very long render times. A portal acts just like a mental ray area light. This light actually gets its brightness and color from the environment already in your scene. With the next step, we continue the example:

8.  In the Main Menu bar, choose Create → Lights → Photometric Lights → mr Sky Portal.

9.  In the Front viewport, drag an mr Sky Portal so it fits the window size in the wall. Then in a Top viewport, move the mr Sky Portal back so it is aligned with the opening of the window inside the room, as shown in Figure 11.118. Make sure the arrow is pointing into the room. Render the Camera viewport again. That helps but is not enough; it is still too dark (Figure 11.119). So it's time to play with exposure controls.

10. In the Main Menu bar, choose Rendering → Exposure Control. Click on Render Preview.

11. Under the mr Photographic Exposure Control rollout, change Exposure Value (EV) from 15 (default) to 12, as shown in Figure 11.120. You should see the rendered preview change to show the update. Render the Camera viewport again to see the difference. It looks good but is still a bit dark, so it's time to add Final Gather bounces.

12. In the Rendered Frame Window mini mental ray controls, change FG Bounces to 5. Render. See Figure 11.121.

**Figure 11.118**
Move the mr Sky Portal to the window in the wall in the Top viewport.

**Figure 11.119**
Rendering with the mr Sky Portal in front of the window is still too dark.

Figure 11.121
**Render with Final Gather Bounces set to 5.**

Figure 11.120
**The mr Photographic Exposure Control rollout**

That is it. If you want to play around some more we recommend moving the light for a more dramatic shadow on the floor. Moving the light can have a dramatic effect on the luminance levels too, so be prepared to edit FG Bounces and Exposure Controls also. For this last render, shown in Figure 11.122 and in the color section of this book, we moved the light and changed the Exposure Value setting to 13.

Figure 11.122
**The final render**

## 3ds Max Lighting with HDRI in mental ray Renderings

High-dynamic-range images (HDRI) are used in CG to create more realistic scenes than the more simplistic lighting models used.

An HDRI is created when several photos at varying exposures are taken of the same subject, ranging from very dark (underexposure) to highlight only the brightest parts of the scene, to very bright (overexposure) to capture the absolute darkest parts of the scene. When these images (typically five or seven images) are compiled into an HDR image, you get a fantastic range of bright to dark for that one subject or environment.

How does that help you light? mental ray can create an environment map in your scene to which you assign an image, usually an HDRI. That environment map uses the brightness of its image to cast light in your scene.

The best type of image to capture for an HDRI is sometimes called a light probe. This is a picture of an environment such as the office reflected in a chrome ball shown in Figure 11.123. You can also take a light probe using a fish-eye camera lens capable of capturing a field of view of close to 180 degrees.

Figure 11.123 shows the middle exposure of five exposures taken of the same office. Figure 11.124 shows the range of photos from underexposed (dark) to overexposed (bright) that were used to compile this sample HDRI.

In the next exercise we will use an HDRI that is from the 3ds Max default HDRI library installed with the program. See Figure 11.125.

Figure 11.123
**A light probe photo of the author's desk, taken with a chrome ball.**

Figure 11.124
**The five exposures that make up a sample HDRI of a desk**

Figure 11.125

**HDR image from the 3ds Max default library**

Figure 11.125

**HDR image from the 3ds Max default library**

Open the `Soldier_Mental Ray_Start.max` file found in the Scenes folder of the mental ray Scene Files project on the companion web page. This scene has the final textured soldier and a tank modeled by Federico Esparza, a student of Randi's, who was inspired by a tank design from the popular video game *Warhammer 40,000: Dawn of War* from THQ. There is a flat plane with some cracked dirt texture on it, and the file is set up with mental ray as the renderer. Nothing too fancy, but it'll get the job done.

Figure 11.126

**Add the HDR image in the Environment map.**

1. When the scene is open, in the Main Menu bar choose Create → Lights → Standard Lights → Skylight. Just click anywhere in your scene to create the Skylight.

2. Next, load the HDRI file into the environment. Choose Rendering → Environment. In the Common Parameters rollout in the Environment tab, click on the None button under Environment Map, as shown in Figure 11.126. This will bring up the Material/Map Browser.

Figure 11.127

**HDRI Load Settings box**

3. Choose Bitmap from the Standard Maps rollout. Navigate to 3ds Max's free library in the Maps folder that is installed when you install the 3ds Max 2011 application (typically here: C:\Program Files\Autodesk\3ds Max 2011\maps\HDRs) and select KC_outside_hi.hdr. The HDRI Load Settings dialog box shows up; hit OK (Figure 11.127).

4. The HDRI that is loaded in the environment needs to have its mapping edited. With the Environment and Effects dialog box still open, open the Slate Material Editor, and place the windows side by side. Drag the Environment Map button in the Environment tab to the view area of the Slate Material Editor. This will open an Instance (Copy) dialog box. Click Instance and then OK to load the HDRI map into the Material Editor. Double-click on the HDRI map node to load the parameters. In the Coordinates rollout, select Environ and change the Mapping drop-down menu to Spherical Environment, as shown in Figure 11.128.

Figure 11.128

**The Mapping parameter set to Spherical Environment**

5. Select the Skylight and in the parameters, under Sky Color, select Use Scene Environment. This will tell the light to refer to the HDRI loaded into the environment for the lighting (Figure 11.129).

Figure 11.129

**Skylight parameters**

6. Render the Camera viewport (see Figure 11.130), and you can see that all the chrome bits on the tank look pretty good, but overall the scene looks fairly dull. It certainly doesn't look like it is outdoors in the daytime on a dry lakebed (Figure 11.130).

We need more light—specifically, sunlight! The Skylight's job is to create the indirect illumination. Now, for the sun. With the Daylight system, the scene had both direct and indirect illumination, but the Daylight system doesn't work with HDRI, so we will need another way of creating sunlight for this scene. For the sun, we can use almost any light that can be directed. We will use the mr Area Spot. These lights work well with mental ray and have parameters very similar to any standard light's. Shadows are turned on and set to Raytraced by default.

Figure 11.130

**A dry lakebed as an example for the lighting of the soldier and tank**

7. In the Main Menu bar, select Create → Lights → Standard Lights → mr Area Spot. To create the light in the viewport, start in the Top viewport and drag from below the soldier and tank and go up, then switch to the Left viewport and move the light up and away from the scene (as shown in Figure 11.131).

Figure 11.131

**Place the mr
Area spotlight.**

Figure 11.132

**mr Area Spotlight
Parameters rollout**

8. With the light selected, go into the Spotlight Parameters rollout in the Command panel and check on Overshoot. This causes a spotlight to flood beyond its falloff area, and cast light in all directions. Set the Falloff amount to 90 (Figure 11.132).

9. In the Intensity/Color/Attenuation rollout, change the Multiplier setting to 0.5. Render the frame and compare it to Figure 11.133. BAM!

With the tank example, the HDRI environment map created an overall fill light for the scene, but also acted as a great reflection environment for the chrome accents on the tank. Adding the extra mr Area Spot light allowed you to create a sunlight for a key light that gave the scene highlights as well as defined directional shadows. HDRI environment maps are very good ways to insert complex lighting scenarios, but are often augmented with standard or photometric lights to really bring out the subject of the scene.

The kind of HDRI map you use will greatly change the effect of the lighting in the scene. Try out some of the other HDRI maps that come with the 3ds Max installation to see how they affect the scene and the reflections in the metal. All these tools and options make mental ray rendering extremely versatile and powerful. This is just the tip of the iceberg; there is much more to experiment with and gain experience on. We encourage you to download HDRIs as well as use different maps that come with the 3ds Max library to see how they change the lighting in any scene.

Figure 11.133

**The final tank and
soldier render**

# Summary

Rendering is the way you get to show your finished scene to the world, or whoever will stop and look. It enables the vector-created scene to be displayed in bitmap images or movie files on any monitor. Getting to this point in your scene takes quite a bit of work, as you can see, but once you see the results playing back on your screen, it all seems worth it. Nothing is more fulfilling than seeing your creation come to life, and that's what rendering is all about. However, don't consider the rendering process merely the last thing to do. Rendering may be the last step of the process, but you should travel the entire journey with rendering in mind, from design to models to animation to lighting. Always allow enough time to ensure that your animations render properly and at their best quality. Most beginners seriously underestimate the time needed to properly complete this step in CG production and don't allow enough time for the render. Lighting and rendering are so important, as a matter of fact, that lighting professionals (who also handle rendering) are among the most sought-after and highest-paid workers in the entertainment CG field.

In this chapter, you learned the basics of rendering with Autodesk 3ds Max 2011. You began by learning about render output and the types of files to which you can render. You rendered the Bouncing Ball exercise from Chapter 8 and enabled motion blur for heightened effect. Then you learned about cameras and rendering separate passes with Render Elements. Additionally, you learned how to render glows and how to use raytracing to render true reflections and refractions in a scene. You put all that to good use in rendering the Red Rocket project that you've worked on throughout the book to a 1.5-second QuickTime file. Then you moved on to various exercises to explore Final Gather and HDRI when rendering with mental ray.

After you have rendered many more scenes, you'll have a much better understanding of how to set up your scene from the very beginning to efficiently achieve a great result. It won't hurt to go over the examples in this chapter more than once and try to render your own scenes in different ways.

# CHAPTER 12

# Particles and Dynamics

*Animating large numbers* of similar objects can be an arduous task to say the least. With hundreds, if not thousands, of individual objects and all of their animated parameters and transforms to consider, this is a task that, one object at a time, could quickly become overwhelming. Luckily, 3ds Max has several tools for animating large numbers of objects in a scene, including instanced objects, externally referencing objects, instanced modifiers, the Crowd utility for characters, and particle systems for controlling any number of particles. *Particles* are usually small objects, often in large numbers, that can represent rain, snow, a swarm of insects, a barrage of bullets, or anything else that requires a large quantity of objects that follow a similar action or are part of a larger system of movement.

Yet another method of creating simultaneous animations for several objects is through the use of *reactor*, the physics engine contained within 3ds Max. Using reactor, you can calculate the interactions between many rigid and soft body objects, or simulate fluids or rope dynamics.

Topics in this chapter include the following:

- **Understanding particle systems**
- **Setting up a particle system**
- **Particle systems and space warps**
- **Using rigid body dynamics**
- **Using soft body dynamics**

# Understanding Particle Systems

Particle systems are a means to manage the infinite possibilities encountered when controlling thousands of seemingly random objects in a scene. The particles can follow a tight stream or emanate in all directions from the surface of an object, for example. The particles themselves can be pixel-sized elements on the screen or instanced geometry from an object in the scene. Particles can react to forces called *space warps,* such as wind and gravity, and bounce off objects called *deflectors* to give them a natural flow through a scene. Particles can even spawn new particles upon collision. There is a wide base of options when you are animating particle systems, especially when you are trying to simulate real-world effects such as smoke or rain.

All particle systems have two common yet distinct components: the emitter and the particles. The *emitter,* as the name suggests, is the object from which the particles originate. The location and, to a lesser extent, the orientation of the emitter are vital to the particles' origination point in the scene. However, emitters are nonrendering objects, making their size and color unimportant.

Particles themselves are the elements that spew from the emitter. The number of particles can range from a few (to simulate a burst from a gun) to thousands (to simulate smoke from a burning building). As you would imagine, the number of particles visible in a viewport can adversely affect the viewport refresh speed and your ability to quickly navigate within the viewports. By default, far fewer particles are shown in the viewports than actually render in the scene. This helps maintain a reasonable system performance level.

## Particle System Types

Two types of particle systems are available in 3ds Max: event-driven and non–event-driven.

### Event-Driven Particle Systems

Event-driven particle systems use a series of tests and operators grouped into components called *events.* An operator affects the appearance and action of the individual particles and can, among many other abilities, change the shape or rotation of the particles, add a material or external force, or even delete the particles on a per-particle basis. Tests check for conditions such as a particle's age, its speed, and whether it has collided with a deflector. Particles move down the list of operators and tests in an event and, if the particles pass the requirements of a test they encounter, they can leave the current event and move to the next. If they do not pass the test, the particles continue down the list in the current event. Particles that do not pass any test in an event commonly are deleted or recycled through the event until they do pass a test. Events are wired together in a flowchart style to clearly display the path, from event to event, that the particles follow.

Particle Flow is the event-driven particle system in 3ds Max, and it is a very comprehensive solution to most particle system requirements. The upper-left pane in the Particle View window in Figure 12.1 shows a partial layout of the events in a Particle Flow setup.

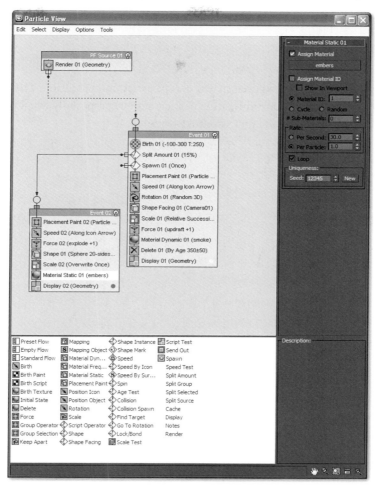

Figure 12.1

**The Particle View window and a Particle Flow emitter**

Events are green circles, operators are gray boxes, and tests appear as yellow diamonds. To the right of the Particle View window is a common example of one of the several emitter types that a Particle Flow can utilize. Using Particle Flow, you can create almost any particle-based effect, including rain, snow, mist, a flurry of arrows and spears, and objects assembling and disassembling in a blast of particles. Unfortunately, an in-depth examination of Particle Flow is beyond the scope of this book. However, we will familiarize you with the fundamentals of particles in the hopes you will be inspired to learn more in the course of your own work—which, when you think about it, is the best way to learn any program.

### Non–Event-Driven Particle Systems

Non–event-driven particle systems rely on the parameters set in the Modify panel to control the appearance and content of the particles, as opposed to passing through events that may alter some of the particles. All particles are treated identically by the system's parameters as a whole; there are no tests to modify the behavior for certain particles within the system. These particles can be bound to space warps to control apparent reactions to scene events, and they can be instructed to follow a path.

Non–event-driven particle systems have been around for a long time; they are stable, easy to learn, and an acceptable solution for many particle requirements. Non–event-driven particle systems are the focus of this chapter and will familiarize you with the workings of 3ds Max's particle workflow.

Six different non–event-driven particle systems are available in 3ds Max; each has its own strengths.

- The SuperSpray particle system
- The Particle Array particle system
- The Particle Cloud particle system
- The Blizzard particle system
- The Spray particle system
- The Snow particle system

They all have similar setups and, after you understand one type, the others are easy to master.

The SuperSpray particle system is the most commonly used non–event-driven particle system in 3ds Max. It features a spherical emitter with a directional arrow to indicate the initial direction of the particles. It has eight rollouts containing the parameters that control the appearance and performance of the particles. The particles can emerge over a specified range of time or throughout the scene's duration. When rendered, they can appear as one of several 2D or 3D shapes, as instanced scene geometry, or as interconnecting blobs that ebb and flow as they near each other. The particles can even spawn additional particles when they collide and load a predesigned series of parameters called a *preset*. The SuperSpray particle system essentially replaced the older, less-comprehensive Spray particle system, and it will be the main focus of this chapter. Figure 12.2 displays a SuperSpray particle system created in a viewport.

Rather than being the emitter, the Particle Array (also known as PArray) particle system, as shown in Figure 12.3, is only a visual link to the particle system emitter itself. The PArray uses an object in the scene as the emitter for the particles. While the parameters are adjusted with the PArray selected, the particles are emitted from the vertices, edges, or faces of the designated scene object. When used in conjunction with the PBomb space warp (discussed later in this chapter) and the Object Fragments setting, acceptable object explosions can be created.

Figure 12.2
**The SuperSpray particle system**

Figure 12.3
**The Particle Array particle system**

The Particle Cloud particle system, as shown in Figure 12.4, contains particles within a volume defined by the emitter or by selecting a 3D object in the scene to act as the constraining volume. When instanced geometry is used as the particle type, an array of space cruisers or a school of fish can be represented by the PCloud system. The PCloud object does not render, and any object used to constrain the particles can be hidden to give the illusion that the particles are not held in place by an external force.

> Instanced geometry takes instanced copies of an object and assigns one instance to the particles in a scene. You can animate a school of fish, for example, by assigning an instanced fish model to particle locations and then animating the particles to school together and swim along.

The Blizzard particle system, which is similar to the SuperSpray particle system in its toolset and capabilities, is shown in Figure 12.5. The presets that ship with Blizzard are designed to simulate the particle motion of rain, snow, or mist. The Blizzard particle system has replaced the less-capable Snow particle system.

Figure 12.4

**The Particle Cloud particle system**

Figure 12.5

**The Blizzard particle system**

The Spray and Snow particle systems, shown in Figure 12.6, are the original particle systems that shipped with the initial release of 3D Studio Max, the first Windows release after four DOS-based versions of 3D Studio. At the time, they were cutting edge and beneficial, but they have not been improved significantly since their implementation. Spray and Snow do not offer primitive or instanced geometry as particles, presets, or particle spawning. The concepts used with these two systems are similar to the other more-advanced systems, but they are seldom used anymore.

Figure 12.6

**The Spray and Snow particle systems**

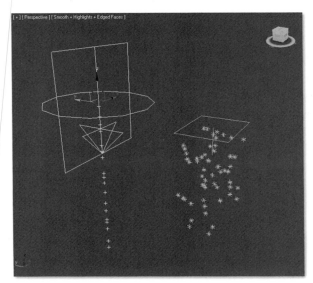

# Setting Up a Particle System

Particles are renderable objects in 3ds Max and are created in the Geometry tab of the Command panel. Like most other objects in 3ds Max, the particle system's parameters can be changed immediately after they are created in the Create panel. Once you deselect the system, however, their parameters must be changed in the Modify panel, just like any other object in 3ds Max. To set up a particle system, follow these steps.

Figure 12.7

**The particle system's parameters**

1. Click Create → Geometry → Particle Systems from the Command panel and then click on the SuperSpray button in the Object Type rollout. The particle system's parameters appear in the Command panel (Figure 12.7).

2. Click and drag in the Perspective viewport to create the SuperSpray emitter. The emitters do not render, so the size does not matter; the arrow will point in the positive Z direction, as shown in Figure 12.8.

3. Drag the Time Slider to the right until the particles extend beyond the limits of the viewport. Frame number 10 should be sufficient. To see the mass of particles, click Zoom Extents to expand your Perspective viewport to show everything in the scene.

   The Basic Parameters rollout controls how the particles spread as they exit the emitter, the size of the emitter, and how they display in the viewports.

4. In the Basic Parameters rollout, set both Spread values to 30 to spread the particles out 30 degrees in both the local X- and local Y-axes of the emitter. The Off Axis parameter rocks the emission direction along the X-axis and the Off Plane parameter rotates the angle of emission around the Z-axis. Both of these should remain at zero. See Figure 12.9.

5. In the Viewport Display area, make sure Ticks is selected and Percentage of Particles is set to 10. This ensures that the particles appear as small crosses in the viewports, regardless of the type of particle used, and that only 10 percent of the particles that are actually emitted are displayed in the viewport. Both of these parameters are used to ensure a minimal loss of performance in the viewport when particles are used.

6. Click the Render button ( 🫖 ) in the Main toolbar. The particles appear as small dots in the Rendered Frame Window. If you cannot see them, try changing the object color in the Name and Color rollout in the Create panel of the Name field, and the color swatch in the Modify panel. In the next section, you will increase the size of the particles in the Rendered Frame Window by increasing the particle's Size parameter. More particles are visible in the rendering than in the viewport because the Percentage of Particles value affects only the viewports and not the renderings.

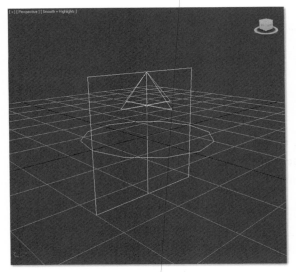

Figure 12.8

**The SuperSpray emitter created in the Perspective viewport**

Figure 12.9

**The Basic Parameters rollout**

## The Particle Generation Parameters

The parameters in the Particle Generation rollout control the emission of the particles, including the quantity, speed, size, and life span. If you can't see any particles in your scene, the first place to look should be the Particle Generation rollout.

Figure 12.10

**The Particle Generation rollout**

1. Expand the Particle Generation rollout (Figure 12.10).

   In the Particle Quantity area, the Use Rate value determines the number of particles emitted at each frame and the Use Total value determines how many particles are emitted over the active life of the system. Only one of these options can be active at a time. Increase the Use Rate value to 12.

2. Increase the Speed value to 15 to increase the velocity of the particles.

3. Below the viewports, next to the timeline, click the Play Animation button ( ▶ ). The particles spew from the emitter briefly and then stop. The particles have a distinct beginning and ending time that controls when the emitter can eject any particles.

4. In the Particle Timing section of the Particle Generation rollout, change the Emit Start value to 10, change the Emit Stop value to 100, and then click the Play Animation button again. The particle system will pause for 10 frames at the beginning of the active time segment and then emit 12 particles every frame for the remaining 90 frames.

5. Drag the Time Slider to frame 50 or so and then zoom out in the Perspective viewport until the limits of the particles' extent are visible. Play the animation again. The particles increase their distance from the emitter until frame 40 and then travel no farther.

There are several parameters that determine when a particle is visible. The Emit Start and Emit Stop parameters mentioned earlier bracket the frames when the particles are emitted. The Display Until parameter in the Particle Timing area defines the last frame when any particle is visible. Regardless of whether this frame falls within the Start and Stop values, when the Display Until frame is reached, no more particles appear in the viewports or in any renderings. Another parameter that controls the display of particles is the Life value. The Life value determines how long each particle exists in a scene—from when it is emitted until it disappears. Currently, the Life value is set to 30 (as seen in Figure 12.10) so that at frame 40, which is 30 frames after the emission begins at frame 10, the particles disappear. Particles that are emitted after frame 10 also live for 30 frames, moving the same distance from the emitter before dying .

6. Change the Life value to 40, allowing the particles to travel one-third farther from the emitter, and change the Variation value, just below Life, to 20, adding randomness to the particle's lifespan.

7. Play the animation. The particles now travel farther from the emitter and die between 34 and 48 frames after being emitted due to the Variation value we changed in step 6.

8. In the Particle Size area of the Particle Generation rollout, change the Size value to 10 and then render one frame of the scene at some point after frame 30. The result should look similar to Figure 12.11.

Figure 12.11

**The SuperSpray particle system rendered in the Perspective viewport**

Notice that the particles are smaller very near the emitter and also very far away from the emitter. By default, the Grow For value causes the particles to grow from a size of zero to full size over the first 10 frames of their lives. The Fade For parameter causes those same particles to shrink from full size to zero size during the last 10 frames of their lives.

9. Change the Fade For value to 0 so the particles retain their size at the end of their lives, and leave Grow For at its default.

10. Render the Perspective viewport again and notice how the particles grow, but never shrink. See Figure 12.12.

Figure 12.12

**The particle system with the Fade For value changed to 0**

## VARIATION

In many situations utilizing particle systems, the particles are intended to appear as many similar but random objects. When the particles all have identical parameters (such as speed, life span, or rotation), the illusion of randomness disappears, which can greatly detract from its sense of reality. To alleviate this situation, in many of the parameter areas of the Super-Spray particle system's rollouts, you will find a Variation parameter. The Variation settings modify their related parameters on a per-particle basis to add seeming randomness to the system. For example, changing the Variation parameter (below the Speed parameter) to 20 will assign a velocity to each particle within 20 percent of the Speed value. When the Speed parameter is set to 10 and Variation is set to 20, each particle is assigned to a random speed between 8 and 12—20 percent on either side of 10.

## Putting It Together

Now that you have a basic understanding of particle systems, you will continue to work with them by creating a system that represents the bullets fired from a gun and the brass expelled from the ejection port. This will require two particle systems, one for each type of object leaving the gun. We will also examine the different particle types that can be emitted.

### Creating the Particle Systems

The basic process of creating a particle system is fairly simple; you place the emitter in the scene, fine-tune its location and orientation, and then adjust the system's parameters. The third item mentioned is the one that will take the most experimentation to perfect.

1.  Open the Particle Gun.max file from the companion web page at www.sybex.com/go/intro3dsmax20011. This file is similar to the completed IK gun file created in Chapter 9, "Character Studio and IK Animation," with a target, floor, materials, lights, and a camera added. The lights and camera have been hidden for clarity.

2.  In the Top viewport, create a SuperSpray particle system. Move and rotate it so that the emitter is recessed slightly into the barrel of the gun, similar to Figure 12.13. Turn on the Angle Snap Toggle ( ) to rotate the system precisely 90 degrees.

Figure 12.13

**The Top and Right viewports showing the proper placement of the SuperSpray particle emitter**

3.  Click the Select and Link button ( ) in the Main toolbar.

4.  Click and hold on the particle system; a rubber-banding line stretches from the emitter to the cursor. Place the cursor over the gun barrel and then release the mouse button. The gun flashes white to indicate that the linking is complete. Any changes in the gun's orientation or position are now passed down to the particle

Figure 12.14

**Changes in the orientation or position are passed down to the particle system.**

Figure 12.15

**The Top and Front viewports showing the proper placement of the second SuperSpray particle emitter**

system, keeping it co-located and oriented with the gun. See Figure 12.14.

5. Rename this particle system **SuperSpray Bullets**.

6. Create a second SuperSpray particle system and place it on the right side of the gun body. Orient the emitter so that the particles are ejected upward and away from the gun, as shown in Figure 12.15.

7. Link this particle system to the gun, just as you did with the other in steps 3 and 4.

8. Rename this system **SuperSpray Brass**.

You may see a random particle or two already emitted by the particle systems. They are caused by the Emit Start time being set to the initial frame of the scene. This anomaly is corrected in the next section.

### Configuring the Particle System Timing

The number of particles emitted over time defines the density of the particles in the scene. The speed of the particles also factors into the proximity of the particles.

1. In the Time Controls area, click the Time Configuration button ( ).

2. In the Time Configuration dialog box, change the Length value to 300, as shown in Figure 12.16, and then click the OK button. At 30 frames per second (fps), the scene is now 10 seconds long.

3. Select SuperSpray Bullets and then click the Modify tab of the Command panel.

4. In the Particle Generation rollout, set the Use Rate to 10, the Speed to 10.0, the Emit Start value to 45, and the Emit Stop value to 300. After a one-and-a-half-second pause, the gun will fire then die off quickly.

5. Change the Display Until value to 300, as shown in Figure 12.17, so that the particles appear in the scene for the entire active time segment. Set the Life value to 300 so the particles do not die out in the scene.

Figure 12.16

**The Time Configuration settings**

Figure 12.17

**Change the Display Until value to 300.**

Figure 12.18

**The rendered Camera viewport showing the particles**

6. In the Particle Size section, change the Size value to 4. Drag the Time Slider to approximately frame 80 and then render the Camera viewport. The scene should look similar to Figure 12.18.

The particles appear as triangles that grow as they travel away from the emitter. When you are creating a traditional gun, this is not the look you want for the particles; the rounds should all appear the same size for the life of the particles. The particle type is covered in the next section and in the "Particle Systems and Space Warps" section later in this chapter. The conditions that allow the particles to pass through the Target object are also addressed.

### Selecting the Particle Type

There are several types of particles that can be emitted by a particle system. Standard particles consist of eight different 2D and 3D particles, including cubes, spheres, and six-pointed stars.

The Facing Standard particle type is a square, 2D particle that maintains a continuous orientation perpendicular to the viewport. Using opacity mapped materials in conjunction with Facing particles can give the illusion of smoke or steam without using a massive number of particles. Facing particles are sometimes referred to as *sprites.*

MetaParticles use what is known as *metaball technology,* where each particle appears as a blob with a sphere of influence surrounding it. Whenever the two spheres of influence from two particles in close proximity overlap, the particles meld together in an organic manner similar to mercury or the wax in a lava lamp. Using MetaParticles can be computationally intensive, so caution should be a priority when that is the selected particle type. Start with a quantity of particles fewer than you would expect to use and then increase the amount, as required, after test rendering the scene.

Geometry that exists in the scene can also be substituted for the particles at render time. Using instanced geometry, a particle system can emit any objects from jet fighters to fire fighters, or nearly any other geometry in the scene, using the material from the object that is instanced. The original scene object can be hidden so as not to appear in the render of the scene, while still being instanced by the particle system.

To resume the Particle System exercise, continue with the following steps:

1. With the SuperSpray Bullets particle system selected, expand the Particle Type rollout.

2. In the Particle Types section, select MetaParticles.

3. From the menu bar, choose Edit → Hold to temporarily save the scene. If rendering the scene causes a system crash, it can be restored to this point using Edit → Fetch. 3ds Max is a stable program, but rendering MetaParticles can significantly task a computer system.

4. Render the scene. The particles that are near to each other combine to form blobs of meshes, as shown in Figure 12.19.

Figure 12.19

**The rendered scene with the MetaParticles effect**

5. In the MetaParticle Parameters section, decrease the Tension setting to 0.1. Tension controls a particle's effort to maintain a spherical shape while in proximity to another particle. Lowering the Tension increases the amount of interparticle combining.

6. Render the scene again to see the effect of the lower Tension value, as shown in Figure 12.20.

Figure 12.20

**The rendered scene with the lower Tension value**

7. MetaParticles would be the solution if this gun were shooting out gobs of melted cheese, rather than working like a conventional machine gun. In this case, instanced geometry is the appropriate particle choice. Mmmmm, melted cheese.

8. Right-click on a blank area of the Active viewport and choose Unhide by Name from the Quad menu. Select the Bullet and Brass objects from the list in the Unhide Objects dialog box and then click the Unhide button. Two small objects, a bullet and a brass casing, appear below the gun.

9. At the top of the Particle Type rollout, select Instanced Geometry for the particle type, as shown in Figure 12.21. In the Instancing Parameters section, click the Pick Object button.

10. Select the Bullet object in the scene. If necessary, press the H key to open the Pick Object dialog box to select the object by name. The bullet flashes white briefly to indicate that the selection is successful and the object name is now identified in the Instancing Parameters section as the instanced geometry object.

11. Render the Camera viewport. There are still a few problems that need to be corrected. The particles are growing as they leave the emitter, the particles grow to be too large for the gun barrel, and the bullets rotate on several axes rather than maintaining a forward orientation, as you can see in Figure 12.22. The bullets also display their object color, the color used by the particle system rather than the material applied to the Bullet object.

12. In the Particle Size section of the Particle Generation rollout, set the Grow For and Fade For parameters to 0. This will cause the particles to maintain a constant size throughout their life spans.

Figure 12.21

**The Particle Type parameters**

Figure 12.22

The rendered scene
showing the large
particles and rotat-
ing bullets

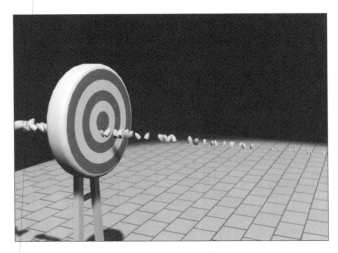

13. When using standard or MetaParticles, the Size parameter defines the size of the particle. When using instanced geometry, however, it becomes a multiplier of the object's actual size. With the current Size value set to 4, the bullets are scaled to four times their modeled size. That's a little big, so set the Size value to 1.

14. Expand the Rotation and Collision rollout. In the Spin Axis Controls section, select Direction of Travel/Mblur to make each bullet's orientation follow its direction of travel, as shown in Figure 12.23.

15. At the bottom of the Particle Type rollout, make sure that the Instanced Geometry radio button is selected and then click the Get Material From button.

16. Render the Camera viewport again. All of the particles are now oriented properly, as you can see in Figure 12.24.

Figure 12.23

The Rotation and
Collision settings

Figure 12.24

The rendered scene with all of the particles oriented properly

### Setting Up the Other Particle System

We have a particle system set up to emit the bullets, and now we need one that ejects the brass casings from the machine gun. In many cases, the same parameters must be maintained among the two systems so these parameters will be wired together, ensuring a common value between them. This way the casings will shoot out with the bullets.

1. Continue with the previous exercise or open the `Particle Gun1.max` file from the companion web page.

2. Select the SuperSpray Brass particle system.

3. In the Particle Generation rollout, set the Size to 1 and set both the Grow For and Fade For values to 0. Set Emit Start to 45, Emit Stop to 300, Display Until to 300, and Life to 300.

4. In the Particle Motion section of the Particle Generation rollout, reduce the Speed value to 5. The rate of particles emitted is still set to 10; the Speed value just determines the velocity of the particles as they leave the emitter.

5. In the Particle Type rollout, choose Instanced Geometry in the Particle Types section and then click the Pick Object button. Select the Brass object as the geometry to be instanced.

6. Select the Instanced Geometry option in the Mat'l Mapping and Source section at the bottom of the Particle Type rollout, and then click the Get Material From button to define the material applied to the particles.

7. In the Rotation and Collision rollout, select the Direction of Travel/Mblur option.

8. Select the Bullet and Brass objects and hide them.

9. Drag the Time Slider, and your bullets and brass should emit together.

### Wiring the Parameters Together

The values that define the parameters unique to each particle system in the scene have been set properly. Several values, such as the Use Rate, must maintain the same value for both particle systems so that, for example, the amount of brass ejected matches the number of bullets fired. These parameters can always be adjusted manually; however, the Parameter Wiring tool forces one object's parameters to drive another's. In the following exercise, the parameter values of the SuperSpray Bullets particle system are used to define the parameter values of the SuperSpray Brass particle system. By wiring parameters together, you can control more than one system by manipulating only one of them.

1. Continue with the previous exercise or load the `Particle Gun2.max` file from the companion web page.

2. Select the SuperSpray Bullets particle system. Right-click in the viewport and choose Wire Parameters from the Quad menu. See Figure 12.25.

Figure 12.25

**Choose Wire
Parameters from
the Quad menu.**

3. From the small pop-up menu that appears, choose Object (SuperSpray) and then Birth Rate from the cascading menu (Figure 12.26). A rubber-banding line connects the particle system to the cursor. At this point, the object to be wired to the SuperSpray Bullet's Birth Rate parameter must be selected.

4. Press the H key to open the Pick Object dialog box, select SuperSpray Brass (Figure 12.27), and then click the Pick button.

5. From the small pop-up menu that appears, choose Object (SuperSpray) and then Birth Rate from the cascading menu (Figure 12.28).

6. The Parameter Wiring dialog box opens, as shown in Figure 12.29. The Birth Rate parameters are highlighted in both the left and right windows. The left side of the dialog box displays the SuperSpray Bullets particle system's parameter, and the right side displays the SuperSpray Brass particle system's parameter.

7. The control direction, defining which parameter controls the other, can be set so that either one of the parameters controls the other, or bidirectional control can be set so that either parameter can change the other. In this case, the bullet rate is used to control the brass rate. Click the right arrow between the two parameter windows, as shown in Figure 12.30.

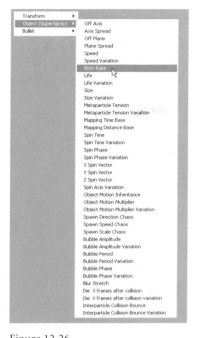

Figure 12.26

**Wire the selected object to the Super-Spray Bullet's Birth Rate parameter.**

Figure 12.27

**Select SuperSpray Brass in the Pick Object dialog box.**

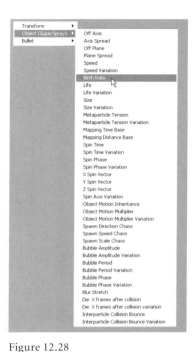

Figure 12.28

**Select Object (SuperSpray) and then Birth Rate.**

8. Complete the wiring process by clicking the Connect button. The parameters in each window will turn a color to indicate that they are wired.

9. Select the SuperSpray Bullets particle system and change the Use Rate setting to 12.

Figure 12.29

**The Parameter Wiring dialog box with the Birth Rate parameters highlighted**

Figure 12.30

**Click the right arrow between the two parameter windows.**

10. Select the SuperSpray Brass particle system and examine its Use Rate. It is now set to 12 as well.

> You can try to change the Use Rate for the SuperSpray Brass particle system, but it won't be effective. The related spinners simply do not work, and they shouldn't because the particle system's Use Rate is defined by the Use Rate of the SuperSpray Bullets particle system. You can highlight and change the value manually; however, nothing will really happen. When you deselect the system and then select it again, the Use Rate reverts to the value set by the other system.

11. Select the Life parameter in both windows; click the right arrow and then the Connect button. The Life parameters are now wired together as well.

> Unfortunately, the Emit Start, Emit Stop, and Display Until parameters are not exposed to the Parameter Wiring dialog box. These values must be changed for each particle system manually.

12. Close the Parameter Wiring dialog box.

13. Drag the Time Slider. The two particle systems emit equal numbers of particles at the same time. The brass ejects in a straight line from the gun body, as shown in Figure 12.31. The straight-line emission is corrected in the next section. You can now change the rate at which the bullets fire, and the brass will eject properly automatically!

The particle systems have been created and linked to the gun so that they maintain the proper position and orientation when the gun moves or rotates. The systems have been adjusted to fire bullets from the barrel and eject brass from the side at an equal and wired rate. The next section covers the processes of adding space warps to interject gravity into the scene and to cause the particles to collide with scene objects.

Figure 12.31

**The straight-line emission**

# Particle Systems and Space Warps

*Space warps* are nonrendering objects that can modify or manipulate the objects in a scene. Modifier-based space warps, for example, deform objects based on the object's proximity to the space warp. In this section, the focus is on the Forces and Deflectors categories of space warps, the space warps that affect particle systems.

The Forces space warps affect particle systems by altering the trajectory of the particles as they move through the scene. Each space warp displays as an icon in the viewports that must be bound to each object that it is designated to affect. The bindings appear as wide gray lines at the top of the Modifier Stack.

The Forces space warps are listed here:

**Motor** Applies a directional spin to the particles, creating a circular movement. The orientation of the Space Warp icon defines the direction of the rotation.

**Vortex** Similar to the Motor space warp, Vortex causes the particles to move in a circular motion but also decreases the radius of the motion over distance, creating a funnel-shaped motion.

**Path Follow** Requires the particles to follow a spline path. The particle timing is controlled by the Path Follow's parameters.

**Displace** Changes the particle trajectory by pushing them based on the space warp's Strength and Decay values. Image maps can also be used to define the amount of displacement.

**Wind** Adds a directional force to the particles based on the space warp's orientation. Randomness can be added to increase the realism of the simulation.

**Push** Applies a constant, directional force to the particles.

**Drag** Rather than changing the direction of the particles, Drag slows the speed of the particles as they pass through its influence.

**PBomb** Disperses particles with a linear or spherical force. This can be effective when used with the Particle Array particle system.

**Gravity** Applies a constant acceleration used to simulate the effect of gravity on the particles. Gravity can be applied in a linear fashion.

## Adding Gravity to a Scene

When looking at the particle systems in the previous exercises, especially the SuperSpray Brass system in our machine gun scene, it's evident that the motion of the particles is not realistic. The particles are emitted at approximately a 45-degree angle up and away from the gun body. The particles maintain a perfectly straight trajectory and never fall to the earth as they should. In this exercise, gravity is added to both particle systems to cause the bullets and brass to drop. To begin the exercise, follow these steps:

1. Continue with the previous exercise or load the Particle Gun3.max file from the companion web page.

2. Drag the Time Slider to frame 100.

3. Click Create → Space Warps. Choose Forces from the drop-down menu if necessary, and then click the Gravity button (Figure 12.32).

Figure 12.32

**The Gravity Button in Space Warps**

4. Click and drag in the Top viewport to place and size the Gravity Space Warp icon. The size and the location are unimportant, but the orientation of the icon defines the direction of the gravitational force. See Figure 12.33.

5. Select the SuperSpray Brass particle system. Click the Bind to Space Warp button (⚋) in the Main toolbar.

6. Click on the Particle System emitter or the particles themselves and drag the cursor toward the Gravity Space Warp icon. A rubber-banding line connects the particle system to the cursor.

7. Place the cursor over the Gravity space warp; when the cursor's appearance changes to identify it as a valid object for binding, release the mouse button. The space warp flashes briefly to indicate a successful binding, and the particles drop through the floor as shown in Figure 12.34.

8. Select the SuperSpray Bullets space warp and bind it to the Gravity space warp as well.

9. Play the animation. The particles from both systems are affected by the gravity, but the bullets drop too far for their distance from the gun to the target. Reducing the amount of gravity isn't appropriate because the brass would fall too slowly and the gravitational force should be consistent throughout the scene. This situation is fixed by increasing the velocity of the bullets as they leave the barrel.

Figure 12.33

**Click and drag in the Top viewport to place and size the Gravity Space Warp icon.**

Figure 12.34

**After the particle system is bound to the Gravity space warp, the particles drop through the floor.**

Figure 12.35

**Click SuperSpray in the Modifer Stack.**

10. The Bind to Space Warp button is still active. Click the Select Object button, and then select the SuperSpray Bullets particle system.

11. Make sure the Time Slider is at a frame well into the animation so that changes to the system are reflected in the viewports.

12. In the Modify panel, click the SuperSpray entry in the Modifier Stack (Figure 12.35) to expose the particle system's parameters.

13. In the Particle Generation rollout, increase the Speed value to 50. The visible trajectories of the particles will flatten out.

At the bottom of the Rotation and Collision rollout, you will find the Interparticle Collisions section. Enabling this parameter causes 3ds Max to calculate and determine the result of any situation where two particles impact each other. This can add a measure of realism to the way the particles react, but it can also consume a significant amount of system resources. Use this feature with caution and always perform an Edit → Hold on the scene prior to enabling or testing the feature.

## Controlling the Particles with Deflectors

As you saw in the previous exercises, particles travel through a scene, guided by space warps but unaffected by geometry. *Deflectors* are a type of space warp that causes the particles that impact the deflectors to bounce as if they have collided with an immovable surface. The amount of bounce assigned to a deflector is a multiplier that defines the velocity of a particle after it impacts the space warp. A Bounce value of 0.5 results in the particle's speed being reduced to 50 percent of the speed it had when it hit the deflector. Most deflectors have Time On and Time Off parameters that control when the deflector is active.

### Deflecting the Brass at the Floor

To get the spent casings to collide with the ground, follow these steps:

1. Continue with the previous exercise or load the `Particle Gun4.max` file from the companion web page.

2. Drag the Time Slider to frame 100.

3. Click Create → Space Warps. Choose Deflectors from the drop-down menu and then click the POmniFlect button (Figure 12.36).

4. In the Top viewport, click and drag to define the two opposite corners of the deflector. The deflector should be similar in size to the Floor object in the scene. Unlike the Forces space warps, deflectors must be positioned in the stream of the particles, as shown in Figure 12.37.

5. Move the deflector 0.3 units in the positive *Z* direction. The impact point is based on the particle location. When using instanced geometry, the particle location is defined by the center point of the geometry. The bullets and brass are about 0.3 units in radius, so moving the deflector up 0.3 units prevents the particles from sinking into the floor.

6. Select the SuperSpray Brass particle system and then click the Bind to Space Warp button in the Main toolbar. Click on the particle system, or particles, drag to the perimeter of the deflector, and then release to bind the deflector to the particle system.

7. Activate the Camera viewport and then play the animation. The particles initially bounce equal in height to their highest point after being ejected, but they discontinue shortly afterward.

8. Select the Deflector object in the viewport, not the deflector binding in the Modifier Stack.

Figure 12.36

**The POmniFlect button for the Deflectors pull-down option**

Figure 12.37

The deflector must be positioned in the stream of the particles.

## UNDERSTANDING DEFLECTOR NAMES

The names assigned to the different deflectors distinguish the shapes and properties of those deflectors. Understanding the deflector naming convention is key to selecting the correct deflector for the task at hand.

- If the deflector name begins with a P or an S, the deflector is Planar or Spherical, respectively.

- If the deflector name begins with a U, this is a universal deflector and any scene geometry can be assigned as a deflector, instead of the Deflector icon itself.

- If the deflector name ends with "OmniFlect," this deflector affects all particles that impact it. The OmniFlect deflectors are more advanced than the simpler space warps that end with "Deflector."

- If the deflector name ends with "DynaFlect," this deflector affects all particles that impact it and, when used with dynamic simulations, can affect other objects in the scene.

Figure 12.38

**POmniFlect
parameters**

Figure 12.38

**POmniFlect
parameters**

9. In the Timing section of the Parameters rollout, set the Time Off value to 300, as shown in Figure 12.38, to leave the deflector on during the entire active time segment.

10. In the Reflection section, set the Bounce value to 0.25 and the Variation value to 10 percent. Increase Chaos to 50 percent so the particles' directions are not constrained to a straight line.

11. In the Common section, increase the Friction value to 4.0 to prevent the particles from spreading too far along the deflector's surface, as shown in Figure 12.38.

12. Play the animation. The brass is ejected from the side of the gun, falls to the floor, and spreads a bit from the point of impact.

### Deflecting the Bullets at the Target

The brass is handled, and now the bullet collisions need to be addressed.

1. Click Create → Space Warps, and then click the UOmniFlect button.

2. In the Top viewport, click and drag to place and size the universal deflector. The size and position do not matter. This is just a visible icon. A scene object will be selected to act as the deflector. See Figure 12.39.

3. Select the SuperSpray Bullets particle system, and bind it to the UOmniflect icon, not the Target object. Bind the particle system to the POmniFlect deflector as well.

4. Click the Select Object button and then select the UOmniFlect icon.

5. In the Modify panel, click the Pick Object button and then select the Target object in the scene.

6. In the Timing section, set the Time Off value to 300.

7. In the Reflection section, set Bounce to 0.01, Variation to 10, and Chaos to 4.

8. Play the animation. The particles hit the target, fall to the floor, and then spread out a bit.

As you can see, the proper use of Force and Deflector space warps, in conjunction with particle systems, can successfully animate thousands of small objects within the constraints of a scene. The completed scene can be examined using the `Particle Gun Complete.max` and `Particle Gun.avi` files on the companion web page. In the remaining sections in this chapter, we will look at the implementation of rigid and soft body dynamics in physics simulations.

Figure 12.39

**In the Top viewport, click and drag to place and size the universal deflector.**

## Using Rigid Body Dynamics

Part of the core package of 3ds Max is the physics engine known as *reactor*. With reactor, complex physical conditions are accurately animated showing the interaction of the scene objects with each other and with external forces such as wind or gravity. Objects are assigned mass, elasticity, and friction properties, and designated as movable or immovable objects. Rigid body dynamics, soft body dynamics, rope, and cloth simulations are all within the limits of reactor's toolset. The Real Time Preview window displays a lower-resolution, unrendered example of the animation to be created to make it easy to visualize how your dynamic simulation will run, without a lot of wait. The reactor engine calculates the animation, but the standard practice of creating keyframes is the final output of the simulations. These keyframes can be edited and manipulated; however, the integrity of the simulation could be compromised.

## Creating the Simulation Objects

In this exercise, a series of primitive objects is dropped onto a complex inclined object to examine the interaction of the scene objects, as shown in Figure 12.40. Although this is a simple example of the use of the physics simulator, reactor can be used to simulate the interactions of very complex scenes with many colliding objects and external forces.

Figure 12.40

**A series of primitive objects is to be dropped onto this complex inclined object.**

1. Open the Rigid.max file from the companion web page. This consists of an inclined box with additional boxes, cylinders, and a hemisphere placed on its surface to make the simulation more complex.

2. Create two rows of spheres above the inclined board. Make sure they are all over the top edge of the board and fit between the two angled rails on the sides.

3. Create a row of small boxes between the rows of spheres as shown, and rotate them each about all three axes to offset them.

4. From the Extended Primitives category of geometry objects, create a Hedra, then go to family group and choose Star 2 and position it near the other objects. The scene should look similar to Figure 12.41.

5. Open the Material Editor and then apply the Checker material to all of the objects you created. The Checker Diffuse Color map helps discern the rotation of each object in the simulation.

Figure 12.41

**The scene after creating additional objects for the simulation**

## Assigning the Physical Properties

Each object in the scene must be assigned the correct properties to define their reactions during the simulation. Note that any objects that are to be stable and immovable are assigned a Mass value of 0.

1. Select all of the objects that make up the inclined board in the scene.

2. Right-click an empty area of the Main toolbar to display a list of available toolbars, then choose reactor. This will bring up the floating toolbar. Right-click on the title bar and choose Dock → Left.

3. From the reactor toolbar, click the Open Property Editor button ( 🖹 ) to open the Rigid Body Properties dialog box shown in Figure 12.42.

4. Make sure Mass is set to 0 in the Physical Properties rollout, and Mesh Convex Hull is selected in the Simulation Geometry rollout.

5. Select all of the spheres that you created. Set their Mass value to 1.0 and choose Bounding Sphere in the Simulation Geometry rollout, as shown in Figure 12.43. When using a spherical object, Bounding Sphere is more accurate and calculates faster than Mesh Convex Hull.

Figure 12.42

**Open the Rigid Body Properties dialog box.**

Figure 12.43

**Choose Bounding Sphere in the Simulation Geometry rollout.**

Most 3D geometry works as expected during a reactor simulation. However, reactor contains its own Plane object for use whenever flat, 2D surfaces are required. When a 3ds Max plane is used instead of a reactor plane, Concave Mesh must be chosen as the Simulation Geometry type.

6. Select all of the boxes that you created, assign a Mass value of 1.0, and choose the Bounding Box option.

7. Select the hedra. Increase its mass to 1.0 and select Mesh Convex Hull for the simulation.

You have now assigned dynamic parameters to the scene objects; however, there is more to do to set up the simulation.

### THE SIMULATION GEOMETRY ROLLOUT

The Simulation Geometry rollout defines how reactor defines the surfaces of an object during the simulation.

- The Bounding Box and Bounding Sphere options place the extents of the objects, as far as the simulation is concerned, at the limits of the smallest possible box or sphere that could encompass them.

- Mesh Convex Hull closely follows the extents of the object, with all vertices included within the simulation volume, while spanning any concave areas. Complicated meshes can increase the calculation time when using Mesh Convex Hull, so the Proxy Convex Hull option allows a less dense substitution object to be used to define the simulation parameters.

- When Concave Mesh is used, the actual surface of the geometry is used. This can drastically increase the calculation time and should be used only when necessary. Using the Proxy Concave Mesh option can reduce the simulation time when using a complicated object.

- 3ds Max assigns the Not Shared option to the selected geometry when multiple objects are selected that do not utilize the same Simulation Geometry setting.

## Creating the Collection

Scene objects must be members of a collection to be included in any simulations. The collections appear as simple icons in the viewports that are selected to access the simulation's parameters, including editing the list of included objects.

1. Continue with the previous exercise or open the Rigid1.max file from the companion web page.

2. Click the Create Rigid Body Collection button () in the reactor toolbar.

3. Click in any viewport to place the Rigid Body Collection icon, as shown in Figure 12.44. The location does not matter.

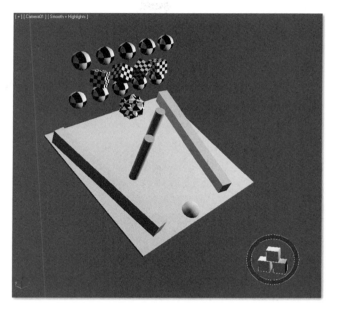

Figure 12.44

**Click in any viewport to place the Rigid Body Collection icon.**

Figure 12.45

**Click the Add button in the RB Collection Properties rollout.**

4. In the Command panel, click the Add button at the bottom of the RB Collection Properties rollout (Figure 12.45).

5. In the Select Rigid Bodies dialog box that opens, select all of the objects in the scene except for the collection itself and then click the Select button; see Figure 12.46. The object names will appear in the Rigid Bodies field in the Command panel.

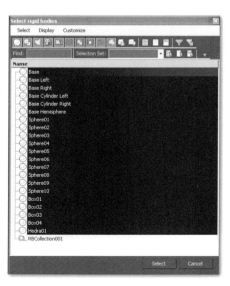

Figure 12.46

**The Select Rigid Bodies dialog box**

In most cases, not every object in a scene is required to be in a simulation. An object should be omitted if its impact on the simulation is not required. For example, in a scene where marbles spill across a table and onto a floor, the marbles, table, and floor must be included, but the nearby lamp or the ceiling should be omitted.

## Testing the Simulation

The reactor engine provides the Real-Time Preview window where you can view the simulation. Materials and lighting are not considered for this preview; therefore, it is much faster, but less accurate, than rendering the animation.

1. Click the Preview Animation button ( ) in the reactor toolbar. The reactor engine analyzes the simulation and then opens the reactor Real-Time Preview window shown in Figure 12.47.

Figure 12.47

**The reactor Real-Time Preview window showing the scene**

Figure 12.48

**The Change Friction property in the Rigid Body Properties dialog box**

2. Press the P key to begin the preview, and then press P again to stop it.

3. After the preview runs its course, choose Simulation → Reset to place the objects at their starting points and review the animation.

You can click and drag in the Preview window to orbit around the simulation objects.

4. The hedra is large for the scene and may cause a bottleneck. Close the Preview window.

5. Select the hedra and reduce its Radius value.

6. Select all of the objects of the inclined board, and then open the Rigid Body Properties dialog box as shown in Figure 12.48.

7. Set the Friction property to 0.1.

8. Select the remaining objects in the scene, and set the Friction to 0.1 as well.

9. Rearrange the objects to change the simulation to your liking.

10. Continue to preview the animation and rearrange the objects until the simulation meets your liking.

## Creating the Animation

The Preview window showed what the animation will be like, but the animation keys have not been created from the simulation. The next exercise creates keys for all the objects in the collection. Creating the keys is not undoable, so it is recommended that an Edit → Hold be performed prior to creating the animation. This will create a return point in the scene in case something goes awry. This way, you can use Edit → Fetch to come back to this place in your workflow.

1. In the Time Configuration dialog box, increase the length of the scene's animation to 200 frames then click OK.

2. Click Edit → Hold from the Main menu.

3. Click the Create Animation button () from the reactor toolbar.

4. Click OK in the reactor dialog box that opens and warns you that the action cannot be undone, as shown in Figure 12.49.

Figure 12.49

**The reactor dialog**

> 3ds Max creates keys at every frame for every object in the simulation. The process of creating keys with reactor cannot be undone, but the objects can be selected and their keys can be deleted in the track bar, the Dope Sheet, or the Function Curve dialog boxes.

5. Play the animation. The scene animates through frame 100 and then stops. The default value for all simulations is 100 frames.

6. To restore the scene to its state before 3ds Max created the animation, click Edit → Fetch from the Main menu and then click the Yes button in the dialog box that opens.

7. Click the Utilities tab (   ) of the Command panel.

8. Click the reactor button in the Utilities rollout.

> In reactor, solvers provide the algorithms that determine each object's reactions in the simulation. The two available solver options in 3ds Max 2011 are Havok 1 and Havok 3. The Havok 1 solver has more functionality and can handle all types of simulation objects. Havok 3 is faster and more accurate, but it can solve only for rigid body objects. If only rigid body objects are used in a simulation, Havok 3 is usually the better choice.

9. In the About rollout, select Havok 3 from the Choose Solver drop-down menu. Havok 3 is the better choice when using only rigid body objects.

10. Expand the Preview & Animation rollout and change the End Frame value to 200.

Figure 12.50

**Click the Create Animation button.**

Figure 12.50

**Click the Create Animation button.**

11. Click Edit → Hold again, and then click the Create Animation button shown in Figure 12.50.

12. 3ds Max creates keys based on the simulation. You can fetch the scene and rearrange the objects as you want to change the simulation parameters and rerun the animation. Remember to hold the scene before creating the animation each time, so you can easily go back to your hold point.

The completed exercise is available as the `Rigid Complete.max` file in the Dynamics Scene Files folder on the companion web page and the final rendering as `Rigid Complete.avi`.

# Using Soft Body Dynamics

Soft body objects differ from rigid body objects in that they can deform upon impact with other objects in the scene. To be included in a simulation as soft body objects, scene objects must have the Soft Body modifier applied and be members of a soft body collection. Soft body objects can interact with rigid body objects in the same simulation. Physical properties are assigned to soft body objects in the same manner that they are assigned to their rigid counterparts.

## Creating the Collections

Before you can simulate the reactions between soft body objects, all objects considered in the simulation must be contained in a collection.

1. Open the `Soft.max` file from the Dynamics Scene Files folder on the companion web page. As you can see in Figure 12.51, this is a simpler version of the project used in the previous exercises.

Figure 12.51

**This is a simpler version of the project.**

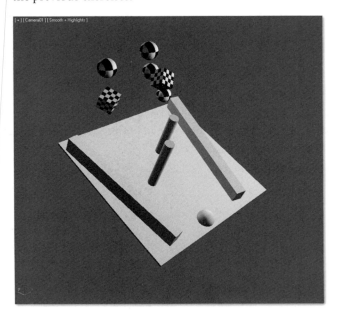

2. Select all of the base objects, and then click the Create Rigid Body Collection button in the reactor toolbar. The icon is placed at the center of the selection, and the selected objects are added to the collection.

3. Select the spheres and boxes with the Checker material applied.

4. Click the Apply Soft Body Modifier button ( ) in the reactor toolbar.

5. With the objects still selected, click the Create Soft Body Collection button ( ) in the reactor toolbar. The falling objects are automatically added to the soft body collection.

6. Move the Collection icons away from the scene geometry. Your Perspective viewport should look similar to Figure 12.52.

Figure 12.52

**The Perspective viewport with the rigid- and soft-body collections**

## Creating the Animation

In the earlier exercise, the Havok 3 solver was selected because of its capabilities when using rigid body objects exclusively. With the combination of both soft and rigid objects in this exercise, the Havok 1 solver is the better choice.

1. In the Utilities panel, click the reactor button and then choose Havok 1 from the drop-down menu in the About rollout, as shown in Figure 12.53.

2. Click the Preview Animation button in reactor and play the animation in the reactor Real-Time Preview window, shown in Figure 12.54. The animation plays slower than the rigid body preview due to the more complex animation required by the deforming meshes.

Figure 12.53

**Select the Havok 1 solver.**

Figure 12.54

**Click the Preview in Window button.**

In a complex scene, or on a slow computer, the reactor Real-Time Preview may display the scene at a rate that is too slow to easily determine the effectiveness of the simulation. In these cases, you need to create the animation and then, if revisions are required, delete all of the simulation objects' animation keys before making any changes and re-creating the animation.

3.  Close the Preview window.

4.  The parameters of individual objects can be set in the reactor SoftBody modifier's settings. Select one of the spheres and then, in the Modify panel, change its Mass to 2, Stiffness to 4, and Friction to 0.1. Repeat this step with one more sphere and one of the boxes. The larger Mass value will cause the object to impact with a greater force.

5.  Test the animation again. Continue to make changes and then, when you are satisfied, hold the scene.

6.  Click the Create Animation button in the reactor toolbar to create the animation using the properties assigned to the objects.

The completed exercise can be found on the companion web page as `Soft Complete.max` and `Soft Compete.avi`.

## Summary

This chapter introduced you to both Max's non–event-driven particle systems and the reactor physics simulation engine. Using particles, thousands of seemingly random or purposeful objects can be animated by effectively manipulating the particle system's parameters. Particles can appear as primitive shapes, interconnecting blobs, or any instanced geometry object from the scene. Particle systems can be affected by external forces, such as gravity, wind, or vortex, and they can bounce off many types of deflectors positioned within the flow of particles.

The reactor component of Max is a powerful tool for creating accurate animations based on the interactions of scene objects. Rigid or soft body objects in collections can impact each other and deform, bounce, or slide away based on the objects' physical properties. Animations can be previewed and then thousands of animation keys can be created quickly to fulfill a scene's physics-based animation requirements.

## So Long, and Thanks for All the Fish

And that's about it for us. (Awkward pause. Do you lean in for a hug, or go for a simple handshake?) We hope you found this text illuminating and helpful in priming you for a fruitful and exciting education in Autodesk's 3ds Max. There are so many resources to be found in bookstores and on the Internet that you should feel confident and secure in jumping into the next step of your CG education.

By now, you should be familiar with the workings of 3ds Max and know what parts of the CG process you find appealing. Whether it's modeling or lighting, animating or dynamics, you now have a firm grasp of how to get things done. If you feel shaky in some areas, we strongly recommend going back to the related chapters and redoing the exercises to build your confidence.

We hope the most important idea you take with you from this book is the notion that proficiency in and mastery of a CG program such as 3ds Max takes patience and practice. The best way to learn is to experience the software in pursuit of your own artistic endeavors. Don't be afraid to throw yourself into your own personal projects, challenging yourself to get better with every effort. Treat this text as a formal introduction to all that 3ds Max has to offer your artistic work, and forge ahead. Have fun, and good luck!

# Index

**Note to the Reader:** Throughout this index **boldfaced** page numbers indicate primary discussions of a topic. *Italicized* page numbers indicate illustrations.